The Legal Regulation of Environmental Crime

Queen Mary Studies
in International Law

Edited by

Malgosia Fitzmaurice

VOLUME 47

The titles published in this series are listed at *brill.com/qmil*

The Legal Regulation of Environmental Crime

The International and European Dimension

By

Valsamis Mitsilegas, Elena Fasoli, Fabio
Giuffrida and Malgosia Fitzmaurice

BRILL
NIJHOFF

LEIDEN | BOSTON

The Library of Congress Cataloging-in-Publication Data is available online at https://catalog.loc.gov
LC record available at https://lccn.loc.gov/2021058061

Typeface for the Latin, Greek, and Cyrillic scripts: "Brill". See and download: brill.com/brill-typeface.

ISSN 1877-4822
ISBN 978-90-04-32308-7 (hardback)
ISBN 978-90-04-50638-1 (e-book)

Copyright 2022 by Koninklijke Brill NV, Leiden, The Netherlands.
Koninklijke Brill NV incorporates the imprints Brill, Brill Nijhoff, Brill Hotei, Brill Schöningh, Brill Fink, Brill mentis, Vandenhoeck & Ruprecht, Böhlau Verlag and V&R Unipress.
All rights reserved. No part of this publication may be reproduced, translated, stored in a retrieval system, or transmitted in any form or by any means, electronic, mechanical, photocopying, recording or otherwise, without prior written permission from the publisher. Requests for re-use and/or translations must be addressed to Koninklijke Brill NV via brill.com or copyright.com.

This book is printed on acid-free paper and produced in a sustainable manner.

Printed by Printforce, United Kingdom

Contents

Notes on Contributors IX

1 Introduction 1

2 Environmental Crime at the International Level
 Criminalisation of Illegal Trade in Wildlife under the Convention on International Trade in Endangered Species of Wild Fauna and Flora (CITES) 7
 1 Introduction 7
 2 CITES and the Provisions for the Prohibition and Penalisation/Criminalisation of Illegal Trade in Wildlife 10
  2.1 *General Provisions and Institutional Structure of CITES* 11
  2.2 *Illegal Trade in Wildlife under CITES in Conjunction with the Other Relevant International Instruments* 13
  2.3 *Prohibition, Penalisation and Criminalisation of Illegal Trade in Wildlife under the Convention* 22
   2.3.1 Implementation of Article VIII.1 of CITES 25
  2.4 *Compliance with Article VIII.1 of CITES* 30
 3 Enforcement of Article VIII.1 of CITES 36
  3.1 *Domestic Enforcement* 37
  3.2 *Enforcement through International Interinstitutional Cooperation* 42
 4 Illegal Trade in Wildlife and Covid-19 48
 5 Concluding Remarks 53
 Acknowledgments 54

3 Environmental Crime at the International Level
 Criminalisation of Illegal Traffic of Hazardous Wastes under the Basel Convention on the Control of Transboundary Movements of Hazardous Wastes and Their Disposal (Basel Convention) 55
 1 Introduction 55
 2 The Basel Convention and the Provisions for the Criminalisation of Illegal Traffic of Hazardous Wastes 58
  2.1 *General Provisions and Institutional Structure of the Basel Convention* 59
  2.2 *Illegal Traffic of Hazardous Wastes under Article 9 of the Basel Convention* 63

2.3   *Criminalisation of Illegal Traffic of Hazardous Wastes under the Basel (and the Bamako) Conventions* 74
   2.3.1   Implementation of Article 9 of the Basel Convention 78
   2.3.2   Compliance with Article 9 of the Basel Convention 84
3   Enforcement of Article 9 of the Basel Convention 86
   3.1   *Domestic Enforcement* 86
   3.2   *Enforcement through International Interinstitutional Cooperation* 91
4   Concluding Remarks 93
Acknowledgments 94

4   Environmental Crime at the International Level
The International Convention for the Prevention of Pollution from Ships (MARPOL) 95
1   Introduction 95
2   The MARPOL Convention: General Introduction 96
3   MARPOL: Structure, Underlying Principles and Enforcement 100
4   Concluding Remarks 108

5   Environmental Crime at the EU Level
Substantive Criminal Law 110
1   Introduction 110
2   The Protection of the Environment within the EU: A Short History 110
3   EU Law and Environmental Crime: Constitutional Perspectives 117
4   The Environmental Crime Directive (2008/99/EC) 121
   4.1   *Actus Reus and Mens Rea* 124
   4.2   *Liability of Legal Persons, Penalties and (Some) Gaps* 133
5   Ship-Source Pollution between EU (Criminal) Law and International Law 140
   5.1   *The Ship-Source Pollution Directive (2009/123/EC)* 140
   5.2   *The* Intertanko *Case and the Autonomy of the Union Legal Order Vis-à-vis International Law* 143
6   Environmental Offences and the Links with Organised Crime and Money Laundering 149
7   The Treaty of Lisbon and the Future of EU Environmental Criminal Law 158

7.1 *Article 83 TFEU and Environmental Crime* 160
7.2 *A New Directive on Environmental Crime: Challenges and Opportunities for the EU Legislator* 164
8 Conclusion 172

6 Environmental Crime at the EU Level
Judicial Cooperation, Conflicts of Jurisdiction and Ne Bis in Idem 175

1 Introduction 175
2 Mutual Recognition Instruments to Fight Environmental Crime 176
   2.1 *Scaling Down Dual Criminality* 180
   2.2 *The Concept of 'Judicial Authority'* 188
   2.3 *Protection of Fundamental Rights* 193
3 Conflicts of Jurisdiction in the European Union 198
4 *Ne Bis in Idem* 203
   4.1 *The Principle of* Ne Bis in Idem *at the European Level* 205
   4.2 Bis, Idem *and Enforcement Condition* 206
      4.2.1 The *'Bis'* Element 207
      4.2.2 The *'Idem'* Element 212
      4.2.3 The Enforcement Condition in Article 54 CISA and Its Relations with Article 50 of the Charter 215
   4.3 *Application of* Ne Bis in Idem *to Criminal and Administrative Proceedings Concerning the Same Facts* 218
      4.3.1 *Bonda, Fransson* and *Grande Stevens*: Incompatibility between Double-Track Systems and *Ne Bis in Idem* 222
      4.3.2 *A and B v Norway, Garlsson, Zecca and Di Puma*, and *Menci:* (Partial) Compatibility between Double-Track Systems and *Ne Bis in Idem* 224
5 Conclusion 231

7 Environmental Crime at the EU Level
The Role of EU Agencies and Bodies 233

1 Introduction 233
2 Europol and Eurojust: Structure, Functioning and Powers 233
   2.1 *Competence of the Two Agencies and Classification of Their Activities* 234
   2.2 *Structure and Operational Activities of Eurojust* 238
   2.3 *Eurojust in Practice: Coordination Meetings, Coordination Centres and Joint Investigation Teams* 241
   2.4 *Structure and Operational Activities of Europol* 244

	2.5	*The Future of Europol in Light of the Revised Regulation* 246
	2.6	*'Non-operational' Tasks of the Two Agencies and the Policy Cycle (EMPACT)* 248
	2.7	*Exchange of Information with National Authorities and the EU Agencies' Evolving Role* 252
3	Europol and Cross-border Environmental Crime 254	
	3.1	*Operational Activities* 254
	3.2	*Non-operational Activities* 260
4	Eurojust and Cross-border Environmental Crime 266	
	4.1	*Operational Activities* 266
	4.2	*Non-operational Activities* 273
5	The European Public Prosecutor's Office 277	
6	Conclusion 283	

8 Conclusion

The Regulation of Environmental Crime in International and EU Law: Coming of Age? 286

1 The Extent and Scope of Criminalisation 286
2 The Organised and Financial Crime Dimension 287
3 Compliance, Enforcement and a Multi-agency Approach 288

Index 289

Notes on Contributors

Elena Fasoli
is Associate Professor of international law at the University of Trento (Italy). She obtained her Ph.D. in international law at the University of Milan. She has been external consultant to the Ministry of the environment of Italy from 2009 to 2013 and was a member of the UNECE Aarhus Convention Compliance Committee from 2014 to 2017. She has published in the fields of international and EU environmental law, international litigation and State responsibility.

Malgosia Fitzmaurice
is Professor of International Law at Queen Mary University of London. She is a member of the *l'Institut de Droit International* and was awarded a Doctoris Honoris Causa of the University of Neuchatel. She is an Editor in Chief of the International Community Law review and book series Queen Mary Studies in International Law. She has published on the subjects of the law of treaties, international environmental law; water law and indigenous peoples.

Fabio Giuffrida
Ph.D. (2019), Queen Mary University of London, is Policy Officer at the European Commission. He has authored several articles and studies concerning different aspects of EU criminal law, including a study on the role of EU agencies in the fight against transnational environmental crime, and recently co-edited a volume on the establishment of the European Public Prosecutor's Office.

Valsamis Mitsilegas
is Professor of European Criminal Law and Global Security at Queen Mary University of London. He has been Director of the Queen Mary Criminal Justice Centre since 2011. He is a member of the European Criminal Law Academic Network (ECLAN) and of the Commission's Expert Group on EU Criminal Policy. He is the author of seven books and over 150 articles and chapters in the areas of European and transnational criminal law, including in the fields of financial and environmental crime.

CHAPTER 1

Introduction

Environmental crime is a global phenomenon. Illegal trade in wildlife, for instance, is amongst the most known areas of environmental crime often linked to organised crime and terrorism,[1] which, in turn, put illegal trade in wildlife in a broader context of global security threat. According to recent data, traffic in wildlife (which coexists with the highly profitable legal trade in wildlife) is worth between USD 7 and 23 billion annually.[2]

This book focuses on the role of criminal law in tackling this global phenomenon and it does so by analysing the measures that have been adopted so far at both international and EU level. It starts from the consideration that no homogenous definition of environmental crime currently exists. Environmental crime is a term that covers a wide variety of conduct ranging from wildlife trafficking to pollution at sea to illicit waste disposal and management.

The first Part looks at environmental crime through the lens of international law. It explores the ways in which selected Multilateral Environmental Agreements (MEAs) criminalise environmentally harmful acts that breach national law implementing those MEAs and that are subject to prosecution and/or to the application of sanctions domestically.

While there are multiple MEAs that are potentially relevant for environmental crime, the first Part focuses primarily on environmentally harmful acts in key sectors, namely, those covered by the Convention on International Trade in Endangered Species of Wild Fauna and Flora (CITES),[3] by the Basel Convention on the Control of Transboundary Movements of Hazardous Wastes and their Disposal (the 'Basel Convention'),[4] and by the Convention on the Prevention of Pollution from Ships (MARPOL).[5] The choice is justified by the fact that the provisions contained in these international instruments, although with different degrees of explicitness, address the issue of illegality and/or that of the criminalisation of the activities falling within their scope of application.

---

1 Already in 2014, the UN Security Council (SC) expressed concern about the convergence between organised crime and terrorism. See Resolution n. 2195 of 19 December 2014, 1.
2 Data available at <https://www.traffic.org/about-us/illegal-wildlife-trade/> accessed 2 June 2021.
3 UN Treaty Series, Vol. 993, 243.
4 UN Treaty Series, Vol. 1673, 57.
5 UN Treaty Series, Vol. 1340, 62; Vol. 1341, 3.

Other MEAs are not so explicit in putting an emphasis on illegality and/or on criminalisation. Usually, MEAs require Parties simply to take the 'necessary measures' in order to implement their obligations. For instance, the Rotterdam Convention on the Prior Informed Consent Procedure for Certain Hazardous Chemicals and Pesticides in International Trade (the 'Rotterdam Convention'), provides that

> [e]ach Party shall take such measures as may be necessary to establish and strengthen its national infrastructures and institutions for the effective implementation of the Convention. These measures may include, as required, the adoption or amendment of national legislative or administrative measures.[6]

The Rotterdam Convention stops short of defining illegal trade in chemicals or of referring to the obligations of Parties for tackling the illegal traffic in toxic chemicals and dangerous products directly.[7] As a consequence, it is domestic laws, including those implementing the Convention, that define the legality (or not) of the production and trade in listed chemicals.[8]

A further example is the Montreal Protocol on Substances that Deplete the Ozone Layer,[9] which does not contain a provision addressing the illegal trade in ozone depleting substances (ODS) in the text. The managing of the illegal trade in ODS thus rests within the activities of the subsidiary bodies established under the Protocol, such as the Meeting of the Parties (MOP) and, for instance, within the creation of a system of licensing the import and export of ODS.[10]

In that regard, CITES, the Basel Convention and MARPOL, although characterised by a different degree of development of their respective architectural and institutional machineries for tackling environmental crime,[11] are similar

---

6   Article 15 of the Rotterdam Convention.
7   Except for a brief reference in the preamble of the Convention which refers to chapter 19 of Agenda 21.
8   UNEP and Grid-Arendal, *The Illegal Trade in Chemicals* (2020) 18.
9   UN Treaty Series, Vol. 1522, 3.
10   See E Clark, 'The Montreal Protocol and OzonAction Networks' in L Elliott and WL Schaedla (eds), *Handbook of Transnational Environmental Crime* (Edward Elgar 2016) 413.
11   For instance, the International Consortium on Combating Wildlife Crime (ICCWC) is much more developed (eg, in terms of the number of entities being members) compared to the Environmental Network for Optimising Regulatory Compliance on Illegal Traffic (ENFORCE) established under the Basel Convention. The first one, which is a collaborative effort between the CITES Secretariat, Interpol, UNODC, the World Bank and WCO, is very focused on enforcement and capacity building as CITES gathers more public and

and, at the same time, different from other MEAs. Since the adoption of the respective texts, they have somehow anticipated the growth of phenomena which have gradually expanded over time (namely, the traffic in wildlife and in hazardous wastes and the illegal discharge of oil and noxious substances from vessels) and they have initially sought to tackle them by highlighting (more or less explicitly) their illegality in the text. Thus, these international instruments oblige (again, more or less explicitly) the Parties to adopt legislative and regulatory frameworks to criminalise these phenomena domestically. As a consequence, CITES, the Basel Convention and MARPOL have been selected as key MEAs for the present (international law) analysis.

Against this backdrop, Chapter 2 explores the existing tools and mechanisms, including their limits, related to the criminalisation of the international illegal trade in wildlife, drawing attention to domestic enforcement and to the activity of the most relevant enforcement agencies and international institutions in the field. The Chapter shows that CITES is amongst the few MEAs that put an emphasis on illegality and criminality, even though, technically, the relevant provision gives no guidance as to the level of punishment required, or any directions as to whether the nature of the penalties should be indeed of a criminal nature. The Chapter argues that despite the multi-agency and multi-level approaches, such as, for example, the establishment of the International Consortium on Combating Wildlife Crime (ICCWC), in many Countries the legislation to tackle wildlife crime is still too weak and the level of prosecution is very low, including because of the limited enforcement capacity. The Chapter concludes with the hope that the progressive increase of public awareness, based on the ever-emerging scientific evidence as to the links between the global health crisis and the illegal trade in wildlife could contribute to include wildlife crime amongst the top priorities for action at the national, as well as international levels.

Chapter 3 deals with the existing tools and mechanisms, including their limits, relating to the criminalisation of the international traffic in hazardous wastes. The Chapter first of all points out that the Basel Convention is the only MEA that explicitly defines in the text a prohibited activity as 'criminal'. However, despite the clear wording in the text, the Basel Convention is a treaty that was not designed to deal with the criminalisation of illegal traffic in any great detail. Because of that, the real 'action' in the criminalisation of the traffic in hazardous wastes lies predominantly in the domestic implementation

---

political attention. ENFORCE is instead less developed and only recently its activities have started to be expanded (eg, in 2020 a formal link between ENFORCE and WCO has been created). See Chapters 2 and 3 for further details.

and enforcement, facilitated by the activity of the most relevant enforcement agencies and international institutions and networks in the field, such as the Environmental Network for Optimising Regulatory Compliance on Illegal Traffic (ENFORCE). The Chapter shows that the penalties and the rate of prosecution are low and usually cases of illegal traffic are resolved by disposing of the waste or requesting the disposal of the waste in another Country or specialised facility. Alternatively, cases are resolved by returning the illegal waste to the Country of export. The Chapter concludes by noticing that waste is progressively taking centre stage, particularly within the discussion about circular economy, e-waste and plastic waste and that it is therefore expected that a higher level of political attention and of financial contribution will be allocated to this phenomenon in the near future.

Chapter 4 addresses MARPOL as another treaty which does not explicitly indicate criminal penalties, but whose provisions are interpreted to allow the use of criminal sanctions for illegal activities falling into its scope of application. MARPOL in fact imposes a general prohibition on all discharges of oil and noxious substances and provides that sanctions shall be established according to the law of the Country under whose authority the ship is operating. Although the nature of these sanctions is not unquestionably and clearly defined in the text, it is assumed that these also include criminal sanctions applied in the context of domestic criminal proceedings.

The second Part of the book examines the evolution and content of European Union (EU) law on environmental crime and evaluates critically the key legal challenges arising in the current state of play. Chapter 5 analyses the harmonisation of substantive criminal law in the field. It places the development of EU substantive criminal law on environmental crime within the broader constitutional context of the evolution of European integration in criminal matters before and after the entry into force of the Treaty of Lisbon. The Chapter analyses the impact of two landmark rulings of the Court of Justice of the European Union on pre-Lisbon EU measures on environmental crime and ship-source pollution and assesses both their constitutional significance and their influence on the development of substantive EU environmental criminal law currently in force. The Chapter covers in detail the provisions of the two main Directives in the field, the Environmental Crime Directive and the Ship-Source Pollution Directive, and includes an analysis of the relationship between international and EU law in relation to the latter. The Chapter evaluates critically the current state of play regarding the implementation of the Environmental Crime Directive and highlights a number of challenges in its operation on the ground. These include the challenge of achieving legal certainty in determining the parameters of criminalisation, the challenge of achieving effective harmonisation in the face of persisting legal diversity, and the challenge of clarifying the relationship between criminal and administrative law regarding the protection of the environment. The Chapter places emphasis on the interrelationship between environmental and organised and financial crime, and stresses the need to address environmental crime also in conjunction with legal instruments focused on money laundering and confiscation. The Chapter is forward-looking, by reflecting on the key challenges for law reform at a time when the Environmental Crime Directive is under revision by EU institutions.

Chapter 6 focuses on criminal procedural law governing environmental crime at EU level. The emphasis here is placed on the operation of the principle of mutual recognition in criminal matters, and the operation of judicial co-operation in the field of environmental crime. The Chapter analyses the key challenges arising from the operation of mutual recognition through two key instruments – the Framework Decision on the European Arrest Warrant and the Directive on the European Investigation Order – and focuses on a number of aspects that are key in the co-operation in the fight against environmental crime (such as the scope of the authorities which can apply mutual recognition, the extent of the waiver of the obligation to verify dual criminality and of the grounds for refusal to recognise and execute a decision across borders). The Chapter examines co-operation from the perspective of the transnational and cross-border dimension of environmental crime. In this context, it also focuses on the EU framework on the settlement of conflicts of jurisdiction and on application of the principle of *ne bis in idem* in the field. The Chapter evaluates critically the application of *ne bis in idem* at both the transnational level (following the Schengen *acquis*) and the domestic level, taking into account the case-law of the Court of Justice and of the European Court of Human Rights on the matter. This in-depth analysis of the application of the *ne bis in idem* principle recognises the fact that legal challenges may arise both in terms of environmental crime prosecutions in multiple jurisdictions, but also in terms of parallel criminal/administrative proceedings on conduct detrimental to the environment also at the national level.

Chapter 7 examines the role of EU bodies and agencies in the fight against environmental crime. The Chapter focuses mainly on the work of Europol and Eurojust, and provides an in-depth and up-to-date analysis of both the operational and the non-operational work of these agencies. The criminal intelligence work of Europol in the field is combined with its strategic work on developing Serious and Organised Crime Threat Assessments and highlighting in this manner the evolving typologies and threats of environmental crime. The Chapter further highlights the co-ordination and awareness-raising work of Eurojust in the field, as well as operational co-operation through the launch of joint investigation teams. A common thread in both cases is the contribution of EU agencies in raising the visibility and knowledge of environmental crime at national level and in strengthening national capacity to tackle the phenomenon. The analysis is complete by a forward-looking overview of the potential of the newly established European Public Prosecutor's Office (EPPO) in the field of environmental crime. The EPPO, which became operational on 1 June 2021, is the first EU body with coercive powers in the field of criminal law, and has a potentially significant role to play in the fight against environmental crime, as long as the latter is related to the offences falling within its current mandate.

The concluding Chapter aims to provide an overview of the key challenges in the evolution of the international and European Union legal framework on environmental crime. This is a dynamic and evolving framework which is gradually coming of age. The conclusion brings together the threads of the analysis running throughout the volume and calls for new thinking in order to achieve legal certainty, effective implementation, and renewed and targeted focus in using criminal law for the effective protection of the environment.

∴

This book is a collaborative work with all Authors involved in the direction and planning of the work, as well as in the drafting of the introduction and the conclusion. Elena Fasoli authored Chapters 2 and 3 (on CITES and the Basel Convention). Malgosia Fitzmaurice authored Chapter 4 (on MARPOL). Valsamis Mitsilegas and Fabio Giuffrida co-authored Chapters 5, 6 and 7 (the EU law Chapters). The opinions expressed by Fabio Giuffrida in these Chapters, the introduction and the conclusion are personal opinions of the Author and do not reflect those of the European Commission.

CHAPTER 2

Environmental Crime at the International Level

Criminalisation of Illegal Trade in Wildlife under the Convention on International Trade in Endangered Species of Wild Fauna and Flora (CITES)

1   Introduction

Illegal trade in wildlife is amongst the most known areas of environmental crime often linked to organised crime and terrorism.[1] According to recent data, traffic in wildlife is worth between USD 7 and 23 billion annually.[2]

Illegal trade in wildlife is a global phenomenon. This is evident, for example, from one of the most recent customs and police transnational operations coordinated by the World Customs Organisation (WCO) and by Interpol, called Operation Thunder 2020. This Operation rallied 103 different States against wildlife and forestry crime and led to large seizures of protected species, triggering arrests and investigations worldwide.[3] This was just the last in a series

---

1   The Chapter focuses on environmentally harmful acts that breach national law implementing multilateral environmental agreements (MEAs) like CITES and that are subject to prosecution and/or to the application of sanctions domestically. The focus is on criminalisation, which according to the UN Commission on Crime Prevention and Criminal Justice (CCPCJ) 'is the harshest form of regulation and involves the most invasive forms of punishment and proceedings. It should thus be used as a last resort when other interventions and sanctions do not or would not have the desired effect. Criminalisation, criminal procedure, and punishment must occur in a proportionate and reasonable manner and should be reserved for serious violations of wildlife, forest, and fisheries laws'. See <https://www.unodc.org/e4j/en/wildlife-crime/module-3/key-issues/criminalization-of-wildlife-trafficking.html> accessed 2 June 2021.
2   Data available at <https://www.traffic.org/about-us/illegal-wildlife-trade/> accessed 2 June 2021. See also UN Secretary General Report on *Tackling Illicit Trafficking in Wildlife*, UN Doc. A/73/947 of 26 June 2019. DP Van Uhm affirms that while these numbers are not to be regarded as accurate since they refer to very rough estimates, at the same time they are able to provide an indication of the value of the illegal wildlife trade (DP Van Uhm, *The Illegal Wildlife Trade: Inside the World of Poachers, Smugglers and Traders* (Springer 2016) 90). For a comprehensive account of the distribution networks in relation to China, see RWY Wong, *The Illegal Wildlife Trade in China, Understanding the Distribution Networks* (Palgrave Macmillan 2019).
3   This operation ran from 14 September to 11 October 2020 and led to 2.082 seizures and apprehended 699 offenders. See <https://www.interpol.int/News-and-Events/News/2020/Wildlife-and-forestry-crime-Worldwide-seizures-in-global-INTERPOL-WCO-operation> accessed 2 June 2021.

of operations carried out annually through a coordinated global action.[4] The Convention on International Trade in Endangered Species of Wild Fauna and Flora (CITES) has operated at the international level since 1975[5] and it tackles this global phenomenon, amongst the other issues deemed within its remit.[6]

CITES requires Parties to have in place legislation that *penalises* international trade that violates the Convention (eg, import or export of CITES specimens without permit or with a forged permit). However, technically the text does not specify whether the violations to which such penalties apply should be considered illegal *per se*, nor whether the nature of the penalties should be criminal.[7] This notwithstanding, the illegality of the violations emerges first of

---

4 See *infra*, section 3.2.
5 UN Treaty Series, Vol. 993, 243. As of January 2021, CITES has 183 Parties, including US and China. See the official website: <https://cites.org/> accessed 2 June 2021. In legal literature, amongst the numerous contributions, see PH Sand, 'Whiter CITES? The Evolution of a Treaty Regime in the Borderline of Trade and the Environment' (1997) 1 *European Journal of International Law* 29; Id, 'Commodity or Taboo? International Regulation of Trade in Endangered Species' (1997) *Green Globe Yearbook* 19; DM Ong, 'The Convention on International Trade in Endangered Species (CITES, 1973): Implications of Recent Developments in International and EC Environmental Law' (1998) 10 *Journal of Environmental Law* 291; J Hutton and B Dickson (eds), *Endangered Species, Threatened Convention: the Past, Present and Future of CITES, the Convention on International Trade in Endangered Species of Wild Fauna and Flora* (Earthscan 2000); R Reeve, *Policing International Trade in Endangered Species: the CITES Treaty and Compliance* (Earthscan 2002); Id, 'The Convention on International Trade in Endangered Species of Wild Fauna and Flora (CITES)' in G Ulfstein (ed), *Making Treaties Work: Human Rights, Environment and Arms* (Cambridge University Press 2007) 134; PW Birnie, AE Boyle and C Redgwell, *International Law and the Environment* (3rd edn, Oxford University Press 2009) 685; M Bowman, P Davies and C Redgwell, *Lyster's International Wildlife Law* (Cambridge University Press 2010) 483–534; W Wijnstekers, *The Evolution of CITES, International Council for Game and Wildlife Conservation* (9th edn, International Council for Game and Wildlife Conservation 2011); PH Sand, 'Endangered Species, International Protection' in R Wolfrum (ed), *Max Planck Encyclopedia of Public International Law* (Oxford University Press 2011) 423–429; Id, 'Enforcing CITES: The Rise and Fall of Trade Sanctions' (2013) 22 *Review of European, Comparative & International Environmental Law* 251; Id, 'International Protection of Endangered Species in the Face of Wildlife Trade: Whither Conservation Diplomacy?' (2017) 20 *Asia Pacific Journal of Environmental Law* 5; P Sands and J Peel, *Principles of International Environmental Law* (4th edn, Cambridge University Press 2018) 409 ff; and R Duffy, 'The Illegal Wildlife Trade in Global Perspective' in L Elliott and WH Schaedla (eds), *Handbook of Transnational Environmental Crime* (Edward Elgar 2016) 109–125.
6 CITES aims at ensuring that international trade in specimens of wild animals and plants used by consumers in their daily lives, for example, for food, healthcare or for fashion purposes does not threaten the survival of the species in the wild.
7 As highlighted by Rose, CITES does not criminalise contraventions of its provisions *per se* (GL Rose, 'International Jurisdictional Challenges in the Suppression of Transnational Environmental Crime' in Elliott and Schaedla (eds) (n 5) 322, 334.

all implicitly from the text: trade which is not undertaken in accordance with the provisions of the Convention is to be considered illegal. By way of example, CITES provides that international trade in endangered species enlisted in Appendix I, the most protected and regulated species,[8] is banned except in presence of exceptional circumstances. Therefore, if this trade is undertaken anyway, in absence of these circumstances, it is illegal. The illegality emerges also when the Standing Committee, which is a subsidiary body to the Convention, recommends Parties to completely suspend trade with States that fail to adopt legislation to penalise illegal trade in wildlife as it was required by the Convention.[9] On the other hand, the emphasis on criminality appears during the implementation phase of the Convention, for example, when the CITES Secretariat encourages Parties to consider maximum terms of imprisonment and fines which are commensurate with felonies or major crimes.[10]

Yet, the textual reference to the penalisation of international trade in wildlife contained in CITES lacks sophistication. One should consider, though, that CITES is a trade treaty, after all. As such, it was not designed to respond to wildlife crime enforcement in any great detail. This is also reflected, for example, in the actors that participate in COPS. Usually these are not law enforcement officers, but environmental biologists, experts with an environmental management or forestry background, who participate with the aim of ensuring that trade is conducted in a sustainable way, without negative impact on the survival of the species. However, one should not disregard the fact that CITES is amongst the very few Multilateral Environmental Agreements (MEAS) that at least puts an emphasis, although limited, on illegality and penalisation.[11]

So where is the real centre of action for the criminalisation of the illegal trade in wildlife? It lies both in domestic enforcement and at the heart of the ever-increasing international liaison of the institutions of CITES, particularly its Secretariat that work in close cooperation with the most important international agencies and institutions on crime and enforcement, such as – but not limited to – the United Nations Office on Drugs and Crimes (UNODC), Interpol and the WCO.[12] Significantly, the cooperation between the institutions

---

8   See *infra* (n 19).
9   This happened, for example, in 2012 in relation to Comoros, Guinea-Bissau, Paraguay and Rwanda. See <https://cites.org/eng/news/pr/2012/20120731_SC62_results.php> accessed 2 June 2021.
10 See *Fourteenth Meeting of the Conference of the Parties the Hague (Netherlands), 3–15 June 2007*, Doc. CoP14 Doc. 24, 2.
11 See also the Basel Convention, Chapter 3 in this volume.
12 In that perspective, MEAS have been described as 'foundational documents of what have become dynamic legal regimes. It is within this dynamism that space has been created

of CITES and the various international enforcement agencies is complementary in nature: the mandate of the latter agencies is essentially crime investigation, yet they need to rely on CITES for establishing what is legal or illegal trade under the Convention. In such a perspective, it should not come as a surprise that the most recent guiding document on drafting domestic legislation (including in terms of prosecution, criminal offences and penalties) to combat illegal trade in wildlife under the Convention has been developed within UNODC, and not within CITES.[13]

Against the above background, the present Chapter explores the existing tools and mechanisms, including their limits, related to the criminalisation of the international illegal trade in wildlife, drawing attention to domestic enforcement and to the activity of the most relevant enforcement agencies and international institutions in the field, but always maintaining as a primary point of view the international law (CITES) perspective.

The Chapter concludes that despite the multi-agency and multi-level approaches through which the fight against illegal wildlife traffic currently takes place, in many Countries (not only in developing ones) the legislation to tackle it is still too weak (often it does not consider wildlife crime as 'serious crime', although this trend is now changing) and the level of detecting and prosecuting wildlife crime is very low, including because of the limited enforcement capacity. Clearly, in many Countries combating wildlife crime is still not a priority. The hope is that the progressive increase of public awareness, based on the ever-emerging scientific evidence as to the links between the global health crisis and the illegal trade in wildlife will contribute to include wildlife crime amongst the top priorities for action at the national, as well as international levels.

2 CITES and the Provisions for the Prohibition and Penalisation/Criminalisation of Illegal Trade in Wildlife

In this section we will first of all briefly introduce the main provisions and institutional structure of CITES (section 2.1). We will then outline the legal, as well as the factual, contours of illegal trade in wildlife under the Convention

---

for normative and operational conversations that have expanded to include the global crime prevention and criminal justice communities of practice' (Elliot and Schaedla, 'Transnational Environmental Crime: Excavating the Complexities – an Introduction' in Elliott and Schaedla (eds) (n 5) 15).

13   UNODC, *Guide on Drafting Legislation to Combat Wildlife Crime* (2018).

(section 2.2). In order to do so, we will start analysing the available data on CITES-related wildlife crime, and then we will address the most important features of the latter within the context of the other relevant international instruments that currently complement (ie, operate alongside or are relevant for) CITES. After that, we will move from the general to the specific, by analysing in detail the provision of CITES that somehow 'talks' in illegality terms of the trade in wildlife, namely, Article VIII.1 (section 2.3). The latter will be thus put in the spotlight, evaluating specific content therein, which, once enriched by the recommendations of the Conference of the Parties (COP) to CITES, as well as by the good practices followed by Parties as identified by the Secretariat, will be assessed, including through its implementation and compliance by Parties.[14] The analysis will highlight both strengths and limitations of Article VIII.1.

2.1 General Provisions and Institutional Structure of CITES

CITES accords varying degrees of protection to more than 38.000 species of animals and plants.[15] Under CITES the 'specimens' may be living or dead and include 'any readily recognizable part or derivative thereof',[16] namely, 'any specimen which appears from an accompanying document, the packaging or a mark or label, or from other circumstances, to be a part or derivative of an animal or plant of a species included in the Appendices'.[17] CITES states that 'species' includes 'any species, subspecies or geographically separate population thereof'.[18]

CITES works through the listing on Appendices of species of wild flora and fauna whose conservation status is threatened by international trade. The level of protection accorded to the species depends upon which Appendix it is listed in.[19] Imports and exports of the species concerned from the different

---

14 Although a forensic distinction between implementation and compliance is difficult to be made, for the purposes of the present Chapter we consider 'implementation' the act of adopting legislative, regulatory and/or administrative domestic measures in order to give effect to the provisions of the Convention; whereas we consider 'compliance' acting in accordance with and in fulfilment of the adopted measures. As highlighted in the document CITES Doc.CoP14 Doc. 24 '[w]ithout compliance, legislative requirements will not achieve their desired results. There cannot be compliance without implementation but there may be implementation without compliance' (3).

15 This number is evolving. See <https://cites.org/eng/disc/species.php> accessed 2 June 2021.

16 Article I(b) of the Convention.

17 CITES Resolution Conf. 9.6 (Rev).

18 Art I(a) of the Convention.

19 Appendix I includes those species threatened with extinction and in respect of which commercial trade is not appropriate or sustainable. Any trade listed in Appendix I species

Countries are subject to a permit system implemented by national management and scientific authorities.

The institutional structure of CITES is composed of the Secretariat, the COP, the Standing Committee,[20] the animals and the plants committees[21] and the management and scientific authorities that operate at the national level.[22] The Secretariat is administered by the United Nations Environment Programme (UNEP) and like for other MEAs it oversees the general application of the Convention. The COP meets every two to three years and it considers and adopts amendments to the Appendices. It also reviews the progress of restoration and conservation of the listed species. The role of the COP is also that of adopting criteria for the granting of permits.[23] The COP discussed,

---

requires prior permits from both the importing and the exporting countries. Certificates are also required for the re-export of species. Appendix II includes those species not necessarily in danger of extinction, but which may become endangered if their trade is not strictly regulated, as well as those for which trade must be strictly regulated to permit effective control. An export permit is required for any trade in Appendix II species and must be presented to the importing State's customs authorities. Appendix III includes those species that Parties choose to make subject to regulation, and which require the cooperation of the other Parties in controlling trade. Trade in Appendix III species requires the management authority of the exporting State to issue an export permit, if it is the State that included the species concerned in Appendix III, or a certificate of origin, if it is another country.

20 The Standing Committee is a permanent advisory body whose members correspond to the six major geographical regions (Africa, Asia, Europe, North America, Central and South America and the Carribean, and Oceania). It provides general policy advice on matters brought to it by the Secretariat and it drafts resolutions for consideration by the COP. The Standing Committee is also responsible, as it will be described further on, for taking decisions in relation to implementation and compliance with the obligations of the Convention.

21 The animals committee and the plants committee are sources of specialised knowledge on certain species that are either controlled by CITES or may become so. They provide for scientific advice on issues relevant to trade in animal and plant species under the Appendices; they undertake periodic reviews on such animal or plant species, and they handle nomenclature issues.

22 The national management authorities instituted by each State Party are competent to grant permits without which the international imports and exports of specimens would be illegal. These authorities also establish the national scientific authorities to advise them on the effects of trade upon any listed species. Although the mandate of these authorities is limited to international trade, some Parties have given them additional responsibilities related to wildlife conservation.

23 For example, the twelfth COP required that all Parties adapt the content and format of their permits to the standardized version; that a security stamp is fixed for each permit; and that no management authority could issue permits retrospectively (CITES Resolution Conf. 12.3 (Rev. CoP14)). See Wijnstekers, *The Evolution of CITES* (n 5) 157–194.

for example, the use of electronic permitting systems for the trade in CITES specimens.[24]

2.2 Illegal Trade in Wildlife under CITES in Conjunction with the Other Relevant International Instruments

Illegal trafficking in wild fauna and flora is a major concern under CITES.[25] Yet, it is difficult to draw an exact picture of the scale of the CITES-related illegal wildlife trade. This is first of all due to the fact that this trade runs in parallel with the legal one; therefore, it is often difficult forensically to distinguish between the two.[26] Secondly, it is only recently that Parties to CITES have started to release more information regarding the cases of illegal trade occurring within their jurisdictions.[27] Especially in the past, Parties may have feared that if they released those data, they could be blamed for not having been able to prevent illegal trade, instead of being seen as victims of it themselves. Nowadays, an increasing number of Parties report cases of illegal traffic occurring within their jurisdiction to the CITES Secretariat (the more Parties in the world are affected, the more they are incentivised to release data). That being said, it is also true that the difficulty to report cases of illegal trade to the Secretariat is not only related to the lack of political will or to the fear of 'name and shame'. Sometimes, national management authorities struggle to collect relevant data from the police, the customs authorities and the judiciary.

The scarcity of data is confirmed also at the regional level. The 2020 evaluation of the European Commission regarding the transposition of the Environmental Crime Directive in the EU's Member States,[28] in relation to wildlife trafficking (along with waste trafficking), indicates that

---

24 See CoP13 Doc. 45. Some Parties expressed the view that the development of such a system would greatly assist in the handling and processing of CITES applications, as well as in the collection and dissemination of CITES trade information.
25 CITES Resolution Conf. 11.3 (Rev. CoP18), Compliance and enforcement, 2.
26 This is the case, for example, of caviar as luxury food that has made sturgeon a protected species. The legal harvesting of caviar coexists with an illegal market where wild sturgeon are poached for their caviar. See T Wyatt, 'The Uncharismatic and Unorganised Side to Wildlife Smuggling' in Elliott and Schaedla (eds) (n 5) 129, 135.
27 In relation to wildlife crime more broadly, as recently highlighted, 'nations generally do not routinely collect, collate, and publish statistical data on environmental crime, environmental offenders, or actions taken against them. Some countries and international organizations have, however, made credible attempts to collect and publish data on environmental crimes' (*The State of Knowledge of Crimes that Have Serious Impacts on the Environment* (UNEP 2018)).
28 On the Environmental Crime Directive see also *infra* section 2.3.1 and, more extensively, Chapter 5 of this book.

[t]here is a general lack of statistical data on environmental crime which makes it difficult to monitor developments and trends. Waste and Wildlife crime belong to the largest and best documented sectors of environmental crime; Member States have identified these as areas where criminal activity is particularly frequent and serious. Both areas have strong cross-border impacts, as they involve illegal trafficking inside the EU but also beyond with the EU as a point of destination, transit or origin.[29]

By contrast, the data regarding specific specimens are somehow easier to collect. By way of example, the Elephant Trade Information System (ETIS), which operates under the supervision of the CITES Standing Committee, since 1998 measures and records on a global basis the levels and trends of illegal trade in ivory and other elephant specimens in elephant range States, ivory consumer States and ivory transit States.[30]

In 2016 the COP has introduced a brand-new reporting tool for the global data on illegal trade in wildlife. Parties have to submit an annual illegal trade report on all seizures for violations involving CITES-listed species, irrespective of whether the seizure was made at an international border or at domestic level (for example, during the search of a private or business property or during inspections at domestic markets).[31] Even though the operation of this new requirement is still at an early stage, it contributes to the efforts made in drawing a clearer picture regarding the scale of the issue. In this respect it is worth anticipating that the data collected in the CITES annual illegal trade reports are shared with the members of the International Consortium on Combating Wildlife Crime (ICCWC) in order to allow data to be used in ICCWC global research and analysis on wildlife and forest crime.[32]

The number of the CITES-related seizures undertaken by Parties is not able, alone, to capture the full extent of the phenomenon under review.[33] Yet,

---

29 European Commission, 'Commission Staff Working Document Evaluation of the Directive 2008/99/ EC of the European Parliament and of the Council of 19 November 2008 on the Protection of the Environment through Criminal Law' SWD (2020) 259 final, 28 October 2020, 8, 9.
30 CITES Conf. 10.10 (Rev CoP18), Trade in elephant specimens, Annex 1.
31 The annual illegal trade report is mandatory, but not subject to compliance procedures. See <https://cites.org/eng/resources/reports/Annual_Illegal_trade_report> accessed 2 June 2021. The data contained in the annual illegal trade reports are then processed, stored and analysed by UNODC. This important activity is currently underfunded, though. See Doc CoP18 Inf 44.
32 See *infra* section 3.2.
33 Already in 2012, the *Wildlife and Forest Crime Analytic Toolkit* prepared by UNODC was warning that '[t]he scale of the problem, the volume of the illegal trade and the number

seizures are a key data point for the analysis of illegal trading. This is shown by the UNODC World Wildlife Crime Report (hereinafter 'the UNODC 2020 Report'), which draws on seizures data and is most relevant for the present analysis.[34] The UNODC 2020 Report testifies first of all to the diversity and constant shifts in trends of wildlife crime.[35] It is reported, for example, that nearly 6,000 species have been seized between 1999 and 2018, including not only mammals but reptiles, corals, birds, and fish. Also, geographical and species trends change over time. By way of example, seizures of rhino horns and pangolins have increased significantly in recent years, whereas agar woods seizures have sharply declined.[36]

The UNODC 2020 Report also describes the critical role played by organised crime within wildlife trafficking. Wildlife markets are in fact particularly vulnerable to criminal infiltration.[37] Organised crime tends to target States where it can operate more efficiently with lower risk of punishment.[38] Since national authorities can choose the level of seriousness to attach to crimes related to specific CITES species,[39] in some Countries, illegal trade, for example, in

---

of people involved in it are largely unknown and often impossible to calculate. The clandestine nature and the lack of comprehensive enforcement and research make it impossible to know the true size of the phenomenon. Indeed, many figures circulated in various reports and articles are the result of guesswork rather than of systematic analysis' (169).

34   UNODC, *World Wildlife Crime Report* (2020). The first edition of the report was released in 2016. The Report draws on seizure data compiled in UNODC's World WISE database. In terms of the nature and breadth of the analysis, the Report indicates that the term 'wildlife crime' refers to harvesting and trade contrary to national law, particularly, but not exclusively, the national laws implemented in fulfilment of CITES obligations.

35   UNODC 2020 Report, 9.

36   ibid 10.

37   On the involvement of organised groups in various environmental crimes, including wildlife crime see, for example, UNEP, *The State of Knowledge of Crimes that Have Serious Impacts on the Environment* (2018) 10, 18, 19. For the difference between organised crime and organised networks see L Elliott, 'Criminal Networks and Illicit Chains of Custody in Transnational Environmental Crime' in Elliott and Schaedla (eds) (n 5) 24, 28. More in general on the role of organised crime see Duffy, 'The Illegal Wildlife Trade in Global Perspective' (n 5) 199 ff.

38   According to UNODC, 'this is the case, for example, with pangolin scale traders who chose to store their stock in the Democratic Republic of Congo as opposed to other source countries due to a perception of lesser capacity for interdiction' (2020 Report, 12).

39   Although, as it will be shown *infra* in this section, the new direction is in the sense to consider wildlife crime involving organised criminal groups as a serious crime. In legal doctrine see, for example, G Broussard, 'Building an Effective Criminal Justice Response to Wildlife Trafficking: Experiences from ASEAN Region' (2017) 26 *Review of European Comparative & International Environmental Law* 118, 121.

pangolins, can be less serious than other species,[40] therefore, organised criminal groups are more inclined to operate there.[41] Organised crime groups also exploit captive breeding for commercial purposes which is legal in several countries (and under the Convention) by using licensed breeding facilities to illegally supply the illegal trade in exotic pets, luxury products and ingredients for traditional medicine.[42] In addition, there has been an increasing concern that such criminal groups might be generating funding to support militias or terrorist networks (wildlife crime can, for example, be associated with threat finance to conflicts or even terrorism),[43] which, in turn, put illegal trade in wildlife in a broader context of global security threat.[44] Taken from this perspective, it does not come as a surprise that in 2014 the UN Security Council (SC) felt the need to express concern about the convergence between organised crime and terrorism.[45] UNODC has estimated that at least 40 percent of internal conflicts in the last 60 years have a link to exploitation or illegal traffic in natural resources.[46]

The breadth of wildlife crime worldwide is not attributable to organised crime only. Corporate crime can also play a role. Legitimate companies, again, thanks to the permeability between legal and illegal activities, can in fact use

---

40   As known, illegal wildlife trade is not exclusively a phenomenon related to high-value wildlife (eg, megafauna like great apes or big cats), but it encompasses also so-called 'uncharismatic' species. See Wyatt, 'The Uncharismatic and Unorganised Side to Wildlife Smuggling' (n 26).

41   UNODC 2020 Report, 27.

42   ibid 13. This permeability between legal and illegal activities has been highlighted also by the European Commission in the recent assessment report on the Environmental Crime Directive (European Commission, 'Commission Staff Working Document Evaluation of the Directive 2008/99/EC' (n 29) 54).

43   UNEP, *The State of Knowledge of Crimes that Have Serious Impacts on the Environment* (2018) 14.

44   The SC has expressed grave concern about, for example, the illegal exploitation of natural resources, including of timber and wildlife, by armed groups and criminal networks, against the peace in the Democratic Republic of the Congo and in the Central African Republic. See SC Resolutions 2463 and 2399 of 2019. In 2014 the SC addressed instead the situation of conflict in the Great Lakes region of Africa with Resolution 2136. In legal doctrine see, for example, L Elliot, 'The Securitisation of Transnational Environmental Crime and the Militarisation of Conservation' in Elliott and Schaedla (eds) (n 5) 68; and F Staiano, 'Wildlife Trafficking under the Lens of International Law: A Threat to the Peace or a Serious Transnational Crime' (2020) 9 *Cambridge International Law Journal* 137.

45   SC Resolution n. 2195 of 19 December 2014, 1.

46   C Nellemann et al, *The Rise of Environmental Crime, A Growing Threat to Natural Resources Peace, Development and Security* (2016) 67.

their legal activities to smuggle wildlife within international trade activities.[47] Additionally, wildlife crime can be also perpetrated by individuals acting alone.[48]

A word of caution is in order here. CITES addresses illegal trade in wildlife with an international dimension. This means that the illegal trade which is captured under the treaty is only that which involves products that have crossed borders in contravention of its provisions. This excludes the domestic, although also relevant, dimension of this type of trade.[49] This applies also to organised crime. In fact, when illegal trade in wildlife is associated with organised crime (as often it is the case), only the activities of organised criminal groups that operate in more than one Country would fall within the scope of CITES.

Moreover, the international trade in wildlife which is relevant for CITES technically differs from what it is known with the expression 'transnational environmental crime' (TEC).[50] While TEC is not the primary subject of the present analysis,[51] Elliott and Schaedla define TEC as

---

47   UNEP, *The State of Knowledge of Crimes that Have Serious Impacts on the Environment* (2018) 9.
48   ibid 8. See also Wyatt, 'The Uncharismatic and Unorganised Side to Wildlife Smuggling' (n 26) 134.
49   According to M Wellsmith, for instance, 'wildlife crime can be considered as occurring at the micro-level (such as subsistence poaching and individual acts of cruelty), meso-level (such as domestic trade in resident vulnerable species and organised illegal hunts) and macro-level (notably import and export of endangered species for international trade)' ('Wildlife Crime: The Problems of Enforcement' (2011) 17 European Journal on Criminal Policy and Research 125, 128).
50   See, amongst many, Elliott and Schaedla (eds) (n 5); V Mitsilegas and F Giuffrida, *The Role of EU Agencies in Fighting Transnational Environmental Crime: New Challenges for Eurojust and Europol* (Brill 2017) 1; J Ayling, 'Prevention of Transnational Environmental Crimes and Regulatory Pluralism' in ed P Drahos (ed), *Regulatory Theory: Foundations and Applications*, (ANU Press 2017) 499–516; and P Stoett, 'Transnational Environmental Crime' in A Swain and J Öjendal (eds), *Routledge Handbook of Environmental Conflict and Peacebuilding* (Routledge 2018) 29–41.
51   We share the view of those that maintain that 'TEC is not a legal category as such. Rather, it is a working definition resulting from the abstraction of concepts elaborated in soft law instruments and information provided by public bodies as well as academic research' and that consider the adoption of an 'additional protocol to the Palermo Convention specifically dealing with environmental crime [...] beneficial in the prevention and prosecution of TEC' (GM Vagliasindi, 'Legal Perspectives on Environmental Crime; the Transnational Dimension of Environmental Crime' in V Mitsilegas et al (eds), *Research Handbook on Transnational Crime* (Edward Elgar 2019) 142, 152, 160). Gregory Rose as well supports the idea of the adoption of an additional Protocol to UNTOC (G Rose, 'International Jurisdictional Challenges in the Suppression of Transnational Environmental Crime' in Elliott and Schaedla (eds) (n 5), 342).

cross-border trading of species, resources, waste or pollutants in violation of prohibitions or regulatory regimes established by multilateral environmental agreements (MEAS), or in contravention of national laws. It includes the trafficking of illegally logged timber (sometimes called 'stolen' timber); the *illegal trade in endangered, threatened and protected species*; the transboundary dumping of toxic and hazardous waste, including electronic waste (e-waste); and the black market in ozone depleting substances (ODS) or other prohibited or regulated chemicals.[52]

Therefore, the international trade in wildlife which is relevant for CITES is the one that infringes upon CITES (international law) provisions directly; whereas TEC, which anyway is not only limited to trade in wildlife, consists in breaches of domestic law (although also derivative of international law provisions, including CITES) characterised by a cross-border or transnational dimension (for example, the activity of laundering outside one Country's jurisdiction the profits of a wildlife crime committed partially inside it, in breach of domestic law).[53] A further distinction is that international trade in wildlife in violation of CITES does not necessarily attract, although being now highly encouraged as will be seen further below, criminal penalties, whereas the latter are usually attached to TEC.

To add another layer to this analysis, when TEC overlaps with breaches of national law that implements CITES and when it is also 'organised',[54] its regime encroaches upon that of the 2000 United Nations Convention on Transnational Organised Crime (UNTOC, so-called 'Palermo Convention').[55]

In 2016 the CITES COP, following-up on a call which had already been made by other international organisations and institutions (above all the General Assembly (GA) to the United Nations with its Resolution 69/314 of 30 July

---

52   Emphasis added. Elliott and Schaedla (eds) (n 5) 3–4.
53   Rose, 'International Jurisdictional Challenges in the Suppression of Transnational Environmental Crime' (n 51) 325.
54   However, let's not forget that while 'transnational crime is heavily associated with organised crime, organization is not a necessary condition of transnational crime' (N Boister, *An Introduction to Transnational Criminal Law* (Oxford University Press 2012) 6.
55   UN Treaty Series, Vol. 2225, 209. The Palermo Convention states that an offence is of transnational nature if: (a) It is committed in more than one State; (b) It is committed in one State but a substantial part of its preparation, planning, direction or control takes place in another State; (c) It is committed in one State but involves an organised criminal group that engages in criminal activities in more than one State; or (d) It is committed in one State but has substantial effects in another State (Article 2).

2015)⁵⁶ recommended Parties to make illegal trafficking in protected species of wild fauna and flora involving organised criminal groups⁵⁷ a 'serious crime' in accordance with their national legislation and Article 2(b) of the Palermo Convention. The COP was thus recommending making it punishable by a maximum deprivation of liberty of at least four years or a more serious penalty.⁵⁸ This clearly included criminal penalties. The advantage of doing so is that States can benefit from mutual legal assistance, joint investigations and from the use of specialised investigative techniques like undercover operations.⁵⁹ In 2019 the GA reiterated this call.⁶⁰ This level of international attention testifies to the increased consideration that wildlife trafficking has now acquired.⁶¹ At the same time, as will be shown further on in the analysis, this does not correspond to a high level of domestic enforcement by the Parties to CITES.⁶² Be that as it may, also the COP to the Palermo Convention, from its part, called upon States Parties to make crimes that affect the environment, in appropriate

---

56 Para 4. See also GA Resolution 68/193 of 18 December 2013. In addition, see ECOSOC Resolution 2013/40 of 25 July 2013 on crime prevention and criminal justice responses to illicit trafficking in protected species of wild fauna and flora, in which the Council encouraged Member States to make illicit trafficking in protected species of wild fauna and flora involving organised criminal groups a serious crime. Similarly, see ECOSOC Resolutions 2003/27, 2008/25, and 2011/36. See also the International Consortium on Combating Wildlife Crime (ICCWC) high-level side event on 'Wildlife and Forest Crime: A Serious Crime' organised in the margins of the 13th United Nations Congress on Crime Prevention and Criminal Justice held in Doha on 13 April 2015. See <https://www.unodc.org/dohadecl aration/news/2015/04/calls-for-wildlife-and-forest-crime-to-be-treated-as-serious-crime .html> accessed 2 June 2021.
57 For the purposes of the Palermo Convention, organised criminal group 'shall mean a structured group of three or more persons, existing for a period of time and acting in concert with the aim of committing one or more serious crimes or offences established in accordance with this Convention, in order to obtain, directly or indirectly, a financial or other material benefit' (Article 2(a)).
58 CITES Resolution Conf. 11.3 (Rev. CoP17), Compliance and enforcement, para 13(g).
59 UNODC 2020 Report, 20.
60 GA Resolution 74/177 of 18 December 2019, para 51.
61 Several other resolutions have been adopted by the GA on trafficking in wildlife. For example, Resolution 69/314 of 30 July 2015, Resolution 70/301 of 9 September 2016, Resolution 71/326 of 28 September 2017, and more recently Resolution 73/343 of 20 September 2019. In the same vein, UNEP has recognised the adverse economic, social and environmental impact of the illegal trade in wildlife and strongly encouraged Member States to take measures to combat it. See, for example, Resolutions 1/3 of 2014 and 2/14 of 2016. In legal doctrine see, particularly, CM Montecorvo, 'Il rilievo internazionale del fenomeno del *Wildlife Trafficking*: ulteriori sviluppi' (2016) *Ordine internazionale e diritti umani* 861.
62 See *infra* section 3.

cases, serious crimes, in accordance with their national legislation, as defined in Article 2(b) of the Convention.[63]

A further element which characterises illegal trade in wildlife under CITES is its links with other crimes, such as, for example, money laundering and corruption.[64] In relation to the former, the GA had in 2015 already called upon Member States to review and amend national legislation as necessary and appropriate so that money laundering offences connected to the illegal wildlife trade are treated as predicate offences, as defined in UNTOC. To that extent, money laundering offences would be actionable under domestic proceeds of crime legislation.[65] The COP to CITES made a similar call in 2016.[66]

In relation to corruption, the GA in 2015 called upon Member States to prohibit, prevent and counter any form of corruption that facilitates illicit trafficking in wildlife and wildlife products.[67] Here, the 2003 United Nations Convention Against Corruption (UNCAC),[68] adopted within UNODC, is the relevant instrument. Even though UNCAC does not explicitly refer to environmental (including wildlife) crime, it nevertheless applies to it. It is indisputable, in fact, that corruption facilitates wildlife crime whilst also weakening the institutional foundations of States.[69] A typical example is the case of a border control or a law enforcement officer who, encouraged by the fact that they would not be (or very seldom) prosecuted,[70] decides to abuse their position of authority, for example, by accepting forged licenses for CITES species in exchange of money. The fact that UNCAC emphasises, for example, the need

---

63   Resolution on Preventing and combating crimes that affect the environment falling within the scope of the United Nations Convention against Transnational Organised Crime (CTOC/COP/2020/L.9/Rev.1, 16 October 2020, para 5).
64   For an overview of all the associated offences that are used to facilitate wildlife crime or that are committed in the aftermath of it, see UNODC, *Wildlife and Forest Crime Analytic Toolkit* (2012) 46–59. See also section 6 of Chapter 5 of this book.
65   CITES Resolution 69/314, 30 July 2015, para 4.
66   CITES Resolution Conf. 11.3 (Rev. CoP17), Compliance and enforcement, para 13(e).
67   GA Resolution 69/314, 30 July 2015, para 10. In legal doctrine see, for example, T Wyatt et al, 'Corruption and Wildlife Trafficking: Three Case Studies Involving Asia' (2018) 13 *Asian Criminology* 35.
68   UN Treaty Series, Vol. 2349, p. 41.
69   See, for example, Broussard, 'Building an Effective Criminal Justice Response to Wildlife Trafficking: Experiences from ASEAN Region' (n 39) 125–126.
70   'Rule of law is undermined through corruption of law enforcement and the judiciary. Government officials, when implicated in transnational crime, are rarely prosecuted, further undermining government legitimacy' (Nellemann et al, *The Rise of Environmental Crime, A Growing Threat to Natural Resources Peace, Development and Security* (n 40) 41).

for effective and coordinated anti-corruption policies for law enforcement officials to ensure that corrupt authorities are held accountable,[71] clearly has a bearing also on wildlife authorities. In 2019, the COP to UNCAC has adopted a resolution on preventing and combating corruption as it relates to crimes that have an impact on the environment. Significantly, the resolution requests UNODC to continue supporting Member States in addressing corruption in their natural resource sectors and continue developing additional tools to that end.[72]

With the same aim, just a few years before, in 2016, the COP to CITES had adopted an unprecedented resolution on prohibiting, preventing, detecting and countering corruption which facilitates activities conducted in violation of CITES.[73] As indicated by one Author, this resolution was the

> first real step to demonstrate a degree of political willingness to tackle this issue and to openly recognize that the problem of corruption within the regulatory agencies of CITES cannot be solved only through internal audits, but it rather requires the intervention of criminal justice institutions.[74]

In that context the COP to CITES also called for the development of guidelines that could 'assist Parties to mitigate the risks of corruption in the trade chain as it relates to CITES-listed specimens'.[75] These new guidelines, which have now been developed by UNODC,[76] suggest, for example, that one of the most effective ways to address wildlife crime and related corruption is for wildlife management authorities to undertake a process of corruption risk management within their institution.[77]

---

71   Article 5 UNCAC.
72   UNCAC Resolution 8/12.
73   CITES Conf. 17.6.
74   Broussard, 'Building an Effective Criminal Justice Response to Wildlife Trafficking: Experiences from ASEAN Region' (n 39) 126.
75   CITES Decision 17.83.
76   UNODC, *Scaling Back Corruption, a Guide on Addressing Corruption for Wildlife Management Authorities*, 2019.
77   ibid x-xi. See also M Yeater, 'Corruption and Illegal Wildlife Trafficking' in UNODC collection of papers on 'Impact of corruption on the environment and the United Nations Convention against Corruption as a tool to address it' fourth Conference of States Parties to the United Nations Convention against Corruption, Marrakesh, Morocco, 26 October 2011, available online.

Finally, a further testament to the importance of UNCAC (along with UNTOC) for the CITES regime is that since 2007 the CITES COP is being recommending that States that are not yet Parties to them consider doing so.[78]

The above-described features are well-known aspects of the illegal trade in wildlife. A less known aspect is perhaps its link with the internet.[79] Like for other products illegally obtained, wildlife and natural resources are now placed on various websites and social media platforms that enable buyers to negotiate prices and place orders. CITES made for the first time the link between illegal wildlife trade and the internet back in 2010. However, it was only in 2016 that the issue was addressed more closely[80] and also in 2019 when the COP discussed and agreed on strengthening the provisions of the Convention to combat wildlife crime linked to the internet.[81] For example, the COP has recommended the Parties to appoint national points of contact with knowledge and training on online investigations, evidence gathering, and prosecutions to serve as focal points for enquiries from other Parties and intergovernmental organisations.[82] In addition, in 2020 the CITES Secretariat in cooperation with Interpol has been developing practical guidelines to assist law enforcement officers to combat wildlife crime linked to the internet.[83]

Against the above background, we will now turn to analyse the specific provision of CITES dedicated to the prohibition and penalisation of the trade in violation of the Convention, ie, Article VIII.1.

2.3 Prohibition, Penalisation and Criminalisation of Illegal Trade in Wildlife under the Convention

CITES does not contain a dedicated article describing what specific conducts should be deemed illegal trade for the purposes of the Convention.[84] However, it emerges anyway when Article VIII.1 requires that Parties

---

78 CITES Resolution Conf. 11.3 (Rev. CoP14), Compliance and enforcement.
79 For the aspects of law enforcement related to cybercrime see also *infra* section 3.1.
80 CITES Decisions 17.92–17.96.
81 CITES Decisions 18.81–18.85 on Wildlife Crime Linked to the Internet.
82 CITES Resolution Conf. 11.3 (Rev. CoP18), Compliance and enforcement, para 12(d).
83 INTERPOL, *Wildlife Crime Linked to the Internet, Practical Guidelines for Law Enforcement Practitioners* (2020). Despite these efforts according to TRAFFIC 'the problem of illegal wildlife trade as linked to the internet, has received insufficient attention internationally. Wildlife cybercrime is not yet regarded as a crime category in its own right in international or national legislation, and related policies and law enforcement actions are not sufficiently comprehensive or targeted' (*Combating Wildlife Crime Linked to the Internet, Global Trends and China's Experiences* (2019) v).
84 By contrast, the Basel Convention does so. See Chapter 3 in this volume.

take appropriate measures to enforce the provisions of the present Convention and to *prohibit trade* in specimens *in violation thereof.* These shall include measures *a*) to *penalise* the trade in, or possession of, such specimens, or both; *b*) and to provide for the *confiscation or return* to the state of export of such specimens.[85]

Illegal trade in wildlife is thus the trade undertaken in a way other than in accordance with the provisions of the Convention. Article VIII.1 gives no guidance as to the level of punishment or any directions on whether the nature of the penalties should be criminal. One Author has noted that 'a penalty imposed by one party may be considered a slap on the wrist by another'.[86] However, if one considers that other MEAs do not put any emphasis on illegality (or criminality),[87] the provisions of CITES might not appear so limited after all. At least, Article VIII.1 goes so far as requiring that Parties need to have in place provisions that will make it illegal to trade other than in accordance with the Convention (ie, prohibition of trade violating CITES); provisions on penalties (ie, penalisation of illegal trade); and provisions on the establishment of

---

85 Emphasis added. As far as confiscation is concerned, CITES requires that confiscated live specimens are either returned to their State of export at the expense of that State or sent to a rescue center or to another appropriate place (Article VIII. 4(b) of the Convention). See Wijnstekers, *The Evolution of CITES* (n 5) 261–298. Some Parties, such as the UK, have adopted legislation that authorises the customs officials to recover the expenses for returning the specimens to the State of origin directly from the importer. The tenth COP upheld this approach and noted that 'the successful recovery of the costs of confiscation and disposal from the guilty Party may be a disincentive for illegal trade' (Resolution Conf. 10.7 (Rev.CoP15)).

86 BL Bacon, 'Enforcement Mechanisms in International Wildlife Agreements and the United States: Wading Through the Murk' (1999) 12 *The Georgetown International Environmental Law Review* 331, 344. Broussard indicates that, for example, all Countries in the ASEAN region have introduced criminal provisions and jail punishment for the most serious wildlife offences (Broussard, 'Building an Effective Criminal Justice Response to Wildlife Trafficking: Experiences from ASEAN Region' (n 39) 119). According to Vagliasindi 'the inclusion of a duty to criminalise within MEAs, including common ranges of criminal sanctions, and the implementation of such a provision at the domestic level would be extremely beneficial in the fight against TEC', even though such a development does not seem feasible for the time being (Vagliasindi, 'Legal Perspectives on Environmental Crime; the Transnational Dimension of Environmental Crime' (n 51) 151).

87 But see the Basel Convention in Chapter 3 of this volume. It is worth mentioning that the *Fourth Programme for the Development and Periodic Review of Environmental Law* (IV Montevideo Programme), amongst the actions to achieve implementation of, compliance with, and enforcement of environmental law, indicates to 'evaluate and, as appropriate, promote the wider use of criminal and administrative law in the enforcement of domestic and national environmental law' (UNEP/Env.Law/2010/1, I.A(j)).

authorities to confiscate what was traded in violation of the Convention (ie, authorisation to confiscate). For the purposes of the present analysis, we will focus on the first and second limbs of this provision.

As far as the first limb is concerned, along with a general clause prohibiting any trade in CITES specimens in violation of the Convention (eg, without a valid permit or certificate), the Party is also required to clearly set out in the legislation the conditions and procedures for the granting of permits and certificates required for trading in CITES specimens in order to ensure that such trade is legal, sustainable and traceable.

As far as the second limb is concerned, CITES requires Parties to include in the domestic legislation a clear definition of the prohibited actions/activities, such as, for example, trade without a valid permit/certificate; possession of specimens that were illegally acquired/introduced; or falsification of documents or mis-declaration of origin/volume of the specimens.

Article VIII.1 of CITES does not exist in isolation. It is enriched by the recommendations of the COP that, although not binding for Parties, play an extremely important role in the evolution of CITES, as well as by the good practices followed by Parties.

The CITES COP has recommended that Parties should designate in the legislation the ministries and agencies and their agents mandated to enforce the Convention, including the necessary powers and authorities to do so; that they should cross-reference to any offences and penalties related to CITES that are provided in customs, general crime/penal, environmental or other legislation; and, most importantly, that they should make illicit trafficking involving organised criminal groups a serious crime.[88]

Moreover, it is a good practice that criminal legislation on regulated or prohibited goods, organised crime, money laundering,[89] controlled deliveries, wiretapping, the use of informants, etc should cover serious offences related to CITES; and that the legislation should also provide offences and penalties for attempted violations, aiding and abetting, corporate and corporate officer liability, recidivism, obstruction of justice, false statement, tampering, and fraud.

---

88   CITES Resolution Conf.11.3, Compliance and enforcement.
89   This is also recommended by the COP, namely, that Parties 'implement national legislation to combat money laundering and facilitate asset forfeiture to ensure that criminals do not benefit from the proceeds of their crimes, stressing that effective prosecutions against money laundering linked to wildlife trafficking benefit from bringing together wildlife trade and money laundering expertise, including from financial intelligence units, as appropriate' (Resolution 11.3 (Rev.CoP18), para 15(f)).

In the next sections we will address Article VIII.1 as implemented and complied with by Parties.

2.3.1 Implementation of Article VIII.1 of CITES

As anticipated, under Article VIII.1 Parties need to have in place provisions that will make it illegal to trade other than in accordance with the Convention as well as provisions on penalties. The requirement to penalise illegal trade does not specify the nature of the penalty to be imposed, even though the COP has now recommended Parties to make illicit trafficking in protected species of wild fauna and flora involving organised criminal groups a serious crime.

Like for any other provision of the Convention, Parties need to give these requirements effect through the adoption of domestic measures that have also to be periodically reported to the Secretariat.[90] Here, a brief mention should also be made to the regional agreements, such as, for example, the Lusaka Agreement on Cooperative Enforcement Operations Directed at Illegal Trade in Wild Fauna and Flora.[91] The Lusaka Agreement can be considered as an agreement to implement CITES, including its Article VIII.1. At least for the African Countries to which it is addressed, it provides that the 'the Parties shall, individually and/or jointly, take appropriate measures in accordance with this Agreement to investigate and prosecute cases of illegal trade'.[92]

Since 1992 a system is in place in order to facilitate Parties in the enactment of adequate legislation. This is unique to CITES and it is called National Legislation Project. The Secretariat of CITES analyses the legislation of Parties and, amongst the different requirements, establishes whether they have in place provisions to prohibit trade in specimens in violation of the Convention and to penalise such trade.[93] Following this assessment, the Parties are classified in three categories: either they have legislation that is considered to meet the requirements for implementation of the Convention (category 1); or they are believed not to meet all of the requirements for implementing CITES

---

90 Article VIII(7) of CITES. Resolution Conf. 11.17(Rev.CoP18), National reports. Parties also have to provide annually information on permits and certificates granted as well as on the States with which the trade occurred and details of traded specimens listed in the Appendices.
91 UN Treaty Series, Vol. 1950, p. 35.
92 Article 4 of the Lusaka Agreement. See <https://lusakaagreement.org/about-us/> accessed 2 June 2021.
93 CITES Resolution Conf. 8.4 (Rev CoP15), National laws for the implementation of the Convention, para 1.

(category 2); or they are considered not to meet any of the requirements (category 3).[94]

From the analysis of the legislation in 2014 it was possible, for example, to notice a certain delay in some Countries in the process of incorporating the amendments (in relation to rosewood from Madagascar) to the CITES Appendices within the national legislation. That was considered to have a bearing on the possibility for the national competent authorities to detect illegal movements of that particular rosewood and to prosecute relevant offenders.[95]

From an assessment conducted in 2016 it appeared instead that 88 Countries and 13 dependent territories needed to strengthen their legal frameworks for the effective implementation of CITES, including in order to penalise trade in violation of the Convention.[96] Morocco, for example, was found without any prison penalty in the legislation. Trafficking in wildlife was clearly not considered as a serious crime. The CITES Secretariat made contact with the Party and they explained that the proposal for a law to that effect did not pass in the national Parliament.[97] At the time, though, the COP had not yet taken the official stance to recommend Parties to consider trafficking involving organised criminal groups as a serious crime, thus, it might be possible that, had a similar situation occurred today, there would be a different outcome. In any case, many States, including developing ones, now have four or more years as their maximum penalty for illegal trafficking involving organised criminal groups,[98] whereas others still struggle with that requirement.

Along with checking national legislation against Article VIII.1, implementation includes adopting guidance materials. By way of example, in 2002 the CITES Secretariat developed a draft Model Law on International Trade in Wild Fauna and Flora, which aimed at facilitating enactment of adequate legislation by indicating the possible content of the domestic provisions to be adopted. In relation to Article VIII.1 the Model Law was specifying that the proposed

---

94 The results of the assessments are available at <https://cites.org/legislation> accessed 2 June 2021. Based on the assessment the Standing Committee is then instructed to determine which Parties have not adopted appropriate measures for the effective implementation of the Convention and to consider appropriate compliance measures, which may include recommendations to suspend trade.
95 *Sixty-Fifth Meeting of the Standing Committee Geneva (Switzerland)*, 7–11 July 2014, SC65 Doc 22, para 12.
96 *Sixty Sixth Meeting of the Standing Committee Geneva (Switzerland)*, 11–15 January 2016, SC66 Doc 26.1, 3.
97 Interview with CITES Secretariat.
98 Amongst many others, this is the case, for example, of Angola, Brunei, China, Fiji, Kenya, Lao PDR, Malaysia, Namibia, Papua New Guinea, South Africa, Tanzania and Viet Nam.

offences could have attracted administrative, civil or criminal penalties; however, in case Parties had decided to prefer criminal penalties an element of intent (*mens rea*) should have been added.[99]

In 2017 the Secretariat, after detecting variations in the national legislation between the definition of offences, the use of criminal and non-criminal sanctions, minimum and maximum penalties, powers of enforcement officers and practices among Parties, committed to have a closer look at those legislations in relation to the obligation to penalise illegal trade and to develop additional guidance documents in the form of sanctioning guidelines.[100]

A year later, UNODC stepped in, and with the collaboration of the CITES Secretariat, developed new guidelines on drafting legislation to combat wildlife crime (the 'UNODC 2018 Guide').[101] Here, one should note that in accordance with the provisions of the Convention, the CITES Secretariat has always been quite keen in not prejudging the discretion left to Parties in selecting the most appropriate type of penalty (whether criminal or not, provided that they were sufficiently deterrent).[102] UNODC seems instead slightly 'criminal justice-prone' in its efforts to harmonise the provisions between the States. The UNODC 2018 Guide states in fact that '[d]etermination of the appropriate penalties has been left to each State, in accordance with its legal system and culture. For most of the offences contained in this Guide, criminal liability will be appropriate'.[103] For other offences, such as simply entering into a protected area, criminal penalties would not be appropriate and domestic legislation should opt for other types of sanctions provided that they are proportional, effective and dissuasive.[104]

---

99   Model Law on International Trade in Wild Fauna and Flora, CITES Secretariat, 12. See also the legislative checklist at <https://cites.org/sites/default/files/eng/prog/Legislation/ChecklistEN.pdf> accessed 2 June 2021.
100   *Sixty-Ninth Meeting of the Standing Committee Geneva (Switzerland), 27 November – 1 December 2017*, SC69 Doc 27, 8.
101   UNODC, *Guide on Drafting Legislation to Combat Wildlife Crime*, 2018. The new UNODC guide declares to draw upon previous UNODC guideline, the CITES Secretariat Model Law as well as upon the processes undertaken during the 2017 Africa-Asia Pacific Symposium on Strengthening Legal Frameworks to Combat Wildlife Crime.
102   The deterrent effect is what is important – this may be different in different countries – hence the discretion.
103   UNODC 2018 Guide, 18.
104   ibid 34. The Guide confirms what it had been already highlighted by the Secretariat that 'States have taken different approaches to criminalising wildlife offences. Some States have introduced specialized legislation while others have incorporated wildlife offences into existing penal codes. States have also made use of a combination of criminal, civil and administrative offences in specialized wildlife legislation' (ibid 2).

Be that as it may, an attempt from the part of UNODC to provide an element of harmonisation between the various national legislations is clear. This should be seen in conjunction with the development by UNODC of another guidance document in order to assist Parties to mitigate the risks of corruption more effectively.[105] The CITES institutions are thus relying more on the work of the most important agencies for crime investigation and prosecution, primarily UNODC, in a mutually beneficial and complementary relationship.[106]

The issue of the harmonisation of criminal penalties also emerged in the context of the implementation of CITES by the EU.[107] The EU became a Party to CITES in 2015 and, like any other Party, it had to implement its provisions.[108] With specific regard to the provisions on the prohibition and penalisation of illegal trade in wildlife, Regulation 338/97 contains a list (which is absent in CITES)[109] of thirteen infringements[110] in relation to which the EU MSs are required to take measures in the form of sanctions that are 'appropriate to the

---

105 See above section 2.2.
106 See *infra* section 3.
107 The EU is one of the largest global markets for wildlife trade, with imports ranging from tropical timber to reptile skins, caviar, orchids and traditional medicines. See, for example, S Theile, A Steiner and K Kecse-Nagy, *Expanding Borders: New Challenges for Wildlife Trade Controls in the EU* (TRAFFIC 2004) 1; and M Engler and RP Jones, *Opportunity or Threat: The Role of the EU in Global Wildlife Trade* (TRAFFIC Europe 2007) 8. See also S Lemaitre and N Hervé-Fournereau, 'Fighting Wildlife Trafficking: an Overview of the EU's Implementation on its Action Plan Against Wildlife Trafficking' (2020) 23 *Journal of International Wildlife Law and Policy* 62. The EU acceded to CITES on 8 July 2015 after the so-called 'Gaborone amendment' entered into force. Before acceding, the EU had only an observer status in the COPs' and other permanent committees' meetings and all the rights of the Parties under the Convention were exercised by the EU Member States 'in the interest' of the EU. On this issue see M Cremona, 'Member States as Trustees of the Community Interest: Participating in International Agreements on Behalf of the European Community' (2009) 17 *European University Institute Working Papers LAW* 8. See the dedicated Chapters on the EU in this book.
108 However, even before the accession, the EU had already in place legislation to implement CITES: Council Regulation No 3626/82 of 3 December 1982 on the implementation in the Community of the Convention on international trade in endangered species of wild fauna and flora [1982] OJ L384/1. In literature see, particularly, TD Mosedale and WC Burns, 'European Implementation of CITES and the Proposal for a Council Regulation (EC) on the Protection of Species of Wild Fauna and Flora' (1997) 9 *Georgetown International Environmental Law Review* 389; and Reeve, *Policing International Trade* (n 5) 112–120. This Regulation was later repealed by Council Regulation 338/97 of 9 December 1996 on the protection of species of wild fauna and flora by regulating trade therein [1997] OJ L61/1.
109 As showed above, CITES does not provide for an article describing what specific conducts should be deemed illegal trade for the purposes of the Convention.
110 For example, the introduction into the EU of specimens without the appropriate permit or certificate.

nature and gravity of the infringements'.[111] These measures can include the seizure, confiscation, or the return of the specimens.[112] However, like CITES, the Regulation does not specify which type of sanction (for example, criminal or administrative) should be applied to a specific infringement.

The rules contained in Regulation 338/97 are complemented by the Environmental Crime Directive,[113] which contains a list of some protected species-related directives whose breach has to be sanctioned when it constitutes an unlawful conduct.[114] The latter condition is satisfied when a non-negligible[115] trading in specimens of protected wild fauna and flora species (or parts or derivatives thereof) is committed, for example, by an individual.[116] Most importantly, the Environmental Crime Directive specifies that the measures to be applied in relation to this non-negligible trading in wildlife should be 'effective, proportionate and dissuasive *criminal* penalties'.[117] It follows, differently from CITES, that the EU rules are a little more explicit as to the type of measures to be taken in case of infringements: the penalties must be of a criminal nature. At the same time, like CITES, the EU rules stop short of defining the specific type or level of these criminal measures.[118] This is due to the limited level of EU harmonisation of (environmental) criminal law at the times when this Directive was adopted.[119] As a result, a considerable variation in the

---

111 Article 16(1) and (2) of Regulation 338/97.
112 Article 16(2) of Regulation 338/97.
113 Directive 2008/99/EC of the European Parliament and of the Council of 19 November 2008 on the protection of the environment through criminal law [2008] OJ L328/28.
114 On the issue that choosing to impose on MSs a duty of criminalisation only when the conducts are unlawful and on the fact that this reflects the accessory nature of environmental criminal law, see more in section 4.1 of Chapter 5 of this book.
115 On the limits of the use of the term 'non-negligible' see M Faure, 'Vague Notions in Environmental Criminal Law (Part 1)' (2010) 18 *Environmental Liability, Law Practice and Policy* 122.
116 Article 3(g) of the Environmental Crime Directive.
117 Emphasis added. Article 5 of the Environmental Crime Directive.
118 In fact, the initially more ambitious aim to provide for minimum sanction levels was abandoned by the EU Commission following a judgment by the European Court of Justice in 2007. See more in section 3 of Chapter 5 of this book. See also European Commission, 'Commission Staff Working Document Evaluation of the Directive 2008/99/EC' (n 29) 9–10, 13.
119 This has to be read also against the constitutional debate over the powers of the EU to criminalise. See V Mitsilegas, M Fitzmaurice and E Fasoli, 'The Relationship Between EU Criminal Law and Environmental Law' in V Mitsilegas et al (eds), *Research Handbook on EU Criminal Law* (Edward Elgar 2016) 272; and R Pereira, 'Towards Effective Implementation of the EU Environmental Crime Directive? The Case of Illegal Waste Management and Trafficking Offences' (2017) 26 *Review of European Comparative & International Environmental Law* 147.

legislation containing the level of punishment is detectable in the EU's MSs. By way of example, according to recent data, the average criminal law sanction in the EU MSs ranges from one year to life imprisonment for natural persons.[120]

Be that as it may, the adoption of non-binding/soft law guidance documents either within or outside CITES is crucial to properly implement CITES and to build on its legal regime (naturally, also the COP Resolutions, similarly not binding, contribute to make such MEA a dynamic legal regime). Given the major role played by customs and other border control officers in CITES matters, one could also mention the guidelines document prepared by the Green Customs Initiative' Secretariat in order to help the customs administrations to conduct documentary and physical inspections, and to check the validity of the documents submitted, that is similarly important.[121]

Yet, States do not seem particularly inclined to take advantage of the tools contained in these guidelines. As highlighted by the UNODC 2020 Report,

> [t]he outstanding question is why more countries are not using such tools to address wildlife crime? The answer likely lies in a combination of a lack of understanding of the nature of these crimes and their broader impact, insufficient prioritization and/or a lack of capacity or resources.[122]

Admittedly, despite the availability of a considerable number of guidance documents, as well as the efforts of the CITES Secretariat to entertain a fruitful, facilitative dialogue with the Parties in order to make sure that they all make the right efforts to achieve the objectives of the Convention, often States do not act in accordance with and in fulfilment of the Convention. In that case, the Secretariat could decide to bring the situation to the attention of the Standing Committee. This possibility will be analysed in the next section.

2.4 *Compliance with Article VIII.1 of CITES*

Compliance matters can be identified through one of the monitoring processes established under the Convention. Amongst them, as seen in the previous section in the context of implementation, Parties need to give effect to the provisions of CITES, including its Article VIII.1, through the adoption of

---

120 Instead, in relation to legal persons the penalties range from below 500,000 to 60,000,000 (European Commission, Commission Staff Working Document Evaluation of the Directive 2008/99/EC' (n 29) 32, 40).
121 UN Environment, *Green Customs Guide to Multilateral Environmental Agreements* (2018).
122 UNODC, *World Wildlife Crime Report* (2020) 19.

domestic measures that have to be periodically reported to the Secretariat.[123] This is the first way to identify a compliance matter.

The Secretariat is also mandated to identify those Parties whose domestic measures do not provide them with the authority to prohibit and penalise the illegal trade.[124] This is relevant not only for implementation, but also for compliance purposes and it constitutes another way to flag out a compliance matter.[125]

Another ground to identify non-compliance, although in relation to a specific species, is the National Ivory Action Plan (NIAP), which is in operation since 2013 in response to the high level of elephant poaching and illegal trafficking of ivory in certain States.[126] Each Plan, upon request of the Standing Committee, has to outline the measures that a Party commits to adopt and it has to include indicators which measure the specific actions in NIAPs, such as, for example, the number of ivory seizures, successful prosecutions, or relevant indicators from the ICCWC Indicator Framework for Combating Wildlife and Forest Crime.[127] This process is relevant for compliance purposes as well. In fact, if a Party has been requested to develop and implement a NIAP and has not done so adequately, the Secretariat and the Standing Committee should consider appropriate measures to ensure compliance with the NIAP process.[128]

Once a compliance matter is identified, the situation may first be handled under Article XIII of the Convention. This has now evolved to become an independent compliance procedure.[129] In essence, the Secretariat carries out an inquiry in the country concerned, this leading to detailed recommendations being made on actions to be taken by the Party. A number of Parties have been or are currently subject to an Article XIII process, such as, for example, Lao People's Democratic Republic (PDR). The CITES Secretariat had received sufficient evidence that ivory, tigers and snakes were traded illegally from and/or through that Country. Information was received, for example, that unregulated breeding facilities were operating, and that Lao PDR did not have proper legislation in place, including a new penal code to address them. The Secretariat

---

123 CITES Resolution Conf. 11.17 (Rev.CoP18), National reports.
124 CITES Resolution Conf. 8.4 (Rev.CoP15), National laws for the implementation of the Convention, para 1.
125 CITES Resolution Conf. 14.3 (Rev.CoP18), CITES Compliance procedures, 3.
126 CITES Resolution Conf 10.10 (Rev.CoP 18), Trade in elephant specimens.
127 ibid 11. See *infra* section 3.2.
128 ibid 13.
129 *Seventeenth Meeting of the Conference of the Parties Johannesburg (South Africa), 24 September -5 October 2016*, CoP17 Doc23, para 19.

first of all made contacts with Lao PDR[130] and once ascertained that the Country was not cooperative enough regarding the measures to be taken, the Secretariat decided to refer the situation to the Standing Committee.

The Standing Committee leads the most important compliance procedure under the Convention. The Committee is mandated to find a solution first of all through offering assistance to the Parties.[131] However, if it finds evidence of unresolved and persistent non-compliance and the Party shows no intent to remedy the issue, the Standing Committee can recommend that trade in specimens of one or more CITES-listed species be suspended with the non-compliant Party.[132] In essence, the Standing Committee can recommend taking a countermeasure in the form of a trade embargo.[133]

---

130   The assessment in relation to law enforcement made by the Secretariat upon a visit in Lao PDR undertaken in 2016 was as follows: 'The Government focused its efforts to curb wildlife crime on strengthening the enforcement capacity of the country. An important amount of financial and technical resources is going into enforcement-related activities. However, despite a reported increase in the number of incidents and investigations, these cases have not yet resulted in arrests, prosecutions and convictions. Three possible factors may explain these low prosecution and conviction rates. First, the focus is on "administrative enforcement" by authorities that are not originally created to enforce criminal laws. Second, laws are vague, ambiguous or inadequate to tackle the problem. The third factor is the lack of sound science. Without knowing the status and characteristics of wild populations, it is very difficult to inspect farms, identify species and have a baseline to measure the impact of enforcement activities on conservation. Additionally, illegal trade in wildlife does not seem to be condemned culturally by society, which explains a certain level of tolerance that may be associated with instances of corruption' (*Sixty-seventh Meeting of the Standing Committee Johannesburg (South Africa)*, 23 September 2016, SC67 Doc 12.1, para 36(c)).

131   The Standing Committee can ask the Party to produce a report on an issue; it can offer a written caution; it can advise as to specific capacity-building issues; it can offer assistance in a given State on invitation by such a State; it can issue a warning that a State is not complying with its obligations and it can ask for a compliance action plan indicating those steps a State will have to take to bring it back into compliance (CITES Resolution Conf. 14.3 (Rev.CoP18) CITES Compliance procedures, para 29).

132   ibid, para 30.

133   The embargo is collectively enforced by States exercising their right under Article XIV.1(a) of the Convention to adopt 'stricter domestic measures regarding the conditions for trade [...] or the complete prohibition thereof' of CITES-listed species with the Country so targeted. Parties are recommended not to accept permits or certificates issued by the Party (or non-Party) affected by the trade measure, even if these documents were issued prior to the decision to suspend trade (unless otherwise stated in the decision to recommend the suspension of trade). It is the responsibility of each national management authority to ensure that its national customs and other relevant enforcement authorities, as well as the regulated community and the general public, are informed of such trade measures. See Sand, 'Enforcing CITES: The Rise and Fall of Trade Sanctions' (n 5) 254.

Over the past three decades, trade embargoes have been enforced against more than forty Parties, especially developing countries, with a good rate of return to compliance.[134] In the case of Lao PDR, for example, in 2018 the Standing Committee agreed to suspend commercial trade in specimens of the genus *Dalbergia spp*.[135] In parallel, the Standing Committee also agreed that Lao PDR must adopt adequate legislative measures to implement the Convention that meet the minimum requirements and that it strengthens the criminal legal framework in relation to illegal trade in wildlife, notably, by amending the penal code to increase penalties for serious wildlife-related offences especially when they are perpetrated through organised groups, transnationally and repetitively.[136] The Standing Committee recommended to Lao PDR that the amended penal code should be disseminated widely among all relevant law enforcement and criminal justice stakeholders.[137]

In August 2019, the Standing Committee noticed that Lao PDR continued to show commitment to work towards the implementation of the Convention and that it submitted a revised NIAP. At the same time, it noticed that Lao PDR had made limited seizures of key species including bears, lions, tigers and pangolins. Therefore, the Committee recommended Lao PDR to make further progress in the enforcement-related activities.[138] From its part, Lao PDR confirmed its continued commitment to make efforts to meet the recommendations of the Standing Committee.[139]

---

134 ibid 161. See also A Lavorgna et al, 'CITES, Wild Plants and Opportunities for Crime' (2018) 24 *European Journal on Criminal Policy and Research* 269, 283. However, the CITES Secretariat warns that it is not in the interest of the CITES's system to issue too many recommendations to suspend trade in so far as they could be somehow disruptive of trade itself and being very difficult for traders to comply with them.

135 The suspension is meant to stay in place until Lao PDR makes scientifically based non-detriment findings for trade in the relevant species, including *D. cochinchinensis* and *D. oliveri*, to the satisfaction of the Secretariat (*Eighteenth Meeting of the Conference of the Parties Geneva, Switzerland, 17 – 28 August 2019*, CoP18 Doc.27, para 21).

136 *Sixty-seventh Meeting of the Standing Committee Johannesburg (South Africa), 23 September 2016*, SC67 Doc. 12.1, para 39.2(b).

137 *Eighteenth Meeting of the Conference of the Parties Geneva, Switzerland, 17 – 28 August 2019*, CoP18 Doc. 27, para 22.

138 More precisely, that Lao PDR 'shall i) investigate and prosecute mid- to high-profile cases involving organised or transboundary illegal trade activities, such as those identified by various international partners; and provide to the Secretariat the results (arrests and prosecutions) of any investigations conducted by competent national authorities to determine the origin of specimens in illegal trade, the identities of individuals involved in smuggling, and the results of any legal proceedings against alleged perpetrators for the period February-December 2019 in the illegal trade report format' (*Seventy-first Meeting of the Standing Committee Geneva (Switzerland), 16 August 2019*, SC71 SR, para 10.1(j).

139 ibid, para 10.1.

Another illustrative case is Guinea. In 2011 the Secretariat, upon information received by NGOs and members of the public, conducted a mission in the Country in order to verify the alleged occurrence of illegal trade. The Secretariat found that there had been significant exports from Guinea (to China) of big apes declared as bred in captivity and that this trade had involved the use of invalid and fraudulent permits and certificates.[140] The Secretariat responded firstly by recommending the adoption of a plan to deploy additional staff to control trade in CITES specimens.[141] After having observed limited progress in meeting these recommendations,[142] the Secretariat noticed that a large number of permits were issued for specimens declared as bred in captivity even though there were no commercial captive-breeding facilities for CITES-listed species in Guinea.[143] As a consequence, the Secretariat referred the situation to the Standing Committee, which in 2013 issued a recommendation to suspend all commercial trade with Guinea.[144] In 2019 the Secretariat reported that the key actors that were involved in the fraudulent issuance of CITES permits had been prosecuted and that they had served a custodial sentence in Guinea. This was confirmed by stakeholders and NGOs operating on the ground. They reported that fraud associated with the use of CITES permits was no longer occurring.[145] Yet, the Secretariat reiterated the importance that legislative measures, continued training and awareness-raising, and increased and systemic transparency are still required to prevent any future incidents in Guinea.[146]

In order to establish a more structured system to respond to persistent compliance issues in specific States, like the ones described above, the COP very recently requested the CITES Secretariat to establish a new Compliance Assistance Programme (CAP). This mechanism is still at a very early stage.[147] CAP is managed by the Secretariat and aims at providing targeted support to

---

140   *Sixty-Second Meeting of the Standing Committee Geneva (Switzerland), 23–27 July 2012,* SC62 Doc. 29, para 22 ff.
141   ibid, para 27.
142   Once asked to clarify the situation, the national management authorities were not able to tell the Secretariat what was happening since they were completely involved in the traffic, and they were issuing the permits unlawfully.
143   ibid, para 30.
144   Notification to the Parties No. 2019/075 (19/12/2019), available at <https://cites.org/sites/default/files/notif/E-Notif-2019-075.pdf> accessed 2 June 2021.
145   *Seventy-First Meeting of the Standing Committee Geneva, Switzerland, 17 – 28 August 2019,* SC71 Doc 10.2, para 12.
146   ibid, para 13.
147   See CITES Decision 18.69 adopted at CoP18.

Parties, in particular where the cause of the non-compliance relates to capacity constraints and not the lack of political will or engagement.[148] CAP is designed to integrate and organise in a more agile manner the assistance provided to Parties with difficulties in achieving compliance. This is made through a programmatic response facilitated by Secretariat staff assigned to each selected Party.[149] This includes the designation of a CAP officer to assist and respond in real time, and when necessary on the ground, to the critical and most urgent needs of the Parties.[150]

At this point of the analysis the question may arise as to whether these compliance procedures, overall, are sufficient to tackle illegal wildlife trafficking effectively. According to one Author this would not be the case and

> [a]lthough praised for its extraordinary effectiveness in quickly eliciting formal compliance by sanctioned states (Sand, 2013), the far-reaching measures of the CITES compliance mechanism have nevertheless not been able to tackle the global phenomenon of illegal wildlife traffic in a comprehensive and effective way.[151]

Admittedly, compliance procedures (coupled with the implementation activities) do not detail how to 'force' or compel compliance and/or to punish non-compliance with the domestic measures derived from CITES. But should they do so? Considering that CITES is first of all a trade treaty and that its approach towards compliance, like for many other MEAs, is by its nature supportive and non-adversarial, probably the answer should be in the negative. CITES was not meant to provide the forum to sit and discuss wildlife crime responses. As clearly put forward by John Sellar:

> You wouldn't appoint someone from the pharmaceutical industry to head a task force combating narcotic trafficking. So why assign a CITES administrator to lead the war against fauna- and flora-related criminal

---

148 'As an accelerator of compliance, the CAP is aimed at enhancing the quality of the assistance provided to Parties concerned by cutting across multiple services, initiatives, donors, providers and settings to facilitate compliance and maximize results regarding the implementation of the Convention' (*Eighteenth Meeting of the Conference of the Parties Geneva, Switzerland, 17 – 28 August 2019*, CoP18 Doc 28, 18).
149 By looking across all Parties, the Secretariat has already identified 10/15 Countries that are eligible to receive this help to deal with recurring compliance issues.
150 ibid 22.
151 A Cardesa-Salzmann, 'Multilateral Environmental Agreements and Illegality' in Elliott and Schaedla (eds) (n 5) 299, 313–314.

activity? If we agree, as I think we should and must, that organised crime now plays a major role in wildlife trafficking, then surely the issue for discussion is not illicit trade, it's crime?[152]

Therefore, since CITES was not designed to deal with the aspects of law enforcement directly, the idea was that it should rely on national enforcement authorities to do so.[153] As a consequence, we need to move away from CITES and its institutions and to turn to the domestic enforcement of Article VIII.1, which is also facilitated by a high degree of interinstitutional cooperation at the international level. There lies in fact the (real) action regarding the criminalisation of the international illegal trade in wildlife. We will address them in the following sections.

3 Enforcement of Article VIII.1 of CITES

Implementation and enforcement are intrinsically linked. On one side, CITES requires Parties to adopt domestic measures that prohibit and penalise trade in specimens in violation of the Convention; on the other, these measures need to be enforced. As it has been pointed out by UNODC,

> recognition of wildlife crime as "serious crime" in relevant legislation is an important first step, but this must be reflected and reinforced throughout national criminal justice systems. Legislation can only have the desired impact if it is effectively implemented, however; in many states, such implementation is still lacking, and combating wildlife and forest crime has not been set as a priority for enforcement by policy and decision-makers.[154]

Enforcement involves a chain of activities including the surveillance, detection, investigation, apprehension, prosecution and conviction of lawbreakers and the seizure and confiscation of their specimens.[155] At the same time, enforcement can be the means through which the objectives of the Convention,

---

152 Quotation contained in Stoett, 'Transnational Environmental Crime' (n 50) 35.
153 Instead for some scholars such as, for example, Duffy, this makes 'the international legal architecture provided by CITES […] ill-equipped to tackle complex transnational illicit trades' (Duff, 'The Illegal Wildlife Trade' in Global Perspective' (n 5) 123).
154 UNODC 2020 Report, 21.
155 *Fourteenth Meeting of the Conference of the Parties The Hague (Netherlands), 3–15 June 2007,* CoP14 Doc.24, para 16.

including in relation to the criminalisation of illegal trade in wildlife, can be achieved, and the major obstacle hindering their realisation.[156]

Enforcement of Article VII.1 of CITES occurs both at the domestic level (section 3.1) as well as at the level of the cooperation of the CITES institutions with the most important international agencies and institutions, such as UNODC, ICCWC and Interpol that specialise in wildlife crime enforcement (section 3.2).

3.1 Domestic Enforcement

Putting in place legislation that prohibits and penalises trade in specimens in violation of the Convention is not a guarantee as such for its effective enforcement. It is also necessary to have operative tools in place at the domestic level, such as detection, investigation, prosecution and conviction of lawbreakers. A study published in 2017 in relation to ASEAN States indicates, for example, that while the laws are 'reasonably well developed', at the same time the enforcement in terms of investigations and convictions is negligible.[157] This led the Author of this study to affirm that 'there is a problem with law enforcement and political will'.[158]

It would be outside the scope of the present analysis to conduct a detailed assessment of all the practices followed in each specific Party to CITES. Instead, through the use of the most relevant and updated reports and analyses available,[159] we will sketch the main shortcomings in domestic enforcement even if they do not purport to exhaust all possible issues in the different legal systems.

---

156 As it has been highlighted 'enforcement is the Achilles' heel of CITES' and 'effective enforcement turns the Convention from paper into actuality. Ineffective enforcement undermines its very objective and every initiative to improve CITES implementation, from the national legislation project to the Significant Trade Review. Model legislation is all very well, but without enforcement its worth is no more than the paper on which it is written; monitoring populations and trade are all very well, but without enforcement CITES may be fiddling while Rome burns. Meanwhile, lack of cooperation and coordination among national, regional and international wildlife authorities, law enforcement agencies and NGOs, plays into the hands of organised wildlife crime networks, whose cooperation and coordination at all levels is more sophisticated' (Reeve, *Policing International Trade* (n 5) 249–252). See also Bowman et al. *Lyster's International* (n 5) 525 and Wijnstekers, *The Evolution of CITES* (n 5) 237.
157 Broussard 'Building an Effective Criminal Justice Response to Wildlife Trafficking: Experiences from ASEAN Region' (n 39) 122.
158 ibid.
159 Such as, for example, UNEP, *Environmental Courts & Tribunals, A Guide for Policy Makers* (2016); LIFE-ENPE, *Environmental Prosecution Report, Tackling Environmental Crime in Europe* (2017) LIFE14 GIE/UK/000043; UNEP, *The State of Knowledge of Crimes that Have Serious Impacts on the Environment* (2018); UN Environment, *Green Customs Guide to Multilateral Environmental Agreements* (2018); UNODC 2020 Report; and European

Amongst the main problems in domestic criminalisation of illegal trade in wildlife there are, for example, the following: low level of political attention to the phenomenon, which is strictly linked to limited public awareness; limited training and financial assistance for law enforcement officers, including those involved in investigation and detection, and for the judiciary.[160]

Wildlife crime is considered less important than other crimes, especially when certain (minor, less charismatic)[161] species are involved. This is linked to the level of political commitment to the fight against wildlife crime, which is clearly not at the top of political agendas.[162] More engagement of private actors, such as local communities and individuals, could increase the social stigma and, therefore, the likelihood that certain behaviors would be addressed and, eventually, prosecuted. From that perspective, more visibility and more political commitment are needed.[163]

At the level of law enforcement agencies involved in investigation, a quite diffuse lack of special training and knowledge has been reported.[164] Wildlife crime, like any other environmental crime, is more difficult to detect. This would call for the establishment of specialised bodies and investigative units.[165]

Commission, 'Commission Staff Working Document Evaluation of the Directive 2008/99/EC' (n 29).

[160] The assessment report released in 2020 by the European Commission in relation to the Environmental Crime Directive also mentions: the lack of cooperation and communication between all levels of the national law enforcement chain, lack of an overarching strategy to combat environmental crime in most Member States; lack of cross-border cooperation; low level of sanctions imposed in practice – most crimes are sanctioned with fines rather than imprisonment; lack of an EU-wide agreed practice on how to use accessory sanctions, mitigating and aggravating circumstances, confiscation and forfeiture; lack of non-binding guidelines concerning prosecution (also with regard to the delineation of administrative procedures) and sentencing; lack of EU-wide minimum criteria for inspections and compliance monitoring at administrative level (European Commission, 'Commission Staff Working Document Evaluation of the Directive 2008/99/EC' (n 29) 34). See more in Chapters 5 and 6 of this book.

[161] As reported in the 2020 UNODC Report, this seems the case, for example, of the pangolins as opposed to elephant poaching for ivory (27). For an account of the great variety of wildlife being trafficked, not only limited to high profile species like tigers, great apes or bears, see Wyatt, 'The Uncharismatic and Unorganised Side of Wildlife Smuggling' (n 26) 129.

[162] UNODC 2020 Report, 21.

[163] L Colantoni and M Bianchi, *Fighting Environmental Crime in Europe, Preliminary Report* (Istituto Affari Internazionali, Ambitus 2020) 36.

[164] See <https://www.unodc.org/e4j/en/wildlife-crime/module-3/key-issues/investigation-measures-and-detection-methods.html> accessed 2 June 2021.

[165] UNODC 2020 Report, 21. For the European region see the results of the study *LIFE-ENPE, Environmental Prosecution Report, Tackling Environmental Crime in Europe* (2017) LIFE 14 GIE/UK/000043.

In the UK, for example, the National Wildlife Crime Unit (NWCU)[166] supports (acting as expert) the investigations conducted by the police since 2003.[167] Part of the NWCU strategy is to identify organised crime groups involved in wildlife crime. Interestingly enough, the lack of funding has been amongst the main challenges related to the practical functioning of the unit, which is, again, a reflection of the fact that wildlife crime is not a priority for the Governments, even the most virtuous ones.[168] In addition, better interagency and trans-disciplinary coordination not only domestic, but also transnational,[169] would be needed. The UNODC 2020 Report indicates that

> [t]here is an urgent need for a trans-disciplinary approach that ties together law-enforcement, wildlife management authorities and other relevant authorities such as financial intelligence unit, public health and safety agencies, administrative and local authorities. Countries could benefit from transnational organized crime units or other agencies coordination/technical working mechanisms, including interagency platforms.[170]

---

166 See <https://www.nwcu.police.uk/> accessed 2 June 2021.
167 By way of example, in August 2020 a Lancashire taxidermy dealer who traded illegally in critically endangered species was sentenced to a total of 56 weeks in custody. The sentence was the result of complex two-and-a-half-year investigation by Lancashire Police and the NWCU. See *Strategic Assessment-UK Wildlife Crime 2020–2022, National Wildlife Crime Unit, Public Version*, 15, available at <https://www.nwcu.police.uk/wp-content/uploads/2021/01/Strategic-Assessment-UK-Wildlife-Crime-November-2020-public-version.pdf> accessed 2 June 2021.
168 See E Fasoli, 'Environmental Criminal Law in the UK' in A Farmer et al (eds), *Environmental Crime in Europe* (Hart 2017) 243, 251. Under-resourcing and marginalisation in relation to enforcement and investigation agencies is also referred to by M Wellsmith ('Wildlife Crime: The Problems of Enforcement' (n 49) 135).
169 As highlighted by Spapens and Mehlbaum, 'a first problem is that in different states competent authorities may vary, and it is often difficult for law enforcement authorities in one state to find the appropriate counterpart in another. When it comes to environmental crimes the problem is even more significant, because law enforcement as well as administrative authorities and customs may be competent in specific cases [...]. Police officers and public prosecutors often have to make a substantial effort to find out which agency or even person they should approach in another state' (T Spapens and S Mehlbaum, 'Policing and Prosecution of Transnational Environmental Crime' in V Mitsilegas et al (eds), *Research Handbook on Transnational Crime* (n 51) 171, 174).
170 UNODC 2020 Report, 23. On the need to have more coordination between multiple organisations or institutions at the national level see <https://www.unodc.org/e4j/en/wildlife-crime/module-3/key-issues/criminal-justice-actors-and-agencies.html> accessed 2 June 2021.

Clearly, the need for better interagency coordination applies also to wildlife crime more generally, not necessarily organised.

The ability to catch up with the new trends, such as internet trade, is another key component for an effective enforcement action. Online trade is particularly difficult to address due to its hidden nature and inconsistent regulatory frameworks.[171] The CITES COP has in fact recommended Parties to establish a unit dedicated to investigating wildlife crime linked to the internet.[172] For example, the UK NWCU has highlighted cybercrime (ie, the use of the internet as an enabler in the facilitation of wildlife crime) amongst the main factors that are allowing criminality to continue or are hindering the effective investigation or prosecution of wildlife offences.[173]

From the criminal justice side, even though more and more criminal justice professionals are realising that wildlife crime is indeed 'a real criminal business with increased sophistication of its modus operandi',[174] the level of detection and prosecution is still very low due to limited law enforcement capacity and training.[175] Sufficient resources are often not available in source, transit and

---

171   UNODC 2020 Report, 25.
172   See, for instance, CITES Conf. 11.3 (Rev. CoP17), Compliance and enforcement, para 11(b). See also above section 2.2.
173   'Very few of the NWCU's investigations into illegal trade in wildlife are without a "cyber" element and the use of on-line tools evidently enables the trade in endangered species to continue unabated'. By way of example, an individual 'pleaded guilty, in September 2018, to selling clothing which was fashioned from endangered big cats. [The individual] illegally listed fur coats, hats and scarves for sale on eBay. The items were leopard, ocelot, lynx and wolf skin. [The individual] was given 200 hours of community service and the garments were seized by the Metropolitan police' (*Strategic Assessment – UK Wildlife Crime 2020–2022, National Wildlife Crime Unit, Public Version*, 16, 18, available at <https://www.nwcu.police.uk/wp-content/uploads/2021/01/Strategic-Assessment-UK-Wildlife-Crime-November-2020-public-version.pdf> accessed 2 June 2021).
174   See, for example, Broussard, 'Building an Effective Criminal Justice Response to Wildlife Trafficking: Experiences from ASEAN Region' (n 39) 118. M Wellsmith refers to the fact that 'wildlife crime is not taken seriously' (M Wellsmith, 'Wildlife Crime: The Problems of Enforcement' (n 49) 137). See also <https://www.unodc.org/e4j/en/wildlife-crime/module-3/key-issues/prosecution-and-judiciary.html> accessed 2 June 2021.
175   As highlighted by UNEP, 'many law enforcement authorities lack the necessary knowledge, training, and equipment to adequately prevent and enforce environmental crime. This gap impacts all actors of the "enforcement chain," including investigators, prosecutors, and judges. As a result, frontline forces responsible for combating environmental crime are severely inhibited' (UNEP, *The State of Knowledge of Crimes that Have Serious Impacts on the Environment* (2018) 21). Here, experts from the UK have reported that a challenge is also constituted by the fact that prosecutors have to properly understand the importance of the issues involved and know the legislation. In order to overcome this problem when, for example, the NWCU takes a case to the magistrates they usually produce an impact statement (which would not be required by law) based on the

destination CITES Parties.[176] One Author suggests that additional resources could be found, for example, through a better allocation of the existing ones in particular by identifying 'hot products' prioritising the action taken.[177] Sometimes it is a problem of absence of sufficient evidence;[178] other times a problem of the case management system.[179] Overall, the UNODC 2020 Report points to a complex situation where, even if large-scale seizures are made by the competent national authorities, at the same time, a low number of investigations, as well as the rarity of prosecutions and subsequent convictions, are detected.[180]

In terms of penalties, it has been recently identified that most crimes are sanctioned only with fines rather than imprisonment.[181] As highlighted by one Author, penalties are 'insufficient, monitoring of exports and imports low, and funding to support national authorities sparse. This results in poor implementation of the Convention at national levels'.[182]

Parties with legislation allowing for high sanctions may find that illegal traders escape heavy fines or imprisonment, for example, because prosecutors, as highlighted above, could not understand (or did not have enough resources to

---

best scientific advice: that evidence is important to make the magistrates understand the importance of the case (interview with Detective Inspector Nevin Hunter Head of Unit-UK National Wildlife Crime Unit conducted within the EFFACE project in 2014, on file with the Author). In this context, a guide commissioned by UNEP lists amongst the possible solutions to improve the environmental rule of law the creation of specialised environmental courts (G Pring and C Pring, *Environmental Courts & Tribunals, A Guide for Policy Makers*, (UNEP, 2016)).

176   As indicated by the UNODC 2020 Report '[o]fficials involved in building cases often have limited training on data management, intelligence analysis or other advanced investigation methods and techniques, which would greatly enhance strategic and tactical decision-making' (19, 21).
177   Lavorgna et al, 'CITES, Wild Plants and Opportunities for Crime' (n 134) 284.
178   According to the UNODC 2020 Report 'many cases end in dismissal or acquittal because the initial charging decisions was made without enough evidence present to successfully prove the charge' (22).
179   As reported by UNODC '[t]he numbers of cases that are dismissed as a result of basic case management deficiencies are unacceptably high. This not only demotivates the prosecutor and frustrates the judiciary, but also undermines the prosecutor/ investigator relationship and damages public confidence in the criminal justice system' (ibid 23). See also M Engler and RP Jones, *Opportunity or Threat: The Role of the EU in Global Wildlife Trade* (TRAFFIC Europe 2007) 14.
180   UNODC 2020 Report, 23.
181   This is for example the current state of affairs in the EU (European Commission, 'Commission Staff Working Document Evaluation of the Directive 2008/99/EC' (n 29) 34).
182   MÁ Clemente-Muñoz, 'The Role of CITES in Ensuring Sustainable and Legal Trade in Wild fauna and Flora' in Elliott and Schaedla (eds) (n 5), 433, 441.

address) the impact that illegal trade could have on species, ecosystems and livelihoods. Correspondingly, when the penalty is too low there is the risk that wildlife crime is perceived, including by the public, as a low importance crime, potentially being under-investigated. That could favour perpetrators of wildlife crimes to the extent that they could select a specific jurisdiction where there are lower penalties or less enforcement action.[183]

3.2 Enforcement through International Interinstitutional Cooperation

Domestic enforcement and transnational interagency coordination are greatly improved through effective international interinstitutional cooperation. The importance of international cooperation has been stressed, for example, in the 2018 Declaration of the London Conference on the Illegal Wildlife Trade:

> We recognise that international cooperation is essential, with full engagement by Governments in relevant bilateral, regional and international mechanisms. Through engagement with local communities, the private sector, NGOs and academia, as well as bringing in new partners, we will build and strengthen sustainable, long-term partnerships to change incentives for those involved in the illegal wildlife trade.[184]

It would be beyond the scope of the present analysis to map exhaustively all the cooperation initiatives that UN bodies, intergovernmental agencies, networks, non-governmental organisations have adopted at the global as well as regional levels.[185] A brief overview of the recent initiatives most relevant for (or that complement) CITES will however be helpful. We will focus on the initiatives undertaken by the International Consortium on Combating Wildlife

---

183 On this aspect see also above n 40 and corresponding text. For further remarks on low penalties and their impact both on the perception of the (lack of) seriousness of environmental crime and the possibility for national authorities to rely on instruments of judicial cooperation at the EU level, see Chapters 5 and 6 of this book.

184 Point 16 of the Declaration, available at <https://www.gov.uk/government/publications/declaration-london-conference-on-the-illegal-wildlife-trade-2018/london-conference-on-the-illegal-wildlife-trade-october-2018-declaration#tackling-the> accessed 2 June 2021.

185 From a green criminology perspective see, for example, G Prink and R White (eds) *Environmental Crime and Collaborative State Intervention* (Palgrave Macmillan 2016). See also Rose, 'International Jurisdiction Challenges in the Suppression of Transnational Environmental Crime' (n 7) 335–340; and L Elliot, 'Cooperation on Transnational Environmental Crime: Institutional Complexity Matters' (2017) 26 *Review of European, Comparative & International Environmental Law* 107.

Crime (ICCWC), by UNODC, by the UN Commission on Crime Prevention and Criminal Justice (CCPCJ) and by Interpol.

Liaisons and cooperative mechanisms between the institutions of CITES and other international bodies and agencies, usually made through memorandum of understanding (MoUs),[186] have been in place for quite some time.[187] However, it is over the last 10 years, especially since the establishment of ICCWC (which is a collaborative effort between the CITES Secretariat, Interpol, UNODC, the World Bank and WCO)[188] that there has been, as one Author points out, a 'paradigmatic shift from the prevention and combat of illegal wildlife trade towards a broader, more aggressive approach that focuses on transnational wildlife and forest crime'.[189] While this is certainly true, this shift did not also entail a governance shift in the sense of a reallocation of competences.[190] It would be wrong to maintain that the CITES institutions somehow relinquished their central role in the fight against illegal trade in wildlife in favour of other international institutions, primarily, UNODC. As already shown above, the CITES institutions never had a crime investigation mandate in the first place. Simply, because of the need to adopt a more aggressive approach towards illegal trade in wildlife, the CITES institutions started to rely more and more on other international institutions that specialise in

---

186   The CITES Secretariat also has longstanding individual MoUs with INTERPOL and WCO, and a more recent agreement with the Lusaka Agreement Task Force.

187   For example, observers from the CITES Secretariat usually participate in the INTERPOL Wildlife Working Group established in order to focus on the expertise and experience of law enforcement officers on the poaching, trafficking or possession of legally protected wild fauna and flora (*INTERPOL and CITES Secretariat, Wildlife Crime Working Group, Practical Guide for the Use of the CITES Management Authorities in Collaboration with the International Criminal Police Organization (INTERPOL)* (INTERPOL and CITES Secretariat 2005)). In literature see, for example, R White, 'What is to be Done About Environmental Crime?' in BA Arrigo and HY Bersot (eds), *The Routledge Handbook of International Crime and Justice Studies* (Routledge International Handbooks 2014) 458.

188   <https://www.cites.org/eng/prog/iccwc.php> accessed 2 June 2021. The mission of ICCWC is to create a more coordinated response against the perpetrators of serious wildlife crimes. The consortium elaborates training materials and guidelines addressed to national officials. In literature see JE Scanlon and L Farroway, 'Organisational Consortiums: The International Consortium on Combating Wildlife Crime' in G Prink and R White (eds) (n 185) 77; and E Van Asch, 'The International Consortium on Combating Wildlife Crime (ICCWC)' in Elliott and Schaedla (eds) (n 5) 469.

189   Cardesa-Salzmann, 'Multilateral Environmental Agreements and Illegality' (n 151) 315.

190   By contrast, Cardesa-Salzmann affirms that '[i]n terms of governance, this shift also encapsulates the gradual reallocation of the institutional center of gravity in the fight against illegal wildlife traffic from CITES to UNODC and its Global Programme for Combating Wildlife and Forest Crime' (ibid).

crime investigation and enforcement. This is the reason why, for example, the more recent guidelines on drafting legislation to combat wildlife crime, as well as the guidance document to mitigate the risks of corruption connected to wildlife crime, have been developed within UNODC (in 2018 and 2019, respectively), and not within CITES.[191] In that perspective, UNODC complements CITES in so far as it strengthens the capacity of governments to prevent, investigate, prosecute and adjudicate wildlife crime.[192] The international institutions that specialise in crime investigation and enforcement like UNODC, in turn, continue to rely on the CITES institutions for the identification of what is legal as opposed to illegal trade in wildlife under the Convention. Therefore, the type of cooperation is complementary in nature, rather than one involving a reallocation of competences. While the institutions of CITES are in charge of identifying, on the basis of the provisions of the Convention, what is illegal trade in wildlife, the international organisations and agencies for crime and enforcement are in charge of combating what has been already defined as such.[193]

In any case, the adoption of a more aggressive approach towards illegal trade in wildlife is clear and UNODC has certainly taken centre stage. As mentioned above, UNODC is amongst the founding partners of ICCWC, whose mission is to strengthen criminal justice systems and provide coordinated support at national, regional and international level to combat wildlife and forest crime.[194] The ICCWC has been active, for example, in the preparation of toolkits to examine how Countries can enhance their responses to fight against wildlife crime. One of the first outputs was a toolkit released in 2012.[195] This toolkit was intended to serve as a set of non-binding guidelines that the Parties could use as a framework to develop their domestic legislation, including the rules and procedures for the criminalisation of illegal trade. Amongst the criteria suggested to national courts when imposing a penalty for a wildlife or a forest offence, there is, for example, the need to deter the offender and other persons from committing the same or a similar offence, also taking into account, for example, the extent of the harm caused (or likely to be caused)

---

191   See above section 2.3.1.
192   Broussard, 'The Evolving Role of the United Nations Office on Drugs and Crime in Fighting Wildlife and Forest Crimes' in Elliott and Schaedla (eds) (n 5) 457.
193   In that perspective, UNODC may be overstepping its mandate if it started to recommend that captive breeding should be banned altogether. In fact, CITES allows and regulates it (interview with the CITES Secretariat).
194   ICCWC Strategic Programme 2016–2020.
195   UNODC, *Wildlife and Forest Crime Analytic Toolkit, Revised Edition* (2012) 133–138.

to the environment.¹⁹⁶ In relation to sentencing, the toolkit highlights that courts should be guided by the gravity of the offence.¹⁹⁷ Interestingly, in order to counter the diffused belief by courts that wildlife and forest offences are less serious offences than other types of crime, the toolkit suggests to set a minimum level of penalties. However, the toolkit points out that this suggestion has received very limited support as it may infringe upon the independence of the judiciary and limit the courts' ability to take into account all relevant circumstances when determining a sentence.¹⁹⁸ Be that as it may, the UNODC 2020 Report indicates that only twelve countries have utilised this Toolkit so far.¹⁹⁹

More recently, in 2016, the ICCWC developed the ICCWC Indicator Framework for Combating Wildlife and Forest Crime in order to enable Parties to measure and monitor the effectiveness of their own law enforcement responses to wildlife and forest crime.²⁰⁰ Interestingly, amongst the indicators identified to expose the critical areas in the respective domestic legislation, the Indicator Framework mentions the assessment of the strength of the existing legislative provisions to combat wildlife crime, the prosecutorial capacity, and the appropriateness of the penalties and verdicts that are handed down in court.²⁰¹ Nevertheless, also in relation to this tool UNODC has detected a very limited use of it (only seven countries).²⁰² It is probably for this reason that the COP to CITES has specifically recommended to Parties to 'make use of the different tools available through ICCWC, in particular the ICCWC Wildlife and Forest Crime Analytical Toolkit and the ICCWC Indicator Framework for Wildlife and Forest Crime, in order to strengthen enforcement related aspects of the implementation of the Convention'.²⁰³

---

196   Other criteria include: the practical measures that could have been taken to prevent, control, abate or mitigate the harm; and the extent to which the person committing the offence has control over the causes that gave rise to the offence and the extent to which they could have reasonably foreseen the harm (ibid 135–136).
197   This is determined by the harm caused and the culpability of the offender with higher penalties reserved for those acting intentionally, knowingly or recklessly, while lower penalties (or no punishment) reserved for offenders acting negligently or with no fault of their own. The toolkit also envisages aggravating circumstances such as the commission of an offence for financial gain or on behalf of a criminal organisation.
198   UNODC, *Wildlife and Forest Crime Analytic Toolkit, Revised Edition* (2012) 136–137.
199   For ten other countries the process in instead underway (UNODC 2020 Report 19).
200   The Framework is composed of the Assessment Guidelines and Assessment Template which provide a standardised approach to measure the effectiveness of national law enforcement responses and enable a country to independently monitor performance over time to identify any changes in the effectiveness of its law enforcement response.
201   See <https://cites.org/eng/prog/iccwc.php/Tools> accessed 2 June 2021.
202   UNODC Report 2020, 19.
203   See, for instance, CITES Conf. 11.3 (Rev.CoP18), Compliance and enforcement, 15(i).

The ICCWC also intervened in the effort to enhance interagency coordination. In 2020 it adopted the Guidelines for Wildlife Enforcement Networks (WENS) whose aim is to support the strengthening of wildlife enforcement networks established at regional and sub-regional levels and also to assist the national agencies responsible for wildlife law enforcement in addressing wildlife crime more effectively, by facilitating increased collaboration and coordination.[204]

The activity of preparing guidance documentation is also complemented by hosting high-profile events. These events organised under the aegis of ICCWC are meant to draw attention to activities for enabling authorities to effectively respond to wildlife crime and the organised crime groups behind such crimes.[205]

On a more operative side, the ICCWC coordinates a number of regional and global operations, such as, for example, Operation Thunderball conducted in June 2019 with Interpol and WCO. This operation involved 109 countries and resulted in over 1,800 seizures across all continents, in the identification of close to 600 suspects, and in the triggering of multiple investigations and prosecutions worldwide.[206]

UNODC also operates in conjunction with the CCPCJ, [207] which prepares the draft resolutions in the field of wildlife crime before endorsement by the Economic and Social Council (ECOSOC).[208]

In 2014 UNODC established a dedicated Global Programme for Combating Wildlife and Forest Crime. It is in that context that, for example, the UNODC 2020 Report (including its 2016 edition) was adopted. The Global Programme works in close coordination with national authorities – ranging from law enforcement and criminal justice agencies, to wildlife, forestry, and fisheries management authorities – and supports them in their efforts to better respond to wildlife crime. The Global Programme addresses the criminal justice systems, for example, in order to strengthen the national capacities for the investigation, prosecution, and adjudication of wildlife crime by delivering highly

---

204 See <https://cites.org/sites/default/files/EST/ICCWC%20WEN%20Guidelines_FINAL_ENG.pdf> accessed 2 June 2021.
205 See, for example, the events organised in 2019: <https://cites.org/eng/news/pr/International_consortium_to_strengthen_global_action_on_combating_wildlife_crime_15082019> accessed 2 June 2021.
206 See further operations at <https://cites.org/eng/prog/iccwc/action.php> accessed 2 June 2021.
207 CCPCJ was established by ECOSOC in 1992 through Resolution 1991/22, upon request of the GA with Resolution 46/152.
208 See above (n 54).

specialised training, developing practical tools and guidelines, and promoting inter-agency cooperation.[209]

Finally, Interpol facilitates the cross-border police cooperation, including that which is related to matters of environmental crime. Amongst the different activities, Interpol is a partner in the ICCWC. Interpol has established the Global Wildlife Enforcement, which aims to facilitate global law enforcement cooperation to disrupt and dismantle transnational organised criminal networks involved in illegal wildlife trade.[210] In addition, the Wildlife Crime Working Group (WCWG) operates as an international platform responsible for devising strategies and initiatives for law enforcement to combat illegal harvest, poaching, and trafficking of wild species of plants and animals on an international scale. A large focus of WCWG's activities is on threatened and endangered species listed under CITES.[211] The WCWG organises annual meetings for operational-level representatives from wildlife and anti-smuggling authorities, customs and national police.[212]

The above overview, although brief, testifies to the existence of a very high number of cooperative international activities that complement CITES and that work to assist (criminal) law enforcement against trade in wildlife in violation of the Convention. One Author suggests, although referring to environmental crime more broadly and not limited to wildlife, that

> the perhaps unintended consequence of [this multilateral collaboration] is that it also increases the sheer extent and scale of surveillance in regard to specific types of criminal activity. It is suggested that this may well constitute a "panopticon effect" in which potential perpetrators of environmental crime, including corrupt government officials, may not know when, where and who is watching them at any point in time. Extensive collaboration, therefore, may be associated with deterrence and crime prevention, as well as detection, investigation and prosecution, precisely because of the sheer number of players involved in the collaborative exercise.[213]

---

209 UNODC, *Annual Report 2019, Global Programme for Combating Wildlife and Forest Crime*, 10.
210 INTERPOL, *Global Wildlife Enforcement, Strengthening Law Enforcement Cooperation Against Wildlife Crime* (2018).
211 G Prink, 'INTERPOL's NEST: Building Capability and Capacity to Respond to Transnational Environmental Crime' in Elliott and Schaedla (eds) (n 5) 444.
212 INTERPOL, *Environmental Compliance and Enforcement Committee Advisory Board, Impact Report 2015–2017*, 5.
213 R White, 'Building NESTs to Combat Environmental Crime Networks' (2016) 19 *Trends of Organised Crime* 88, 95–96.

4 Illegal Trade in Wildlife and Covid-19

Throughout the analysis we were in search of the (real) centre of action in the criminalisation of the international illegal trade in wildlife. We discovered that in terms of distribution of competences under the design of the Convention, the enforcement action has always been lying outside CITES. In fact, the latter was not designed to deal with enforcement in the first place. At the same time, the CITES institutions more and more rely on the international institutions that specialise in crime investigation and prosecution, since especially over the last few years, there has been a shift towards a more aggressive approach in the fight against wildlife crime. That being said, Covid-19 has somehow road-tested this distribution of roles.

Up until a few years ago, the implementation of CITES was not exactly a priority for many Parties.[214] Suddenly, around February 2020, CITES started to receive a lot of attention.[215] During the first months of the pandemic, when the indications as to the possible links between the human consumption of wild animals and Covid-19 were starting to emerge, it was somehow suggested that the CITES institutions should have done more in relation to zoonotic diseases, including through tackling more forcefully illegal trade in wildlife (especially the species that were posing a threat to human health).[216] This prompted the

---

214 By way of example, in 2016 Clemente-Muñoz highlighted that '[i]n recent times, CITES has seen less attention from some Parties, possibly because it is now one of an increasing number of conventions that require implementation. The global economic crisis may also have affected resource allocations to the Convention. Many Countries have reduced the staff in CITES Management Authorities and the funding for implementation. This reduces the engagement of enforcement bodies and affects the implementation of national legislation on CITES' (Clemente-Muñoz, 'The Role of CITES in Ensuring Sustainable and Legal Trade in Wild Fauna and Flora' (n 182) 441).

215 'Reports that the Covid-19 outbreak originated from illegally sourced wildlife has brought about a significant and increased global interest in the Illegal Wildlife Trade' (*Strategic Assessment-UK Wildlife Crime 2020–2022, National Wildlife Crime Unit, Public Version*, 15, available at <https://www.nwcu.police.uk/wp-content/uploads/2021/01/Strategic-Assessment-UK-Wildlife-Crime-November-2020-public-version.pdf> accessed 2 June 2021).

216 The principal suspect of the so-called 'spillover' is the pangolin, which is listed in Annex I of CITES, therefore, it enjoys the highest level of protection. Commercial trade in all eight species of these threatened mammals is illegal. At the same time, they are the most illegally trafficked mammals in the world. As reported by Nellemann et al, 'the scale of illegal, illicit and unregulated trade in pangolin parts is under-documented, making it difficult to precisely ascertain the size of the trade' (Nellemann et al, *The Rise of Environmental Crime, A Growing Threat to Natural Resources Peace, Development and Security* (n 46) 44). See, for example, one of the biggest cases of this kind in recent years: 'Chinese Gang of Pangolin Smugglers Jailed over US$17.6 Million Haul of Scales', published on *South China Morning Post*, 6 January 2021. By contrast, other scientific models exonerate the pangolin

swift reaction by the CITES Secretariat that in March 2020 distanced itself from those allegations.²¹⁷

While there is ever-increasing evidence demonstrating that zoonotic diseases, including Covid-19, are facilitated, amongst other factors, by wildlife crime (the risk of, for example, unsanitary conditions are more likely to be present in the context of the illegal trade rather than the legal one),²¹⁸ the Secretariat was responding to those allegations by pointing out that CITES was not designed to tackle wildlife crime directly, even less so to deal with its impacts on human health. Indeed, as amply demonstrated in the previous sections, CITES provides for a regulatory framework for the import and export of wildlife products, it even goes as far as requiring States to penalise illegal trade, however, when it comes to managing the aspects of criminalisation more

---

from the 'spillover' effect. These models argue that it is far from sure that the coronavirus that originates in bats was transferred to humans via the pangolin. See, for instance, R Frutos et al, 'Covid-19: Time to Exonerate the Pangolin from the Transmission of SARS-Cov-2 to Humans' (2020) *Infection, Genetics and Evolution* 1.

217 In essence, the Secretariat maintained that 'matters regarding zoonotic diseases are outside of CITES' mandate, and therefore the CITES Secretariat does not have the competence to make comments regarding the recent news on the possible links between human consumption of wild animals and Covid-19'. See the statement at<https://cites.org/eng/CITES_Secretariat_statement_in_relation_to_COVID19#:~:text=Matters%20regarding%20zoonotic%20diseases%20are,wild%20animals%20and%20COVID%2D19.> accessed 2 June 2021.

218 In this perspective, Sustainable Development Goal 15, the one dedicated to life on land, indicates that surging wildlife crime, land use changes such as deforestation, and habitat encroachment are primary pathways of transmission for emerging infectious diseases, including Covid-19, threatening public health and the world economy. See <https://unstats.un.org/sdgs/report/2020/goal-15/> accessed 2 June 2021. The UN *Framework for the Immediate Socio-Economic Response to Covid-19*, 2020, states that 'the success of post-pandemic recovery will also be determined by a better understanding of the context and nature of risk. In view of the Covid-19 crisis, this includes developing and maintaining a global mapping of encroachment, illegal trade, wet markets, etc. that are pathways for future pathogen transmission and thus potential future zoonoses identified. It will also mean supporting efforts to arrest ecosystem encroachments and harmful practices, restore degraded ecosystems, close down illegal trade and illegal wet markets, while protecting communities that depend on these for their food supply and livelihoods' (28). The UNODC 2020 Report indicates that: '[w]hen wild animals are poached from their natural habitat, butchered and sold illegally, the potential for transmission of zoonotic diseases is increased. [...] Stopping the trafficking in wildlife species is a critical step not just to protect biodiversity and the rule of law in line with the Sustainable Development Goals, but to help prevent future public health emergencies' (27). The 2020 *IPBES Workshop Report on Biodiversity and Pandemics, Intergovernmental Science-Policy Platform on Biodiversity and Ecosystem Services* reports instead of an unsustainable illegal wildlife trade having multiple implications for health (29).

directly, it relies on domestic enforcement facilitated by the many international interinstitutional cooperation activities that are in place. Public health considerations were not amongst the aims of the Convention, certainly not amongst the main ones. The only link to public health is contained in Article XIV.2 of CITES, which, in a form of a saving clause, provides that the provisions of CITES shall in no way affect the domestic provisions that Parties might have in place, including in relation to public health.[219] Therefore, it was a deliberate decision of the drafters of the Convention to refrain from dealing with that particular risk to human health.

Taken from this perspective, it seems that the CITES Secretariat was right when it maintained that the mandate given to the Convention was limited to regulating international trade in wildlife only, irrespective of its possible impact on human health.

The CITES Secretariat also made clear, through the statement put forward in March 2020, that for it to stay in line with its mandate, the right course of action for tackling more forcefully illegal trade in wildlife, even the one more dangerous for human health, should have been to (continue to) collaborate 'with source, transit and destination countries through compliance assistance and enforcement activities, including with the partners of the International Consortium on Combating Wildlife Crime (ICCWC) so that Parties are supported where needed and have the tools they need to combat illegal wildlife trade'.[220]

The stance taken by the CITES Secretariat in this matter confirms the existence of a 'paradigmatic shift' towards a more aggressive approach to tackle wildlife crime that was described in the previous section.[221] The right path should be the collaboration of the CITES institutions with the most important international agencies that specialise in crime investigation and enforcement, notably the ICCWC, and not a complete reallocation of competences in the fight against illegal wildlife crime. Again, CITES is a trade treaty after all.

Admittedly, this approach is not set in stone. The Parties to CITES (ie, almost all Countries of the world) could agree, for example, to give a more

---

219   More specifically, Article XIV of CITES provides that '[the] provisions of the present Convention shall in no way affect the provisions of any domestic measures or the obligations of Parties deriving from any treaty, convention, or international agreement relating to other aspects of trade, taking, possession or transport of specimens which is in force or subsequently may enter into force for any Party including any measure pertaining to the customs, public health, veterinary or plant quarantine fields'.
220   Above (n 216).
221   See above section 3.2.

prominent role to human health considerations in the Treaty. This could include the possibility for the COP to CITES (or more likely for the Standing Committee under the COP's mandate) to recommend to a specific Party to stop a domestic trade, to close a domestic market or to eliminate the consumption for food of certain CITES-listed species that were found to constitute a threat to human health. Here, the trade could be either legal or illegal or both under CITES. For such a proposal an amendment to CITES would be required and it should be made allowed under the Convention that not only Parties unilaterally,[222] but that also the COP could recommend a specific State to adopt such types of measures. However, the limitation inherent in such a proposal is that the amendment would probably fall outside the scope of the Convention since, as known, CITES only addresses trade in wildlife with an international dimension (ie, products that cross a border) and not purely domestic trade.[223]

A proposal that could be more in line with the scope of the Convention was put forward in the first months of the Covid-19 pandemic. A suggestion was made that the Parties to CITES should completely prohibit trade in wildlife, especially that which is particularly dangerous for human health. However, as the example of pangolins shows,[224] it is not by prohibiting trade in certain species altogether that international trade will stop and the risk to human health significantly reduces. As long as demand exists of that particular species, the result of such measure, as confirmed by the experts,[225] may be that trade would be simply driven underground.[226]

A more drastic option could be to draft a brand-new agreement that regulates more restrictively the trade (both domestic and international) of the CITES-listed species that are most problematic for human health. However,

---

[222] In February 2020 China notified the CITES Secretariat of a domestic measure, which was then communicated to CITES Parties in March 2020, prohibiting the consumption for food of wild animals to safeguard people's lives and health. See <https://cites.org/sites/default/files/notif/E-Notif-2020-018.pdf> accessed 2 June 2021.

[223] Are of this view also N De Sadeleer and J Godfroid, 'The Story Behind Covid-19: Animal Diseases at the Crossroads of Wildlife, Livestock and Human Health' (2020) 11 *European Journal of Risk Regulation* 210, 223.

[224] See above (n 128).

[225] Interview with the CITES Secretariat.

[226] Some authors call for measures and incentives to reduce demand for illegal wildlife products domestically. See, for example, J Ayling, 'Reducing Demand for Illicit Wildlife Products, Crafting a "whole-of society" Response' in Elliott and Schaedla (eds) (n 5) 346.

here the criticism would probably be that the new instrument would constitute a duplication of CITES.²²⁷

A further solution would entail to look, again, 'outside' CITES. John Scanlon, who served as CITES Secretary-General from 2010 to 2018, suggested, for example, that a good course of action could be to add a health aspect to the already existing discussion as to the adoption of a new Protocol to the Palermo Convention.²²⁸ He suggested that the new Protocol should address wildlife crime.²²⁹ In that perspective, the aspects of criminalisation would be at the forefront. Therefore, in a fashion similar to the content of Article 5 of the Protocol against the illicit manufacturing of and trafficking in firearms to the Palermo Convention, one could imagine that the new Protocol against the illicit trafficking in wildlife can provide, for example, that each State Party shall adopt such legislative and other measures as may be necessary to establish as criminal offences, when committed intentionally, the illicit trafficking in specimens, especially those that constitute primary pathways of transmission for emerging infectious diseases, including through falsification of the documents of origin/volume of these specimens. However, even in this case, the downside would be that the specific scope of application of these Protocols (like the Palermo Convention) only includes the offences that are transnational in nature and that also involve organised criminal groups. Therefore, the new Protocol could not be able to capture the purely domestic dimension of the illegal trafficking, including illegal conducts such as, for example, operating illicit wet markets without the involvement of organised criminal groups.

---

227   See, for example, the view of some US based NGOs, such as the Association of Zoos&Aquariums, at <https://www.aza.org/aza-news-releases/posts/testimony-of-dan-ashe-on-stopping-the-spread> accessed 2 June 2021.

228   On the Palermo Convention, see also above (n 49) and corresponding text. The Palermo Convention is already supplemented by three Protocols which target specific areas and manifestations of organised crime: the Protocol to Prevent, Suppress and Punish Trafficking in Persons, Especially Women and Children; the Protocol against the Smuggling of Migrants by Land, Sea and Air; and the Protocol against the Illicit Manufacturing of and Trafficking in Firearms, their Parts and Components and Ammunition.

229   This suggestion is retrieved from the interview available at <https://earth.org/covid-19-pandemic-deepens-global-wildlife-treaty-cites-faces-an-identity-crisis/> accessed 2 June 2021. Recently, a proposal for a new Protocol on the illicit trafficking of wildlife has been tabled by the Global Initiative to End Wildlife Crime (<https://endwildlifecrime.org/untoc-wildlife-protocol/> accessed 5 December 2021). By contrast, according to other experts a Protocol to UNTOC should not be developed for each type of crime, especially considering that, for example, the Protocol related to trafficking in persons has not been used much. According to this latter view, it would be advisable to stick to the already existing instruments UNTOC and UNCAC.

Be that as it may, the CITES Secretariat has in the meantime already started to liaise with important international organisations dealing with health issues, such as, for example, the World Organisation for Animal Health (OIE), based in Paris.[230] It is interesting to note that before the burst of the Covid-19 pandemic worldwide, OIE's activities were not devoted much to wildlife health considerations for the sake of human health. Now things have changed[231] and a closer relationship with CITES has been set up precisely in order to ensure a better collaboration between, for example, veterinarians and CITES management authorities. Clearly, pending the discussion as to the adoption of a possible new instrument or amending/using the existing ones, CITES has already entered into a mutually beneficial relationship with the other international organisations active in the area.

5 Concluding Remarks

CITES is a dynamic legal regime and amongst the few MEAS that put an emphasis on illegality and criminality, even though, technically, the relevant provision (Article VIII.1) gives no guidance as to the level of punishment or any directions as to whether the nature of the penalties should be indeed of a criminal nature. As a result, there is a considerable variation in the level of penalties applied across Parties.

In 2016 the COP to CITES, following-up on a call which had already been made by other international organisations and institutions (eg, GA, ECOSOC, UNODC), has taken the official stance to recommend Parties to make illegal wildlife trafficking that involves (as it is often the case) organised criminal groups, a 'serious crime' in accordance with UNTOC. In essence, the COP called upon Parties to apply the most serious penalties (therefore, including criminal ones) to wildlife trafficking. The result is that now more and more States, including developing ones, have four years or more as their maximum penalty for illegal trafficking involving organised criminal groups in their legislation.

However, putting in place legislation that penalises trade in specimens in violation of the Convention is not a guarantee for its effective enforcement.

---

230 See the official website at <https://www.oie.int/en/> accessed 2 June 2021.
231 See the dedicated webpage at <https://www.oie.int/en/scientific-expertise/specific-information-and-recommendations/questions-and-answers-on-2019novel-coronavirus/expert-groups-and-guidance/> accessed 2 June 2021. OIE acknowledges, for example, that although the origin of the virus causing Covid-19 has not been confirmed yet, it is highly suspected to have emanated from poorly regulated wildlife.

It is also necessary to have operative tools in place at the domestic level (such as detection, investigation, prosecution and conviction of lawbreakers). This also includes a good transnational interagency coordination. Many cooperation initiatives that exist at the international level, thanks to the work of UN bodies, intergovernmental agencies, networks and non-governmental organisations, such as the ICCWC, which constitutes the main cooperation forum for combating illegal wildlife traffic, are in place precisely to facilitate domestic enforcement.

Despite these efforts, though, in many Countries (not only in developing ones) the level of detecting and prosecuting wildlife crime is very low, including because of the limited enforcement capacity. Countries with high penalties might see perpetrators escape punishment, for example, because of the lack of proper judicial awareness and training, whereas in countries with low penalties wildlife offences might be considered less serious than other types of crimes. Sometimes, this is because 'less charismatic' species are involved.

Yet, it might be the case that it is precisely from one of these 'less famous' species that the Covid-19 outbreak has started.[232] This proves first of all that not only high-profile species should be protected. All wildlife, if trafficked, could pose a threat to human health. It also points to the need of more engagement of private actors, including the public, so that the social stigma could be increased, ultimately leading to more political commitment. In (too) many Countries, in fact, combating wildlife crime is still not a priority. The hope is therefore that the progressive increase of public awareness, based on the ever-emerging scientific evidence as to the links between the global health crisis and the illegal trade in wildlife will contribute to include wildlife crime amongst the top priorities for action at the national, as well as international levels.

Acknowledgments

This Chapter has been enriched by the research material and experience generously shared by Ms. Sofie Hermann Flensborg from the CITES Secretariat. The interview with Ms. Hermann Flensborg was held on 24 November 2020. Dr. Raffaella D'Antonio, from Newcastle University, also contributed with her excellent research assistance.

---

232 See above (n 215).

CHAPTER 3

Environmental Crime at the International Level

Criminalisation of Illegal Traffic of Hazardous Wastes under the Basel Convention on the Control of Transboundary Movements of Hazardous Wastes and Their Disposal (Basel Convention)

1   Introduction

Illegal traffic of hazardous waste, along with wildlife crime is amongst the most recognised areas of environmental crime.[1] It involves, for example, electrical and electronic waste (e-waste), which is currently the fastest growing waste stream in the world.[2]

---

1   As recently highlighted by the European Commission, 'waste and wildlife crime belong to the largest and best documented sectors of environmental crime; Member States have identified these as areas where criminal activity is particularly frequent and serious' (European Commission, 'Commission Staff Working Document Evaluation of the Directive 2008/99/EC of the European Parliament and of the Council of 19 November 2008 on the protection of the environment through criminal law' SWD (2020) 259 final, 28 October 2020, 8). The present Chapter focuses on environmentally harmful acts that breach national law implementing Multilateral Environmental Agreements (MEAs), such as the Basel Convention, and that are subject to prosecution and/or to the application of sanctions domestically. The focus is on criminalisation, which according to the UN Commission on Crime Prevention and Criminal Justice (CCPCJ) 'is the harshest form of regulation and involves the most invasive forms of punishment and proceedings. It should thus be used as a last resort when other interventions and sanctions do not or would not have the desired effect. Criminalisation, criminal procedure, and punishment must occur in a proportionate and reasonable manner and should be reserved for serious violations of wildlife, forest, and fisheries laws'. See <https://www.unodc.org/e4j/en/wildlife-crime/module-3/key-issues/criminalization-of-wildlife-trafficking.html> accessed 2 June 2021.
2   Within East Asia and the Pacific, China is the main destination for e-waste, even though the Country banned the import of used electronic and electrical equipment in 2000. Globally, it is estimated that 80% of e-waste is shipped to Asia (including India) – with 90% of that amount destined for China. The main sources of e-waste reaching China are the EU, Japan and the United States. Such shipments are in breach of the law in the countries of export as well as in China. Secondary centers for e-waste trade in the region include Indonesia, Thailand and Viet Nam. See <https://www.unodc.org/documents/toc/Reports/TOCTA-EA-Pacific/TOCTA_EAP_c09.pdf> accessed 2 June 2021. For the European perspective see J Huisman et al, *Countering WEE Illegal Trade (CWIT) Summary Report, Market Analysis, Legal Analysis, Crime Analysis and Recommendations Roadmap* (2015) available online.

In the past, exporting hazardous wastes to countries with lower environmental standards was a diffuse practice potentially leading to illegal conducts. Several episodes started to show to the worldwide public the downsides of that worrying phenomenon.[3] This was certainly the case of the illegal dumping of a residue of caustic soda by the tanker *Probo Koala* in the port of Abijan (Ivory Coast) in 2006, that caused the killing of 15 people, the hospitalisation of 69 and that required an additional 108,000 other people to seek medical treatment.[4] As highlighted by Tatiana Terekhova

> hazardous wastes, if improperly handled, can have adverse effects on human health and the environment. For example, persistent exposure to dioxins – unwanted by-products of incineration and manufacturing processes such as those involved in the bleaching of paper pulp – are known to result in skin lesions and altered liver function in the short-term, and impairment to the immune system and even cancer in the long-term.[5]

The Basel Convention on the Control of Transboundary Movements of Hazardous Wastes and their Disposal (the 'Basel Convention')[6] was in operation

---

3   I Rucevska et al, *Waste Crime-Waste Risks: Gaps in Meeting the Global Waste Challenge* (UNEP 2015).
4   See T MacManus, *State-Corporate Crime and the Commodification of Victimhood: The Toxic Legacy of Trafigura's Ship of Death* (Routledge 2018).
5   T Terekhova, 'Transboundary Movements of Hazardous Wastes and Corruption: The Special Case of E-waste in West Africa' in UNODC, *Corruption, Environment and the United Nations Convention against Corruption* (2012) 13.
6   In legal literature, amongst the numerous contributions, see K Kummer, 'The International Regulation of Transboundary Traffic in Hazardous Wastes: the 1989 Basel Convention' (1992) 41 *International and Comparative Law Quarterly* 530; S Choksi, 'The Basel Convention on the Control of Transboundary Movements of Hazardous Wastes and Their Disposal: 1999 Protocol on Liability and Compensation' (2001) *Ecology Law Quarterly* 509; TR Subramanya, 'The Basel Convention on the Control of Transboundary Movements of Hazardous Wastes and their Disposal of 1989 and Related Developments: an Overview' (2006) 46 *The Indian Journal of International Law: A Quarterly* 406; A Shibata, 'Ensuring Compliance with the Basel Convention – its Unique Features' in U Beyerlin, PT Stoll and R Wolfrum (eds), *Ensuring Compliance with Multilateral Environmental Agreements: a Dialogue between Practitioners and Academia* (Martinus Nijhoff Publishers, 2006) 69; L Widawsky, 'In My Backyard: How Enabling Hazardous Waste Trade to Developing Nations Can Improve the Basel Convention's Ability to Achieve Environmental Justice' (2008) *Environmental Law* 577; K Kummer, 'International Chemicals and Waste Management' in M Fitzmaurice et al (eds), *Research Handbook on International Environmental Law* (Edward Elgar 2010) 637; and T Terekhova, 'The Basel Convention: a Tool for Combating Environmental Crime and Enhancing the Management of Hazardous and other Wastes' in L Elliott and WH Schaedla (eds), *Handbook of Transnational Environmental Crime* (Edward Elgar 2016) 422.

well before the *Probo Koala* accident, and amongst its aims was to respond to the growing international concern over the disproportionate environmental burdens borne by developing Countries from transboundary movements in hazardous wastes. The Convention was adopted in 1989 and entered into force in 1992.[7]

The Basel Convention requires that waste should be moved only between those Countries that have appropriate facilities to treat it or to dispose of it in an environmentally sound way, otherwise the activity would be conducted illegally. Waste crime occurs when the trade, treatment or disposal of hazardous wastes is undertaken in a way that breaches the Convention and that causes harm or risk to the environment and to human health.[8] This is the case, for example, of the transboundary movement of hazardous wastes taking place without the consent of the State of import or if consent is obtained by falsification, misrepresentation, or fraud.

The Basel Convention is the only Multilateral Environmental Agreement (MEA) that explicitly defines in the text a prohibited activity as 'criminal'. The Convention is clear in prescribing that the Parties should 'consider that illegal traffic in hazardous wastes or other wastes is criminal' (Article 4(3)). This is quite a forward statement, especially considering that other MEAs, such as for example CITES, put an emphasis on the criminalisation in the text only implicitly.[9] Yet, the fact that the Basel Convention states that Parties are required only 'to consider' the illegal traffic as criminal might appear weak and leaving too much discretion to Parties as whether to actually adopt measures in that direction. However, one should consider that the Basel Convention is a treaty essentially regulating the management of hazardous wastes including their transboundary movement and disposal. Therefore, it was not designed to deal with the criminalisation of the illegal traffic in hazardous wastes in any great detail. At the same time, the emphasis on criminalisation emerges, for example, from the Guide for the development of national legal frameworks to implement the Basel Convention adopted in 2019.[10]

---

7 UN Treaty Series, Vol. 1673, 57. As of June 2021, it has 188 Parties. See the official website of the Basel Convention at <www.basel.int> accessed 2 June 2021.
8 L Bisschop, 'Illegal Trade in Hazardous Waste' in Elliott and Schaedla (eds) (n 6) 190. For the economic aspects of the international traffic of waste see D Kellenberg, 'The Economics of the International Trade of Waste' (2015) 7 *Annual Review of Resource Economics* 109.
9 See Chapter 2 in this book.
10 See Committee Administering the Mechanism for Promoting Implementation and Compliance: Guide for the Development of National Legal Frameworks to Implement the Basel Convention, UNEP/CHW.14/13/Add.2/Rev.1, 20 June 2019, para 101. The Guide has been adopted through Decision -14/15.

Under this perspective the real 'action' in the criminalisation of the traffic in hazardous wastes predominantly lies in the domestic implementation of the Convention by Parties.

Against the above background, this Chapter explores the existing tools and mechanisms, including their limits, relating to the criminalisation of the international traffic in hazardous wastes. It does so by drawing attention to the domestic enforcement and to the activity of the most relevant enforcement agencies and international institutions in the field, but always maintaining the point of view represented by the international law (the Basel Convention) as the primary perspective.[11]

The chapter concludes by noticing that waste is progressively taking centre stage, particularly within the discussion about circular economy, e-waste and plastic waste. It is therefore expected that a higher level of political attention and of financial contribution will be allocated to this phenomenon in the near future.

2   The Basel Convention and the Provisions for the Criminalisation of Illegal Traffic of Hazardous Wastes

In this section we will briefly introduce the main provisions and institutional structure of the Basel Convention (section 2.1). We will then outline the nature of the illegal traffic in hazardous wastes under the Convention by relying on the available data and also by looking at the links between the Basel Convention and the other international instruments that play a role in the fight against illegal traffic in hazardous waste (section 2.2). The attention will be set on the provisions of the Basel Convention that, combined, require Parties to consider illegal traffic as 'criminal' (section 2.3). The implementation of (and compliance with)[12] these provisions by Parties will be also assessed (sections 2.3.1 and 2.3.2).

---

11   For a broader overview of the international legal frameworks that, besides the Basel Convention, carry implications for the illegal traffic in hazardous wastes see, for example, L Bisshop, 'Illegal Trade in Hazardous Waste' (n 8).

12   Although a forensic distinction between implementation and compliance is difficult to make, for the purposes of the present Chapter we consider 'implementation' the act of adopting legislative, regulatory and/or administrative domestic measures to give effect to the provisions of the Convention, whereas we consider 'compliance' acting in accordance with and in fulfilment of the adopted measures.

2.1 General Provisions and Institutional Structure of the Basel Convention

The Basel Convention is the main regime that regulates the transboundary movement and disposal of hazardous and other wastes. It covers hazardous wastes based on their origin and/or their composition and characteristics (e.g., explosive, flammable, toxic, or corrosive) and only two types of 'other wastes', namely, household wastes and incinerator ash. Wastes are defined as 'substances or objects which are disposed of or are intended to be disposed of or are required to be disposed of by the provisions of national law'.[13]

In order to minimise the transboundary movement of hazardous and other wastes, the Basel Convention advocates both non-trade-based and trade-based measures. The Parties to the Basel Convention are first of all required to adopt appropriate measures to minimise the generation of hazardous and other wastes and to ensure adequate disposal facilities within the generating State. Such measures are intended to ultimately reduce the transboundary movement of wastes.

However, the core of the Convention is that of regulating trade by providing control measures over the transboundary movement of hazardous and other wastes. Parties are required to ensure environmentally sound management (ESM)[14] of hazardous waste and to reduce the frequency of such movements. The importance of ESM in relation to waste has been recently stressed, for example, by the UN Environmental Assembly of the UN Environment Programme (UNEA).[15]

The Basel Convention envisages five natural or legal persons that can be involved in the transport of hazardous wastes.[16] The first is the 'generator', i.e. the entity whose activity has produced the wastes or, in cases where the entity is not known, the person who has possession or control over the wastes.[17] The second one is the 'exporter' who arranges for the export of hazardous wastes and who is under the jurisdiction of the exporting State.[18] The 'carrier' is the

---

13   Article 2(1) of the Basel Convention.
14   The concept of environmentally sound management (ESM) finds expression through a series of technical guidelines developed in relation to the management of specific wastes streams by the Working Group, a subsidiary body to the Conference of the Parties. See <http://www.basel.int/Implementation/CountryLedInitiative/EnvironmentallySoundManagement/ESMToolkit/Overview/tabid/5839/Default.aspx> accessed 2 June 2021.
15   UNEA Resolution 4/7 of 15 March 2019 on ESM of waste.
16   See TG Puthucherril, 'Two Decades of the Basel Convention' in S Alam et al (eds), *Routledge Handbook of International Environmental Law* (Routledge 2013) 298–299.
17   Article 2(18) of the Basel Convention.
18   Article 2(15) of the Basel Convention.

performing carrier,[19] while the 'importer' is any person under the jurisdiction of the importing State who imports the hazardous wastes.[20] The final player, the 'disposer', receives the hazardous cargo for disposal.[21]

Article 4 of the Convention gives each Party a right to prohibit the import of Basel wastes into its borders and impose upon each Party a corresponding obligation not to permit the export of wastes to any State of import that has not specifically consented to the import. The Basel Convention requires the so-called 'prior informed consent' (PIC) procedure, which obliges each exporting Party to prohibit generators or exporters from commencing movements of waste unless the States of import are informed of the intended wastes movements. The State of export has to receive written consent and confirmation of a contract between the exporter and the disposer certifying ESM techniques from the State of import. Each State of export also has a duty to prohibit exportation, find an alternate facility, or re-import wastes if there is reason to believe the wastes will not be handled in an environmentally sound manner in the intended State of import.

The Basel Convention allows Parties to enter into bilateral, multilateral or regional agreements regarding movements of wastes with other Parties, or even non-Parties, to the Basel Convention provided that the Secretariat is notified of this and that such agreements are at least as environmentally sound as the Basel Convention requires. This is provided in Article 11.[22] This means that the transboundary movement with non-Parties not undertaken pursuant to Article 11 of the Basel Convention is prohibited. As a consequence, any movement undertaken by a Party, for instance, with the United States, which are not a Party to the Basel Convention,[23] needs to be made pursuant to Article 11 agreements.

---

19   Article 2(17) of the Basel Convention.
20   Article 2(16) of the Basel Convention.
21   Article 2(19) of the Basel Convention.
22   The list of Article 11 agreements is available at <http://www.basel.int/Countries/Agreements/tabid/1482/Default.aspx> accessed 2 June 2021. Article 11 can also be interpreted to support regional agreements initiated by developing nations desiring a total ban on all imports of wastes into their region (L Widawsky, 'In My Backyard: How Enabling Hazardous Waste Trade to Developing Nations Can Improve the Basel Convention's Ability to Achieve Environmental Justice' (n 6) 589). In this regard, it should be noted that the Basel Convention requires Parties to prohibit the export of hazardous wastes to States, particularly developing Countries, which belong to an economic or political integration entity that has prohibited by legislation all such imports (TG Puthucherril, 'Two Decades of the Basel Convention' (n 16) 300).
23   But they are Party to the OECD Council Decision C(2001)107/FINAL concerning the revision of Decision C(92)39/Final on the control of transboundary movements of wastes destined for recovery operations, 15 May 2004.

In 1995 the Parties to the Basel Convention sought to introduce a ban on the export of hazardous wastes for final disposal from the Organization for Economic Co-operation and Development (OECD) to non- OECD Countries. This is known as 'the Ban Amendment'.[24] The rationale behind this Ban is essentially that of reducing wastes production in so far as generators would not be able to export their wastes to the developing world anymore. The Ban Amendment entered into force only very recently in December 2019. This major delay was due to the opposition of both developed countries (for example, Australia and Canada were requesting a differentiation between waste for final disposal and waste for recycling or recovery purposes) and the developing ones. Interestingly, the latter felt that their economies could suffer from the economic loss deriving from the recovery of materials from hazardous wastes.[25] In any case, after years of stalling in the negotiations,[26] the Ban eventually reached the necessary number of ratifications.[27] The Ban Amendment now provides for the prohibition by OECD Countries, EU and Liechtenstein, of all transboundary movements to non-OECD States of hazardous wastes covered by the Convention that are intended for final disposal, and of all transboundary movements to non-OECD States of hazardous wastes covered by Article 1.1(a) of the Convention[28] that are destined for reuse, recycling or recovery operations.

The Basel Convention has also taken steps against plastic pollution. Plastics account for ten per cent of the waste generated worldwide and some 500 billion plastic bags are used globally each year.[29] Various calls have already been made to respond to this global concern. For example, in the area of pollution

---

24 The Ban Amendment was adopted as a decision (Decision III/1) of the third meeting of the Conference of the Parties (COP). This Decision bans export of hazardous wastes intended for final disposal and those for recycling from what are known as Annex VII Countries (Basel Convention Parties that are members of the EU or OECD and Liechtenstein) to non-Annex VII Countries (all other Parties to the Convention).
25 See TG Puthucherril, 'Two Decades of the Basel Convention' (n 16) 303; and L Widawsky, 'In My Backyard: How Enabling Hazardous Waste Trade to Developing Nations Can Improve the Basel Convention's Ability to Achieve Environmental Justice' (n 6) 614.
26 <http://www.basel.int/Implementation/LegalMatters/CountryLedInitiative/tabid/1339/Default.aspx> accessed 2 June 2021.
27 BC-14/12, Amendments to Annexes II, VIII and IX to the Basel Convention. For all previous decisions adopted on the Ban Amendment see <http://www.basel.int/Implementation/LegalMatters/BanAmendment/Decisions/tabid/3597/Default.aspx> accessed 2 June 2021.
28 Article1(1)(a) of the Basel Convention: '[w]astes that belong to any category contained in Annex I, unless they do not possess any of the characteristics contained in Annex III'.
29 *Global Waste Management Outlook* (2015) 103, available online.

by marine plastics and microplastics, already in 2017 UNEA was 'inviting relevant international and regional organisations and conventions [...] including the Basel Convention as appropriate within their mandates, to increase their action to prevent and reduce marine litter and microplastics and their harmful effects and to coordinate where appropriate to achieve that end'.[30] In 2019, a series of amendments were introduced to the Basel Convention, which entered into force very rapidly in January 2021 thanks to the existence of a broad international consensus on this issue. These amendments have widened the scope of the plastic wastes covered by the Convention (that in the past were instead treated as non-hazardous) and which will be now subject to the PIC procedure, to the provisions pertaining to waste minimisation, as well as to ESM.[31]

Finally, the Basel Convention is compounded by the Basel Protocol on liability and compensation for damage resulting from transboundary movements of hazardous wastes and their disposal adopted by the fifth Conference of the Parties (COP) in 1999. The Protocol would seek to provide a regime to address liability issues and to assure compensation that is adequate for damages deriving from transboundary movement of hazardous and other wastes and also for incidents that happen due to illegal traffic.[32] However, the Protocol has so far attracted very limited ratifications (only twelve) and its entry into force is quite unlikely.[33]

As far as the institutional structure of the Basel Convention is concerned, the COP is the governing body of the Convention and it comprises all States. The COP is empowered to take action to achieve the purposes of the Convention, to promote harmonisation of policies, strategies and measures that seek to minimize harm to human health and to the environment. The COP adopts protocols and establishes subsidiary bodies. The Secretariat arranges the meetings of the COP and provides assistance to Parties in coordinating the implementation of the Convention. It holds the task to assist Parties upon request in their identification of cases of illegal traffic and circulates to the Parties concerned any information it has received regarding the traffic (however, as we will see, this will be described as a rather weak supervisory function).[34]

---

30   UNEA Resolution 3/7 of 30 January 2018, para 8. See also UNEA Resolution 4/6 of 28 March 2019, eight preambular paragraph.
31   <http://www.basel.int/Implementation/Plasticwaste/PlasticWasteAmendments/Overview/tabid/8426/Default.aspx> accessed 2 June 2021.
32   See < http://www.basel.int/TheConvention/Overview/LiabilityProtocol/tabid/2399/Default.aspx> accessed 2 June 2021.
33   See <http://www.basel.int/Countries/StatusofRatifications/TheProtocol/tabid/1345/Default.aspx> accessed 2 June 2021.
34   Article 16(i) of the Basel Convention. See *infra* section 2.3.

In addition, any Party which has reason to believe that another Party is acting or has acted in breach of its obligations under the Convention, including in cases of illegal traffic, may inform the Secretariat thereof, and in such an event, shall simultaneously and immediately inform, directly or through the Secretariat, the Party against whom the allegations are made.[35] Finally, the Basel Convention established in 2002 a body that administers the Mechanism for Promoting Implementation and Compliance, namely the Implementation and Compliance Committee (ICC). Its objective is to assist Parties to comply with their obligations under the Convention, including those related to illegal traffic, and to facilitate, promote, monitor and secure their implementation of and compliance with.[36]

2.2 Illegal Traffic of Hazardous Wastes under Article 9 of the Basel Convention

The Basel Convention deals with the transboundary movement of hazardous wastes. A recent study undertaken by the United Nations Environment Programme (UNEP) highlights that '[t]he drivers and incentives of engaging in illegal trade and disposal of hazardous waste and chemicals [...] include profit, weak enforcement systems, the complexity of rules and range of actors involved in the global chemicals, and waste trade chain'.[37] One commentator also adds that '[a] major incentive for illegal traffic is the low effort required and the huge profits that can be drawn in comparison with legal shipment'.[38]

---

35 Article 19 of the Basel Convention.
36 The ICC has a double mandate: under its specific submission mandate, the Committee shall consider any submission made to it in accordance with the terms of reference with a view to determining the facts and root causes of the matter of concern and assist in its resolution; under its general review mandate, the Committee shall, as directed by the Conference of the Parties, review general issues of compliance and implementation under the Convention. See <http://www.basel.int/TheConvention/Implementation ComplianceCommittee/Overview/tabid/2868/Default.aspx> accessed 2 June 2021.
37 UNEP, *The State of Knowledge of Crimes that Have Serious Impacts on the Environment* (2018) 3.
38 J Albers, *Responsibility and Liability in the Context of Transboundary Movements of Hazardous Wastes by Sea* (Springer 2014) 24. The Author also highlights that '[i]llegal trafficking is fostered by the lack of sufficient governmental structures and enforcement capabilities especially in developing countries and, above all, by the huge profits that can be made by the persons involved. A further common way to circumvent legal requirements regarding the transboundary movement of hazardous wastes is the pre-treatment of such wastes. By mixing hazardous and non- hazardous wastes or by selling wastes as products or raw materials, attempts are made to avoid trade restrictions and requirements' (ibid 26).

The illegal traffic which is captured under the Convention is only that involving wastes that have crossed borders in contravention of its provisions. The illegal traffic differs from what it is known with the expression 'transnational environmental crime' (TEC).[39] The former is the one that infringes upon the Basel Convention's (international law) provisions directly; whereas TEC, which is not only limited to movement in hazardous waste, consists in breaches of domestic law (although also derivative of international law provisions, including the Basel Convention) characterised by a cross-border or transnational dimension (for example, the activity of laundering outside one Country's jurisdiction the profits of a waste crime committed partially inside it, in breach of domestic law). A similarity between the two is instead that both international movement in hazardous wastes in breach of the Basel Convention and TEC related to waste should attract criminal penalties.[40]

Article 9 of the Basel Convention is clear in describing what specific conducts (involving a transboundary movement) are to be considered illegal traffic for the purposes of the Convention. For instance, illegal traffic occurs if the movement of waste is made without notification to all States concerned, or if it is undertaken without the consent of a State concerned, or through consent obtained by falsification, misrepresentation or fraud. It is also a case of illegal movement if it does not conform in a material way with the documents required or when the movement results in deliberate disposal of hazardous wastes in contravention of the Convention and of the general principles of international law. Specific methods of illegal traffic include making false declarations, the concealment, mixture or double layering of the materials in a shipment and the mislabelling of individual containers. One expert from the UK Environment Agency has also identified the increasingly emerging threat of the export of waste as non-waste.[41]

---

39 See, amongst many, Elliott and Schaedla (eds) (n 6); V Mitsilegas and F Giuffrida, *The Role of EU Agencies in Fighting Transnational Environmental Crime, New Challenges for Eurojust and Europol* (Brill 2017) 2 ff; J Ayling, 'Prevention of Transnational Environmental Crimes and Regulatory Pluralism' in P Drahos (ed), *Regulatory Theory: Foundations and Applications* (ANU Press, 2017) 499; and P Stoett, 'Trasnational Environmental Crime', in A Swain and J Öjendal (eds), *Routledge Handbook of Environmental Conflict and Peacebuilding* (Routledge 2018) 29.

40 See *infra* section 2.3.

41 R Harwood, 'Current Challenges and Success for the Enforcement of the Basel Convention in Relation to the Repatriation of Plastic Wastes – Environment Agency, England' Information sessions on the Basel Convention's Plastic Waste Amendments, 30 September 2020, available at <http://www.brsmeas.org/Portals/2/docs/webinars-recordings/20200930_BC_PWAs-Enforcement.mp4> accessed 2 June 2021.

Under Article 9(3) of the Basel Convention, if the illegal traffic arises as a result of conduct on the part of the importer or disposer, the State of import is internationally responsible for ensuring ('shall ensure') that the waste is disposed of in an environmentally sound manner by the importer or disposer, or if necessary, by itself.[42] Likewise, under Article 9(2) of the Basel Convention, if the illegal traffic is deemed to result from the conduct on the part of the exporter or generator, the State of export *shall ensure* that the waste is taken back (this is called repatriation of waste), or, if impracticable, that the waste is disposed of in accordance with the provisions of the Convention.[43]

However, at times the process can operate differently. Countries of import might demand that those of export take back the waste even if the waste is not hazardous (therefore, even if technically it would not be a case of illegal traffic). According to some Parties this could be made under Article 4(11) of the Convention, whereby Parties could impose 'additional requirements that are consistent with the provisions of this Convention and are in accordance with the rules of international law, in order to better protect human health and the environment'.[44] Under this reading of Article 4(11) (but other Parties object to it), the additional requirements that the Parties could adopt would apply to both hazardous and non-hazardous wastes. For example, Parties could require (by adopting national legislation to this effect) an additional permit for recycling facilities to import non-hazardous plastic waste in their territory. In this context, if illegal traffic occurs, the obligation to take back the waste would then apply to a case of non-hazardous waste. This is called 'political return', and it is made, for example, when the Country of export prefers to take back the waste rather than running the risk of incurring in a public scandal. The expert interviewed[45] has reported, for example, of recent cases of illegal shipments towards Asia of plastic wastes that were treated as not hazardous, and that eventually were taken back by the Countries of export under their good will. Technically, the latter could have refused to do so, since, as said, it was not a case of illegal traffic in hazardous wastes under the Convention. One should

---

42 See Guidance on the Implementation of the Basel Convention Provisions Dealing with Illegal Traffic (Paragraphs 2, 3 and 4 of Article 9) (UNEP 2019) 27 ff.
43 ibid, 21 ff.
44 In practice, a Party to the Basel Convention could, for example, decide (through the adoption of national law) that all the computing equipment which is older than 10 years is to be considered 'Basel waste'. The Party then has to inform the Basel Secretariat of the national decision and, as a result of that, if some other Country wants to send computing equipment of that type to this Party, they will have to do so by applying the PIC procedure.
45 See the acknowledgment at the end of the Chapter.

recall, though, that the Plastic Amendment has now entered into force.⁴⁶ The rationale of this amendment was to clarify the different types of plastic waste: *a*) that requires special consideration and subject to PIC procedure, *b*) presumed to be hazardous and subject to PIC procedure or *c*) presumed to be non-hazardous (destined for recycling and almost free from contamination) and not subject to PIC procedure.⁴⁷ Therefore, it is now clearer which categories of plastic waste will be considered hazardous and subject to the provisions of the Convention, including that on the repatriation of waste under Article 9 in the context of a case of illegal traffic. This will entail that political returns will be progressively reduced in the future, at least in relation to plastic waste.

Be that as it may, the above provisions of the Basel Convention involve the responsibility of the State of import or that of the State of export towards other Parties of the Convention. These obligations are legally binding as to the result to be achieved. In fact, they impose on States firstly a duty to ensure vigilance on the activities undertaken by the private operators in order to make sure that they are in accordance with the domestic law implementing the Convention, which requires ESM. At the same time, these provisions entail an obligation for the Parties to ensure that they dispose of the waste in an environmentally sound way in case the private operators do not operate properly (ie, operate illegally). The manual for the implementation of the Convention developed in 2015 makes this very useful example

> E exports hazardous waste from State A to State B, for disposal by disposer D without notifying State B or obtaining its consent. On receipt of the waste, D is suspicious and alerts the competent authority in State B. The waste is analysed and is confirmed as hazardous. The competent authority of State B requests its counterpart in State A to arrange for the waste to be taken back by E within 30 days, but E is bankrupt and has no means to manage the waste in an environmentally sound manner. State A obtains the agreement of State B to take the waste back within two months, during which time it makes arrangements for the ESM of the waste. E is convicted of a criminal offence under State A's national legislation implementing Article 9(5) of the Convention.⁴⁸

---

46 See above text corresponding to footnote n 31.
47 This tripartition is contained, respectively, in the changes to the three annexes of the Basel Convention adopted through the COP Decision BC-14/12, namely, Annex II: Y48; Annex VIII: A3210; and Annex IX: B3011.
48 UNEP, *Manual for the Implementation of the Basel Convention* (2015) 22.

In such a context, the private operator should be punished for illegal traffic. Article 9(5) of the Convention in fact provides that '[e]ach Party shall introduce appropriate national/domestic legislation to prevent and punish illegal traffic. The Parties shall co-operate with a view to achieving the objects of this Article'. This aspect will be analysed further.[49]

Interestingly, the Basel Convention also provides that in cases where the responsibility for the illegal traffic cannot be assigned to one of the private companies involved (eg the generator, the exporter, the importer or the disposer), it falls on the States the obligation to cooperate in order to make sure ('shall ensure') that the waste is disposed of as soon as possible in an environmentally sound manner.[50] This again, is an obligation of result and it reflects the general principle of cooperation in good faith, which is contained in many treaties and international acts, and which is supported by state practice, particularly in relation to hazardous activities.[51]

Against the above background, the exact size of the illegal movement in hazardous waste is currently unknown both at the global[52] and at the regional levels. As to the latter, the 2020 evaluation of the European Commission regarding the transposition of the Environmental Crime Directive in the European Union's (EU) Member States (MSs)[53] in relation to waste trafficking (along with wildlife trafficking) indicates that

> [t]here is a general lack of statistical data on environmental crime which makes it difficult to monitor developments and trends. Waste and Wildlife crime belong to the largest and best documented sectors of environmental crime; Member States have identified these as areas where criminal activity is particularly frequent and serious. Both areas have strong cross-border impacts, as they involve illegal trafficking inside the EU but also beyond with the EU as a point of destination, transit or origin.[54]

---

49   See *infra* section 2.3.1.
50   Article 9(4) of the Basel Convention.
51   P Sands and J Peel, *Principles of International Environmental Law* (4th edn, Cambridge University Press 2018) 620.
52   I Rucevska et al, *Waste Crime-Waste Risks: Gaps in Meeting the Global Waste Challenge* (n 3) 6.
53   On the Environmental Crime Directive see also *infra* section 2.3.1 and, more extensively, Chapter 5 of this book.
54   European Commission, 'Commission Staff Working Document Evaluation of the Directive 2008/99/EC' (n 1) 8, 9.

Notwithstanding this, efforts have been put in place in order to flag out at least the most relevant traffic patterns. Starting from 1998 the Basel COP has requested Parties to bring any cases or alleged cases of illegal traffic to the attention of the Secretariat.[55] Very recently, for example, the Basel COP has encouraged Parties to provide information (under the existing reporting procedures) to the Secretariat about cases of illegal traffic and trade in wastes and chemicals covered by the Basel Convention and by the Rotterdam[56] and the Stockholm[57] Conventions. These Conventions are in fact the primary instruments for tracking and managing hazardous waste and chemicals. In spite of this, the collection of this data has never been an easy task and over the years very few cases were reported. Parties may have feared that if they released the data, they could be blamed for not having been able to prevent illegal traffic. In any case, Parties have never demonstrated to be very collaborative with the Secretariat on this issue.[58] The question therefore may arise as to whether the Parties to the Basel Convention are fulfilling the obligation to cooperate ('shall cooperate') with a view to achieving the objects of Article 9.

In 2016, Parties to the Basel Convention were given the opportunity to report confirmed cases of illegal traffic through the national reporting system, which is an obligation under the Convention. This process is called 'table 9' of the national reports.[59] Even though the completeness of this data is still problematic, and only half of the Parties are actually providing data, it is certainly a good source of information. For example, by looking at the table 9 data regarding the UK in relation to the last four years, it emerges that the most common measures including punishment taken in relation to illegal waste traffic do not go further than either 'warning letters and waste returned to England' or 'container stopped and no further action' taken.[60] This reflects what in the next

---

55 See <http://www.basel.int/Procedures/ReportingonIllegalTraffic/tabid/1544/Default.aspx> accessed 2 June 2021.
56 Rotterdam Convention on the Prior Informed Consent Procedure for Certain Hazardous Chemicals and Pesticides in International Trade, adopted on 10 September 1998. UN Treaty Series, Vol. 2244, 337.
57 Stockholm Convention on Persistent Organic Pollutants, adopted on 22 May 2001. UN Treaty Series, Vol. 2256, 119.
58 See also *infra* section 3.1.
59 <http://www.basel.int/Countries/NationalReporting/NationalReports/BC2018Reports/tabid/8202/Default.asp> accessed 2 June 2021.
60 See the table 9 data of UK related, for example, to 2018 at <http://ers.basel.int/ERS-Extended/FeedbackServer/fsadmin.aspx?fscontrol=respondentReport&surveyid=77&voterid=50019&readonly=1&nomenu=1> accessed 2 June 2021.

sections will be described as a very low rate of prosecution in relation to waste trafficking.[61]

The ICC plays a much more prominent role than the Secretariat in the collection of data regarding the illegal traffic of hazardous waste under the Basel Convention. In 2019 the Basel COP asked the ICC to undertake, under its general review mandate,[62] a scoping exercise of the extent of illegal traffic with a view to estimating how many cases of illegal traffic there were, with respect to which waste and in which regions, and how the cases were resolved.[63] Interestingly, the Basel COP recommended to base this evaluation on the information provided by Parties in the table 9, on the communications sent to the Secretariat, and also on the information provided by the relevant international organisations and entities, such as the International Criminal Police Organization, the World Customs Organization (WCO), the United Nations Office on Drugs and Crime (UNODC), UNEP, the United Nations University, the Organization for Security and Cooperation in Europe, the Basel Convention regional and coordinating centres,[64] and the European Union Network for the Implementation and Enforcement of Environmental Law (IMPEL).[65] This list includes the most relevant international agencies and institutions for the fight against traffic in hazardous wastes upon which the Basel Convention's institutions rely for extracting the available data on illegal traffic. For instance, WCO, UNEP and the regional centers of the Basel Convention report of a situation whereby cases of illegal traffic are much higher than those reported through the procedures set up by the Basel Convention.[66]

The report on scoping the extent of illegal traffic in hazardous wastes under the Convention was ready by May 2020 (hereinafter 'the scoping report') and it contains the data on reported cases of illegal traffic for the year 2017.[67] This scoping report does not draw a completely exhaustive picture of the phenomenon, since only around 50 Parties answered to the call to report cases.[68] As a result of the irregular reporting, data was not easily comparable.[69] The scoping

---

61 See *infra* section 3.1.
62 Above n 36.
63 Annex to Decision BC-14/15.
64 For details on the regional networks see *infra* section 3.1.
65 Annex to Decision BC-14/15.
66 Illegal Traffic, Scoping Exercise, Note by the Secretariat, UNEP/CHW/CC.14/4/Add.1, 7 May 2020, 17.
67 ibid.
68 More precisely, 101 Parties required to do so have transmitted their national report for 2017.
69 For example, some Parties declared the amount of waste movements in liters/kg instead of metric tons.

report itself, in fact, warns that on the basis of the available data it is only possible 'to get an impressionistic global view of the wastes that are subject to illegal traffic'.[70] Notwithstanding this, the outcomes of this assessment are certainly an important step in the right direction.[71]

The first element which emerges from the scoping report is that Parties reported a low number of cases of illegal traffic in the year 2017. Seventy per cent of the respondents indicated that there were no cases of illegal traffic closed in the reporting year, whereas only twenty-seven Parties reported existing cases.[72] Of the latter, many concerned electric waste and electronic equipment (e-waste), end-of-life vehicles and plastic wastes.[73] Therefore, it is confirmed that the Parties to the Basel Convention find it difficult to collect and share information on illegal traffic. Sometimes this is due to a lack of capacity. Just to mention a few examples, Iraq stated that there is a lack of means for detecting hazardous waste in imported goods, and a lack of expertise to detect hazardous waste and illegal traffic crossing the border, whereas El Salvador reported on its part that there has been no detection or knowledge of illicit trafficking in hazardous wastes.[74] In 2019, the Basel COP has invited 'Parties to continue to share information, through the Secretariat, on best practices in preventing and combating illegal traffic, and to report confirmed cases of illegal traffic to the Secretariat using the prescribed form for confirmed cases of illegal traffic'.[75]

In terms of the regions affected by the phenomenon, the vast majority of exports come from Western European Countries and by far the largest number

---

70 Illegal Traffic, Scoping Exercise, Note by the Secretariat, above footnote n 66, 11.
71 In any case, in 2019 the Basel COP has requested the Secretariat to 'continue to maintain a collection of best practices for preventing and punishing illegal traffic, forms for reporting confirmed cases of illegal traffic, information on national definitions of hazardous wastes, including national lists, as well as information on import or export restrictions or prohibitions, and to continue to make that information available on the Convention website' (Decision BC-14/17, National legislation, notifications, enforcement of the Convention and efforts to combat illegal traffic, para 9).
72 Illegal Traffic, Scoping Exercise, Note by the Secretariat, above footnote n 66, 6. Of the 27 Parties having reported closed cases of illegal traffic, 14 (50%) were from the Western European and Others Group (WEOG) region, 8 (29%) were from the Eastern Europe region, 2 (7%) were from the Group of Latin America and the Caribbean (GRULAC), 4 (14%) were from the Asia and Pacific region and none were from the African region.
73 ibid, 11.
74 Illegal Traffic, Report on Additional Steps, Note by the Secretariat, UNEP/CHW/CC.13/ /10, 17 August 18, 38–39.
75 Decision BC-14/17, National Legislation, Notifications, Enforcement of the Convention and Efforts to Combat Illegal Traffic, UNEP/CHW.14/28, para 5.

of reported imports are into African Countries. Now that the Ban Amendment has entered into force it might be possible that the assessment will be different in the upcoming years. Since the Ban Amendment entails that generators are not able to export their wastes to the developing world anymore, the companies operating in developed Countries might decide to reduce waste production at the source. More realistically, these companies could simply decide to direct the illegal movements elsewhere. The scoping report highlights an interesting trend in this regard. Eastern European Countries have started to become an importing region with appreciable and increasing numbers of imports of illegal waste.[76]

Amongst the reasons why certain regions, like Africa, became key destinations for large-scale imports of hazardous wastes, there is a lack of resources for monitoring and control especially at the enforcement level.[77] This lack of control minimises the risk and makes it particularly appealing to organised criminal groups, whose activities undermine both the reputation and the competitive situation of the legal businesses. Only the latter in fact need to bear the costs of complying with the environmental guidelines and with the health protection regulations of their employees and those related to handling and tracking toxic material.[78] One expert from the UK Environment Agency has, for example, identified the recent increase in organised crime groups exploiting the plastic waste market for unlawful financial gain.[79]

The relevance of organised crime is confirmed also at the regional level. The 2020 evaluation of the European Commission regarding the transposition of the Environmental Crime Directive in the EU MSs reports an increased involvement of organised criminal groups in waste crime. For instance, the UK (up until very recently in the EU) is witnessing a 'steady rise in organised, large-scale waste crime'[80] mostly coming from existing organised crime groups that are already involved in other types of crime and are now getting interested into the waste and recycling markets.[81] Also in Italy the illegal management of

---

76 Illegal Traffic, Scoping Exercise, Note by the Secretariat, above (n 66) 12.
77 See *infra* section 3.1.
78 C Nellemann et al, *The Rise of Environmental Crime, A Growing Threat to Natural Resources Peace, Development and Security* (2016) 62.
79 R Harwood, 'Current Challenges and Success for the Enforcement of the Basel Convention in Relation to the Repatriation of Plastic Wastes – Environment Agency, England' (n 41).
80 L Noel et al, 'Independent Review into Serious and Organised Crime in the Waste Sector' (2018) 3, available at <https://www.gov.uk/government/publications/serious-and-organised-waste-crime-2018-review> accessed 2 June 2021.
81 European Commission, 'Commission Staff Working Document Evaluation of the Directive 2008/99/EC' (n 1) 53.

waste is considered a growing activity with an increasing transnational dimension, in part as a result of the involvement of organised crime groups.[82]

Differently from other MEAS, above all CITES, the relevance of organised crime for the illegal traffic in hazardous wastes under the Basel Convention has not determined any particular action taken at the level of the Basel COP.[83] For example, the latter has not recommended, as did the CITES COP, that the Parties make illegal trafficking in hazardous wastes involving organised criminal groups as a 'serious crime' in accordance with Article 2(b) of the 2000 United Nations Convention on Transnational Organised Crime (UNTOC), so-called 'Palermo Convention' (i.e., to make it punishable by a maximum deprivation of liberty of at least four years or a more serious penalty).[84] It may be that on this aspect the Basel COP preferred not to take a specific action to criminalise further the illegal traffic in hazardous wastes involving organised crime, so to consider it not just 'criminal',[85] but also as a 'serious crime'.

A further element which characterises illegal movement in hazardous waste under the Basel Convention is its link with other crimes, such as corruption and fraud. The former facilitates waste crime whilst also weakening the institutional foundations of the States, such as in the case of a lack of appropriate control of the documents by a customs officer in exchange of money. As highlighted by Tatiana Terekhova,

> corruption can affect the proper implementation and enforcement of the various obligations enshrined in the Basel Convention. With respect to ESM, corruption may take place in the process of licensing disposal facilities or authorizing persons to transport hazardous wastes. With regards to transboundary movements of wastes, corruption may occur at any given time, for instance when the State of export authorizes that the prior informed consent (PIC) procedure be initiated.[86]

---

82 ibid.
83 See in this volume Chapter 2.
84 UN Treaty Series, Vol. 2225, p. 209. For the purposes of the Palermo Convention, organised criminal group 'shall mean a structured group of three or more persons, existing for a period of time and acting in concert with the aim of committing one or more serious crimes or offences established in accordance with this Convention, in order to obtain, directly or indirectly, a financial or other material benefit' (Article 2(a)).
85 See the next section.
86 T Terekhova, 'Transboundary Movements of Hazardous Wastes and Corruption: The Special Case of E-waste in West Africa' (n 6) 13–14.

The fact that illegal waste traffic is a 'safe harbour' for corruption did not lead the Basel COP to recommend making greater use of the 2003 United Nations Convention Against Corruption (UNCAC).[87] Even though UNCAC does not explicitly refer to environmental (including waste) crime, it nevertheless applies to it. The fact that UNCAC emphasises the need for effective and coordinated anti-corruption policies for law enforcement officials to ensure that corrupt authorities are held accountable,[88] clearly has a bearing also on the authorities involved in waste controls. However, as said, the Parties to the Basel Convention preferred to not make a link between the two issues (corruption and illegal waste traffic) by adopting a decision to that effect.

The link between illegal traffic and fraud emerges instead, for example, from the operations conducted by Interpol.[89] An operation in 2016 resulted in the identification of trafficking routes used by criminal networks: 300 tonnes of hazardous waste from Cyprus were intended to be sent to Central America using fraudulent documents.[90]

Finally, a mention should be made of the impact of Covid-19 to the illegal traffic in hazardous wastes. A waste shipment specialist at the Scottish Environmental Protection Agency (SEPA), also Chair of the Environmental Network for Optimizing Regulatory Compliance on Illegal Traffic (ENFORCE),[91] has highlighted that criminal activities could take advantage of the higher rates of transboundary movements of hazardous wastes, including healthcare waste, due to the limited recycling capacity as a result of the lockdown.[92] Illegal operators could also capitalise on the reduced enforcement presence (i.e., fewer controls by inspectors and customs officers). Some Countries, such as Romania, have identified an increase on illegal imports during the pandemic. In terms of the destinations for the illegal shipments of particular types of waste, in the year 2020 the inspections have showed that most of the shipments were made intra-EU. The same expert also reported that, thanks to the

---

87   UN Treaty Series, Vol. 2349, 41.
88   Article 5 UNCAC.
89   See *infra* section 3.2.
90   UNEP, *The State of Knowledge of Crimes that Have Serious Impacts on the Environment* (2018) 12.
91   See *infra* section 3.2.
92   K Olley, 'Overview of the Impact of Covid-19 on Transboundary Movements of Hazardous and Other Waste and Illegal Traffic' Twelfth Meeting of the Open-ended Working Group (OEWG) of the Basel Convention, online event held in September 2020. Available at <https://unep-brs.webex.com/recordingservice/sites/unep-brs/recording/30ef4ac473a34 e5b8a37b0ab1a9e2754/playback> accessed 2 June 2021.

inspections made in 2020, significant quantities of tyres being illegally shipped were prevented from being exported to India.[93]

2.3 Criminalisation of Illegal Traffic of Hazardous Wastes under the Basel (and the Bamako) Conventions

The Basel Convention goes further than just providing that '[e]ach Party shall introduce appropriate national/domestic legislation to prevent and punish illegal traffic'.[94] In fact, it is the only MEA that goes as far as requiring that Parties define a prohibited activity as 'criminal'. This is stated in Article 4(3) of the Convention whereby '[t]he Parties *consider* that illegal traffic in hazardous wastes or other wastes is criminal'.[95]

Other MEAs that with the Basel Convention share the common objective of protecting human health and the environment from hazardous substances, namely, the Rotterdam and the Stockholm Conventions that deal with illegal trade in chemicals, stop short of doing that. As it has been highlighted, '[t]he Rotterdam and Stockholm Conventions are less prescriptive [than the Basel Convention] although they too require Parties to take the necessary legal and administrative measures to ensure that imports and exports of chemicals are undertaken in accordance with their provisions'.[96]

At the same time, the Basel Convention does not impose a clear obligation to make illegal traffic 'criminal'. The Convention in fact states that the Parties just have to 'consider' it to be criminal.[97] The fact that the Basel Convention states that Parties are required only 'to consider' the illegal traffic as criminal might appear weak and leaving too much discretion to Parties on whether to decide to actually adopt measures to fight it through criminal law. In fact, no further detail is given in relation to these criminal measures. However, it could be argued that the very fact that the Convention uses the word 'prohibit' in relation to the import/export of hazardous wastes should be seen as tantamount to

---

[93] The data referred to by the Expert were collected in the context of the project SWEAP. See <https://www.sweap.eu/> accessed 2 June 2021.
[94] Article 9(5) of the Basel Convention.
[95] Emphasis added.
[96] *Analysis on Possible Synergies in Preventing and Combating Illegal Traffic and Trade in Hazardous Chemicals and Wastes, Secretariat of the Basel, Rotterdam and Stockholm Conventions* (2017) 10, para 32.
[97] See, for example, GM Vagliasindi, 'Legal Perspectives on Environmental Crime; the Transnational Dimension of Environmental Crime' in V Mitsilegas et al (eds), *Research Handbook on Transnational Crime* (Edward Elgar 2019) 150.

an obligation to criminalise illegal traffic in national legislation.[98] In addition, as it will be seen further on,[99] the Guide for the development of national legal frameworks to implement the Basel Convention adopted in 2019 specifies that the criminalisation of illegal traffic must clearly emerge from domestic law, for example, from a specialised environmental legislation or from the penal code.

In any case, one should consider that the Basel Convention is a treaty essentially regulating the management of hazardous wastes including their transboundary movement and disposal. Therefore, it was not designed to deal with the criminalisation of the illegal traffic in hazardous wastes in any great detail. Under this perspective, although the Basel Convention provides for a role of the Secretariat with respect to illegal traffic,[100] the States negotiating Basel were not prepared to provide for the Secretariat to act on their own initiative; instead, the Secretariat's action is triggered on request.[101] From this it could be inferred that States wished to exercise a degree of control over the Secretariat's actions in this sensitive area. The Basel Secretariat cannot go further and, for example, trigger the ICC on the basis of the available information it has received on illegal traffic. As suggested by one Author, it seems that 'the Basel Convention's treaty bodies – especially the Secretariat – were equipped with remarkably weak supervisory functions'.[102]

Since the Basel Convention, in essence, established rules designed to regulate trade in hazardous wastes,[103] regional conventions were later adopted in order to address the issue regarding the criminalisation of shipments of hazardous wastes, especially towards developing Countries. Article 11 of the Basel Convention in fact encourages parties to enter into bilateral, multilateral and regional agreements on hazardous waste to help achieve the objectives of the Convention.

---

98 National Legislation: Strategies to Promote Full Legislative Implementation, Note by the Secretariat, UNEP/CHW/CC.11/9, 8 July 2014, Annex, paras 21-28. Paragraph 24 seems to imply that there is an obligation to criminalise illegal traffic without explicitly saying so.
99 See *infra* section 2.3.1.
100 Article 16(1)(h) of the Basel Convention may relate to illegal traffic (although not exclusively). However, the provision does not provide for the Secretariat to take initiative, since it will only be triggered upon request (see next footnote).
101 The Secretariat can assist Parties upon request in their identification of cases of illegal traffic and in circulating any information it has received from them (Article 16(1)(i) of the Basel Convention).
102 A Cardesa-Salzmann, 'Multilateral Environmental Agreements and Illegality' in Elliott and Schaedla (eds) (n 6) 299, 310.
103 P Sands and J Peel, *Principles of International Environmental Law* (n 51) 620.

Two Conventions are important in this regard. The Bamako Convention on the Ban of the Import into Africa and the Control of Transboundary Movement and Management of Hazardous Wastes within Africa, which was adopted in 1991 within (at that time) the Organisation of African Unity,[104] and the Convention to Ban the importation into Forum Island Countries of Hazardous and Radioactive Wastes and to Control the Transboundary Movement of Hazardous wastes, known also as Waigani Convention, which was adopted in 1995 within the South Pacific Region.[105]

The Bamako Convention tackles the practice under which developed nations export toxic wastes specifically to Africa. The *Probo Koala* case mentioned at the beginning of this Chapter is just one egregious example. To avoid the occurrence of such types of accidents the Bamako Convention prohibits the import of all hazardous and radioactive wastes into the African continent for any reason; it aims at minimising and controlling transboundary movements of hazardous wastes within the African continent; it prohibits all ocean and inland water dumping or incineration of hazardous wastes; and it aims at ensuring that disposal of wastes is conducted in an environmentally sound manner. The Waigani Convention was modelled after the Bamako Convention and it bans the import of hazardous and radioactive waste and regulates the transboundary movement of such waste.[106] Both the Bamako and the Waigani Conventions contain provisions on criminalisation. However, we will focus only on the ones contained in the former since it bears grater implications for the purposes of the present analysis.[107]

The Bamako Convention provides that the Parties shall introduce appropriate legislation at the national level for imposing criminal penalties on all persons who have planned, carried out, or assisted in illegal imports of hazardous

---

104 UN Treaty Series, Vol. 2101, 177. The Convention entered into force in 1998. See the official website <https://www.unenvironment.org/explore-topics/environmental-rights-and-gov ernance/what-we-do/meeting-international-environmental> accessed 2 June 2021.
105 UN Treaty Series, Vol. 2161, 91. The Convention entered into force in 2001.
106 P Sands and J Peel, *Principles of International Environmental Law* (n 51) 624.
107 The Waigani Convention provides that Each Pacific Island Developing Party shall take appropriate legal, administrative and other measures within the area under its jurisdiction to ban the import and/or export of hazardous and radioactive wastes and that such import and/or export 'shall be deemed an illegal and criminal act' (Article 4(1)(a) and (b)). As far as the implementation of the Convention is concerned, the ninth COP was held in 2017 and it also included the topic of the efforts to combat illegal trafficking. See <https://www.sprep.org/attachments/Publications/Corporate_Documents/report_9th _waigani_convention_eng.pdf> accessed 2 June 2021.

wastes.[108] Interestingly, the Bamako Convention goes as far as specifying that such criminal penalties shall be sufficiently high to both punish and deter such conduct.[109] The Bamako Convention thus goes a little bit further than the Basel Convention because it details a little more the criminal measures that should be applied to illegal traffic of hazardous wastes.

As far as the implementation of the Bamako Convention is concerned, after a stalling in the activities (the first Bamako COP was held only in 2013), in 2018 and in 2020 the second and third COPs were held. Also, the number of ratifications of the Convention has slightly increased.[110] This notwithstanding, the progress to tackle the illegal trade in hazardous wastes is only in its infancy. Within the second Bamako COP a call was made, for example, by the Deputy Executive Director of UNEP to the African Countries most affected by the hazardous waste dumping to take responsibility for the fight against environmental crime, since the Countries which benefited from it would not do it for them.[111] Amongst the decisions taken in 2020 the third Bamako COP in fact decided to urge Parties to better implement the provisions of the Convention, namely, 'to urge parties and other African States that have not yet done so to enhance or supplement existing legislation to prevent illegal and unwanted traffic in hazardous and other e-waste from entering their territory and the African continent'.[112] A call was also made to request Parties and other African Countries to strengthen the level of international interinstitutional cooperation, including by participating in partnerships and entities such as ENFORCE, the International Network for Environmental Compliance and Enforcement (INECE), and Interpol.[113] As we will see, the international interinstitutional cooperation is key for an effective enforcement of the provisions also of the Basel Convention.[114]

---

108   Article 9(3) of the Bamako Convention.
109   ibid. To this effect in 2013 the COP adopted Decision 1/14 on illegal traffic that requested 'the Secretariat to assist Parties in developing national legislation and administrative procedure for the prevention, monitoring, repression and remediation of illegal traffic'.
110   There are 29 Member States of the African Union as of June 2021 (out of the 55 African States) that have ratified or acceded to the Bamako Convention.
111   *Rapport de la Conférence des Parties à la Convention de Bamako sur l'interdiction d'importer en Afrique des déchets dangereux et sur le contrôle des mouvements transfrontières et la gestion des déchets dangereux produits en Afrique sur les travaux de sa deuxième reunion*, UNEP/BC/COP.2/11, 25 avril 2018, para 4.
112   Decision CB.3/9: Prevention of electronic hazardous waste and the import and dumping of end-of-life waste electrical and electronic equipment in Africa, para 1.
113   ibid, para 6.
114   See *infra* section 3.2.

2.3.1 Implementation of Article 9 of the Basel Convention

Article 4(4) of the Basel Convention provides that each Party 'shall take appropriate legal, administrative or other measures to implement [...] the provisions of the Basel Convention'. As already seen above, Article 9(5) complements this provision and further states that '[e]ach Party shall introduce appropriate national/domestic legislation to prevent and punish illegal traffic. The Parties shall co-operate with a view to achieving the objects of this Article'.[115] Parties enjoy flexibility in designing those measures in accordance with their national practices and policies.

The strategic framework for the implementation of the Basel Convention 2012–2021 has considered as an indicator for measuring the achievement of the goals of the Convention, including Article 9, the fact that 'Parties have reached an adequate level of administrative and technical capacity (in the form of customs, police, environmental enforcement and port authorities, among others) to prevent and combat illegal traffic and judicial capacity to deal with cases of illegal traffic'.[116] While the assessment as to the achievement of this goal is at present still ongoing,[117] the Basel institutions throughout this period have undertaken a wide array of activities and initiatives. A brief overview of the most important ones will be helpful.

Parties have first of all an obligation to report to the Secretariat on the measures adopted to implement Article 9.[118] In this context, a recent call has been made by the Basel COP to the ICC to review the information provided by Parties as to whether their national legislation contains provisions to prevent illegal traffic of hazardous and other wastes as well as provisions that make illegal traffic criminal.[119] A large majority of the Parties that have responded to the questionnaire[120] have reported that their legislation does make reference to the prevention of illegal traffic of hazardous and other wastes. Almost the same majority indicated that their legislation indeed provides that illegal traffic is criminal. In most cases the Countries reported that the punishment for it

---

[115] Article 9(5) of the Basel Convention. See also above section 2.2.
[116] Decision BC-10/2, Strategic Framework for the Implementation of the Basel Convention for 2012–202.
[117] <http://www.basel.int/Implementation/StrategicFramework/Evaluation/Finalevaluation/tabid/6108/Default.aspx> accessed 2 June 2021.
[118] Article 13(3)(c) of the Basel Convention.
[119] See Illegal Traffic, Responses to Question 1(c) of the Reporting Format, Note by the Secretariat, UNEP-CHW-CC.14-4-Add.4, 7 May 2020, para 8.
[120] As of 1 January 2020, 101 Parties out of the 183 Parties of the Basel Convention required to do so, have transmitted their national report for 2017.

included fines;[121] fewer of them included prison. Only twelve Parties, developing Countries in particular, did not provide that illegal traffic is criminal within their legislation.[122]

Overall, the ICC indicates that the current reporting system 'does not generate adequate information to assess either general trends in the enforcement of provisions on illegal traffic, or the effectiveness of different means of enforcement and different penalties within Parties'.[123] For that reason, the ICC stated that it was considering 'including in its proposed work programme for 2022–2023 that it identify best practices and case studies in enforcement and punishment of illegal traffic, and to consider how to assess whether Parties' current efforts are on target to achieve best practices'.[124]

In 2019 the Basel COP has also urged 'Parties to fulfil their obligations set out in paragraph 4 of Article 4 and paragraph 5 of Article 9 of the Convention, including by updating or developing stringent legislation on the control of transboundary movements of hazardous wastes and by incorporating into their national legislation appropriate sanctions or penalties for illegal traffic in hazardous wastes and other wastes'.[125]

Along with looking at the already existing domestic legislation adopted by Parties, the Basel institutions also provide technical assistance, especially to developing country Parties and Parties with economies in transition, to assist them in fulfilling their obligations. In 2019 the Basel COP has, for example, invited Parties to provide information to the Secretariat on their needs in terms of technical assistance and on their difficulties in implementing the Basel Convention.[126] In the questionnaire that Parties were required to fill and send back to the Secretariat by 31 March 2020, they were encouraged, if

---

121 An example is the UK. The case of the breach of the duty of care for waste (including hazardous) is considered an offence, but it can be dealt with by means of a fixed penalty notice (FPN). The person who is served with a FPN is not obliged to pay the penalty. But if that person does pay the penalty, they cannot be prosecuted. If they do not pay the penalty they can, and probably will, be prosecuted. See *Waste Duty of Care Code of Practice, November 2018, Presented to Parliament and to the National Assembly for Wales pursuant to Section 34(9) of the Environmental Protection Act 1990*.

122 These are Andorra, Argentina, Colombia, Venezuela, Democratic Republic of the Congo, Egypt, Rwanda Japan, Lebanon, Republic of Pakistan, Moldova (Illegal Traffic, Responses to Question 1(c) of the Reporting Format, Note by the Secretariat, UNEP-CHW-CC.14-4-Add.4, 7 May 2020, para 15).

123 ibid, para 29.

124 ibid, para 30.

125 Decision BC-14/17, National Legislation, Notifications, Enforcement of the Convention and Efforts to Combat Illegal Traffic, UNEP/CHW.14/28, para 3.

126 Decision BC-14/18.

needed, to ask for technical assistance on prevention and combating illegal traffic. They could also request further assistance including support with the identification of cases of illegal traffic, which, as seen above, is an area where Parties usually struggle.[127] Technical assistance is also delivered through the regional centres, which are a network of 14 regional and coordinating centres for capacity building and technology transfer.[128] Amongst the reported activities there is, for example, capacity building and assistance for custom officers that have to monitor, detect and prevent illegal traffic.[129]

Technical assistance can also be delivered for waste traffic and trade in chemicals, thanks to a synergy amongst the activities of the Basel, Stockholm and Rotterdam Conventions. Amongst the priority areas of this synergy there is that of enhancing national capacities to deal with illegal traffic of hazardous chemicals and wastes. In this context, hands-on training can be offered also for collecting information on possible collaborations in preventing and combating illegal traffic and trade in hazardous chemicals and wastes.[130]

As part of the technical assistance, mention should be made also to the ongoing projects supporting the implementation of the Basel Convention. Norad-1 is a four-year project (started in 2018) funded by the Norwegian Agency for Development Cooperation, which aims at preventing and reducing marine litter and microplastics in Bangladesh and Ghana.[131] Part of the activities of Norad-1 is devoted to enhancing legal, policy and institutional capacity in order to prevent cases of illegal traffic. Another relevant project was known as the 'e-waste Africa project'. It was undertaken by the Basel Secretariat from 2008 to 2012 after it was discovered that West Africa was serving as the major trading route for used electrical and electronic equipment into the African continent, with Ghana and Nigeria as the main import hubs.[132] The project

---

127   See <http://www.brsmeas.org/Implementation/TechnicalAssistance/NeedsAssessment/tabid/4898/language/en-US/Default.aspx> accessed 2 June 2021.
128   See <http://www.basel.int/Partners/RegionalCentres/Overview/tabid/2334/Default.aspx> accessed 2 June 2021.
129   See <http://www.basel.int/Partners/RegionalCentres/ActivityReports/tabid/2992/Default.aspx> accessed 2 June 2021.
130   <http://www.brsmeas.org/Implementation/TechnicalAssistance/CapacityDevelopment/Enhancingnationalcapacities/tabid/5925/language/en-US/Default.aspx> accessed 2 June 2021.
131   See <http://www.basel.int/Implementation/Plasticwaste/Technicalassistance/Projects/BRSNorad1/tabid/8343/Default.aspx> accessed 2 June 2021.
132   T Terekhova, 'Transboundary Movements of Hazardous Wastes and Corruption: The Special Case of E-waste in West Africa' (n 6) 15.

aimed at building local capacity in order to discourage corruption while distinguishing between e-wastes and electrical and electronic products destined for reuse.[133]

The Basel Convention's institutions, according with a practice commonly used also in the context of other MEAs, adopt guidance (soft law) documents in order to assist Parties in implementing and potentially harmonising the provisions of the Convention. Overall, these guidelines attempt to respond to the difficulties encountered by the actors involved at the different levels in implementing the measures that are mandated by the Basel Convention. They also attempt to address the need to further develop training and share data for the benefit of both administrative and judicial operators at the domestic level. Some of these guidance documents, particularly those most relevant for illegal traffic in hazardous wastes, will be now briefly described.

Amongst the most recent documents, the Guidance on the Implementation of the Basel Convention Provisions Dealing with Illegal Traffic (Paragraphs 2, 3 and 4 of Article 9) was developed in 2019 with a view to providing guidance to Parties on how to implement in practice the aforementioned provisions dealing with the consequences of illegal traffic under the Convention.[134] Another relevant guidance, developed in 2017, aims at clarifying the terminology used in the Basel Convention. At times, in fact, the same substance/object can be considered Basel waste in one Country and non-waste in another, or hazardous in one and non-hazardous in another.[135] The Glossary of Terms has been adopted[136] specifically to provide legal clarity in relation to the distinction between wastes and non-wastes, as this has a bearing on the illegal cross-border transports of used substances or objects intended for re-use and also on the application of the PIC procedure.

In 2017 the ICC developed also a guide for the development of national legal frameworks to implement the Basel Convention. It indicates the possible

---

133 See 'Where are WEee in Africa?', Findings from the Basel Convention E-Waste Africa Programme, 2011, available online.
134 See above (n 42).
135 As it has been highlighted '[w]hile the concept of "waste" is well-understood in the context of materials destined for final disposal, a lack of clarity and divergent interpretations have attended the transboundary movement of materials destined for further use. Many Parties consider that such materials are not waste if destined for various modes of re-use. This is especially true for materials that require no repair, refurbishment, reassembly, or similar processing' (Report on the Implementation of the Basel Convention as it Relates to the Interpretation of Certain Terminology, UNEP/CHW.11/INF/2, 1 February 2013, para 2).
136 *Basel Convention, Glossary of Terms* (UN Environment 2017).

content of the domestic provisions, as well as providing examples of tools to respond to non-observance of national law to fight against illegal traffic.[137] In relation to the criminal penalties, it indicates fines, imprisonment and closure.[138] The updated version of this guide adopted by the ICC in 2019, also adds the consideration that in order to make illegal traffic a criminal offence it must be drafted as such in the Basel Convention implementing legislation or another national law. For example, it should be contained in a specialised environmental legislation or in the penal code.[139]

Finally, the issue of the harmonisation of criminal penalties also emerged in the context of the implementation of the Basel Convention by the EU. The latter, together with its MSs, has been a Party to the Basel Convention since 1994. The international obligations contained in the Basel Convention have been implemented mainly through Regulation 1013/2006 on shipments of waste (so-called 'Basel Regulation'), which applies a major distinction between shipments of wastes between the MSs and shipments outside of the EU.[140] The Basel Regulation requires that the EU MSs lay down rules on penalties applicable in case of illegal shipments of wastes and that they 'take all measures necessary' to ensure that these rules are implemented. However, the Basel Regulation does not specify the type (eg, administrative or criminal) and content of these measures.[141] It only requires that the penalties must be 'effective, proportionate and dissuasive'.[142]

The Basel Regulation has to be read in conjunction with Directive 2008/99/EC on protection of the environment through criminal law (so-called 'Environmental Crime Directive').[143] This Directive contains, in its Annexes, a

---

137   Committee Administering the Mechanism for Promoting Implementation and Compliance: Guide for the Development of National Legal Frameworks to Implement the Basel Convention, Note by the Secretariat, UNEP/CHW.13/INF/27, 3 February 2017, 34 ff.
138   ibid, para 93.
139   Committee Administering the Mechanism for Promoting Implementation and Compliance: Guide for the Development of National Legal Frameworks to Implement the Basel Convention (n 10) para 101.
140   Regulation (EC) No 1013/2006 of the European Parliament and of the Council of 14 June 2006 on shipments of waste [2006] OJ L190/1. This Regulation has been amended by the Regulation (EU) No 660/2014 of the European Parliament and of the Council of 15 May 2014 amending Regulation (EC) No 1013/2006 on shipments of waste [2014] OJ L189/135.
141   Article 50(1) of Regulation (EC) No 1013/2006, as amended by Regulation (EU) No 660/2014.
142   ibid.
143   Directive 2008/99/EC of the European Parliament and of the Council of 19 November 2008 on the protection of the environment through criminal law [2008] OJ L328/28.

list of waste-related directives whose breach has to be sanctioned by the MSs through effective, proportionate and dissuasive *criminal* penalties, provided that the violation is unlawful and meets the requirement under Article 3(b) of the Environmental Crime Directive, ie, the shipment of waste is undertaken in a non-negligible quantity.[144] It should be noted that the Environmental Crime Directive covers both hazardous and non-hazardous wastes within its remit.

It follows from the above that the EU provisions on criminalisation go a bit further than the Basel Convention, since they detail the criminal measures (effective, proportionate, and dissuasive) that should be applied to illegal traffic of hazardous wastes. In addition, the EU provisions expand the scope of the waste-related activities that could be potentially criminalised so as to include also non-hazardous wastes compared with the Basel Convention, which instead covers only hazardous wastes. Both the EU provisions and those contained in the Basel Convention stop short of prescribing specific types and levels of criminal penalties leaving the choice of measures to the discretion of the States.[145] As a result, as it occurs globally, there is a considerable variation in the level of punishment at the MSs' level. By way of example, according to recent data the average criminal law sanction in the EU MSs ranges from one year to life imprisonment for natural persons.[146]

---

144 For more in-depth remarks on the Environmental Crime Directive, including on the issue of choosing to impose on MSs a duty of criminalisation only when the conduct is unlawful and on the fact that this reflects the accessory nature of environmental criminal law, see Chapter 5 of this book.

145 This is due to the limited level of EU harmonisation of environmental criminal law at the time of adoption of the Environmental Crime Directive. In addition, this has to be read against the constitutional debate over the powers of the EU to criminalise. See V Mitsilegas, M Fitzmaurice and E Fasoli, 'The Relationship Between EU Criminal Law and Environmental Law' in V Mitsilegas et al (eds), *Research Handbook on EU Criminal Law* (Edward Elgar 2016) 272. See more in Chapter 5 of this book. For a comparative study on the possibility that the absence of specification about the types and levels of penalties in the Environmental Crime Directive could compromise its effective implementation and enforcement by the Member States see R Pereira, 'Towards Effective Implementation of the EU Environmental Crime Directive? The case of Illegal Waste Management and Trafficking Offences' (2017) 26 *Review of European Comparative & International Environmental Law* 147.

146 Instead, in relation to legal persons the penalties range from below 500,000 to 60,000,000 (European Commission, 'Commission Staff Working Document Evaluation of the Directive 2008/99/EC' (n 1) 40).

2.3.2 Compliance with Article 9 of the Basel Convention

As anticipated above,[147] the Basel Convention established a non-compliance procedure[148] that within its general review mandate[149] plays an important role in the collection of data regarding the illegal traffic. The ICC is the subsidiary body that in 2019 was entrusted by the Basel COP to undertake the scoping exercise of the current extent of illegal traffic.[150] The same Basel COP also requested the ICC to undertake a number of other activities aimed at improving compliance with obligations pertaining to preventing and combating illegal traffic in hazardous wastes and other waste. Amongst these there is the review of the existing cooperative arrangements with international organisations or entities with a mandate regarding preventing and combating illegal traffic, and the exploration of modalities for disseminating, especially to enforcement entities, existing guidance and technical assistance tools developed under the Convention to assist Parties to prevent and combat illegal traffic. These activities will be analysed more in detail in the sections dedicated to enforcement.[151]

The core activity of the ICC within its specific submission mandate[152] is determining the facts and causes of non-compliance (therefore, also in relation to Article 9) and assisting the Parties by providing them with advice, non-binding recommendations and information. The ICC examines the submissions by the Parties relating to a specific Party's failure to comply (although, so far, no Party has made use of this possibility),[153] as well as the self-submissions by them.

The Secretariat cannot trigger the ICC on the basis of the available information it has received on illegal traffic. However, it can still trigger the ICC for a failure of a Party to comply with its reporting obligations, such as that of the transmission of information, including national reporting.[154] This may well expose failures to introduce implementing legislation at the domestic level, including those related to the criminalisation of illegal traffic.

---

147   See above section 2.1.
148   In general, see A Shibata, 'Ensuring Compliance with the Basel Convention – its Unique Features' (n 6) 69–87; and A Fodella, 'Mechanism for Promoting Implementation and Compliance with the 1989 Basel Convention on the Transboundary Movements of Hazardous Wastes and their Disposal' in T Treves et al (eds), *Non-Compliance Procedures and Mechanisms and the Effectiveness of International Environmental Agreements* (TMC Asser Press, 2009) 33.
149   See above (n 36).
150   See above section 2.2.
151   See *infra* section 3.2.
152   See above (n 36).
153   It should be noted that Party to Party submissions are anyway rare also in the context of other MEAs.
154   Article 9(c) of the terms of reference of the ICC.

An illustrative example is Togo. In 2010 the Secretariat triggered the ICC in relation to Togo for difficulties with its reporting obligations under Article 13(13) of the Basel Convention.[155] By 2016 this issue was resolved after Togo submitted its national reports for the year 2015 and the subsequent ones complete and on time.[156] At the same time, the scrutiny undertaken on its national reporting brought to light difficulties also to fully comply with the obligations under Article 4(4) and Article 9(5) of the Basel Convention. In June 2016 Togo submitted that, despite its best efforts, it was unable to fully comply with the aforementioned obligations to establish national legislation for the prevention and fight against illegal traffic.[157] The self-submission of the State of Togo highlighted in particular that measures were completely absent in that regard. Togo committed to take action in order to overcome the issue by transmitting a draft compliance action plan.[158] At present, the ICC is still dealing with the self-submission by Togo, since the latter did not transmit on time the copy of a new decree law thereby completing the activities of its approved compliance action plan.[159]

Another illustrative case is Liberia. In 2010 the Secretariat decided to activate the ICC since Liberia never submitted a national report as it is required under Article 13(13) of the Basel Convention.[160] Later on, Libera submitted a voluntary compliance action plan in order to resolve the matter of concern regarding reporting obligations. Interestingly, part of the assistance activity was to support Liberia in introducing criminal penalties in its national legislation.[161]

In spite of this, the fact that the ICC was not triggered by Ivory Coast in the *Probo Koala* case has been interpreted by one Author as a signal that the Parties 'seem to expect little relief from [the ICC]'.[162] This is true and Parties seem to prefer to keep the burden of the action in relation to the criminalisation of illegal traffic in hazardous wastes primarily at the level of the domestic enforcement, including through the assistance of the guidance documents

---

155 See submission CHW/CC/9c/2010/9.
156 UNEP-CHW-CC.12-CC-12-11.
157 See submission of Togo CHW/CC/9a/2016/1.
158 Decision CC-12/11. Togo committed, for example, to 'develop and submit for adoption national legal, administrative and other mechanisms/measures to implement and enforce the provisions of the Basel Convention, in particular to prevent and punish conduct in contravention of the Convention as well as to develop legislation to prevent and punish illegal traffic' (ibid).
159 UNEP-CHW-CC.14-CC-14-3-Add.1.
160 See submission CHW/CC/9c/2010/5.
161 See Annex to UNEP-CHW-CC.12-CC-12-7.
162 Cardesa-Salzmann, 'Multilateral Environmental Agreements and Illegality' in Elliott and Schaedla (eds) (n 6) 311.

prepared by the Basel institutions for the benefit of both administrative and judicial operators on the ground, as well as through international interinstitutional cooperation.

3 Enforcement of Article 9 of the Basel Convention

Enforcement refers to the range of procedures and actions employed by a State, its competent authorities, and its agencies to ensure that organisations or persons can be brought or returned into compliance and/or punished including through criminal action.[163]

Enforcement of Article 9 of the Basel Convention occurs both at the domestic level (section 3.1), as well as, at least to a certain extent, at the level of the cooperation of the Basel institutions with the most important international agencies and institutions, such as WCO and Interpol, also specialised in waste crime enforcement (section 3.2).

3.1 *Domestic Enforcement*

The Basel Convention requires Parties to enact appropriate legal, administrative and other measures to prevent and criminalise illegal traffic in hazardous wastes. These measures can only have the desired impact if they are effectively enforced, including through the national criminal justice systems.

It would be outside the scope of the present analysis to undertake an extensive review of all the practice followed in each Party to the Basel Convention. We will therefore limit the present assessment to an analysis of the main shortcomings in domestic enforcement arising out of the most relevant and updated reports and analyses available.

Amongst the main issues in domestic criminalisation of illegal trade in hazardous wastes there is first of all a low level of political attention to the phenomenon (even lower than in relation to, for example, CITES). On one hand this is linked to public awareness. An expert from the UK Environment Agency has highlighted the importance for the public to share concerns and information with the enforcement agencies so that they can prioritise and act on the different issues.[164]

---

163 *Manual on Compliance with and Enforcement of Multilateral Environmental Agreements* (UNEP 2006) 33.
164 R Harwood, 'Current Challenges and Success for the Enforcement of the Basel Convention in Relation to the Repatriation of Plastic Wastes – Environment Agency, England' (n 41).

On the other hand, this is also linked to the level of financial contributions from the Parties for the functioning of the Basel Convention. While in the past illegal traffic in hazardous waste has not attracted too much attention and, for example, the Basel Convention could not benefit from international funds, things are now changing. Waste is progressively gaining centre stage as it is considered also a resource, particularly within the discussion about circular economy; i.e., waste recycling. The debate in relation to e-waste and plastic waste has also grown. In recent years especially the latter has received international attention and, consequently, a higher level of financial contributions.[165]

Another issue in domestic criminalisation is the low level of training and financial assistance for law enforcement officers and for the judiciary. Here, Parties should find guidance in the documents that the Basel institutions and the other international and domestic organisations have developed throughout the years. At the UK level, for example, in 2017 the Environmental Services Association has published its second report on waste crime (ESA report).[166] Amongst the key recommendations the ESA report indicated the need to modernise the regulatory waste regime by introducing competency tests for all operators and by mandating the use of electronic waste transfer notes to track waste from cradle to grave.[167]

In relation to customs officials, training in how to recognise and respond to illegal shipments of hazardous wastes is critical. Customs officers are in fact in a unique position to detect illegal trafficking in wastes at border crossings.[168] Lack of legal clarity may in fact lead to both unintentional and intentional breaches of the regulations dealing with waste management and transboundary movement. Grey zones and different national legislations are clear challenges for the law enforcement community.[169] Customs and other border control officers might find assistance, for example, in the guidelines document prepared by the Green Customs Initiative's Secretariat in order to help the customs administrations to conduct documentary and physical inspections.[170]

---

165 See, for example, the projects within the technical assistance activities. See above text corresponding to footnote n 131.
166 ESAET, *Rethinking Waste Crime* (2017) available online.
167 ibid, 6.
168 UNEP, *Basel Convention Training Manual on Illegal Traffic for Customs and Enforcement Agencies* (2006) 7.
169 I Rucevska et al, *Waste Crime-Waste Risks: Gaps in Meeting the Global Waste Challenge* (n 3) 7.
170 UN Environment, *Green Customs Guide to Multilateral Environmental Agreements*, 2018. A less recent training document is the *Manual for Customs Officers on Hazardous Chemicals and Wastes under the Basel, Rotterdam and Stockholm Conventions*, UNEP, 2014.

The ICC, since 2009, has developed assistance on-demand for States Parties by establishing a directory of training institutions offering activities aimed at improving capacity for detection, prevention and prosecution of cases of illegal traffic.[171] However, the real issue remains the need for the enforcement agencies to receive more resources. The same waste expert from the UK Environment Agency mentioned above, highlighted in fact that financial assistance would enable them to make a greater impact on preventing illegal exports of waste.[172] This is confirmed by the ESA report, which has also recommended to secure sources of funding for enforcement action.[173]

As an example of best practices at the level of enforcement officers it is worth mentioning the National Environmental Standards and Regulations Enforcement Agency (NESREA) in Nigeria, which has been established within the Ministry of Environment. Nigeria is currently facing the challenge of managing waste electrical and electronic equipment (WEEE) either generated domestically or imported illegally as goods of second hand. Thanks to the collaboration between NESREA and the Basel Secretariat, INECE and Interpol (but also through enhanced monitoring of the imported goods, such as the Nigeria Integrated Customs Information System), the Government was able to better control the e-waste imports into the Country and the volumes of the imported waste have drastically reduced.[174]

As to the guidance documents developed to the benefit of law enforcement agencies involved in investigation and prosecution of waste crimes, it is important to mention the instruction manual prepared in 2012 by the Basel Secretariat on the prosecution of illegal traffic of hazardous wastes.[175] This document has been very recently complemented by the Guidance for prosecutors of waste crime within the WasteForce project, which provides information on prosecution practices in the European Union and South East Asia, and on investigation and evidence collection.[176]

---

171   See <http://www.basel.int/Implementation/LegalMatters/IllegalTraffic/InternationalCooperation/tabid/3425/Default.aspx> accessed 2 June 2021.
172   R Harwood, 'Current Challenges and Success for the Enforcement of the Basel Convention in Relation to the Repatriation of Plastic Wastes – Environment Agency, England' (n 41).
173   ESAET, *Rethinking Waste Crime* (n 166) 7.
174   See <http://www.basel.int/Implementation/Ewaste/EwasteinNigerandSwaziland/tabid/7610/Default.aspx> accessed 2 June 2021.
175   *Basel Convention Instruction Manual on the Prosecution of Illegal Traffic of Hazardous Wastes or other Wastes* (2012).
176   WasteForce, *Guidance for Prosecutors of Waste Crime* (2020). A less recent guidance document on prosecution is *Guidance Elements for Detection, Prevention and Control of Illegal Traffic in Hazardous Wastes*, approved by Decision VI/15 of the COP at its sixth meeting, available online.

A very much related issue in domestic criminalisation is the prosecution rate: 'even in instances where illegal trade or traffic is detected, prosecution seldom takes place and, even if a prosecution is successful, ultimate penalties may be low'.[177] One should also consider that each State has its own means of investigation and enforcement and application of national offences and penalties. A study conducted in 2014 also highlighted the issue of the lack of involvement and awareness of the judiciary eventually leading to 'fails in prosecution and sanctioning'.[178]

This trend is confirmed in the scoping report undertaken by the ICC for the year 2017.[179] The analysis was also directed to estimate how cases of illegal traffic were eventually resolved domestically. It emerged that the rate of prosecution is very low like the level of penalties.

> Globally, a considerable majority of the cases of illegal traffic were resolved by disposing of the waste or requesting the disposal of the waste in another country or specialised facility. The second most used method of resolving illegal shipments was returning to a country of export (or the waste concerned did not leave the country of export). Not quite so many illegal shipments were punished, although in general the penalties do not seem to have been particularly high. There was only one reported incidence of imprisonment, only two reported fines exceeding USD 50,000, and only two reported fines between USD 5000 and USD 50.000, with the vast majority of fines appearing to be below USD 5,000.[180]

It may be that the penalty is too low also because waste traffic is perceived as a low importance crime. This calls even more the need to engage with the public so that the issue can be moved further up in the domestic political agendas. In that context, dissemination of the available tools and guidance documents to the benefit of all operators in the waste enforcement chain becomes essential.

---

177 *Analysis on Possible Synergies in Preventing and Combating Illegal Traffic and Trade in Hazardous Chemicals and Wastes, Secretariat of the Basel, Rotterdam and Stockholm Conventions* (2017) 12. See <http://www.brsmeas.org/> accessed 2 June 2021.
178 N Isarin, *Overview of the Challenges and Needs of Parties and Various Stakeholders in Preventing and Combating Illegal Traffic in Line with the Requirements of the Basel Convention* (2014) 7.
179 Above (n 66).
180 ibid, para 36(g). For further remarks on the similar situation in the EU, see Chapters 5 and 6 of this book.

After detecting a widespread lack of awareness of, and the failure to disseminate, existing guidance tools, in 2019 the Basel COP has encouraged Parties to disseminate at the national level, through coordination or other communication mechanisms, to all stakeholders involved in the enforcement chain, the guidance and training tools aimed at preventing and combating illegal traffic developed under the Convention.[181] On the same line of intervention in 2019, the Basel COP requested the ICC to develop a better understanding of the reasons for the limited amount of information on illegal traffic shared with the Secretariat and what can be done to enhance coordination and increase the flow of information, in order to better assist the Parties to strengthen coordination between their competent authorities and enforcement entities.[182] From the analysis conducted by the ICC it emerged that amongst the most important reasons for the limited amount of information shared with the Secretariat there is the lack of communication between the entities at the national level, lack of clear assignment of responsibilities between them, and failure to establish coordinating mechanisms between competent authorities and enforcement entities.[183] These mechanisms (eg, domestic steering committees) are useful tools to coordinate the work, for example, of the different ministries and they contribute to make sure that the flow of information between the enforcement entities is conducted effectively. For that reason, the ICC encouraged Parties to establish these types of mechanisms and to improve cooperation between organisations with a mandate to assist the competent authorities and various enforcement entities with preventing and combating illegal traffic.[184] Following-up on this call, the UK for example, has recently set up a new taskforce dedicated to tackling serious and organised waste crime, such as falsely labelling waste so it can be exported abroad to unsuspecting Countries. The Joint Unit for Waste Crime for the first time brings together law enforcement agencies, environmental regulators, HM Revenue & Customs and the National Crime Agency in the fight against waste crime.[185]

---

181 Illegal Traffic, Dissemination of Guidance and Tools, Note by the Secretariat, UNEP/CHW/CC.14/4/Add.6, 4 May 2020, paras 25 and 26(e).
182 Annex to Decision BC-14/15, para 1(2)(b). Therefore, a questionnaire to that effect was prepared and distributed to Parties.
183 Illegal Traffic, National Coordination Mechanisms, Note by the Secretariat, UNEP/CHW/CC.14/4/Add.2, 4 May 2020, paras 18-22.
184 ibid.
185 See <https://www.gov.uk/government/news/clock-is-ticking-for-waste-criminals-as-new-taskforce-launched> accessed 2 June 2021.

3.2 *Enforcement through International Interinstitutional Cooperation*
Domestic enforcement is greatly improved by effective interinstitutional cooperation.[186] The Basel institutions are progressively enhancing the collaborations and cooperative arrangements with the most relevant international agencies and institutions that deal with crime investigation and enforcement. There is in fact a wide consensus among these organisations on the need of an international approach to environmental (including waste) crime due to its global environmental, social, political and economic impact.[187]

It would be outside the scope of the present analysis to refer to all the activities that UN bodies, intergovernmental agencies, networks, non-governmental organisations have adopted at the global as well as regional levels. However, a brief overview of the most recent and relevant ones will be helpful.

In 2013, the Basel COP initiated ENFORCE,[188] which is a network of relevant experts that aims at promoting Parties' compliance with the provisions of the Basel Convention pertaining to preventing and combating illegal traffic in hazardous wastes and other wastes through the better implementation and enforcement of national law.[189] ENFORCE also aims at improving cooperation and coordination between relevant entities, such as WCO and Interpol, with a specific mandate to deliver capacity-building activities and tools for preventing and combating illegal traffic.[190]

In 2019 ENFORCE participated in the review process led by the ICC that mapped the existing cooperative arrangements with international organisations or entities with a mandate regarding preventing and combating illegal traffic (amongst these, International Criminal Police Organization, WCO, UNODC, UNEP, United Nations University, OSCE, Basel Convention regional

---

[186] See <http://www.basel.int/Implementation/TechnicalAssistance/Enforcement/tabid/2555/Default.aspx> accessed 2 June 2021.

[187] Study on the Implementation of Directive 2008/99/EC on the Protection of the Environment Through Criminal Law, available at <https://www.eufje.org/images/docPDF/Study-on-the-implementation-of-Directive-2008_99_ENEC_SEO_BirdLife_May2016.pdf> accessed 2 June 2021.

[188] Decision BC-11/8, 2013. See <http://www.basel.int/Implementation/TechnicalAssistance/Partnerships/ENFORCE/Overview/tabid/4526/Default.aspx> accessed 2 June 2021.

[189] The stock-taking of the activities of ENFORCE, including the roadmap 2020–2021, is available at <http://www.basel.int/Implementation/TechnicalAssistance/Partnerships/ENFORCE/Overview/tabid/4526/Default.aspx> accessed 2 June 2021.

[190] Terms of reference for cooperative arrangements on preventing and combating illegal traffic: The Environmental Network for Optimizing Regulatory Compliance on Illegal Traffic (ENFORCE), available online.

and coordinating centres and IMPEL) with a view to strengthening such arrangements.[191]

The activities undertaken by ENFORCE have been recently expanded and are now divided between priority activities and supporting ones. The former aim at improving the understanding of the challenges and needs of Parties in preventing and combating illegal traffic in line with the requirements of the Basel Convention.[192] The latter include sharing training tools and materials, facilitating information exchange on success stories, techniques, expertise and dissemination of good practices, and reporting on the progress and effectiveness of training activities and modules.[193]

In 2020 a formal link between ENFORCE and WCO has been established. In the past, the WCO used to participate as an observer to the meetings of ENFORCE. Recently, WCO became a full member in 2020 to better integrate customs enforcement initiatives within the Network and give greater prominence to the role played by customs in environmental matters.

The WCO priority in 2020 was environmental sustainability. The WCO intelligence network, which comprises 11 Regional Intelligence Liaison Offices, customs laboratories, and the CENcomm (Customs Enforcement Network Communication) was established, as well as the Harmonized System for classifying goods in relation to waste.[194] WCO also coordinated a number of operations in the field, such as the various DEMETER operations that started in 2009. The most recent one, DEMETER VI, conducted in 2020 resulted in a total of 131 seizures, including almost 99,000 tonnes of waste and an additional 78,000 pieces of waste materials, particularly metal, plastic and e-wastes.[195] The Countries that reported most of the seizures of waste products were Belgium, Canada, China, Poland, and Denmark.[196]

Interpol facilitates the cross-border police cooperation, including that related to waste crime. In 2017, the Interpol Pollution Crime Working Group coordinated a major operation called 'Operation 30 days of action' in order to gather more information on waste crimes and to encourage international

---

191   Annex to Decision BC-14/15, para 1(2)(e).
192   UNEP/CHW/ ENFORCE.5/2, 11 January 2021, para 11.
193   ibid.
194   Report of the fourth meeting of the Environmental Network for Optimizing Regulatory Compliance on Illegal Traffic (Geneva, 30 September-1 October 2019), UNEP/CHW/ENFORCE.4/3, 26 December 2019, para 30.
195   <http://www.wcoomd.org/en/media/newsroom/2020/october/operation-demeter-vi-thwarts-transboundary-shipments-of-illegal-waste-and-ozone-depleting-substances.aspx> accessed 2 June 2021.
196   ibid.

cooperation in the fight against illegal waste activities. The operation uncovered 664 cases of criminal and administrative waste violations, of which 238 cases of waste activities on site and 423 cases of waste shipments (3 cases were unspecified). As a result of the operation, 483 individuals and 264 companies were reported and over 1.5 million tonnes of illicit waste were detected.[197] Of particular relevance, although less recent, is also the project EDEN to target the illegal trade and disposal of waste launched in 2013 at the Interpol-UNEP International Environmental Compliance and Enforcement Conference held in Kenya.[198]

On a final note, one should mention the non-profit organisations such as, for example, the Basel Action Network (BAN),[199] that play a considerable role in gathering, compiling and disseminating relevant information to national authorities and to the wider public, including participating actively to the meetings of the Basel Convention. UNEP regularly invites BAN to participate as an NGO expert and stakeholder in internal meetings and policy deliberations regarding waste matters.[200]

4   Concluding Remarks

The Basel Convention is the only MEA that explicitly defines in the text a prohibited activity as 'criminal'. The Convention is clear in prescribing that the Parties should 'consider that illegal traffic in hazardous wastes or other waste is criminal' (Article 4.3). At the same time, no further detail is given in relation to these criminal measures. Parties are therefore given much flexibility in designing measures in accordance with their national practices and policies. This is a consequence of the fact that the Basel Convention is a treaty that was not designed to deal with the criminalisation of illegal traffic in any great detail. At its core it regulates the management of hazardous wastes including their transboundary movement and disposal. This does not mean that the Parties to the Basel Convention are not committed to fight against this worrying phenomenon. Rather, it means that the real 'action' in the criminalisation of the traffic in hazardous wastes lies predominantly in the domestic implementation and enforcement, which, as a result of the choice of measures left to States,

---

197   See the key operational findings at <https://www.interpol.int/Crimes/Environmental-crime/Pollution-crime> accessed 2 June 2021.
198   See <https://actionguide.info/m/inits/152/> accessed 2 June 2021.
199   <http://www.ban.org/> accessed 2 June 2021.
200   <https://www.ban.org/advocacy> accessed 2 June 2021.

is characterised by a considerable diversity and variation between them. This holds particularly true in relation to the level and type of the penalties applied at the domestic level, at least in relation to those cases in which prosecution is actually carried out. Overall, the penalties and the rate of prosecution are low. Usually, cases of illegal traffic are resolved by disposing of the waste or requesting the disposal of the waste in another Country or specialised facility. Alternatively, they are resolved by returning the illegal waste to the country of export.

It may be that the rate of prosecution and the level of the penalty are too low also because waste traffic is perceived as a low importance crime. This has a bearing on the basic level of training and of financial assistance for law enforcement officers and for the judiciary, which could certainly be improved though further enhancing the international interinstitutional cooperation currently in place. A call has been made recently to enhance the flow of information regarding illegal traffic in hazardous waste through the establishment of coordinating mechanisms at the domestic level, such as task forces or steering committees with stakeholders' participation.

Now that waste is progressively taking centre stage, particularly within the discussion about circular economy, e-waste and plastic waste, one would expect that a higher level of political attention and of financial contribution, as well as enhanced coordination will be devoted to this phenomenon in the near future. Public engagement will also be key in order to move the issue of the illegal traffic in hazardous wastes further up in the domestic as well as international political agendas.

Acknowledgments

This Chapter has been enriched by the research material and experience generously shared by Ms. Tatiana Terekhova from the Basel Secretariat. The interview with Ms. Terekhova was held on 10 December 2020. Dr. Raffaella D'Antonio, from Newcastle University, also contributed with her excellent research assistance. Mr. Alistair McGlone provided insightful comments on an earlier version of this Chapter.

CHAPTER 4

Environmental Crime at the International Level

The International Convention for the Prevention of Pollution from Ships (MARPOL)

1 Introduction

The general framework dealing with all sources of marine pollution is included it the 1982 United Nations Convention on the Law of the Sea (the UNCLOS).[1] Article 192 of the UNCLOS imposes a general obligation for States to protect the marine and coastal environment and its resources requiring them to establish, prescribe, and enforce vessel source pollution rules and standards as well as to cooperate among themselves to that end, either directly or through the 'competent international organization', which is the International Maritime Organisation (the IMO). Therefore, the UNCLOS includes three types of jurisdiction: to prescribe, to enforce and to adjudicate.[2] Article 211 (2) of the UNCLOS stipulates that flag States regulation of the vessel source pollution must 'at least have the same effect as that of generally accepted international rules and standards established through the competent international organization or general diplomatic conference'. Such rules are considered to be embodied in the MARPOL Convention, in its two first Annexes as mandatory and widely ratified by States.[3] The flag State has the primary responsibility to regulate vessel-source pollution (Article 211(1)). According to Article 217(8), penalties provided for by laws and regulations by a flag State shall be adequate in severity to discourage violations. Article 217 provides wide obligations on a flag State of enforcement jurisdiction. One of the most important is the certification obligation by the flag State to ensure that ships under its jurisdiction and control carry a certificate required and issued pursuant to international rules and standards.[4] Further, a coastal State has a far–reaching jurisdiction

---

1 See generally on marine pollution, Y Tanaka, *The International Law of the Sea* (3rd edn, CUP 2019).
2 311; UN Law of the Sea Convention: signed: 10 December 1982; entered into force 16 November 1994. D Bodansky, 'Protecting the Marine Environment from Vessel-Source Pollution: UNCLOS and Beyond' (1991) 18 *Ecology* 719, 723.
3 Tanaka (n 1) 334, 351.
4 ibid 352.

concerning vessel-sources pollution (Articles 211(4) and 21 (2)) in its territorial sea and exclusive economic zone (Article 215(5) and (6)).[5] Finally, the UNCLOS has introduced the port State jurisdiction.[6] As Tanaka has observed, '[u]nder Article 218, the port State would assume the role of an agent of an organ of the international community in the protection of the marine environment and safety at sea'.[7] However, the implementation of this provision is not straightforward, as the UNCLOS is restrictive in the respect of port State jurisdiction, the State jurisdiction is permissive not an obligation and it is almost impossible to detect discharges in marine environment outside the areas of the State jurisdiction.[8]

2   The MARPOL Convention: General Introduction

About 11 billion tons of goods are transported by ship each year. This represents 1.5 tons per person based on the current global population,[9] which

---

5   Article 220 includes provisions concerning the enforcement of the jurisdiction of coastal States and provisions concerning a violation of relevant rules. Article 220(2) and (3) provides as follows: 2. 'Where there are clear grounds for believing that a vessel navigating in the territorial sea of a State has, during its passage therein, violated laws and regulations of that State adopted in accordance with this Convention or applicable international rules and standards for the prevention, reduction and control of pollution from vessels, that State, without prejudice to the application of the relevant provisions of Part II, section 3, may undertake physical inspection of the vessel relating to the violation and may, where the evidence so warrants, institute proceedings, including detention of the vessel, in accordance with its laws, subject to the provisions of section 7'.

        3. 'Where there are clear grounds for believing that a vessel navigating in the exclusive economic zone or the territorial sea of a State has, in the exclusive economic zone, committed a violation of applicable international rules and standards for the prevention, reduction and control of pollution from vessels or laws and regulations of that State conforming and giving effect to such rules and standards, that State may require the vessel to give information required to establish whether a violation has occurred'. Tanaka (n 1) 253.

6   Article 218(1) provides that: 'When a vessel is voluntarily within a port or at an off-shore terminal of a State, that State may undertake investigations and, where the evidence so warrants, institute proceedings in respect of any discharge from that vessel outside the internal waters, territorial sea or exclusive economic zone of that State in violation of applicable international rules and standards established through the competent international organization or general diplomatic conference'.

7   Tanaka (n 1) 355.
8   ibid 356.
9   See International Chamber of Shipping, 'Shipping and World Trade: Driving Prosperity' <https://www.ics-shipping.org/shipping-fact/shipping-and-world-trade-driving-prosperity/> accessed 5 February 2021; World Economic Forum, 'Here's how we Can Reduce Emissions from the Shipping Industry' <https://www.weforum.org/agenda/2020/10/shipping-industry-carbon-emissions-climate-change-environment-ocean/> accessed 5

accounts for over 95 per cent of world trade,[10] which is considered to be the most environmentally friendly form of transport.[11] The popular view is that 'the shipping industry is responsible for a significant proportion of the global climate change problem. More than three percent of global carbon dioxide emissions can be attributed to ocean-going ships'.[12] However, this contentious area of shipping is constantly undergoing major changes. Since 1 January 2015, Annex VI (prevention of air pollution from ships) has established a Sulphur limit of 0.10 per cent for ships operating in so-called Emission Control Areas (ECA), in the North Sea, the Baltic Sea, designated areas off the United States (US) and Canada and the US Caribbean Sea. In 2016, a new deadline (1 January 2020) was set for the regulations to come into effect for ships sailing in areas outside the designated ECAs. The limit for the Sulphur content of ship's fuel oil, which was 3.5 per cent mass by mass until 31 December 2019, was to be reduced to 0.50 per cent mass by mass. Meanwhile, a new low Sulphur fuel has been tried, using cooking oil.[13] We also know that due to the existence of the MARPOL Convention,[14] oil spills account for just 12 per cent of the oil in our oceans. Three times as much oil is carried out to sea via runoff from our roads, rivers and drainpipes.[15]

Shipping contributes to a limited extent to marine pollution from human activities, in particular when compared to pollution from land-based sources.[16]

February 2021; and A Michaelowa and K Krause, 'International Maritime Transport and Climate Policy' (2000) 35 *Intereconomics* 127, 128.

10   Michaelowa and Krause (previous n) 28.
11   See Oceana Europe, 'Climate Change: Shipping Pollution' <https://europe.oceana.org/en/shipping-pollution-1> accessed 5 February 2021.
12   ibid.
13   RM van Pallandt, 'Pollution from Ships and Protection of the Environment: The IMO, MARPOL and Cooking Oil' *Prospect Law* (19 February 2020) <https://prospectlaw.co.uk/pollution-from-ships-and-protection-of-the-environment-the-imo-marpol-and-cooking-oil/> accessed 5 February 2021.
14   Adopted on 2 November 1973, entered into force on 12 October 1983, 1340 UNTS 184. See further Md S Karim, *Prevention of Pollution of the Marine Environment from Vessels: The Potential and Limits of the Maritime International Organization* (Springer International Publishing 2015), in particular chapter 3.
15   Conservation International, 'Ocean Pollution: 11 Facts you Need to Know' <https://www.conservation.org/stories/ocean-pollution-11-facts-you-need-to-know> accessed 5 February 2021.
16   See IMO, 'Marine Environment' <https://www.imo.org/en/OurWork/Environment/Pages/Default.aspx> accessed 16 January 2021. See generally on MARPOL and Annex 1, M Szepes, 'MARPOL 73/78: The Challenges of Regulating Vessel-Source Oil Pollution' (2013) 2 *Manchester Student Law Review* 74, 74–109. See generally on vessel source pollution, A Khee-Jin Tan, *Vessel-Source Marine Pollution: The Law and Politics of International Regulation* (CUP 2005); see also Karim (n 14).

Protection of the environment was not the IMO's original mandate. Its main interest was maritime safety. The IMO's activities in the area of marine environmental protection started in 1954 when the Organisation became the depository of the first International Convention for the Prevention of Pollution of the Sea from Oil (the OILPOL Convention),[17] which only related to pollution caused by tankers during their routine operations such as the washing of cargo tanks and camping of resultant oily water in the ocean.[18] The OILPOL was amended several times but was very limited as it only covered one source of pollution. At present, the protection of the marine environment constitutes a significant part of the IMO's functions. The body whose function is protection of the marine environment is the Marine Environment Protection Committee (the MEPC).[19] One of the factors which contributed to the adoption of the MARPOL Convention was the *Torrey Canyon* incident.

The conference that adopted the MARPOL Convention was convened in October-November 1973, but preparatory meetings began in 1970. The International Conference on Tanker Safety and Pollution Prevention convened in February 1978 andadopted a Protocol to the 1973 MARPOL Convention. It absorbed the 1973 Convention and expanded on the requirements for tankers to help make them less likely to pollute the marine environment. The MARPOL Convention has incorporated much of the OILPOL and its amendments into Annex I, which has broadened and improved the OILPOL, while other Annexes covered chemicals (Annex II), harmful substances carried in packaged form (Annex III), sewage (Annex IV), and garbage (Annex V). The new Annex VI on Air Pollution was added and entered into force on 19 May 2005. The MARPOL Convention has established a number of 'Special Areas' in which more stringent discharge standards were applicable. Standards relating to Special Areas would be implemented when the coastal States concerned had provided adequate reception facilities for dirty ballast and other oily residues. However, the slow progress at ratifying the Convention has become a major concern.[20]

---

17 Adopted on 12 May 1954, entered into force on 26 July 1958, 327 UNTS 3. See further JV Crayford, 'Forthcoming Changes to the International Convention for the Prevention of Pollution from Ships' in MH Nordquist and JN Moore (eds), *Current Maritime Issues and The International Maritime Organization* (Kluwer Law International/Martinus Njihoff Publishers 1999) 133.

18 OILPOL was the first international Treaty that attempted to protect the sea from pollution from oil tankers.

19 A Chircop, 'The IMO's work on Environmental Protection and Global Ocean Governance' in DJ Attard (ed), *The IMLI Treatise on Ocean Global Governance Volume III: IMO and Global Ocean Governance* (OUP 2018) 176.

20 Crayford (n 17) 135.

It may be said that MARPOL is a very robust and dynamic Convention responding quickly to changes in the world's environment. An example of this is the response of MARPOL to climate change and greenhouse gases. At the same time, additional measures for tanker safety were incorporated into the 1978 Protocol to the 1974 International Convention for the Safety of Life at Sea (SOLAS).[21] Further amendments to the MARPOL Convention, particularly to Annex I, were developed in response to major oil spills which indicated the necessity for stricter Regulations, such as the 1989 *Exxon Valdez*, the 1999 *Erika*, and the 2002 *Prestige* incidents. Due to these incidents, the IMO introduced mandatory double-hulls for tankers and the subsequent phasing out of single-hull tankers. The Marine Environment Protection Committee (the MEPC) has agreed to make mandatory double hulls or alternative designs (Regulation 19) for prevention of oil pollution in the event of collision or stranding. The sinking of the *Erika* accelerated the phase out schedule for single-hull tankers, ie it resulted in the revision of the old Regulation 13G of MARPOL. It is recognised that MARPOL has eliminated most of operational discharges and has led to safer vessels, with a notable decrease of oil spills from them. There is a response in place to address occasional spills.[22]

As a result of the *Erika* incident, the IMO also adopted the following measures in response:

1. the 2000 amendments raising by 50 per cent the limits of compensation payable to victims of pollution by oil from oil tankers under the International Convention on Civil Liability for Oil Pollution Damage[23] (CLC Convention) and the International Convention on the Establishment of an International Convention on the Establishment of an International Fund for Compensation for Oil Pollution Damage[24] (IOPC Fund) were adopted;

2. in 2000, the MSC adopted amendments to the Guidelines on the Enhanced Programme of Inspections During Surveys of Bulk Carriers and Oil Tankers (Resolution A.744(18)) in relation to the evaluation of the longitudinal strength of the hull girders of oil tankers);

---

21   Adopted on 1 November 1974, entered into force on 1 May 1991, 1184 UNTS 3; see Crayford (n 17) 136.
22   RC Prince, 'Oil Pollution from Operations and Shipwrecks' in S de Mora, T Fileman and T Vance (eds), *Environmental Impact of Ships* (CUP 2020) 68.
23   Adopted on 29 November 1969, entered into force on 19 June 1975, replaced by 1992 Protocol (adopted on 27 November 1992, entered into force on 30 May 1996) 973 UNTS 3.
24   Adopted on 27 November 1992, entered into force on 30 May 1996, 1953 UNTS 330.

3. other measures aimed at enhancing safety and minimizing the risk of oil pollution.

The *Prestige* incident led to further amendments to the phase out schedule for single-hull tankers.[25]

It may be added that the standard setting by the IMO is based on the principle of non-discrimination, but with the application of the principle of common but differentiated responsibilities to developing States through means of technical and financial assistance.[26] The process of standard setting by the IMO is based on an ongoing evaluation of standards to combat pollution from ships. Amendments to Annexes are done through the tacit acceptance procedure, in order to speed up the procedure to respond to changing conditions.[27]

3   MARPOL: Structure, Underlying Principles and Enforcement

As the main international instrument which deals with pollution from operational and accidental spillages from ships (Annexes I and II regulate only operational spillages), MARPOL is a multilateral Convention whose Parties constitute 98 per cent of the world's merchant tonnage. As of 16 January 2021, there are 159 States Parties (the combined merchant fleets of which constitute approximately 98 per cent of the gross tonnage of the world's merchant fleet).[28]

MARPOL covers a multitude of instruments. It consists of an 'umbrella Convention' (which sets out the main rights and obligations of States) and six Annexes, which cover the areas under the MARPOL's jurisdiction. All Annexes have been amended several times, therefore their content has undergone radical changes. However, not all States Parties have accepted all amendments and this has resulted in an extremely complex nexus of differentiated obligations of States under these Annexes.

---

25 See IMO, 'Tanker Safety – Preventing Accidental Pollution' <https://www.imo.org/en/OurWork/Safety/Pages/OilTankers.aspx> accessed 16 January 2021; and IMO, 'MARPOL Annex I – Prevention of Pollution from Ships' <https://www.imo.org/en/OurWork/Environment/Pages/OilPollution-Default.aspx> accessed 16 January 2021. To date, MARPOL (Annexes I and II) have been ratified by 150 countries representing over 99 per cent of world merchant-shipping tonnage.
26 J Harrison, *Saving Ocean through Law: The International Legal Framework or the Protection of the Marine Environment* (OUP 2017) 219.
27 ibid 119.
28 IMO, 'Status of Treaties' <https://wwwcdn.imo.org/localresources/en/About/Conventions/StatusOfConventions/StatusOfTreaties.pdf> accessed 16 January 2021.

The Convention as a global instrument comprises 'generally accepted international rules and standards' as formulated in Article 211 of the UNCLOS (see the previous section). These rules and standards constitute the minimum standards prescribed by flag States for their merchant ships and have become binding on third States through the working of customary international law.[29] It may be presumed that the criterion of the minimum standard is applicable to the umbrella Treaty itself and the two first Annexes (acceptance of which was mandatory for States ratifying MARPOL). The acceptance by States of other Annexes is not so extensive.[30]

Apart from the Annexes, the MARPOL Convention has also two Protocols: Protocol I, Provisions concerning Reports on Incidents Involving Harmful Substances (in accordance with Article 8 of the Convention); and Protocol II, on Arbitration. The amendments to MARPOL itself, the Protocols, and the Annexes are governed by Article 16 of the 1973 original Convention, which is very complex and combines the system of tacit approval/opting out system. The above-mentioned tacit acceptance/opting out system is based on the principle that a State Party to the Convention may 'opt out' from accepting a new amendment within a prescribed period of time, and as a result is not bound by it.

In the IMO practice, all decisions, including the adoption of amendments, are taken by consensus. In case of a lack of consensus, both SOLAS and MARPOL provide that a two-thirds majority of the parties adopts amendments.[31] It appears that, at least within the framework of the IMO sponsored treaties, tacit acceptance/opting out is a simplified and effective method of speeding up the entry into force of amendments.[32]

The procedure has resulted in a patchy application of the Convention (including Annexes) and it complicates the issue of whether some particular regulations are 'generally accepted' for the flag State to apply in the sense of Article 211 of UNCLOS. Under MARPOL, the Parties undertake to give effect to the provisions of the Convention and those Annexes, which bind them, in order to prevent pollution of the marine environment by the discharge of

---

29 P Birnie, A Boyle and C Redgwell, *International Law and the Environment* (OUP 2009) 404.
30 Annex III entered into force on 1 July 1992; Annex IV entered into force on 27 September 2003; Annex V entered into force on 31 December 1988; Annex VI entered into force on 19 May 2005.
31 In the SOLAS, a two-thirds majority of the contracting governments and in the MARPOL a two-thirds majority of the parties (ibid).
32 D Lost-Sieminska, 'The International Maritime Organization' in MJ Bowman and D Kritsiotis (eds), *Conceptual and Contextual Perspectives on the Modern Law of Treaties* (CUP 2018) 920.

harmful substances or effluents containing such substances in contravention of the Convention.

Under Annexes I (Prevention of pollution by oil), II (Control of pollution by noxious liquid substances), IV (Prevention of pollution by sewage from ships) and V (Prevention of pollution by garbage from ships), the MARPOL Convention introduces certain sea areas as 'special areas' in which, for relating to their oceanographical and ecological reasons and to their sea traffic, the adoption of special mandatory methods for the prevention of sea pollution is required. Under the Convention, these special areas are provided with a higher level of protection than other areas of the sea. Annex VI (Regulations for the Prevention of Air Pollution from Ships) establishes certain sulphur oxide (SOx) Emission Control Areas with more stringent controls on sulphur emissions and nitrogen oxides (NOx) Emission Control Areas for Tier III NOx emission standards. Under MARPOL, there are also Particularly Sensitive Sea Areas (PSSAS), which are designated by the MEPC. PSSAS are defined 'as areas that need special protection through action by the IMO because of their significance for recognised ecological, socio-economic, or scientific attributes, where such attributes may be vulnerable to damage by international shipping activities'.[33]

Annex VI (Regulations for the Prevention of Air Pollution from Ships) establishes certain sulphur oxide (SOx) Emission Control Areas with more stringent controls on sulphur emissions and nitrogen oxides (NOx) Emission Control Areas for Tier III NOx emission standards.

Under the enforcement regime of MARPOL, flag States are primarily responsible for enforcing its provisions. Article 3 states that the MARPOL provisions apply to ships entitled to the flag State party to the Convention and also to ships which operate under the authority of this latter, even if they are not entitled to fly its flag. MARPOL also applies to ships in the Exclusive Economic Zone (EEZ) of a State party to the MARPOL Convention.

Article 4(1) of MARPOL provides a double system of national prohibitions and sanctions. First, violations are to be prohibited and sanctions to be established under the law of the Administration of the ship concerned, wherever the violation occurs. Secondly, violations are to be prohibited and sanctions established under the law of the Party within whose jurisdiction they occur (Article 4(2)). According to MARPOL, the flag State has to ensure that its ships comply with all the required technical standards. In order to achieve this end,

---

33 IMO List of MARPOL Special Areas and Particularly Sensitive Sea Areas <https://www.nepia.com/industry-news/imo-list-of-marpol-special-areas-and-particularly-sensitive-sea-areas/> accessed 17 May 2021.

the State has to conduct inspections and issues an 'international oil pollution prevention certificate'.

Article 5 of the Convention introduced the far-reaching jurisdiction of the port State. It provides that an inspection must be carried out to confirm that the ship is in possession of a valid certificate to assess the condition of the ship when there are 'clear grounds' for believing that its condition does not conform substantially to the certificate.[34]

In cases of stated non-compliance with the MARPOL certificate, Article 7 imposes a duty upon the port State not to allow the ship to leave port, unless it can do so without presenting an unreasonable threat or harm to the marine environment. However, the port State has an obligation not to delay ships unduly. In the event of such violation, within the jurisdiction of a Party, according to Article 4(2), a Party can either start proceedings in accordance with its own law, or furnish such information and evidence as it may have possession that violation has occurred to the Administration of the ship concerned.[35] Article 4(1) further provides that, if the Administration of the ship involved in a violation is informed of it and is satisfied that sufficient evidence is available to enable proceedings to be brought, that Administration shall initiate such proceedings as soon as possible, in accordance with its law. It may also be noted that 'any violation' in Article 4(2) means that it applies to operational and discharge standards, as well as to design and equipment standards of the Convention. The MARPOL Convention provides that the Parties to the Convention 'shall cooperate in the detection of violations and the enforcement of the provisions of the Convention, using all appropriate and practicable measures of detection and environmental monitoring, adequate procedures for reporting and accumulation of evidence'.[36] Further, it states:

> any Party shall furnish to the Administration evidence, if any, that the ship has discharged harmful substances or effluents containing such substances in violation of the provisions or the Regulations. If it is practicable to so, the competent authority of the former party shall notify the master of the ship of the alleged violation.[37]

---

34 R Becker, 'MARPOL 73/78: An Overview in International Environmental Enforcement' (1998) 19 *The Georgetown International Environmental Law Review* 625.
35 MARPOL, Article 4(2a-b).
36 ibid, Article 6(1).
37 ibid, Article 6(3).

Parties have the duty to furnish the Administration with information on the discharge of harmful substances or effluents. Upon the receipt of such evidence, the Administration so informed is to investigate the matter and may request the other Party to furnish further better evidence of the alleged contravention. If the Administration is satisfied that sufficient evidence is available to enable proceedings to be taken in accordance with its law, it shall do so as soon as possible. The Administration shall promptly inform the Party that has reported the alleged violation, as well as the IMO, of such actions.[38] Article 4(4) stipulates that the Parties shall adopt laws giving effect to agreed Regulations by prohibiting prescribed acts and omissions and by specifying penalties under their domestic laws which are 'adequate in severity to discourage violations'.

The Convention imposes a general prohibition of all discharges of oil and noxious substances and provides that sanctions shall be established according to the law of the State under whose authority the ship is operating.[39] These penalties 'shall be adequate in order to discourage violation and shall be equally severe irrespective of where the violations occurred'.[40] Although the nature of these sanctions is not unquestionably and clearly affirmed, it has to be assumed that these also include criminal sanctions applied in the context of criminal proceedings. For instance, in the US, MARPOL is implemented through the Act to Prevent Pollution from Ships,[41] which establishes that the knowing violation of the Convention, of the Act itself, or of other Regulations relating to wastes from ships, including garbage, oil, and hazardous substances shall be sanctioned with imprisonment up to ten years and/or fines.[42]

The MARPOL Convention excludes from its jurisdiction any warship, naval auxiliary, or other ship owned or operated by a State and used on government non-commercial service.[43] However, the Convention imposes an obligation on these ships to act in a manner consistent with the Convention, as long as it is practicable. As it is evident that national governments and their agencies are quite prodigious polluters, the provision excluding such entities undermines the purpose of MARPOL, and the insertion of 'the best effort clause' constitutes a weak attempt to ensure State compliance. The 'best effort clause' was the result of a compromise among the Parties to the MARPOL Convention.[44]

---

38   ibid, Article 6(4).
39   ibid, Article 4.
40   ibid.
41   Act to Prevent the Pollution from Ships, 33 USC 1901 et seq.
42   See 18 USC 3571.
43   MARPOL, Article 3(3).
44   DW Abecassis, RM Jarvis and RM Jarashow (eds), *Oil Pollution from Ships: International, United Kingdom and United States Law and Practice* (Stevens 1985) 38.

Negotiating States had argued that such vessels should not be subject to other States' inspection, as it would compromise national security. However, it is suggested that States can comply with the requirements of the Convention avoiding compromising national security, by assuming more responsibility for monitoring compliance (eg flag States could conduct an annual MARPOL inspection of their ships, or introduce a random inspection to which their ships would be subjected at any time). The existing provision appears to send a wrong message and should be changed to make it clear that these ships are immune from the MARPOL Regulations.[45]

With respect to the ships of non-Parties to the MARPOL Convention, Article 5 provides that Parties are to apply such requirements as may be necessary to ensure that no more favourable treatment is given to such ships. The measures under Article 5 are the source of some doctrinal controversy in so far as they purport to apply to ships flying the flag of non-Parties. As an exercise of jurisdiction of the coastal State over foreign ships, these provisions cannot, according to one author, restrict the rights enjoyed by non-Parties under the general international law principle of *pacta tertiis nec nocent nec prosunt*.[46]

In case of punitive measures to be adopted, the flag State must impose penalties that are 'adequate in severity to discourage violations of the present Convention and shall be equally severe irrespective of where the violations occur'.

According to these provisions, any violation of the requirements of MARPOL shall be prohibited and sanctions shall be established under the law of the Administration of the ship concerned wherever the violation occurs. Annexes 1 and 2 of the MARPOL prohibit some types of discharges especially in the so-called special areas (Annex 1) and within the territory of 12 miles of the nearest land (Annex II).

The MARPOL Convention, although very far-reaching in protecting the environment and innovative in enforcing environmental regulations, does not include an express provision on the precautionary principle. However, the MEPC adopted, on 15 September 1995, a Resolution on Guidelines on the Incorporation of the Precautionary Approach in the Context of Specific IMO Activities.[47] The inherent vagueness of 'scientific uncertainty' and the risk of long term irreversible adverse effects on the environment are counterbalanced by the presence of the environmental impact assessment, the duty to inform,

---

45   ibid.
46   J Willisch, *State Responsibility for Technological Damage in International Law* (Decker and Humbolt 1987) 115.
47   Annex 10, MEPC 37/22, Add. 1.

and the use of the best available technology and best environmental practice (the BATBEP), which are the most tangible constitutive elements of this approach.

MARPOL establishes a general prohibition of all discharges of oil and noxious substances. Regulation 11 of Annex I and Regulation 6 of Annex II provide for a set of exceptions according to which discharges are permitted in three cases: a) where necessary to secure the safety of a ship or save life at sea; b) where the discharges into the sea of oil or oily mixture result from damage to a ship or its equipment provided that i) 'all reasonable precautions' were taken 'after the occurrence of the damage or discovery of the discharge' for the purposes of preventing or minimising the discharge; and that ii) the owner or the master did not act either with intent to cause damage, or recklessly and with knowledge that damage would probably result; and (c) where approved by both the flag State and any Government in whose jurisdiction it is contemplated the discharge will occur, in order to combat a specific pollution incident for minimising the damage from pollution. The MARPOL Convention considers a discharge being 'reckless' only if made with 'knowledge that damage would probably result'. In the MARPOL Convention, the exclusion from liability for discharges operates only if the master or the owner did not act either with intent to cause damage, or recklessly and with knowledge that damage would probably result. The literal wording of the provision seems to suggest that the acts of persons other than the owner or master are completely irrelevant in the case of discharge resulting from damage to the ship or its equipment. Discharge would appear to be prohibited only where one of these two persons acted with intent or recklessly and with knowledge that damage would probably result. On this point, some Authors have highlighted that such an interpretation of MARPOL would lead to the rather illogical result that, for example, a person who caused intentional damage to a ship or its equipment could escape liability as long as neither the master nor the owner acted with intent or recklessly.[48]

There are several cases that have originated from the breaches of MARPOL, such as the famous *Erika* case.[49] It has been said that '[t]he effective implementation and the successful attainment of the objectives of the civil and criminal liability regimes for oil marine pollution depend upon national courts. French

---

48 A Pozdnakova, *Criminal Jurisdiction over Perpetrators of Ship-Source Pollution: International Law, State Practice and EU Harmonisation* (Martinus Nijhoff Publishers 2013) 224–225.

49 For an in-depth analysis of this case see S Kopela, 'Civil and Criminal Liability as Mechanism for the Prevention of Oil Marine Pollution: The *Erika* case' (2011) 20 RECIEL 313.

criminal courts in the Erika case have interpreted these regimes in a radical, though inspiring, way'.[50] In 1999, the Maltese-flagged tanker *Erika* sunk off the coast of Brittany, spilling 19,800 tonnes of heavy fuel oil and polluting roughly 400 km of coastline, which has resulted in criminal charges against a number of persons, both natural and legal, involved in the accident for, *inter alia*, offences against pollution of waterways on the basis of French law.[51] The criminal liability of the persons involved in the accident concerned the compatibility of French law criminalising marine pollution caused by negligent behaviour with international law and particularly MARPOL (Article 4).

In broad brushstrokes, both the Tribunal de Grand Instance (TGI) and the Court of Appeal found that the national law was compatible with the MARPOL Convention. The Court of Appeal pursued a purposive interpretation of MARPOL and concluded that, *inter alia*,

> the definition of discharge in Article 2(3)(a) of MARPOL does not make a distinction between voluntary or accidental discharges; what is more, the Preamble of the Convention makes it clear that its objective is to reduce both deliberate discharges as well as those caused by negligence or accidents.[52]

The Court also found that interpretation of Regulations 9 and 11 in such a way as to allow unintentional discharges is contrary to the objective of the Convention as identified in the Preamble and that such an interpretation would create incoherence.[53] The Court of Appeal 'acknowledged that the defences recognized by Regulation 11 [of MARPOL] were not recognized in the French law'.

In this respect, the Court analysed whether France could enact stricter legislation in its EEZ on the basis of Article 211(5) of the UNCLOS.[54] The Court interpreted this provision in light of the object and purpose as referring to laws 'rendering effective' international rules. From this point of view, the French law was found compatible with the MARPOL Convention, whose purpose is to provide severe sanctions in order to prevent the occurrence of polluting incidents.

---

50 ibid 313.
51 ibid 314.
52 ibid 315.
53 ibid.
54 ibid 316.

4   Concluding Remarks

MARPOL (as the CITES) are considered successful Multilateral Environmental Agreements. The success of the MARPOL Convention is definitely a result of its reception in national laws of the State parties and due to the enforcement by national and European courts. It is a global Convention, thus its application and implementation is worldwide. Due to its strict rules, vessel pollution is greatly reduced. However, as the *Erika* case has evidenced, there are certain open questions regarding the MARPOL interpretation by domestic courts, especially its relationship with the national legal order.

One of the possible drawbacks of the MARPOL implementation is its very complicated structure. The Annexes are quite numerous and only the first two of them are compulsory. That means that the ratification of the four remaining Annexes is very patchy. They are also subject to many amendments through tacit acceptance/opting out procedure; hence, not all of them are accepted by all parties that adopted the original Annex. This patchwork of different obligations makes the enforcement and the management of the MARPOL quite difficult and unwieldy.

There are certain problems in national laws concerning the implementation of this Convention, such as over-reliance on flag State enforcement, which can be one of the major causes of worldwide enforcement deficiency of the MARPOL Convention.[55] As was noted, 'a huge number of ships are registered in so-called open registries. Some of these open registry countries are very reluctant to prescribe or enforce stringent regulation on ships entitled to fly their flag. The relation of this registry with their ships is a relation of service provider and client. Some of these countries give registration to ships owned by foreign citizens to earn some money'.[56] Another question is that developing countries have grave problems in complying with the MARPOL both as coastal and port States due to financial difficulties (eg the lack of reception facilities). It is argued that the MARPOL has been drafted in such a way as to make the developing countries feel that they have no legal obligation to provide reception facilities.[57] Further, '[o]ne of the main challenges for developing countries is the implementation of the MARPOL Convention in the domestic legal framework. Many States consider it against the sovereignty to apply an international convention directly in the domestic arena'.[58] The additional

---

55   Md S Karim, 'Implementation of the MARPOL Convention in Developing Countries' (2010) 79 *Nordic Journal of International Law* 303, 319.
56   ibid.
57   ibid.
58   ibid 327.

problem is the insufficient use of experts regarding the implementation of the MARPOL Convention in developing countries, notwithstanding many of them trained in the IMO.[59] The main problem is financial in relation to the MARPOL implementation in developing countries, as evidenced by the lack of reception facilities.[60]

On the other hand, as Karim states:

> ... developing countries should not use the lack of financial assistance as an excuse for non-compliance with global standards. If there is firm determination at least some of the international conventions may be implemented in full or in part without any external help. Moreover, to get assistance from donor agencies and international financial institutions, the government of the respective country has to first initiate the proposal.[61]

Despite these justifiably critical comments, in view of present Author, the MARPOL Convention has been remarkably useful in the protection of the marine environment, in particular due to its certification procedure and the enforcement by States parties.

---

59   ibid 327–8.
60   ibid 334.
61   ibid 337.

CHAPTER 5

Environmental Crime at the EU Level
Substantive Criminal Law

1   Introduction

EU environmental law and EU criminal law share a similar history. Whereas the founding Treaties did not provide for any competence of the Communities on environmental and criminal law matters, the European Union is now competent to adopt legislation in both areas. In this chapter, the history of the protection of the environment within the EU is first addressed (section 2). Section 3 explains the importance that the protection of the environment has had for the development of EU constitutional and criminal law before the entry into force of the Treaty of Lisbon. This will set the scene for the analysis of the two most relevant EU substantive criminal law instruments in the field, namely Directive 2008/99/EC on the protection of the environment through criminal law (section 4) and Directive 2009/123/EC on ship-source pollution (section 5). Section 6 discusses the links between environmental crime and organised crime, pointing out the rules and gaps in EU legislation, while section 7 focuses on the future of EU environmental criminal law in the light of the Treaty of Lisbon. Against this backdrop, section 8 draws some conclusions, paving the way for the analysis of the EU instruments of judicial cooperation that can be used to counter environmental crime.

2   The Protection of the Environment within the EU: A Short History

The environment first appeared in the Treaties with the Single European Act (SEA), which was signed in 1986 and entered into force in 1987.[1] Article 25 SEA introduced Title VII in the Treaty Establishing the European Economic Community ('EEC Treaty'): Title VII was composed of three articles devoted to the environment (Articles 130r, 130s, and 130t EEC Treaty). After the entry into force of the Treaty of Lisbon (2009), the Treaty on the Functioning of the

---

[1] This section and the following one draw upon V Mitsilegas and F Giuffrida, 'The Role of EU Agencies in Fighting Transnational Environmental Crime. New Challenges for Eurojust and Europol' (2017) 1 *Brill Research Perspectives in Transnational Crime* 1, 21ff.

European Union (TFEU) still includes a title entirely dedicated to the environment and composed of three provisions, which are very similar to the original ones.

Article 191 TFEU sets out the *objectives* of the Union policy on the environment, namely to preserve, protect and improve the quality of the environment, protect human health, guarantee a prudent and rational utilisation of natural resources, and promote measures at international level to deal with environmental problems.[2] The first three objectives were already mentioned in the SEA, whereas the fourth was added by the Treaty of Maastricht, which entered into force in 1993.

Article 191 TFEU also lists the *principles* on which the Union environmental policy should be based, as well as the *elements* that this policy should take into account. As far as the former are concerned, they are the precautionary principle and the principles that preventive action should be taken, that environmental damage should as a priority be rectified at source, and that the polluter should pay.[3] These principles already featured in the SEA, with the only exception of the precautionary principle, which was introduced by the Treaty of Maastricht. The elements to be taken into account in the Union environmental policy are identical to those listed in the SEA: 'available scientific and technical data, environmental conditions in the various regions of the Union, the potential benefits and costs of action or lack of action, the economic and social development of the Union as a whole and the balanced development of its regions'.[4]

Finally, similarly to Article 130r EEC Treaty, Article 191(4) TFEU allows the Union and the Member States to cooperate with third countries and competent international organisations. Since the beginning, therefore, the EU action in the field of environmental protection has encompassed an external dimension. The Communities first, the Union then, have taken part in different international agreements and conventions concerning the protection of the

---

2 Article 191(1) TFEU.
3 Article 191(2) TFEU. For further remarks on the listed principles and the historical development of EU environmental law, see E Orlando, 'The Evolution of EU Policy and Law in the Environmental Field: Achievements and Current Challenges' (2013) Transworld Working Paper 21 <http://www.iai.it/sites/default/files/TW_WP_21.pdf> accessed 2 June 2021; N de Sadeleer, *EU Environmental Law and the Internal Market* (OUP 2014) 7ff; M Lee, *EU Environmental Law, Governance and Decision-Making* (2nd edn, Hart 2014) 1–27; R Pereira, *Environmental Criminal Liability and Enforcement in European and International Law* (Brill 2015) 173ff. On the precautionary principle, see also the *'Communication from the Commission on the precautionary principle'* COM (2000) 1 final, 2 February 2000.
4 Article 191(3) TFEU.

environment,[5] including the Basel Convention on the Control of Transboundary Movements of Hazardous Wastes and their Disposal ('Basel Convention') and the Convention on International Trade in Endangered Species of Wild Fauna and Flora (CITES).[6]

Whereas Article 193 TFEU, like Article 130t EEC Treaty, acknowledges that Member States can maintain or introduce more stringent protective measures, insofar as the latter are compatible with the Treaties, Article 192 TFEU regulates the EU's decision-making procedure when actions need to be taken in order to achieve the Union's objectives in the field.

The environment falls within those areas in which the EU shares its competences with the Member States,[7] with the consequence that the Member States could regulate the matter inasmuch as the EU has not exercised its competence. The EU can thus adopt legally binding acts in the field, but only and in so far as the objective of the proposed action cannot be sufficiently achieved by the Member States; in other words, EU action should comply with the principle of subsidiarity.[8]

Against this backdrop, Article 192 TFEU provides that, when the EU exercises its competence in environmental matters, it should follow the ordinary legislative procedure, in which the Council of the European Union (hereinafter: the 'Council') and the European Parliament have the role of co-legislators. In Article 130s EEC Treaty as introduced by the SEA, the rule was instead that the Council had to act unanimously. In some sensitive fields, the Council can still act unanimously, after consulting the European Parliament, the Economic and Social Committee, and the Committee of the Regions: for instance, this special legislative procedure applies when provisions primarily of a fiscal nature – still concerning the environment though – have to be adopted.[9]

In addition to Articles 191–193 TFEU, other provisions of the Treaties acknowledge the importance of protecting the environment at the EU level. For example, Article 2 EEC Treaty was modified by the Treaty of Maastricht so

---

5 See also T Fajardo, 'Revisiting the External Dimension of the Environmental Policy. Some Challenges Ahead' (2010) 7 *Journal of European Environmental Law* 365; E Morgera (ed), *The External Environmental Policy of the European Union. EU and International Law Perspectives* (Cambridge University Press 2012).
6 On CITES and the Basel Convention see, respectively, chapters 2 and 3 of this book.
7 Article 4(2)(e) TFEU.
8 Article 5(3) Treaty on the European Union. On subsidiarity in EU environmental law see N de Sadeleer, 'Principle of Subsidiarity and the EU Environmental Policy' (2012) 9 *Journal of European Environment and Planning Law* 63; Lee (n 3) 20ff.
9 Article 192(2)(a) TFEU. Article 192(2) TFEU lists the cases in which the special legislative procedure applies.

as to include a reference to the respect of the environment among the principles to observe in the establishment of the common market. The Treaty of Amsterdam (entered into force in 1999) introduced in the same Article a reference to the improvement of the quality of the environment. After Lisbon, this provision has been replaced by Article 3 of the Treaty on the European Union (TEU), whose paragraph 3 now reads as follows:

> [t]he Union shall establish an internal market. It shall work for the sustainable development of Europe based on balanced economic growth and price stability, a highly competitive social market economy, aiming at full employment and social progress, and a *high level of protection and improvement of the quality of the environment*.[10]

The Treaty of Amsterdam had also introduced a new Article 3c in the Treaty establishing the European Community, which had repealed the EEC Treaty since the entry into force of the Treaty of Maastricht. The content of that provision can now be found in Article 11 TFEU, which states that 'environmental protection requirements must be integrated into the definition and implementation of the Union's policies and activities, in particular with a view to promoting sustainable development'.[11] This is the so-called environmental integration principle.[12] The protection of the environment has progressively become a horizontal interest of the EU as it should be respected in the framework of all EU policies.

Furthermore, the Treaty of Lisbon recognised the Charter of Fundamental Rights of the European Union (CFR or 'Charter') the same legal value as the Treaties.[13] As a consequence, the Charter now confers on individuals rights that are directly applicable in the context of national proceedings before national courts.[14] This is possible when Member States are implementing EU law[15] and

---

10 Article 3(3) TEU. Emphasis added.
11 Article 11 TFEU.
12 See, for instance, Lee (n 3) 24.
13 Article 6(1) TEU.
14 For example, with regard to the right not to be tried or punished twice, see Case C-537/16 *Garlsson Real Estate SA and others*, EU:C:2018:193, para 68.
15 Article 51(1) CFR. In *Fransson*, the Court of Justice adopted a broad interpretation of the application of the Charter, including in cases where national legislation does not implement expressly or directly an EU criminal law instrument (Case C-617/10 *Åklagaren v Hans Åkerberg Fransson*, EU:C:2013:105, para 26). The Court developed its approach in *Siragusa*, where it ruled that the concept of 'implementing Union law', as referred to in Article 51 of the Charter, requires a certain degree of connection above and beyond the matters being closely related or one of those matters having an indirect impact on the other

only when a right – and not a principle – comes into play. The Charter makes a distinction between the two categories: principles have to be 'observed' and implemented either by EU institutions and bodies or by acts of the Member States, whereas rights have to be 'respected'.[16] An example of a directly applicable right is the right not to be tried or punished twice for the same criminal offence (*ne bis in idem*), which is enshrined in Article 50 of the Charter and further discussed in the next chapter.

Nevertheless, as Lee argues, the impact that the Charter may have on the environmental field is rather limited. It is true that Article 37 CFR regulates the principle of environmental protection, stating that '[a] high level of environmental protection and the improvement of the quality of the environment must be integrated into the policies of the Union and ensured in accordance with the principle of sustainable development'. However, Article 37 CFR is clearly phrased as a principle, and not a right,[17] so that it does not seem directly enforceable before domestic courts. As the explanations to the Charter recognise, the content of Article 37 CFR is based on the above-mentioned Article 3(3) TEU and Article 191 TFEU,[18] as well as Article 11 TFEU. In other words, 'given its similarity to existing language, and its status as a principle, it seems unlikely that Article 37 CFR will have a dramatic effect on environmental law'.[19]

Beside the Treaty and the Charter, further EU instruments and measures have addressed issues connected with the protection of the environment, even before the entry into force of the SEA. For instance, the first Environmental Action Programme (EAP) was launched in 1973.[20] Even though it 'provided only a broad framework of principles and objectives', 'it inaugurated what

---

(Case C-206/13 *Siragusa v Regione Sicilia – Soprintendenza Beni Culturali e Ambientali di Palermo*, EU:C:2014:126, para 24). See V Mitsilegas, *EU Criminal Law after Lisbon. Rights, Trust and the Transformation of Justice in Europe* (Hart 2016) 10–11.

16   Article 51(1) CFR. See also the explanation to Article 51 CFR in the 'Explanations relating to the Charter of Fundamental Rights' [2007] OJ C303/17, 35. In the literature see, for instance, J Krommendijk, 'Principled Silence or Mere Silence on Principles? The Role of the EU Charter's Principles in the Case Law of the Court of Justice' (2015) 11 *European Constitutional Law Review* 321.

17   T Lock, 'Rights and Principles in the EU Charter of Fundamental Rights' (2019) 56 *Common Market Law Review* 1201, 1214–1215.

18   'Explanations relating to the Charter of Fundamental Rights' (n 16) 27.

19   Lee (n 3) 24. For further remarks on Article 37 CFR, see N de Sadeleer, EU *Environmental Law and the Internal Market* (n 1) 108ff.

20   Declaration of the Council of the European Communities and of the representatives of the Governments of the Member States meeting in the Council of 22 November 1973 on the programme of action of the European Communities on the environment [1973] OJ C112/1.

has become an established practice':[21] since that Programme, other EAPs have been implemented in the EU. Adopted by the Council and Parliament in accordance with the ordinary legislative procedure, the 7th EAP covered the period until 2020.[22] The 8th EAP covers instead the period 2021–2030.[23]

Due to the lack of relevant primary law provisions before the entry into force of the SEA, the Council used the Articles of the Treaties on the common market and the flexibility clause to regulate environmental issues. Since national environmental regulation could represent a burden on the undertakings, and therefore hamper their fair competition and the enjoyment of fundamental freedoms, the Community institutions began to approximate national legislation on the matter through the competence they had – and still have, in accordance with Articles 114 and 115 TFEU – in the field of the common (now internal) market.[24]

The Court of Justice endorsed this approach. In *Commission v Italy* (1980), ruling on Italy's failure to implement a Council Directive on the approximation of the laws relating to the sulphur content of certain liquid fuel, the Court held that that measure was well founded on Article 100 EEC Treaty (now Article 115 TFEU), since 'provisions which are made necessary by considerations relating to the *environment* and health may be a *burden* upon the undertakings to which they apply and if there is no harmonization of national provisions on the matter, *competition* may be appreciably distorted'.[25]

---

21 Orlando (n 3) 4.
22 Decision No 1386/2013/EU of the European Parliament and of the Council of 20 November 2013 on a General Union Environment Action Programme to 2020 "Living well, within the limits of our planet" [2013] OJ L354/171. For some remarks on the Programme, including its silence on environmental crime, see T Fajardo, 'European Environmental Law and Environmental Crime: An Introduction' in A Farmer, M Faure and GM Vagliasindi (eds), *Environmental Crime in Europe* (Hart 2017) 10–12. The competence of the European Parliament and the Council to adopt the Programme, acting in accordance with the ordinary legislative procedure, is enshrined in Article 192(3) TFEU.
23 The European Commission tabled a proposal for the 8th EAP in October 2020 (Commission, 'Proposal for a Decision of the European Parliament and of the Council on a General Union Environment Action Programme to 2030' COM (2020) 652 final, 14 October 2020).
24 See de Sadeleer, EU *Environmental Law and the Internal Market* (n 1). See also I von Homeyer, 'The Evolution of EU Environmental Governance' in J Scott (ed), *Environmental Protection: European Law and Governance* (OUP 2009) 12ff; N Giovannini, L Melica, M Giannotta et al, 'Compendium of International and EU Law Instruments' (Droit au Droit 2013) 19ff <http://www.dadinternational.org/images/PDF/DRD-Compendium.pdf> accessed 2 June 2021.
25 Case 92/79 *Commission v Italy*, EU:C:1980:86, para 8. Emphasis added. The Directive at stake was Council Directive 75/716/EEC of 24 November 1975 on the approximation of the laws of the Member States relating to the sulphur content of certain liquid fuels [1975] OJ L327/22.

Whereas in this judgment the Court mainly looked at the environment through economic lenses, five years later it took a step further in *ADBHU* (1985), where it upheld the validity of a Directive that imposed on the undertakings that wanted to dispose of waste oils an obligation to obtain a permit to this end. The limits to the free trade deriving from the Directive were necessary to ensure an adequate protection of the environment, which was defined as 'one of the Community's essential objectives'.[26] The Court recalled this judgment in some other decisions, such as the so-called *Danish Bottle* case (1988), where it underlined that the fact that the protection of the environment is an essential objective of the Community 'is ... confirmed by the Single European Act'.[27]

Even though the SEA introduced an *ad hoc* Title on the environment in the EEC Treaty, measures concerning environmental issues continued to be adopted also in accordance with other legal bases. In the so-called *Titanium Dioxide* case (1991), for instance, the Court annulled a Directive adopted on the basis of the above-mentioned Article 130s EEC Treaty (now Article 192 TFEU), ie the provision – introduced by the SEA – which regulated the decision-making procedure in the environmental field. In that case, the Court found that the Directive at stake should have been adopted on the basis of the Article on the harmonisation of national regulations for the better functioning of the internal market (Article 100a EEC Treaty, now Article 114 TFEU).[28] The difference in the legal basis was not irrelevant since, in accordance with Article 130s EEC Treaty, the Council acted unanimously, whereas the so-called 'cooperation procedure' applies pursuant to Article 100a EEC Treaty (now Article 114 TFEU); under this procedure,

> the Council acts by a qualified majority where it intends accepting the amendments to its common position proposed by the Parliament and included by the Commission in its re-examined proposal, whereas it must secure unanimity if it intends taking a decision after its common position has been rejected by the Parliament or if it intends modifying the Commission's re-examined proposal.[29]

---

26 Case 240/83 *Procureur de la République v Association de défense des brûleurs d'huiles usagées*, EU:C:1985:59, para 13. In that case, the validity of Council Directive 75/439/EEC of 16 June 1975 on the disposal of waste oils ([1975] OJ L194/23) was questioned before the Court.
27 Case 302/86 *Commission v Denmark*, EU:C:1988:421, para 8.
28 Case C-300/89 *Commission v Council*, EU:C:1991:244.
29 ibid, para 19.

As anticipated, the Court argued that the Directive on procedures for harmonising the programmes for the reduction and eventual elimination of pollution caused by waste from the titanium dioxide industry should have been adopted as a measure related to the internal market. The reasons of such conclusion are the following: i) pursuant to Article 130r(2) EEC Treaty (now Article 191 TFEU), the environmental protection should be a component also of other policies of the Community; ii) the harmonisation of national measures on the environment can be necessary to avoid unnecessary burdens on the undertakings and the distortion of fair competition (as already pointed out in *Commission v Italy*); iii) the provision on the harmonisation of national laws for the functioning of the internal market (then Article 100a(3) EEC Treaty, now Article 114(3) TFEU) expressly requires that the European Commission (hereinafter: the 'Commission'), in its proposals for the measures intended to pursue such harmonisation, should take as a base a high level of protection, when these measures concern environmental protection.[30]

This decision confirms therefore that the protection of the environment is an EU's horizontal interest that is to be ensured in the framework of any EU policy. As the next sections show, this was not the only case where environmental matters turned out to be a battlefield among EU institutions.

3   EU Law and Environmental Crime: Constitutional Perspectives

The founding Treaties did not regulate the Communities' competence in the field of criminal law. After the entry into force of the Treaty of Lisbon, the Communities have been incorporated in the European Union and no more dualism exists. However, at the times of the Treaty of Amsterdam, the European Community represented the first pillar of the three-pillar EU structure and, within its framework, it was not possible for the European legislator (the European Parliament and the Council) to adopt legal instruments defining or introducing criminal offences and criminal sanctions.[31] Provisions that obliged Member States to criminalise criminal conduct could only be adopted in the context of the former intergovernmental third pillar, by means of legal instruments such as Framework Decisions. It was however debated whether, in light of the growing importance of the protection of the environment at the European level, the Community could adopt first-pillar legal instruments

---

30   ibid, paras 22–24. For further considerations on the case law mentioned in this section, see Orlando (n 3) 5ff.
31   See more in V Mitsilegas, *EU Criminal Law* (Hart 2009) 65ff.

to oblige the Member States to punish environmental violations with *criminal penalties*. The dispute on the correct legal basis for the adoption of EU legislation aimed at the protection of the environment by means of criminal law lies at the heart of two landmark decisions of the Court of Justice, the so-called *Environmental Crime* and *Ship-Source Pollution* cases.[32]

In 2003, the Council adopted a Framework Decision on the protection of the environment through criminal law, with the intent to harmonise Member States' legislation.[33] Arguing that the protection of the environment was a first pillar objective, the Commission challenged the legality of the 2003 Framework Decision's legal basis before the Court of Justice. The Luxembourg Court shared the view of the Commission and annulled the Framework Decision in the *Environmental Crime* case.[34] Recalling both the *ADBHU* (1985) and the *Danish Bottle* (1988) decisions, the Court focused on the protection of the environment as an *essential objective* of the Community. It also reminded that, according to settled case law, the choice of the legal basis must rest on objective factors that are amenable to judicial review, including in particular the aim and content of the measure. In those circumstances, the aim was the protection of the environment and the content particularly serious environmental offences.[35]

Therefore, the essential character of environmental protection as a Community objective was crucial to determine whether criminal law could be used to achieve such an objective in the Community pillar. According to the Court, the fact that the Community did not enjoy any direct power in the field of criminal law did not prevent the Community itself,

---

32 For further remarks on these cases and their impact on the development of EU criminal law see, eg, M Dougan, 'From the Velvet Glove to the Iron Fist: Criminal Sanctions for the Enforcement of Union Law' in M Cremona (ed), *Compliance and the Enforcement of EU Law* (OUP 2012) 97ff.

33 Council Framework Decision 2003/80/JHA of 27 January 2003 on the protection of the environment through criminal law [2003] OJ L29/55. On this Framework Decision see HE Zeitler, 'Environmental Criminal Law' (2006) 77 *Revue Internationale de Droit Pénal* 255.

34 Case C-176/03 *Commission v Council*, EU:C:2005:542. For some recent commentaries on this historical decision see M Kaiafa-Gbandi, 'C-176/03 – *Commission of the European Communities v Council of the European Union*. The "Constitutional" ECJ Ruling on the Enforcement of Community Law (C-176/03) and Its Impact on EU Law', and S Miettinen, 'C-176/03 – *Commission of the European Communities v Council of the European Union*. EU Substantive Criminal Competence and the Court of Justice: Reactions to the Case Law' in V Mitsilegas, A di Martino and L Mancano (eds), *The Court of Justice and European Criminal Law. Leading Cases in a Contextual Analysis* (Hart 2019), respectively 137–150 and 151–163.

35 Case C-176/03 *Commission v Council* (previous n), paras 41 and 45–47.

when the application of effective, proportionate and dissuasive criminal penalties by the competent national authorities is an *essential* measure for combating serious environmental offences, from taking measures which relate to the criminal law of the Member States which it considers *necessary* in order to ensure that the rules which it lays down on environmental protection are fully effective.[36]

In other words, the European Community was deemed to be competent – in the circumstances pointed out by the Court – to adopt directives that contained criminal law provisions, namely provisions imposing on the Member States the duty to criminalise conduct affecting the environment.[37] The legal basis for such harmonisation would be represented by Article 175 of the Treaty on the European Community, ie what was in its first version Article 130s EEC Treaty and what is now Article 192 TFEU.

After this seminal ruling, a number of questions remained open. Among the others, the Court did not specify whether the Community competence in criminal law was limited to the definition of criminal offences or extended also to criminal sanctions.[38] This issue was dealt with by the Court in another relevant judgment, the *Ship-Source Pollution* case. In 2005, the European Parliament and the Council adopted Directive 2005/35/EC,[39] which aimed to incorporate international standards for ship-source pollution into Community law (Article 1), namely those provided for in the 1973 Convention on the Prevention of Pollution from Ships (MARPOL).[40] Adopted on the basis of Article 80(2) of the Treaty on the European Community on the transport policy of the Communities, the 2005 Directive (first-pillar instrument) had been originally accompanied by Framework Decision 2005/667/JHA (third-pillar

---

36 ibid, para 48. Emphasis added. For further remarks on the judgment and the reactions it triggered see, eg, Mitsilegas, *EU Criminal Law* (n 31) 70ff; Pereira, *Environmental Criminal Liability* (n 3) 186 ff.
37 V Mitsilegas, M Fitzmaurice and E Fasoli, 'The Relationship between EU Criminal Law and Environmental Law' in V Mitsilegas, M Bergström and T Konstadinides (eds), *Research Handbook on EU Criminal Law* (Edward Elgar 2016) 275.
38 Mitsilegas, *EU Criminal Law* (n 31) 74.
39 Directive 2005/35/EC of the European Parliament and of the Council of 7 September 2005 on ship-source pollution and on the introduction of penalties for infringements [2005] OJ L255/11.
40 MARPOL 1973, the original Treaty, was modified by a 1978 Protocol and the combined instrument (then sometimes referred to as 'MARPOL 73/78') entered into force in 1983. See more in chapter 4 of this book.

instrument),[41] which imposed on the Member States the duty to *criminalise* conduct defined in the Directive. The adoption of these two instruments was prompted by the dramatic shipwreck of the tanker *Prestige* in 2002.[42]

Once again, the Commission challenged the legality of the adoption of a third-pillar instrument on ship-source pollution, arguing that parts of that Framework Decision should have been adopted under the first pillar. However, the Commission did not bring to the fore the articles on the Communities environmental policy, rather focused its arguments on Article 80 of the Treaty on the European Community concerning transport policy. Also in this case, the Court of Justice shared the Commission's view and annulled Framework Decision 2005/667/JHA.

In essence, the Court restated what it had ruled in the *Environmental Crime* case, but clarified that the competence of the Community in the field of criminal law could not include the determination of the type and level of sanctions.[43] In assessing whether Framework Decision 2005/667/JHA affected the Community's competence on transport under Article 80(2) of the Treaty on the European Community, the Court followed a twofold approach: it examined the nature of Community competence on transport in the general Treaty framework; and it linked the Community transport policy with the objective of environmental protection.[44] On the latter issue, the Court reminded that environmental protection, namely one of the essential objectives of the Community, had to be integrated in the definition and implementation of the Community policies, according to the above-mentioned Article 6 of the Treaty on the European Community (now Article 11 TFEU). Of course, this provision concerned also the common transport policy: '[t]he Community legislature may therefore, on the basis of Article 80(2) EC and in the exercise of the powers conferred on it by that provision, *decide to promote environmental protection*'.[45]

---

41 Council Framework Decision 2005/667/JHA of 12 July 2005 to strengthen the criminal-law framework for the enforcement of the law against ship-source pollution [2005] OJ L255/164.
42 See Recitals 2–4 of Council Framework Decision 2005/667/JHA. The *Prestige* was a tanker that sank off the Spanish coast in November 2002. Its sinking led to a large oil spill that caused extensive damage to the environment. On the effects of this dramatic shipwreck on EU and international environmental law, see V Frank, 'Consequences of the *Prestige* Sinking for European and International Law' (2005) 20 *The International Journal of Marine and Coastal Law* 1.
43 Case C-440/05 *Commission v Council*, EU:C:2007:625.
44 Mitsilegas, *EU Criminal Law* (n 31) 82.
45 Case C-440/05 *Commission v Council* (n 43), para 60. Emphasis added.

The Court also specified that, since some Articles of the Framework Decision were 'designed to ensure the efficacy of the rules adopted in the field of maritime safety, noncompliance with which may have serious *environmental consequences*, by requiring Member States to apply criminal penalties to certain forms of conduct', those articles must have been regarded as 'being essentially aimed at improving maritime safety, as well as *environmental protection*, and could have been validly adopted on the basis of Article 80(2) EC'.[46]

The protection of the environment has therefore been of utter importance in the history of the European Communities, and then of the European Union. The Union has been paying an increasing attention to the matter despite the silence of the founding Treaties. Its criminal law competences were for the first time acknowledged precisely in the field of environmental law. Against this backdrop, the sections below analyse the two EU substantive criminal law instruments concerning environmental crime, namely the 2008 Directive on the protection of the environment through criminal law and the 2009 Directive on ship-source pollution.

4 The Environmental Crime Directive (2008/99/EC)

The annulment of the 2003 Framework Decision on the protection of the environment through criminal law was followed by the adoption of Directive 2008/99/EC on the protection of the environment through criminal law ('Environmental Crime Directive'),[47] which largely replicates the content of the Framework Decision. Adopted by the Council and the European Parliament before the entry into force of the Treaty of Lisbon and in accordance with Article 175 of the Treaty on the European Community (currently Article 192 TFEU), the Environmental Crime Directive is the first European instrument introducing duties of criminalisation for the Member States outside the framework of the third pillar.[48] Similar duties had been previously provided for by the Convention on the Protection of the Environment through Criminal Law, which was concluded under the aegis of the Council of Europe in 1998

---

46   ibid, para 69. Emphasis added.
47   Directive 2008/99/EC of the European Parliament and of the Council of 19 November 2008 on the protection of the environment through criminal law [2008] OJ L328/28.
48   On the political background to the Environmental Crime Directive see, eg, GF Perilongo and E Corn, 'The Ecocrime Directive and Its Translation into Legal Practice. EU Green Offences and Their Impact at National Level According to the Results of a Recent Survey' (2017) 8 *New Journal of European Criminal Law* 236, 243–246.

(hereinafter: '1998 Council of Europe Convention').[49] As the Convention was signed by 14 out of 47 Parties to the Council of Europe and ratified only by Estonia,[50] it never entered into force.

The Environmental Crime Directive's objective is to ensure more effective protection of the environment,[51] in this way addressing the concerns connected to the rise in environmental offences, which 'are increasingly extending beyond the borders of the States in which the offences are committed'.[52] Nowadays, there are even more sources and data confirming that environmental crime is '[u]sually transnational in nature'.[53] While Sheptycki and Bisschop argued, respectively in 2007 and 2011, that crimes against the environment were neglected by the criminological literature on transnational crime,[54] (legal and) criminological studies on environmental crime have recently become more and more numerous.[55]

---

49 Convention on the Protection of the Environment through Criminal Law, ETS No 172, Strasbourg, 4 November 1998 ('1998 Council of Europe Convention'), which was largely inspired by the debates and academic initiatives on environmental crime that had previously spread in Europe (see more in M Faure, 'The Revolution in Environmental Criminal Law in Europe' (2017) 35 *Virginia Environmental Law Journal* 321, 342–344. On the Convention and its relations with the Environmental Crime Directive see Pereira, *Environmental Criminal Liability* (n 3) *passim*; GM Vagliasindi, 'The EU Environmental Crime Directive' in Farmer, Faure and Vagliasindi (eds) (n 22) 35–36, who also notes that the Committee of Ministers of the Council of Europe had already suggested to adopt measures to tackle environmental crime back in 1977 (ibid 33–34, with reference to the 'Resolution (77) 28 on the contribution of criminal law to the protection of the environment').

50 For further information see the Council of Europe's website at <https://www.coe.int/en/web/conventions/full-list/-/conventions/treaty/172/signatures?module=treaty-detail&treatynum=172> accessed 2 June 2021.

51 See Recitals 5 and 14 and Article 1 of the Environmental Crime Directive. For further remarks on the Commission's stance that mostly, if not only, criminal law measure can ensure the effective protection of the environment, see J Öberg, *Limits to EU Powers. A Case Study of EU Regulatory Criminal Law* (Hart 2017) 80–84, where the author concludes that the Commission failed to provide sufficient evidence to 'support the claim that criminal sanctions are superior to other, non-criminal sanctions' (ibid 84).

52 Recital 3 of the Environmental Crime Directive.

53 N Boister, *An Introduction to Transnational Criminal Law* (OUP 2018, 2nd edn) 200.

54 JWE Sheptycki, 'Transnational Crime and Transnational Policing' (2007) 1 *Sociology Compass* 485, 488; L Bisschop, 'Transnational Environmental Crime: Exploring (Un) charted Territory' in M Cools, B De Ruyver, M Easton et al (eds), *EU Criminal Justice, Financial & Economic Crime: New Perspectives* (Maklu 2011) 156ff.

55 See, eg, L Elliott and WH Schaedla (eds), *Handbook of Transnational Environmental Crime* (Edward Elgar 2016); T Spapens, R White and W Huisman (eds), *Environmental Crime in Transnational Context* (Routledge 2016).

There are no doubts that many forms of environmental crime are transnational and that their effects do not stop at the national borders,[56] yet not all the types of environmental crime can be regarded as transnational. Fly-tipping, for instance, does not usually involve more than one country,[57] and the same goes for other conduct that falls within the remit of the Directive (eg discharge of material into purely national soil).[58] The emphasis of the Directive's Preamble on cross-border environmental crime may be explained by the need to justify the compliance of this instrument with the principle of subsidiarity. As mentioned above, the subsidiarity principle prescribes that EU action in areas of shared competence should aim to achieve results that cannot be sufficiently achieved by the Member States, either at central level or at regional and local level, and that can be better achieved at Union level, because of the scale or effects of the proposed action.[59] Furthermore, irrespectively of the effects of environmental crime on one or more Member States, the harmonisation promoted by the Union can be necessary to ensure that environmental legislation – being as consistent as possible throughout the EU – does not hamper fair competition:[60] as noted in the literature, the 'need to ensure a level playing-field among the economic actors, albeit not explicitly mentioned in

---

56   See, among the many, the examples mentioned by T Spapens and W Huisman, 'Tackling Cross-Border Environmental Crime. A "Wicked Problem"' in Spapens, White and Huisman (eds) (previous n) 27ff. See also R White, 'Transnational Environmental Crime' in M Natarajan (ed), *International Crime and Justice* (Cambridge University Press 2010) 195–196; G Wright, 'Conceptualising and Combating Transnational Environmental Crime' (2011) 14 *Trends in organized crime* 332, 333; L Elliott, 'Fighting Transnational Environmental Crime' (2012) 66 *Journal of International Affairs* 87, 89.
57   E Watkins, 'A Case Study on Illegal Localized Pollution Incidents in the EU'. A study compiled as part of the EFFACE project (IEEP 2015).
58   Member States shall criminalise this conduct, mentioned in Article 3(a) of the Environmental Crime Directive, when further conditions are met – see section 4.1 below.
59   Article 5(2) of the Treaty Establishing the European Community in its Amsterdam-version (now Article 5(3) TEU). On the Environmental Crime Directive's compliance with the principle of subsidiarity, see Recital 14. That EU instruments on environmental crime are ideal examples of supranational legal instruments respecting the subsidiarity principle is also argued by the drafters of the 'Manifesto on European Criminal Policy' (2009) 4 *Zeitschrift für Internationale Strafrechtsdogmatik* 707, 713 ('The principle of subsidiarity is also respected in fields of criminal law which involve offences that are by trend committed transnationally and cannot be prevented on national level only. Crimes concerning ... the environment belong to this category because ... the impact of the offence [does] not stop at borders'). They add a caveat though: 'Although the principle of subsidiarity will most likely be met in these cases this does not imply that all aspects of these crimes have to be dealt with on an inter-national level' (ibid).
60   On the Court's approach to environmental issues from a similar economic perspective, see section 2 above.

the [Environmental Crime Directive] or in the explanatory memorandum to the proposal for a directive, certainly played a role in assessing the need for approximation of environmental criminal law'.[61] The following section analyses the *actus reus* and *mens rea* requirements as defined in the Directive. Section 4.2 looks at the rules on the liability of legal persons and penalties, while at the same time pointing out some gaps in the Directive when compared to more recent EU criminal law instruments.

4.1 Actus Reus *and* Mens Rea

Article 3 of the Environmental Crime Directive obliges Member States to ensure that nine categories of conduct constitute criminal offences, provided that two conditions are met: they have to be *unlawful* and committed *intentionally*, or at least with *serious negligence*.[62]

As for the latter requirement, although the extension of *mens rea* to serious negligence extends the scope of criminalisation, the literature welcomed the EU legislator's choice to provide for a duty of criminalisation that is limited to cases of 'serious' negligence, as this would be in line with the *extrema ratio* principle underpinning criminal law.[63] Member States remain however free to adopt more severe measures in the implementation of the Directive, including provisions founding criminal liability on simple negligence.[64] The reference to 'serious negligence', without any further specification, allows the Member States to accommodate the Directive within their criminal justice systems. At the same time, however, this wording may jeopardise the principle of legal certainty.[65] The Court of Justice addressed this issue in the different, albeit analogous, context of ship-source pollution.

In the *Intertanko* judgment,[66] the Court of Justice found that the use of 'serious negligence' in Directive 2005/35/EC on ship-source pollution, without the

---

61 Vagliasindi, 'The EU Environmental Crime Directive' (n 49) 45.
62 Article 3 of the Environmental Crime Directive.
63 Vagliasindi, 'The EU Environmental Crime Directive' (n 49) 46–47. See also Pereira, *Environmental Criminal Liability* (n 3) 235–236.
64 'Explanatory Memorandum to the Proposal for a Directive of the European Parliament and of the Council on the protection of the environment through criminal law' COM (2007) 51 final, 9 February 2007, 6.
65 Mitsilegas, Fitzmaurice and Fasoli (n 37) 287. For an in-depth analysis of several issues connected with legal (un)certainty in environmental criminal law, see the study by E Lees, *Interpreting Environmental Offences. The Need for Certainty* (Hart 2017), which focuses on the UK legal system.
66 Case C-308/06 *International Association of Independent Tanker Owners (Intertanko) v Secretary of State for Transport* 9, EU:C:2008:312. For a commentary, see E Denza, 'A Note on *Intertanko*' (2008) 33 *European Law Review* 870.

concept being further defined therein, does *not* infringe the principle of legal certainty, which is a fundamental principle of Community (now EU) law.[67] The Court made express reference to the principle of legality of criminal offences and penalties as a specific expression of legal certainty.[68] It is in this context that the Court examined the principle of serious negligence. It first referred to the use of the principle in the legal systems of Member States, but then went further to actually define the concept of serious negligence for the purposes of the 2005 Directive on ship-source pollution. In this context, serious negligence 'must be understood as entailing an unintentional act or omission by which the person responsible commits a patent breach of the duty of care which he should have and could have complied with in view of his attributes, knowledge, abilities and individual situation'.[69] Although the Court emphasised in the judgment that the actual definition of the infringements provided for by the Directive results from the transposition of the Directive in the Member States,[70] its foray into defining fundamental concepts and principles of criminal law is striking and goes further than the mere confirmation that such principles constitute general principles of Union (and in this case Community) law.

The second requirement laid down by the Environmental Crime Directive for the conduct to be criminalised, ie its being 'unlawful', is not less contentious. While 'unlawfulness' does not imply that conduct shall necessarily be active, since the 'failure to comply with a legal duty to act can have the same effect as active behaviour',[71] it means that the nine categories of conduct – which are mentioned immediately below – have to be criminalised when they infringe either the legislation adopted pursuant to the European Treaties to be found in Annexes A or B to the Directive, or a national piece of legislation, a national regulation, or a decision taken by a national authority giving effect to the legislation adopted pursuant to the Treaties.[72] In Annex A, for instance, the Regulation 338/97 implementing CITES is mentioned.[73]

By imposing a duty of criminalisation when the conduct is 'unlawful', the EU has followed the path of many national legislators. In most jurisdictions,

---

67   Case C-308/06 *Intertanko* (previous n), paras 69–80. For further details on the Directive(s) on ship-source pollution, see section 5 below.
68   ibid, para 70.
69   ibid, para 77.
70   ibid, para 78.
71   Recital 6 of the Environmental Crime Directive. As a consequence, failures to comply with a legal duty to act should also be subject to criminal penalties, if they meet the other requirements laid down in the Directive (ibid).
72   Article 2(a) of the Environmental Crime Directive.
73   On CITES, see more in chapter 2 of the book.

environmental criminal law is strictly intertwined with other branches of law (usually administrative law), and it looks as an 'accessory' to them rather than a self-standing matter. As Faure argues, in many legal systems

> the major part of environmental criminal law simply consists of provisions incorporated in environmental statutes of an administrative nature (for example, a Clean Water Act) and have as their main function the enforcement of compliance with administrative obligations. A great deal of environmental criminal law is therefore not formulated in an independent manner but is rather formulated as *accessory* to regulation. In legal practice, an important part of environmental criminal law will therefore consist of violations of a regulatory nature. For example, the polluter will be prosecuted for discharging certain substances into the environment without a permit or for violating permit conditions.[74]

The obligation for the Member States to criminalise conduct that is 'unlawful' confirms the accessory nature of environmental criminal law. The dependence of criminal law on administrative legislation may be interpreted, at the same time, as a safeguard of, and a risk for the principle of legal certainty. On the one hand, if criminal liability follows from the violation of administrative law provisions (with or without further requirements set out in criminal legislation), 'usually the criminal behaviour will *ex ante* be relatively clear'.[75] On the other hand, however, it is admittedly difficult for an individual to understand whether a given behaviour amounts to a criminal offence if criminal legislation cross-references further (often technical and complex) instruments of administrative law.[76] The Annexes to the Directive list *more than seventy* legal

---

[74] M Faure, 'Environmental Crimes' in G De Geest (ed), *Encyclopedia of Law and Economics*, vol 3 (2nd edn, Edward Elgar 2009) 320. Emphasis added. Other authors speak of 'dependency' or 'dependence' of criminal law on administrative law (respectively, Pereira, *Environmental Criminal Liability* (n 3) 222 and Vagliasindi, 'The EU Environmental Crime Directive' (n 49) 47). See also DM Uhlmann, 'Prosecutorial Discretion and Environmental Crime' (2014) 38 *Harvard Environmental Law Review* 159, 162ff; M Luchtman, 'Procedural Safeguards and the Interaction between Administrative and Penal Enforcement' (2016) 87 *Revue International de Droit Pénal – Protection of the Environment through Criminal Law* (ed by JL de La Cuesta et al) 221.

[75] M Faure, 'The Evolution of Environmental Criminal Law in Europe: A Comparative Analysis' in Farmer, Faure and Vagliasindi (eds) (n 22) 272. The same author lists several reasons that justify his conclusion according to which 'probably some link between environmental criminal law and administrative law should be retained' (ibid 273).

[76] See also P Beauvais, 'Les Limites de l'Internationalisation du Droit Pénal de l'Environnement' in L Neyret (ed), *Des Écocrimes à l'Écocide. Le Droit Pénal au Secours de*

instruments adopted by the Union, so that in many instances it is not immediately clear if and when a conduct is criminal, nor it is easy to prove the intentional subjective element of this illegal conduct. This becomes even more controversial if one bears in mind that the list seems currently outdated. Recital 15 of the Directive sets out a mechanism to regularly update the text but it has not been used.[77]

The shortcomings of defining environmental crime by references to instruments listed in the Annexes to the Directive are highlighted in the Commission's recent evaluation of the Environmental Crime Directive: it is noted that the Annexes defining the material scope of the Directive are outdated and a feasible mechanism to ensure that new relevant legislation comes under the scope of the Directive is missing; and that the Directive does not cover instruments such as the EU Timber Regulation, the Invasive Species Regulation and the REACH (Registration, Evaluation, Authorisation and Restriction of Chemicals) Regulation – with such inconsistencies potentially growing over time, as environmental legislation is constantly changing and as there are cases where substantive ecological damage goes unpunished because it does not violate any environmental legislation.[78]

With regard to the nine categories of conduct of natural persons[79] which Member States have to criminalise, they can be classified according to the legislative technique used to define them. Four of these categories of conduct have to be criminalised when they *cause*, or are *likely to cause*: i) death or serious injury to any person; or ii) 'substantial damage' to the quality of air, soil, water, or to animals or plants. These four conducts are:

---

l'Environnement (Bruylant 2015) 13–14; Perilongo and Corn (n 48) 243. The lack of clarity of the Environmental Crime Directive is also pointed out in the 'Manifesto on European Criminal Policy' (n 59) 713.

[77] See also L Krämer, 'Forty Years of EU Measures to Fight Wildlife Crime' (2019) 22 *Journal of International Wildlife Law & Policy* 305, 316, who argues that this 'leaves a considerable part of EU environmental legislation falling outside the field of application of Directive 2008/99', and mentions examples such as Regulation (EC) 1907/2006 on chemicals [2006] OJ L396/1, and Directive 2007/60/EC on the assessment and management of flood risks [2007] OJ L288/7. Recital 15 of the Environmental Crime Directive reads as follows: 'Whenever subsequent legislation on environmental matters is adopted, it should specify where appropriate that this Directive will apply. Where necessary, Article 3 should be amended'.

[78] Commission, 'Commission Staff Working Document Evaluation of the Directive 2008/99/EC of the European Parliament and of the Council of 19 November 2008 on the Protection of the Environment through Criminal Law' SWD (2020) 259 final, 28 October 2020, 63.

[79] The following section deals with the liability of legal persons.

- the discharge, emission or introduction of materials or ionising radiation into air, soil or water (Article 3(a));
- the collection, transport, recovery or disposal of waste, including the supervision of such operations and the aftercare of disposal sites, and including action taken as a dealer or a broker (waste management) (Article 3(b));
- the operation of a plant in which a dangerous activity is carried out or in which dangerous substances or preparations are stored or used (Article 3(d));[80] and
- the production, processing, handling, use, holding, storage, transport, import, export or disposal of nuclear materials or other hazardous radioactive substances (Article 3(e)).

Requiring Member States to criminalise these conducts when they cause death, serious injury, or some of the other above-mentioned consequences, the Directive endorses the model of offences that are based on the harm they cause. Nevertheless, since these categories of conduct shall be criminalised also when they are concretely apt to endanger persons, animals, plants, air, soil or water – even without damaging them – the Directive also accepts that environment can be sufficiently protected by the so-called concrete endangerment offences.[81] When transposed into national substantive criminal law, the cause-effect relationship between a conduct and its (potential) impact on persons or the environment may represent a challenge for national authorities, since in most of the cases this link is difficult to prove.[82] As Mégret underlines,

> environmental crime often lacks the single-event character typical of ordinary localized crime, and consequently may be *much more about process than a one-time occurrence*. ... While crimes against the environment may be committed gradually, the criminal law traditionally looks to an identifiable event (an actus reus) and, more often than not, clearly and relatively immediately ascertainable damage (e.g., bodily harm, death, or

---

80 In this case, the Directive requires that the operation of the plant causes or is likely to cause death or serious injury to any person or substantial damage to the quality of air, the quality of soil or the quality of water, or to animals or plants 'outside the plant' (Article 3(d) of the Environmental Crime Directive).
81 See Pereira, *Environmental Criminal Liability* (n 3) 227; Faure, 'The Revolution' (n 49) 346ff; Vagliasindi, 'The EU Environmental Crime Directive' (n 49) 48.
82 See, for instance, Eurojust, 'Strategic Project on Environmental Crime. Report' (November 2014) 55–56; M Duțu and A Duțu, 'Environmental Crime in the EU: Is There a Need for Further Harmonisation or for New Enforcement Tools?' (2016) 87 *Revue International de Droit Pénal – Protection of the Environment through Criminal Law* (ed by JL de La Cuesta et al) 107, 115; Krämer, 'Forty Years' (n 77) 317.

damage to property). The problem that this presents for the criminalization of environmental harm is magnified when the damage is not only *geographically* but also *temporally diffuse*. In some cases, for example, the existence of harm may only be ascertainable with a substantial passage of time, and might only affect future generations.[83]

Further complications arise since the Directive relies on unclear benchmarks against which criminalisation should follow at the national level, such as 'serious' injury to any person and 'substantial' damage to the quality of air, soil, water, or to animals or plants. It has been noted that the notion of 'substantial damage' is 'too vague and not clear enough' and that 'criteria, guidelines or instructions to define [this and other notions] are absent or insufficient'[84] at the national level. Some authors have however pointed out that more detailed rules would have been difficult to agree on the political level and would have limited the leeway of Member States to accommodate the Directive in their legal systems.[85]

As per Recital 12, since the Directive lays down minimum requirements only, Member States remain free to adopt or maintain more stringent measures regarding the effective criminal law protection of the environment. They may for instance decide to strengthen such protection by regulating the above-listed categories of conduct as abstract endangerment offences,[86] that is, criminalise them as such without taking into account their (real or potential) consequences. The Directive embraces this model of *abstract endangerment* offences with regard to three other categories of conduct:[87]

---

83 F Mégret, 'The Problem of an International Criminal Law of the Environment' (2011) 36 *Columbia Journal of Environmental Law* 195, 222. Emphasis added. Similarly, E Pirjatanniemi, 'Desperately Seeking Reason – New Directions for European Environmental Criminal Law' (2009) 54 *Scandinavian Studies in Law* 409, 418.

84 GENVAL, 'Final report on the 8th round of mutual evaluations on "The practical implementation and operation of the European polices on preventing and combating Environmental Crime"' Council doc 14852/19, 5 December 2019 ('GENVAL final report') 56. On GENVAL, see immediately below in this section.

85 Vagliasindi, 'The EU Environmental Crime Directive' (n 49) 47.

86 ibid 48. Vagliasindi however warns that, since abstract endangerment offences are usually sanctioned with low penalties, this may violate the Member States' obligation to provide for effective and dissuasive penalties; hence, 'abstract endangerment offences could be provided by Member States only in addition to concrete endangerment or harm-based offences covering the most serious cases' (ibid).

87 ibid 48. Cf also Pereira, *Environmental Criminal Liability* (n 3) 227–228; Faure, 'The Revolution' (n 49) 346ff.

- the illegal shipment of waste, as regulated by Article 2(35) of Regulation 1013/2006, when the illegal shipment is undertaken in a non-negligible quantity and whether it is executed in a single shipment or in several shipments which appear to be linked (Article 3(c)); Regulation 1013/2006 is also known as the 'Basel Regulation' since it implements, in the EU, the 1989 Basel Convention.[88] The shipment of waste is illegal when, for instance, it takes place without the previous notification or consent of the competent authorities as required by the Basel Regulation.[89] The provision on illegal shipment of waste is an example of the legal uncertainty that may follow from the text of the Directive: Article 3(c) refers to the shipment of waste, which falls within the scope of Article 2(35) of Regulation 1013/2006, which in turn defines 'illegal shipment' as any shipment of waste effected – among the others – in violation of further Articles of that Regulation or of the procedures set out in the Annexes to that Regulation.[90] These cross-references are likely to hamper a clear understanding of what conduct amounts to a criminal offence;
- trading in specimens of protected wild fauna or flora species – or parts or derivatives thereof – except for cases where the conduct concerns a 'negligible quantity' of such specimens and has a 'negligible impact' on the conservation status of the species (Article 3(g)). Like the illegal shipments of waste, also the illegal trade in protected species had been regulated at the international level before the adoption of the Environmental Crime Directive. The landmark multilateral agreement in the field is CITES. Even though the EU has formally become a party to the CITES only in 2015, already in 1982 the Convention had been implemented in the Community with Regulation 3626/82, subsequently repealed by Regulation 338/97.[91] Whereas all these instruments – including the Basel Convention on the shipment of waste – provided broad rules on the measures to take against the phenomena at

---

88 The European Union is a party to the Basel Convention since 1994. On the Basel Convention, see more in chapter 3 of this book.
89 See Article 2(35)(a) and (b) of Regulation No 1013/2006.
90 See Article 2(35)(f) and (g) of Regulation No 1013/2006.
91 Council Regulation (EEC) No 3626/82 of 3 December 1982 on the implementation in the Community of the Convention on international trade in endangered species of wild fauna and flora [1982] OJ L384/1, which was repealed by the Council Regulation (EC) No 338/97 of 9 December 1996 on the protection of species of wild fauna and flora by regulating trade therein [1997] OJ L61/1. See more in, eg, I Kouvaras, 'EU Confronting Wildlife Trafficking' (2016) 25 *European Energy and Environmental Law Review* 76, 78ff. On CITES, see more in chapter 2 of this book.

issue,[92] the Environmental Crime Directive has clarified that such measures should be of penal nature; and
- the production, importation, exportation, placing on the market or use of ozone-depleting substances (Article 3(i)).

Abstract endangerment offences, while in theory ensuring a better protection of the environment as they criminalise an unlawful conduct as such, may raise concerns as regards the compliance with the fundamental principles of criminal law, including the principle of *extrema ratio*.[93]

The two remaining categories of conduct are instead exclusively conceived as harm-based offences, since the Directive obliges Member States to criminalise:
- the killing, destruction, possession, and taking of specimens of protected wild fauna or flora species,[94] except for cases where the conduct concerns a 'negligible quantity' of such specimens and has a 'negligible impact' on the conservation status of the species (Article 3(f)); and
- any conduct that causes the significant deterioration of a habitat within a protected site (Article 3(h)).

Some of the above-mentioned provisions include a reference to 'negligible impact' and 'negligible quantity',[95] which leaves the Member States free to implement the Directive in a way that is compatible with their legal systems and tradition – the limited European harmonisation of environmental offences that follows from these rules being the obvious flipside.

Finally, inciting and aiding and abetting the nine above-mentioned categories of conduct, when the latter are intentional, are to be criminalised as well.[96]

---

92 Article 16(1) of Regulation 338/97 provides that Member States shall take 'appropriate measures' to ensure the imposition of sanctions for at least some of the infringements of the Regulation listed therein, whereas Article 16(2) specifies that such measures 'shall be appropriate to the nature and gravity of the infringement and shall include provisions relating to the seizure and, where appropriate, confiscation of specimens'. See also Elliott, 'Fighting Transnational Environmental Crime' (n 56) 96. See more in chapters 2 and 3 of this book.

93 See, for instance, Pereira, *Environmental Criminal Liability* (n 3) 227–228.

94 Unlike Article 3(g) of the Environmental Crime Directive on the trading in specimens of protected wild fauna or flora species (see above in the text), the further specification on 'parts or derivatives' of specimens of protected wild fauna or flora species is not mentioned in the provision on the killing, destruction, possession, and taking of these specimens.

95 On the ambiguous notions of 'negligible impact' and 'negligible quantity', see M Faure, 'Vague Notions in Environmental Criminal Law (part 1)' (2010) 18 *Environmental Liability, Law Practice and Policy* 119, 122ff.

96 Article 4 of the Environmental Crime Directive.

The Directive differs from many other instruments of EU criminal law in so far as it does not require the criminalisation of the *attempt* to commit environmental crimes. It is instead consistent with them when it obliges Member States to ensure that inchoate offences (inciting and aiding and abetting) are punishable as criminal offences and yet does not define them. Member States remain therefore free to adopt their own standards and rules in that regard as well.

The overview of the offences provided for by the Environmental Crime Directive lends support to the well-known argument according to which the boundaries of the notion of 'environmental crime' are unclear. Similarly to the definition of environment itself, 'environmental crime' is a broad concept encompassing very different phenomena,[97] and not all of them are included in Article 3 of the Directive. For instance, the Directive does not provide for any rule on crimes concerning food safety or animal welfare,[98] as well as illegal, unreported and unregulated fishing or trade in hazardous chemicals.[99]

The Environmental Crime Directive's impact on the substantive criminal law of Member States has been subject to different studies, including the already mentioned EFFACE project, as well as to the eighth round of mutual evaluation carried out within the Council's Working Party on General Matters including Evaluations (GENVAL), which was devoted to the 'practical implementation and operation of European policies on prevention and combating environmental crime'[100] and concluded in December 2019. By means of both a questionnaire and visits of small groups of experts in each EU country, this round of evaluation focused on Member States' actions and legislation concerning illegal trafficking in waste and the illegal production or handling of dangerous materials. The evaluation concluded that, despite the desired harmonisation at

---

[97] For different views on this topic see, for instance, P Cleary Yeager and SS Simpson, 'Environmental Crime' in M Tonry (ed), *The Oxford Handbook of Crime and Public Policy* (OUP 2009) 325; S Chin, W Veening and C Gerstetter, 'EFFACE Policy Brief 1: Limitations and Challenges of the Criminal Justice System in Addressing Environmental Crime' (2014) 4–5; A Farmer, AR Germani and R Sollund, 'Conclusions of the EFFACE Case Studies' (2015) 7–10; EnviCrimeNet, 'Report on Environmental Crime' (2016) 4 <www.envicrimenet.eu/images/docs/envicrimenet%20report%20on%20environmental%20crime.pdf> accessed 2 June 2021.

[98] EnviCrimeNet and Europol, 'Intelligence Project on Environmental Crime. Report on Environmental Crime in Europe' (2015) 11 <http://www.envicrimenet.eu/reports> accessed 2 June 2021.

[99] Pereira, *Environmental Criminal Liability* (n 3) 255–261.

[100] GENVAL Final report (n 84).

the EU level and the fact that all Member States have in principle implemented the Environmental Crime Directive,[101] national legal systems still provide for very different rules and procedures concerning environmental crime.[102] The recent evaluation of the Environmental Crime Directive by the Commission reached similar conclusions.[103] Differences among Member States also exist with regard to the place of environmental criminal law within the national systems, since the relevant offences can be found in criminal codes, special *ad hoc* legislation or even in administrative statutes, with further consequences in terms both of the (im)possibility for individuals and law enforcement authorities to be easily aware of these provisions and of higher or lower social disapproval of the illegal conduct.[104] Some Member States, such as Sweden, reportedly did not take any measure to implement the Directive as they already complied with the obligations set out therein.[105]

4.2 *Liability of Legal Persons, Penalties and (Some) Gaps*

The Directive obliges the Member States to ensure the liability of legal persons where the offences listed in the Directive (including inchoate offences) are committed for the benefit of legal persons 'by any person who has a leading position within the legal person, acting either individually or as part of an organ of the legal person'.[106] Likewise, legal entities should also be liable where the commission of an environmental offence (including an inchoate offence) is due to the lack of supervision or control, by a person in a leading position,

---

101 Several authors however criticise the accuracy of such implementation in some Member States – for a comparative overview, see Faure, 'The Evolution of Environmental Criminal Law in Europe' (n 75) 304–309.
102 GENVAL Final report (n 84) 55. See also Pereira, *Environmental Criminal Liability* (n 3) 328–334; Faure, 'The Evolution of Environmental Criminal Law in Europe' (n 75) 268ff.
103 Commission, 'Commission Staff Working Document Evaluation of the Directive 2008/99/EC' (n 78).
104 Faure, 'The Evolution of Environmental Criminal Law in Europe' (n 75) 271. For instance, in Finland, 'the most serious acts that attract prison sentences have been gathered under Chapter 48 of the Criminal Code. The reason why environmental offences were included as a separate entity in the Criminal Code is to emphasise the *blameworthiness* of the acts' ('Evaluation report on the eighth Round of Mutual Evaluations "The practical implementation and operations of European policies on preventing and combating environmental crime" – Report on Finland' Council doc 8430/1, 11 June 2018, 51, emphasis added).
105 Faure, 'The Evolution of Environmental Criminal Law in Europe' (n 75) 305.
106 Article 6(1) of the Environmental Crime Directive. This provision further clarifies that such a leading position within the legal entity shall be based on: '(a) a power of representation of the legal person; (b) an authority to take decisions on behalf of the legal person; or (c) an authority to exercise control within the legal person' (ibid).

on persons under his or her authority.[107] For the purpose of its application, the Directive defines a 'legal person' as any legal entity having such status under the applicable national law but it expressly excludes States, public bodies exercising State authority, and public international organisations.[108] Such an exception can be found in some national systems as well,[109] and is often justified because the costs of the potential fines issued against a public body would be paid by means of public money and, consequently, would eventually fall upon the shoulders of the citizens.[110] Nonetheless, some criticism has been voiced against the exclusion of public bodies from the remit of the Directive, as this overlooks those cases where 'the actions or omissions of administrative bodies or public companies ... impact on the environment or human health'.[111]

Member States should ensure that penalties against legal persons are 'effective, proportionate and dissuasive',[112] while the nature of such penalties (criminal, administrative, and/or civil) is not specified. This is due to the fact that some Member States had, and still have, reservations about the *criminal* liability of legal persons.[113] The Environmental Crime Directive's provisions on legal persons are nonetheless to be welcomed, as there is increasing evidence on the paramount role that legal entities play in the commission of environmental crimes.[114]

The link between the liability of legal persons and the benefit they gain from environmental offences allows to adequately address those cases where such crimes have not been committed, or at least not only, for purely personal interests. Legitimate companies can often decide to 'behave' in an illegal way to avoid relevant costs linked with their activities, such as those concerning waste disposal. In the literature, these phenomena are defined as 'organisation

---

107 Article 6(2) of the Environmental Crime Directive.
108 Article 2(d) of the Environmental Crime Directive.
109 This is the case, for instance, of Italy (cf Article 1(3) of the Legislative Decree No 231/2001).
110 cf G Grasso and F Giuffrida, 'Ai Confini tra il Giudice Contabile e il Giudice Penale: I Rapporti tra le Giurisdizioni e la Problematica Nozione di "Ente Pubblico"' [2016] *L'Indice Penale* 894, 921.
111 Pereira, *Environmental Criminal Liability* (n 3) 269. Cf I Plakokefalos, 'Criminal Liability of States for Environmental Crimes: The Perspective of International Law' (2016) 87 *Revue International de Droit Pénal – Protection of the Environment through Criminal Law* (ed by JL de La Cuesta et al) 283.
112 Article 7 of the Environmental Crime Directive.
113 For a recent overview on the matter, see K Ligeti and F Giuffrida, 'The (Criminal) Liability of Legal Persons and Heads of Business: Strengths and Weaknesses of the European Union's Approach' (2020) *Revue Pénale Luxembourgeoise* 2.
114 See Vagliasindi, 'The EU Environmental Crime Directive' (n 49) 48.

crime'[115] or 'organisational crime', which refers 'to violations of criminal statutes committed in the context or in pursuit of the goals of legitimate organizations, organizational subunits, or work groups'.[116] In theory, the difference between organisational crime and organised crime is crystal-clear, with the consequence that – for example – only in the latter case it would be necessary to punish all the members of the criminal syndicate. In the case of a crime committed by a corporation, it would instead be illogical to sanction all the employees,[117] and it is for this reason that the Environmental Crime Directive lists some conditions to be met to issue penalties against legal persons. Nevertheless, the boundaries between organised and organisational crime can sometimes become quite blurred in practice, 'as when legitimate businesses are converted gradually into criminal ones, or when they serve as nothing more than a respectable-appearing shell for activities that are largely, if not exclusively, criminal'.[118] At any rate, according to the GENVAL final report and the Commission's evaluation of the Environmental Crime Directive, all Member States have introduced the liability of legal persons at least for waste-related crimes, albeit in different forms (criminal or administrative).[119]

Unlike the penalties for legal persons, those for individuals who commit the offences listed in the Environmental Crime Directive shall not only be 'effective, proportionate and dissuasive', bus also of 'criminal'[120] nature. The

---

115 T Fajardo, 'Organised Crime and Environmental Crime: Analysis of EU Legal Instruments'. Study in the framework of the EFFACE Research Project (University of Granada 2015) 20–21.
116 N Shover and J Scroggins, 'Organizational Crime' in Tonry (ed) (n 97) 273. For further remarks on 'corporate environmental crime', see Faure, 'Environmental Crimes' (n 74) 330–333.
117 I Rodopoulos, 'Les Activités Criminelles Organisées en Matière Environnementale: Quelque Réflexion en Vue d'une Réponse Pénale Internationale' in Neyret (ed) (n 76) 169–171.
118 Shover and Scroggins (n 116) 276. See also, for instance, AR Germani, G D'Alisa, PM Falcone et al, 'Victims in the "Land of Fires": Illegal Waste Disposal in the Campania Region, Italy' in R Sollund, CH Stefes and AR Germani (eds), *Fighting Environmental Crime in Europe and Beyond. The Role of the EU and Its Member States* (Palgrave Macmillan 2016), where the authors highlight the involvement of legal businesses – in addition to that of organised crime groups – in waste-related crimes. The need to regulate corporate liability in the field of environmental crime was also pointed out by M Faure and G Heine, *Criminal Enforcement of Environmental Law in the European Union* (Kluwer Law International 2005) 87–88.
119 GENVAL final report (n 84) 13, where it is also specified that in the Member States 'where only corporate fines have been provided for, such fines have been considered insufficient' (ibid); Commission, 'Commission Staff Working Document Evaluation of the Directive 2008/99/EC' (n 78) 33 and 36.
120 Article 5 of the Environmental Crime Directive.

Commission's proposal for a Directive on the protection of the environment through criminal law included further details concerning penalties for natural persons.[121] However, in line with the *Ship-Source Pollution* case of the Court of Justice that prevented the Community from regulating criminal sanctions,[122] the final text of the Environmental Crime Directive does not specify the type and level of criminal penalties. As this leaves a considerable margin of discretion to the Member States in the implementation of the Directive, the impact of the latter on national systems has been limited also in that regard.[123] At the national level, maximum imprisonment penalties for individuals range from six months to life imprisonment,[124] in addition to further differences concerning fines and complementary sanctions (such as the order to repair the damage caused by the offence).[125]

Even though in some countries the penalties for environmental crimes can be high, they are deemed to be on average quite mild in most EU Member States.[126]

---

121   See Article 5 of the 'Commission's proposal for a Directive of the European Parliament and of the Council on the protection of the environment through criminal law' COM (2007) 51 final, 9 February 2007.
122   See section 3 above.
123   Eurojust, 'Strategic Project on Environmental Crime. Report' (n 82) 36; Chin, Veening and Gerstetter, 'EFFACE Policy Brief 1' (n 97) 2; G Giardi, 'Fighting the European Ecomafia. Organised Trafficking in Waste and the Need for a Criminal Law Response from the EU' (2015) 6 *New Journal of European Criminal Law* 229, 248ff; C Gerstetter, C Stefes, A Farmer et al, 'Environmental Crime and the EU. Synthesis of the Research Project "European Action to Fight Environmental Crime" (EFFACE)' (2016) 31–34.
124   Mitsilegas, Fitzmaurice and Fasoli (n 37) 286. See Commission, 'Commission Staff Working Document Evaluation of the Directive 2008/99/EC' (n 78) 32.
125   Commission, 'Commission Staff Working Document Evaluation of the Directive 2008/99/EC' (n 78) 32. See also Faure, 'The Evolution of Environmental Criminal Law in Europe' (n 75) 309–314; Pereira, 'Towards Effective Implementation of the EU Environmental Crime Directive? The Case of Illegal Waste Management and Trafficking Offences' (2017) 26 *Review of European Community & International Environmental Law* 147, 153ff. According to some authors, however, the differences in sanctions that emerge from the law in the books 'seem to disappear when moving from theory to practice. Although the available data do not lead to unambiguous conclusions on this point, incarcerations seem to range from an average of 6/7 months to a maximum of 2 years. Coherently, prison sentences are almost automatically suspended under probation. As for monetary sanctions, criminal fines for natural persons generally amount to 5,000€ and rarely exceed 10,000€' (Perilongo and Corn (n 48) 251).
126   See, eg, EnviCrimeNet, 'Report on Environmental Crime' (n 97) 11–13; Perilongo and Corn (n 48) 251. As for wildlife crime, the European Economic and Social Committee (EESC) bemoaned 'the laxity of existing penalties' (European Economic and Social Committee, 'Opinion on the "Communication from the Commission to the Council and the European Parliament on the EU Approach against Wildlife Trafficking" – COM (2014) 64 final' [2014] OJ C424/52, para 3.1.1.

On the one hand, severe sanctions do not *per se* ensure the effectiveness of the fight against environmental crime, since 'the legally defined maximum sentence says relatively little on the sanctions that are *effectively* imposed by the judiciary'.[127] For instance, a survey on prosecutions against environmental crime in Ireland between 2004 and 2014 found that no imprisonment sentence was issued in any of the cases where the competent courts found that an environmental crime had been committed.[128] On the other hand, however, the choice of keeping penalties (too) low can hamper an effective response to these crimes for different reasons. Low penalties are usually interpreted as a sign that a crime is not very serious, so that resources and people are to be better employed in the fight against more serious offences. In some countries, furthermore, the most intrusive investigative measures, eg wiretapping, can be adopted only if a given threshold of penalty is met.[129] Similarly, also the limitation period of crimes can depend upon the maximum penalty applicable, with the consequence that the lower is the sanction the shorter is the period needed for the crime to become time barred.[130] As the next chapter shows, low penalties can also hamper the procedures of judicial cooperation at the supranational level.

A broader question of legitimacy lurks behind the EU legislator's choice to introduce criminal penalties for environmental crimes, namely whether it is more efficient to tackle these offences by means of criminal law, or whether the environment would be better protected by stepping up measures and sanctions of administrative (or even civil) law. The Preamble to the Environmental Crime Directive touches upon the issue and claims that '[e]xperience has shown that

---

127 Gerstetter, Stefes, Farmer et al, 'Environmental Crime and the EU' (n 123) 34. Emphasis added.
128 MJ Lynch, PB Stretesky and MA Long, 'Environmental Crime Prosecutions in Ireland, 2004–2014' (2019) 43 *International Journal of Comparative and Applied Criminal Justice* 277, 284, where the authors also note that 'Under some environmental statutes in Ireland, it is possible for Higher Courts to punish directors or managers of corporations with prison terms of up to 10 years for significant environmental violations. Thus, the absence of any prison sentences in these data suggest that the responsible courts did not view the violation as sufficient enough for a prison term' (ibid).
129 See, for instance, Article 266(1)(a) of the Italian Code of Criminal Procedure, which allows wiretapping for any intentional crime that is punished with a maximum penalty of at least 5 years. For further examples see Pereira, *Environmental Criminal Liability* (n 3) 339; M Kusak, *Mutual Admissibility of Evidence in Criminal Matters in the EU* (Maklu 2016) 66–68. It is thus not surprising that, as noted in the GENVAL final report (n 84) 14, '[i]n some Member States the use of special investigative techniques (such as observation, infiltration, telephone tapping, etc.) to investigate environmental crime, including waste-related crimes, is not allowed, unless there is a link with economic and financial offences'. See more in section 6 below.
130 See, for instance, Article 157 of the Italian Penal Code.

the existing systems of penalties have not been sufficient to achieve complete compliance with the laws for the protection of the environment'.[131] Although it is unclear if and to what extent this 'experience' is empirically grounded, the Directive states that such compliance with environmental legislation 'can and should be strengthened by the availability of criminal penalties, which demonstrate a social disapproval of a qualitatively different nature compared to administrative penalties or a compensation mechanism under civil law'.[132] Albeit endorsed by the EU legislator with regard to several areas of crime, the presumption that, almost by definition, criminal sanctions are more effective and dissuasive[133] than other punitive measures is subject to fierce debates in the literature,[134] even beyond the field of environmental criminal law.[135] What is sure, however, is that criminal penalties are more powerful than other measures on a symbolical level, so that EU action in all the cases where criminal law is preferred over other measures could arguably be explained by reference to at least 'the Union's need to reaffirm its core values and to strengthen its political identity'.[136]

---

131   Recital 3 of the Environmental Crime Directive.
132   ibid. On the reasons behind the choice of the EU legislator to opt for criminal measures, including the strong stigma attached to criminal sanctions, see, eg, Duţu and Duţu (n 82) 109–110.
133   See also Recital 5 of the Environmental Crime Directive, which claims that '[i]n order to achieve effective protection of the environment, there is a particular need for more dissuasive penalties for environmentally harmful activities …'. For some arguments in favour of the criminalisation of conduct affecting the environment, especially but not only on the international level, see Mégret (n 83) 227ff.
134   See, for instance, J Öberg, 'Criminal Sanctions in the Field of EU Environmental Law' (2011) 2 *New Journal of European Criminal Law* 402; Pereira, *Environmental Criminal Liability* (n 3) 292ff; A Lucifora, 'Spunti di Comparazione e Nuove Prospettive di Armonizzazione del Diritto Penale dell'Ambiente: Scelte di Politica Criminale e Tecniche di Tipizzazione' [2019] *Rivista Trimestrale di Diritto Penale dell'Economia* 190, 228ff. According to the 'Manifesto on European Criminal Policy', the 'criminalisation of administrative offences does not comply with the European principle of proportionality and its sub-principle, the principle of ultima ratio. Furthermore, in such cases no interests that require protection by means of criminal law are at risk' ('Manifesto on European Criminal Policy' (n 59) 711). See also M Faure, 'The Development of Environmental Criminal Law in the EU and its Member States' (2017) 26 *Review of European Community & International Environmental Law* 139, 143–144.
135   For some remarks and references, see F Giuffrida, 'Effectiveness, Dissuasiveness, Proportionality of Sanctions and Assimilation Principle: The Long-Lasting Legacy of the *Greek Maize* Case' in Mitsilegas, di Martino and Mancano (eds) (n 34) 116–117.
136   Öberg, *Limits to EU Powers* (n 51) 193. On the expressive dimension of (EU) criminal law see more in, inter alia, J Iontcheva Turner, 'The Expressive Dimension of EU Criminal Law' (2012) 60 *American Journal of Comparative Law* 555.

Finally, in addition to those on penalties, further silences of the Environmental Crime Directive can be mentioned. Especially when compared to the most recent EU substantive criminal law directives, the 2008 Directive looks rather basic, although one should bear in mind that it was adopted in a different legal and political scenario.[137] The Directive does not include, for instance, any provision requiring Member States to introduce an aggravating circumstance if crimes are committed within the framework of a criminal organisation[138] or to establish jurisdiction on environmental crimes when some conditions are met.[139] The statute of limitation of environmental offences is not addressed in the Directive either, although this is a key element to take into account in the fight against (environmental) crime. At the time of writing, only one EU criminal law instrument lays down some rules on the statute of limitation of offences harmonised at the EU level (the so-called 'PIF Directive'),[140] and it is thus unsurprising that the Environmental Crime Directive did not tackle the issue more than ten years ago.

---

137 The Treaty of Lisbon brought about several and considerable changes to EU powers in the field of criminal law. For an overview, see Mitsilegas, *EU Criminal Law after Lisbon* (n 15) 4ff.
138 On the links between environmental crime and organised crime, see more in section 6 below.
139 Pereira, *Environmental Criminal Liability* (n 3) 219. For some examples of rules on jurisdiction to be found in other EU directives see, for instance, Article 10(1) of Directive 2011/36/EU of the European Parliament and of the Council on preventing and combating trafficking in human beings and protecting its victims [2011] OJ L101/1, which requires Member States to take the necessary measures to establish their jurisdiction over the offences regulated in the Directive where: '(a) the offence is committed in whole or in part within their territory; or (b) the offender is one of their nationals'. Member States may also decide to establish further jurisdiction over those offences when committed outside their territory also when '(a) the offence is committed against one of [their] nationals or a person who is an habitual resident in [their] territory; (b) the offence is committed for the benefit of a legal person established in [their] territory; or (c) the offender is an habitual resident in [their] territory' (Article 10(3) of Directive 2011/36/ EU). For very similar provisions, see also Article 11(1) and (3) of Directive (EU) 2017/1371 of the European Parliament and of the Council of 5 July 2017 on the fight against fraud to the Union's financial interests by means of criminal law [2017] OJ L198/29.
140 Article 12 of Directive (EU) 2017/1371 (previous n). 'PIF' stands for '*protection des intérêts financiers*'. See more in F Giuffrida, 'The Protection of the Union's Financial Interests After Lisbon' in R Sicurella, V Mitsilegas, R Parizot et al (eds), *General Principles for a Common Criminal Law Framework in the EU. A Guide for Legal Practitioners* (Giuffrè 2017) 267–268.

5 Ship-Source Pollution between EU (Criminal) Law and International Law

In the same way as the annulment by the Court of Justice of the 2003 Framework Decision on the protection of the environment through criminal law prompted the adoption of the 2008 Environmental Crime Directive, the annulment of the 2005 Framework Decision created a legal vacuum that was filled by Directive 2009/123/EC on ship-source pollution and on the introduction of penalties for infringements ('Ship-Source Pollution Directive').[141] The following section analyses this Directive, while section 5.2 examines the above-mentioned *Intertanko* case that, apart from setting out the Court of Justice's view on the meaning of 'serious negligence',[142] offers an interesting insight on the relations between Community/EU law and international law in the field of ship-source pollution.

5.1 *The Ship-Source Pollution Directive (2009/123/EC)*

The Ship-Source Pollution Directive is a further testament to the fact that environmental criminal law is rarely a stand-alone subject: unlike the Environmental Crime Directive, Directive 2009/123/EC does not even contain a list of conduct to be criminalised, it rather modifies an existing piece of EU legislation concerning ship-source pollution (the above-mentioned Directive 2005/35/EC), introducing in it some articles that provide that (some) infringements of the Directive have to be punished by the Member States with criminal sanctions.[143] Apart from this structural difference, however, the Ship-Source Pollution Directive is largely similar to the Environmental Crime Directive.

---

141 Directive 2009/123/EC of the European Parliament and of the Council of 21 October 2009 amending Directive 2005/35/EC on ship-source pollution and on the introduction of penalties for infringements [2009] OJ L280/52. See Recital 2 on the need for this Directive to 'fill the legal vacuum following the judgment' of the Court of Justice in the *Ship-Source Pollution* case.

142 Case C-308/06 *Intertanko* (n 66). See section 4.1 above.

143 Once again, the EU legislator emphasises that the existing set of rules and penalties is not sufficient to adequately ensure maritime safety and prevent ship-source pollution, so that the more several criminal penalties, which demonstrate a higher social disapproval than administrative penalties, are needed (cf Recitals 3 and 4 of the Ship-Source Pollution Directive). On Directive 2005/35/EC, see more in Mitsilegas, Fitzmaurice and Fasoli (n 37) 279–283, where it is also noted that, in requiring the introduction of *criminal* penalties, Directive 2009/123/EC goes beyond the unclear MARPOL provisions on sanctions. The same has been argued by, eg, Pozdnakova: 'UNCLOS and MARPOL merely encourage States to adopt adequate penalties for pollution violations. Neither treaty specifies the nature of such penalties. Accordingly, merely by requiring the Member States to introduce criminal sanctions for discharge violations, the Directives have already gone further

First, the infringements mentioned in the Directive, and namely the 'ship-source *discharges* of polluting substances ... into any of the areas referred to in Article 3(1)'[144] of Directive 2005/35/EC, should be criminalised when they are committed intentionally or unintentionally ('recklessly or with serious negligence').[145] Article 3(1) of Directive 2005/35/EC refers to: a) internal waters, including ports, of a Member State, in so far as the MARPOL regime is applicable; b) territorial sea of a Member State; c) straits used for international navigation subject to the regime of transit passage, as laid down in the 1982 United Nations Convention on the Law of the Sea (UNCLOS), to the extent that a Member State exercises jurisdiction over such straits; d) exclusive economic zone or equivalent zone of a Member State, established in accordance with international law; and e) the high seas. As for the unintentional character of the conduct, more precisely, the Directive does not only mention the 'serious negligence', as the Environmental Crime Directive does, but it also prescribes the criminalisation of *reckless* conduct.[146] Article 3(2) of Directive 2005/35/EC

---

than the international treaties' (A Pozdnakova, *Criminal Jurisdiction over Perpetrators of Ship-Source Pollution: International Law, State Practice and EU Harmonisation* (Brill 2012) 214).

144 Article 4(1) of Directive 2005/35/EC, as amended by the Ship-Source Pollution Directive. Emphasis added. As Pozdnakova notes, since the Directive refers to discharges only, it does not require criminal penalties for 'serious safety violations that have not yet resulted in pollution. It is up to the individual Member States to decide whether such violations should be criminalized' (Pozdnakova (previous n) 214). However, '[i]n the light of accidents such as the *Erika* and the *Prestige*, it may be reasonable to extend criminal liability to serious omissions or failures that have the potential to cause major pollution' (ibid).

145 Article 4(1) of Directive 2005/35/EC, as amended by the Ship-Source Pollution Directive (see immediately below in the text). As noted in the literature, 'The pollutant substances included in the [Ship-Source Pollution Directive] are the same as those of the Directive 2005/35/EC, which comply with the Annexes to the Marpol Convention. They are hydrocarbons (petroleum in any form, including crude oil, fuel oil, sludge, oil refuse and refined products), mixtures thereof, and noxious liquid substances carried in bulk. The noxious liquid substances carried in bulk, if discharged into the sea from tank cleaning or deballasting operations, present a hazard (ranging from slight to severe) to either marine resources or to human health or cause harm to amenities or other legitimate uses of the sea' (F Pellegrino, 'The Introduction of Penalties for Ship-Source Pollution in Community Law: Recent Developments' (2011) 48 *European Transport\Trasporti Europei* 99, 106; see also GM Vagliasindi, 'Directive 2008/99/EC on Environmental Crime and Directive 2009/123/EC on Ship-source Pollution'. Study in the framework of the EFFACE research project (University of Catania 2015) 15).

146 Article 4(1) of Directive 2005/35/EC, as amended by the Ship-Source Pollution Directive. For the definition of 'serious negligence' according to the Court of Justice, see section 4.1 above. See more in Pereira, *Environmental Criminal Liability* (n 3) 235ff. In MARPOL, in addition to intent and recklessness, there is also a reference to 'knowledge that damage would probably result' from the conduct, while nothing similar can be found in the

further clarifies that, while applying to the discharges of polluting substances from any ship, irrespective of its flag, the Directive's provisions do not concern warships, naval auxiliaries or other ships owned or operated by a State and used, for the time being, only on government non-commercial service.

The Directive requires a further element for the above-mentioned conduct to be criminalised, that is, it should cause deterioration in the quality of water.[147] It follows that, if ship-source discharges of polluting substances do not cause such deterioration, Member States are free not to punish these 'minor cases'[148] with criminal sanctions.[149] However, when similar minor cases are repeated, and therefore result in deterioration in the quality of water not individually but in conjunction, this exception does not apply and they should be treated as criminal offences.[150]

Second, also the Ship-Source Pollution Directive obliges the Member States to criminalise inchoate offences (incitement and aiding and abetting)[151] but is silent on the criminalisation of the attempt. Third, it requires penalties for natural persons to be effective, proportionate, dissuasive, and of criminal nature;[152] being it a legal instrument adopted before the entry into force of the Treaty of Lisbon and in the framework of the then first pillar, the Directive does not lay down any further rule on penalty threshold. Fourth, the Ship-Source Pollution Directive, after emphasising that 'frequently ship-source pollution offences are committed in the interest of legal persons or for their benefit',[153] regulates the liability of legal persons in a very similar way to the Environmental Crime Directive, since it: i) mentions that the crime connected with the ship-source discharges of polluting substances should be committed for the benefit of the

---

Directive (Pozdnakova (n 143) 218; cfr Annex I of MARPOL 73/78, Regulation 11; Annex II of MARPOL 73/78, Regulation 6; Annex VI of MARPOL 73/78, Regulation 3).

147 Recital 9 of the Ship-Source Pollution Directive. Cf Article 5a(2) of Directive 2005/35/EC, as amended by the Ship-Source Pollution Directive. See more in Pereira, *Environmental Criminal Liability* (n 3) 241–242.
148 Article 5a(2) of Directive 2005/35/EC, as amended by the Ship-Source Pollution Directive.
149 Further exceptions to the criminalisation obligations set out in the Directive can be found in Article 5 of Directive 2005/35/EC, as amended by the Ship-Source Pollution Directive (see also Pereira, *Environmental Criminal Liability* (n 3) 247–248; Mitsilegas, Fitzmaurice and Fasoli (n 37) 280–281). This is a further example of the complex drafting of EU environmental criminal law instruments, as this provision refers back to some Annexes to MARPOL, which set out the conditions that, if met, do not require Member States to criminalise the ship-source discharges of polluting substances.
150 Article 5a(3) of Directive 2005/35/EC, as amended by the Ship-Source Pollution Directive.
151 Article 5b of Directive 2005/35/EC, as amended by the Ship-Source Pollution Directive.
152 Article 8a of Directive 2005/35/EC, as amended by the Ship-Source Pollution Directive.
153 Recital 6 of the Ship-Source Pollution Directive.

legal persons; ii) makes a distinction between the cases where the crime is perpetrated by persons who have a leading position and those who do not have such position;[154] iii) excludes from the scope of corporate liability the States, public bodies in the exercise of State authority, and public international organisations;[155] and iv) does not formally require the penalties for the legal persons to be of criminal nature.[156] Finally, the Ship-Source Pollution Directive shares the same silences of the Environmental Crime Directive, as it does not include any rule on jurisdiction[157] and statutes of limitation.

In sum, many of the observations and concerns that have been discussed above with respect to the Environmental Crime Directive are also valid vis-à-vis the Ship-Source Pollution Directive, which is drafted in a very similar way. In this context, it is instead worth looking more closely at the *Intertanko* judgment where, as mentioned, the Court of Justice interpreted the notion of 'serious negligence' and examined the relations between Community/EU law and international law in the field of ship-source pollution.[158]

5.2 The Intertanko *Case and the Autonomy of the Union Legal Order Vis-à-vis International Law*

In *Intertanko*, the Court of Justice was faced with a preliminary reference from the High Court of England and Wales concerning the validity of the liability provisions of Directive 2005/35/EC.[159] As illustrated above, the Directive requires the Member States to adopt national legislation introducing extensive liability for ship-source pollution, including extending the *ratione personae* scope of those liable for pollution and extending the criteria for liability, including liability for serious negligence. The adoption of the parallel third pillar Framework Decision on criminal sanctions for ship-source pollution (later

---

154 Article 8b of Directive 2005/35/EC, as amended by the Ship-Source Pollution Directive.
155 Article 2(5) of Directive 2005/35/EC, as amended by the Ship-Source Pollution Directive.
156 Article 8c of Directive 2005/35/EC, as amended by the Ship-Source Pollution Directive.
157 The only reference to jurisdictional issues can be found in Recital 12 of the Ship-Source Pollution Directive, according to which '[j]urisdiction with regard to criminal offences should be established in accordance with the national law of Member States and in accordance with their obligations under international law'. It is evident that this Recital has little added value in practice, as it merely refers to existing or future national or international rules without setting out any harmonised provision on the matter. Jurisdiction in case of ship-source pollution, and problems thereof, are extensively analysed by Pozdnakova (n 143) especially 236ff (with regard to jurisdiction in the EU).
158 The issue of 'serious negligence' is discussed in section 4.1 above, while the next section focuses on the part of the Court's ruling on the relationship between Community law and international law.
159 The following remarks draw upon Mitsilegas, Fitzmaurice and Fasoli (n 37) 288ff.

annulled by the Court of Justice) triggered a sharp reaction from the shipping industry and Member States with major shipping economic interests: namely Cyprus, Greece and Malta. The latter were outvoted in the adoption of Directive 2005/35/EC, which, unlike its third pillar counterpart, was adopted under qualified majority voting in the Council.[160]

In light of the perceived challenges to its interests, the shipping industry took a case to the High Court challenging the validity of Directive 2005/35/EC, prior to the adoption of domestic implementing law in the United Kingdom.[161] The arguments put to the High Court centred on the incompatibility between Community law and international law of the sea under the MARPOL 73/78 Convention and UNCLOS.[162] It was argued in particular that it was unlawful for the Community to legislate independently of MARPOL for third country vessels on the high seas or in the Exclusive Economic Zone and that it was unlawful for the European Community to legislate in relation to activities in the territorial sea otherwise than in accordance with MARPOL. It was also argued that, under UNCLOS, passage affected by negligent or serious negligent pollution remained lawful and that any attempt to lower this legality threshold would amount to an unlawful interference with the right of innocent passage.[163] The High Court decided to refer these questions to the Court of Justice[164] where the applicants (representing a variety of shipping interests) and the Greek, Cypriot and Maltese Governments submitted that Articles 4 and 5 of Directive 2005/35/EC did not comply with international law in particular by establishing a stricter liability regime for accidental discharges than that laid down in MARPOL.[165]

In addressing these questions, the Court was called primarily to assess the compatibility of Community law with international law on pollution at sea. The Court reiterated the principle of primacy of international agreements concluded by the Community over secondary Community legislation[166] and

---

160 Greece and Malta voted against the text of the Directive and Cyprus abstained (see 'Council adopts new measures on the prevention of ship source pollution' Council doc 11138/05 (Presse 188), 12 July 2005).
161 S Boelaert-Suominen 'The European Community, the European Court of Justice and the Law of the Sea' (2008) 23 *The International Journal of Marine and Coastal Law* 643, 702.
162 On MARPOL, see chapter 4 of this book.
163 R Barnes and M Happold 'Current Legal Developments. United Kingdom' (2007) 22 *The International Journal of Marine and Coastal Law* 331.
164 Case C-308/06 *Intertanko* (n 66), para 29. For a commentary on this decision see, for instance, Pozdnakova (n 143) 217ff.
165 Case C-308/06 *Intertanko* (n 66), para 37.
166 ibid, para 42.

acknowledged that the validity of a measure of secondary Community legislation may be affected by the fact that it is incompatible with such rules of international law.[167] The review of the validity of Community law in this context takes place under two conditions: that the Community is bound by the international agreements in question;[168] and that review is not precluded by the nature and the broad logic of the international agreement and that the latter's provisions appear, as regards their content, to be unconditional and sufficiently precise.[169] The Court applied this two-fold test at two levels: to assess the validity of the ship-source pollution Directive in the light of MARPOL; and to assess the validity of the Directive in the light of UNCLOS. In both cases, but via a different reasoning in each case, the Court shielded the 2005 Directive on ship-source pollution from a review in the light of international law.

As regards the assessment of the Directive's validity in the light of MARPOL, the Court stated from the outset that the Community is not a party to that Convention.[170] It added that it does not appear that the Community has assumed, under TEC, the powers previously exercised by the Member States in the field to which MARPOL applies, nor that, consequently, its provisions have the effect of binding the Community.[171] The Court distinguished MARPOL from the GATT (General Agreement on Tariffs and Trade) Convention within the framework of which the Community progressively assumed powers previously exercised by the Member States, with the consequence that it became bound by the obligations flowing from that agreement and found that the GATT case law could not be applied to MARPOL.[172] The fact that all the Member States of the Community are parties to MARPOL does not change this finding as, in the absence of a full transfer of the powers previously exercised by the Member States to the Community, the latter cannot, simply because all those States are parties to MARPOL, be bound by the rules set out therein, which it has not itself approved.[173] The assessment of whether the validity of Directive 2005/35/EC can be evaluated in the light of MARPOL thus fell at the very first hurdle, namely to establish whether the Community is bound by the international convention in question. Not even the acknowledgement by the Court of the

---

167 ibid, para 43.
168 ibid, para 44.
169 ibid, para 45, where the Court referred to its *IATA* ruling (Case C-344/04 *IATA* and *ELFAA*, EU:C:2006:10).
170 Case C-308/06 *Intertanko* (n 66), para 47.
171 ibid, para 48.
172 ibid.
173 ibid, para 49.

contested fact that the Directive has the objective of incorporating certain rules set out in that Convention into Community law was deemed sufficient to allow such review.[174]

The Court did further examine whether the Directive could be reviewed in the light of rules of customary international law, but found that in the specific case in question the relevant MARPOL provisions did not codify such rules.[175] Therefore, the Court stated unequivocally that the validity of Directive 2005/35/EC could not be assessed in the light of MARPOL, even though the latter binds the Member States.[176] This is a far-reaching conclusion, as it creates a fundamental tension between Member States' obligations under international law and their duties under Community law.[177] In declining to review the validity of the Directive in the light of that Convention, the Court has effectively allowed, under certain conditions, Member States to disregard their international law obligations when legislating at EU level.

The Court's assessment of whether it could review the validity of the 2005 Directive on ship-source in the light of UNCLOS clearly passed the first hurdle of the two-fold test, namely establishing that the Convention is binding upon the Community–with the Court stressing again that its provisions form an integral part of the Community legal order.[178] The Court then went on to examine whether the nature and the broad logic of UNCLOS, as disclosed in particular by its aim, preamble and terms, preclude examination

---

174   ibid, para 50. The Preamble to the Directive recognises the need to harmonise the implementation of MARPOL at Community level (Recital 3). The text of the Directive is however less clear–in accordance with Article 1(1), its purpose is 'to incorporate international standards for ship-source pollution into Community law *and* to ensure that persons responsible for discharges are subject to adequate penalties' (emphasis added). It is not clear from Article 1(1) whether the introduction of provisions on liability for ship-source pollution in the Directive is a separate objective from the incorporation of international standards–the use of the cumulative 'and' indicates that these are separate objectives. For a view in favour of the purpose of the Directive being to implement international law see Boelaert-Suominen (n 161) 701–702 (noting also the cross-references to MARPOL and UNCLOS in the text of the Directive and its annex). For a different view, see P Eeckhout, who points out that it has been unclear during negotiations whether the purpose of the Directive was to implement international standards (see P Eeckhout, 'Case C-308/06, *The Queen on the application of Intertanko and others v Secretary of State for Transport*, judgment of the Court of Justice (Grand Chamber) of 3 June 2008' (2009) 46 *Common Market Law Review* 2041, 2043).

175   Case C-308/06 *Intertanko* (n 66), para 51.
176   ibid, para 52.
177   On this point, see also Eeckhout (n 174) 2052.
178   Case C-308/06 *Intertanko* (n 66), para 53, referring to Case C-459/03 *Commission v Ireland*, EU:C:2006:345 (the *Mox Plant* case).

of the validity of Community measures in the light of its provisions.[179] In its assessment, the Court distinguished between the effects of UNCLOS on States and its effects on individuals. It found that UNCLOS' main objective is to codify, clarify and develop the rules of general international law relating to the peaceful cooperation of the international community when exploring, using and exploiting marine areas[180] and concluded that, for the areas where it is applicable, UNCLOS seeks to strike a fair balance between the interests of States as coastal States and the interests of States as flag States, which may conflict.[181] On the contrary, individuals are in principle not granted independent rights and freedoms by virtue of UNCLOS.[182] In stark contrast with the Opinion of Advocate General Kokott,[183] the Court found that UNCLOS does not establish rules intended to apply directly and immediately to individuals and to confer upon them rights or freedoms capable of being relied upon against States.[184] It therefore follows, according to the Court, that the nature and broad logic of UNCLOS prevent the Court from being able to assess the validity of a Community measure in the light of that Convention.[185] Therefore, the review of the validity of the 2005 Directive on ship-source pollution in the light of UNCLOS failed the second hurdle of the Court's reviewability test.

The Court's reasoning with regard to the reviewability of Community law in the light of international law reflects a traditional view of public international law concerning primarily the regulation of relations between States. This approach, which reflects some of the arguments in the more recent *Kadi* litigation,[186] has led like-minded commentators to endorse the Court's ruling in *Intertanko*.[187] In this context, it should be noted that the Court in *Intertanko* did not follow – at least procedurally – a purely international law approach, in that it employed a Community law methodology focusing on the individual to ascertain whether Community law could be reviewed in the light of international law. However, the outcome of this approach has been criticised from a Community law perspective on two main grounds: on the ground that it has

---

179 Case C-308/06 *Intertanko* (n 66), para 54.
180 ibid, para 55.
181 ibid, para 58.
182 ibid, paras 59 and 60–63.
183 See ibid, paras 49ff.
184 ibid, para 64.
185 ibid, para 65.
186 Joined Cases C-584/10 P, C-593/10 P and C-595/10 P *European Commission v Kadi*, EU:C:2013:518.
187 See in particular Denza (n 66) 875.

departed from earlier external relations case law in reintroducing the test of whether an international agreement has an effect on the individual for it to form the basis of review of secondary Community law;[188] and on the ground that the finding that UNCLOS does not affect directly individuals, but regulates merely inter-state relations, is unpersuasive.[189] While the UNCLOS pollution provisions differ from the Security Council norms under litigation in *Kadi* in that they constitute measures of general application and not measures addressed specifically to individuals, their impact on the rights of the individual cannot be underestimated. This was in particular the case in the dispute in question, which concerned the liability of individuals for ship-source pollution.

While criticised as being at odds with its earlier formulation of Community external relations law, the Court's ruling in *Intertanko* can be better understood if read in the context of parallel *internal* constitutional developments in the Community. *Intertanko* has not been the only case where the Court had to deal with the imposition at Community level of liability for ship-source pollution. Some months earlier, the Court had issued the above-mentioned judgment in the *Ship-Source Pollution* case,[190] where it clarified its earlier, seminal ruling in the *Environmental Crime* case.[191] Indicative of the high political importance and sensitivity of the issue of Community criminal law competence has been that no less than 20 Member States intervened in the ship-source pollution competence litigation to argue against first pillar Community competence. In the *Ship-Source Pollution* case, the Court however confirmed Community competence in the field, albeit in narrow terms and without entirely clarifying the extent of such competence. In this light, it would have been unlikely for the Court to be willing to reopen the highly politicised debate on the criminalisation of ship-source pollution in *Intertanko* by reviewing the content of the Directive in the light of international law.[192]

---

188 Boelaert-Suominen notes that by ruling that UNCLOS is not directly effective as it confers no rights or obligations directly on *individuals*, the Court seems to have put stricter conditions for the 'invocability' of international (environmental) agreements than in earlier case law (Boelaert-Suominen (n 161) 707). See also M Mendez 'The Legal Effect of Community Agreements: Maximalist Treaty Enforcement and Judicial Avoidance Techniques' (2010) 21 *European Journal of International Law* 83.
189 See Eeckhout (n 174) 2056.
190 Case C-440/05 *Commission v Council* (n 43).
191 Case C-176/03 *Commission v Council* (n 34). See section 3 above.
192 As Eeckhout notes, the Court 'may not have been convinced that it was possible to interpret the Directive in conformity with Marpol 73/78 and with UNCLOS' (Eeckhout (n 174) 2056).

While in the *Ship-Source Pollution* case the Court affirmed internally the autonomy of the Community legal order with regard to the Union legal order, in *Intertanko* the Court did the same externally, by affirming the autonomy of the Community legal order with regard to international law. The Court thus boosted the autonomy of both the constitutional and the political choices on the criminalisation of ship-source pollution by the Community.[193] The affirmation of internal autonomy in criminal matters had however significant implications for the treatment of criminal law (and its implications for the individual) by Community law: rather than it being viewed as a special case, or a specific area of Community action, the Court viewed criminal law as a means to an end, the end being the effective achievement of Community objectives. The Court thus prioritised broader constitutional considerations of competence in relation to an examination of the impact of Community law criminalisation on the individual. A similar logic permeates the Court's ruling in *Intertanko*. Whereas in *Kadi* the Court's assertion of the autonomy of the Community legal order was linked to the need to take into account the centrality of the position of the individual in such legal order and the protection of fundamental rights, in *Intertanko* the assertion of the autonomy of Community law may have the opposite effect by extending the scope of criminalisation and thus aggravating the position of the individual at EU level.

6 Environmental Offences and the Links with Organised Crime and Money Laundering

There is strong evidence that organised crime groups are increasingly involved in some forms of environmental crime,[194] especially illegal trafficking in waste and protected species.[195] The GENVAL final report encourages the Member

---

193 This is in particular the case if one considers that the scope of both MARPOL and UNCLOS is much broader than the specific issue of liability for ship-source pollution at stake in the proceedings and that their adoption (and ratification by the Community/EU and/or its Member States) predated the development of the specific Community response to pollution at sea triggered by a major incident taking place in European waters.

194 See, most recently, DP van Uhm and RCC Nijman, 'The Convergence of Environmental Crime with Other Serious Crimes: Subtypes within the Environmental Crime Continuum' [2020] *European Journal of Criminology* 1.

195 See, for instance, M Luna and W Veening, 'EFFACE Policy Brief 2: Organised Environmental Crime' (2014); Report of the 'European action against the involvement of Organized Crime and Mafia-related crime in Waste Trafficking, in cooperation with Europol, owing to the emergence of the trans-national phenomenon' Council doc 16605/14, 8 December 2014, 31ff; Giardi (n 123) *passim*; Rodopoulos (n 117) 165–182; GM Vagliasindi, 'Organised

States to 'consider environmental crime, and more specifically illegal shipment of waste ... as a part of economic crime frequently committed by organised crime groups, and to take into consideration its economic aspects and its financial implications for the natural environment and society'.[196] Similarly, the Council included the fight against organised crime groups involved in environmental crime (and especially wildlife and illicit waste trafficking) among the eight priorities for the fight against organised and serious international crime between 2018 and 2021.[197] Among the priorities for the period between 2022 and 2025, under 'Environmental Crime', the Council stated that this priority's aim is 'to disrupt criminal networks involved in all forms of environmental crime, with a specific focus on waste and wildlife trafficking, as well as on criminal networks and individual criminal entrepreneurs with a capability to infiltrate legal business structures at high level or to set up own companies in order to facilitate their crimes'.[198]

Environmental crime is appealing to criminal syndicates for its 'high profit-low risk' nature.[199] This expression could be found already in the 2004 'European Union Organised Crime Report' issued by Europol, where it was also stated that a little was known about the involvement of organised crime groups in this 'non-traditional' area of crime.[200] Several studies point out that the magnitude, consequences, damages, and costs of (organised) environmental crime

---

Environmental Crime' in A Farmer, V Mitsilegas, M Faure et al, 'Evaluation of the Strengths, Weaknesses, Threats and Opportunities Associated with EU Efforts to Combat Environmental Crime'. Study in the framework of the EFFACE research project (2015) 87–104; L Elliott and WH Schaedla, 'Transnational Environmental Crime: Excavating the Complexities – An Introduction' in Elliott and Schaedla (eds) (n 55) 4ff; Gerstetter, Stefes, Farmer et al, 'Environmental Crime and the EU' (n 123) 40–41; P Crowe and P Lynch, 'Fly-Tipping: Organised Crime behind Large Rise' BBC News (13 February 2020) <www.bbc.com/news/uk-england-50660138> accessed 2 June 2021.

196 GENVAL final report (n 84) 16.
197 'Council conclusions on setting the EU's priorities for the fight against organised and serious international crime between 2018 and 2021 – Council conclusions (18 May 2017)' Council doc 9450/17, 19 May 2017. On these priorities and their impact on the activities of EU agencies, see more in chapter 7 of this book.
198 'Council conclusions setting the EU's priorities for the fight against serious and organised crime for EMPACT 2022–2025' Council doc 8665/21, 12 May 2021, 10.
199 See EnviCrimeNet, 'Report on Environmental Crime' (n 97) 7. See also, for instance, J Schneider, 'Endangered Species Markets. A Focus for Criminology?' in Natarajan (ed) (n 56) 208–209; C Gibbs, EF McGarrell and B Sullivan, 'Intelligence-led Policing and Transnational Environmental Crime: A Process Evaluation' (2015) 12 *European Journal of Criminology* 242, 243.
200 Europol, '2004 European Union Organised Crime Report' (2004) 17.

can hardly be determined in an accurate way,[201] as is the case for organised crime more in general.[202] However, the existing (tentative) data lead to the conclusion that environmental crime is a lucrative field for organised criminality, be it an Italian criminal syndicate or a loose criminal network.[203] The 2016 Assessment on environmental crime released by Interpol and the United Nations Environmental Programme (UNEP) reports that the annual losses for the illegal trade and dumping of hazardous waste range between 10 and 12 billion dollars, whereas those for illegal logging and trade are worth between 50.7 and 152 billion dollars.[204] According to the EU Action Plan against Wildlife Trafficking, launched by the Commission in February 2016, the price of rhino horn in the black market is believed to be higher than that of gold.[205]

Although the phenomenon of organised environmental crime is on the rise, as acknowledged most recently by the 'EU Strategy to tackle Organised Crime 2021–2025',[206] the Environmental Crime Directive and the Ship-Source Pollution Directive do not include any provision on organised crime. It has

---

201 See, for instance, A Illes, S Newman, E Watkins et al, 'Understanding the Damages of Environmental Crime. Review of the Availability of Data'. Study in the framework of the EFFACE research project (2014); Elliott and Schaedla, 'Transnational Environmental Crime' (n 55) 4; Gerstetter, Stefes, Farmer et al, 'Environmental Crime and the EU' (n 123) 12–19; GENVAL final report (n 84) 21–26.

202 J Finckenauer 'Organized Crime' in Tonry (ed) (n 97) 307–309; M Levi, M Innes, P Reuter et al, 'The Economic, Financial & Social Impacts of Organised Crime in the EU' (2013) Study for the European Parliament, especially 8–22; P Andreas, 'Illicit Globalisation Myths and Misconceptions' in V Mitsilegas, P Alldridge and L Cheliotis (eds), *Globalisation, Criminal Law and Criminal Justice. Theoretical, Comparative and Transnational Perspectives* (Hart 2015) 49–52.

203 In 2012, Klaus von Lampe, assessing the state of empirical research on transnational organised crime, argued that '[t]here seems to be a growing consensus among scholars that typically offender structures resemble "networks" rather than "organizations"' (K von Lampe, 'Transnational Organized Crime Challenges for Future Research' (2012) 58 *Crime, Law and Social Change* 179, 183). At the same time, trafficking in waste and toxic waste was identified as one of the five main activities of Italian organised crime groups (see Europol, 'Threat Assessment. Italian Organised Crime' (2013) 15).

204 C Nellemann, R Henriksen, A Kreilhuber et al (eds), 'The Rise of Environmental Crime – A Growing Threat To Natural Resources, Peace, Development And Security. A UNEP-INTERPOL Rapid Response Assessment' (United Nations Environment Programme and RHIPTO Rapid Response–Norwegian Center for Global Analyses 2016) 20.

205 'Commission Staff Working Document accompanying the Communication on the EU Action Plan against Wildlife Trafficking' SWD (2016), 26 February 2016, 7.

206 Commission, 'Communication from the Commission to the European Parliament, the Council, the European Economic and Social Committee and the Committee of the Regions on the EU Strategy to tackle Organised Crime 2021–2025' COM (2021) 170 final, 14 April 2021, 16.

therefore been argued that 'environmental criminal law is only integrated to a very small extent into organised crime legislation at the international, European and national level (with the exception of Italy)'.[207] As far as the international scenario is concerned, the most known piece of legislation on organised crime is the 2000 United Nations Convention on Transnational Organized Crime ('Palermo Convention' or UNTOC). The aim of the Convention is to promote cooperation to prevent and combat transnational organised crime more effectively (Article 1). To this end, it lays down some rules concerning inter alia mutual legal assistance (Article 18), joint investigations (Article 19), and special investigative techniques (Article 20).[208] The Preamble of the Convention mentions the 'illicit trafficking in endangered species of wild flora and fauna' as one of those crimes against which the tools provided for by the Convention can be used.

The Convention however applies only in cases of 'serious crimes', if the offence is transnational in nature and an organised criminal group is concerned (Article 3(1) UNTOC). If some forms of environmental crime can be transnational in their very essence, the problems in the application of the Convention concern the concept of 'serious crime', since the latter 'shall mean conduct constituting an offence punishable by a maximum deprivation of liberty of at least four years or a more serious penalty'.[209] For the purposes of the Convention, the notion of 'serious crime' is also recalled in the definition of 'organised criminal group', since the latter 'shall mean a structured group of three or more persons, existing for a period of time and acting in concert with the aim of committing one or more *serious crimes* or offences established in accordance with [the] Convention, in order to obtain, directly or indirectly, a financial or other material benefit'.[210]

As a consequence, if national legislation on environmental crime does not provide for high penalties, domestic judicial and police authorities cannot rely on the Palermo Convention to fight the phenomenon at issue.[211] Since this

---

207 Gerstetter, Stefes, Farmer et al, 'Environmental Crime and the EU' (n 123) 40. See also L Krämer, *EU Environmental Law* (7th edn, Sweet & Maxwell 2012) 413; Rodopoulos (n 117) 175ff.
208 On the Palermo Convention and its applicability to environmental crime, see JAE Vervaele, 'International Cooperation in the Investigation and Prosecution of Environmental Crime. Problems and Challenges for the Legislative and Judicial Authorities' (2016) 87 *Revue International de Droit Pénal – Protection of the Environment through Criminal Law* (ed by JL de La Cuesta et al) 249–250 and 253–256.
209 Article 2(b) of the Palermo Convention.
210 Article 2(a) of the Palermo Convention. Emphasis added.
211 Eurojust, 'Strategic Project on Environmental Crime. Report' (n 82) 93. On the limited applicability of the Palermo Convention to environmental crime, see A Cabrejo le

instrument has not been used frequently in practice,[212] some authors have floated the idea of a Protocol to the Palermo Convention on environmental crime to allow the application of the Convention even if the high thresholds provided for therein are not met.[213]

The EU took part in the negotiations for the drafting of the Convention and is a party to it.[214] On its basis, the 2008 Framework Decision on the fight against organised crime was adopted.[215] The Framework Decision provides for a sophisticated framework of criminalisation on participation in a criminal organisation,[216] but no specific reference to environmental crime can be found. The definition of 'criminal organisation' recalls that of the Palermo Convention, since it

> means a structured association, established over a period of time, of more than two persons acting in concert with a view to committing offences which are punishable by deprivation of liberty or a detention order of a maximum of at least four years or a more serious penalty, to obtain, directly or indirectly, a financial or other material benefit.[217]

Roux, T Reitano and M Shaw, 'Tightening the Net: Toward a Global Legal Framework on Transnational Organized Environmental Crime' (WWF-Global Initiative Against Transnational Organized Crime 2015) 30ff.

212 See Commission, 'Communication to the European Parliament, the Council, the European Economic and Social Committee and the Committee of the Regions. EU Action Plan Against Wildlife Trafficking' COM (2016) 87 final, 26 February 2016, 5–6. See also Elliott, 'Fighting Transnational Environmental Crime' (n 56) 95.

213 Cabrejo le Roux, Reitano and Shaw (n 211) 35.

214 On the EU's participation in the procedures that led to the adoption of the Palermo Convention, see V Mitsilegas, 'The European Union and the Global Governance of Crime' in Mitsilegas, Alldridge and Cheliotis (eds) (n 202) 157ff.

215 Council Framework Decision 2008/841/JHA of 24 October 2008 on the fight against organised crime [2008] OJ L300/42, which repealed the previous Joint Action of 21 December 1998 adopted by the Council on the basis of Article K.3 of the Treaty on European Union, on making it a criminal offence to participate in a criminal organisation in the Member States of the European Union (98/733/JHA) [1998] OJ L351/1. On the Joint Action and its relations with the Palermo Convention, see V Mitsilegas, 'Defining Organised Crime in the European Union: The Limits of European Criminal Law in an Area of "Freedom, Security and Justice"' (2001) 26 *European Law Review* 565. For a detailed overview of the EU's legal framework on organised crime, see S Hufnagel, 'Organized Crime' in Mitsilegas, Bergström and Konstadinides (eds) (n 37) 355–375.

216 V Mitsilegas, 'The Council Framework Decision on the Fight against Organised Crime: What Can Be Done to Strengthen EU Legislation in the Field?'. Note for the European Parliament (2011) 5 <www.europarl.europa.eu/document/activities/cont/201206/20120627ATT47779/20120627ATT47779EN.pdf> accessed 2 June 2021.

217 Article 1(1) of Framework Decision 2008/841/JHA.

The Framework Decision therefore leaves a wide margin of discretion to the Member States, since the elements of a criminal organisation are defined broadly and with flexible criteria.[218] According to some authors, this choice is not necessarily blameworthy, since 'legal diversity can in fact promote the fight against cross-border organized crime, providing practitioners with a high level of flexibility in choosing strategies and jurisdictions to carry out certain measures (e.g. wiretapping, surveillance, arrest)'.[219] The impact of this instrument on national legislation has however been very limited, as the Commission acknowledged in the 2016 Report on the implementation of the Framework Decision.[220]

This Report also revealed a quite patchy implementation in the Member States as far as the predicate offences of the criminal organisation are concerned: at the time of the Report, only four Member States had implemented the provision of the Framework Decision on the minimum threshold of maximum penalty of four years, whereas others had chosen a lower threshold, others a higher one, some others had not indicated any threshold for the predicate offence so that every criminal offence could be covered.[221] Given the mild penalties provided on average for environmental crimes, the choice of decoupling the application of the legislation on organised crime from the threshold of the penalties provided for predicate offences would allow a better fight against organised environmental crime, at least on paper.

The Report from the Commission on the implementation of the Framework Decision on organised crime was based on information provided by the Member States and on a detailed external study, which demonstrated that, when national authorities deal with organised crime, they are likely to be better equipped to curb criminal phenomena than when they investigate other

---

218 Mitsilegas, 'The Council Framework Decision' (n 216) 5–6. See also M Fichera, 'Organised Crime: Development and Challenges for an Enlarged European Union' in C Eckes and T Konstadinides (eds), *Crime within the Area of Freedom, Security and Justice. A European Public Order* (Cambridge University Press 2011) 173ff; F Calderoni, 'A Definition that Does Not Work: The Impact of the EU Framework Decision on the Fight against Organized Crime' (2012) 49 *Common Market Law Review* 1365.

219 Hufnagel, 'Organized Crime' (n 215) 367. For further remarks on the inherent ambiguity of the notion of 'organised crime' under both a criminological and a legal perspective, see also Finckenauer (n 202) 304–307; A Goldsmith, 'Organized Crime' in M Marmo and N Chazal, *Transnational Crime & Criminal Justice* (SAGE 2016) 117–118.

220 Commission, 'Report to the European Parliament and the Council based on Article 10 of Council Framework Decision 2008/841/JHA of 24 October 2008 on the fight against organised crime' COM (2016) 448 final, 7 July 2016, 10. See also Calderoni (n 218) 1385–1390.

221 Commission, 'Report to the European Parliament and the Council based on Article 10 of Council Framework Decision 2008/841/JHA' (previous n) 4–5.

crimes (including environmental crime).²²² When they investigate organised crime, it is indeed common for national authorities to be able to rely on special and effective investigative tools and impose high penalties or accessory penalties such as confiscation. The study also showed that the legal provisions on the participation in a criminal organisation are deemed to be very useful in case of organised crime groups involved in illegal trafficking, be it of drugs or human beings. In general, the study concluded that 'the more "intellectual" the crime was, the more difficult it was to prove participation and therefore such offences became less useful' and that 'the usefulness was highest for offences whose commission in practice required some *sort of criminal organisation behind it*'.²²³ Even though neither the Report nor the study took into account organised environmental crime, it can be argued that the application of the provisions on organised crime can be useful to combat environmental crimes in their organised dimension – therefore especially in cases of illegal trafficking (either of waste or of protected species).²²⁴

Apart from criminalising the participation in a criminal organisation as such, the EU legislator also requires the Member States to treat this conduct as an *aggravating circumstance* for a series of other offences harmonised at the EU level. For instance, Member States shall take the necessary measures to ensure that when offences such as attacks against information systems,²²⁵ trafficking in human beings,²²⁶ and fraud affecting the Union's financial

---

222 A Di Nicola, P Gounev, M Levi et al, 'Study on Paving the Way for Future Policy Initiatives in the Field of Fight against Organised Crime: The Effectiveness of Specific Criminal Law Measures Targeting Organised Crime. Final Report' (Rand 2015) 207 <www.rand.org/randeuropa/research/projects/organised-crime.html> accessed 2 June 2021. See also ibid 223–337.

223 ibid 207–208. Emphasis added.

224 In the literature, it has likewise been argued that 'crimes against the environment are rarely prosecuted or punished *as such*. Even though certain environmental offences can *in theory* be subject to severe punishment, this occurs *in practice* only when–and almost only *because*–they are part of an organised crime scheme and/or they affect human health. Serious environmental offences are thus prosecuted as organised crimes or as crimes against life and individual safety, and the impact they have on the environment is seldom the focus of prosecution' (Perilongo and Corn (n 48) 253; emphasis in the original).

225 Article 9(4)(a) of Directive 2013/40/EU of the European Parliament and of the Council of 12 August 2013 on attacks against information systems and replacing Council Framework Decision 2005/222/JHA [2013] OJ L218/8.

226 Article 4(2)(b) of Directive 2011/36/EU of the European Parliament and of the Council on preventing and combating trafficking in human beings and protecting its victims, and replacing Council Framework Decision 2002/629/JHA [2011] OJ L101/1.

interests[227] are committed within a criminal organisation, this shall be considered to be an aggravating circumstance. The use of participation in a criminal organisation as an aggravating circumstance reflects a view of the value of participation not as a 'self-standing' criminal offence, but rather as conduct that may be taken into account when other offences are prosecuted. The fact that the Environmental Crime Directive does not provide for such an aggravating circumstance is therefore a missed opportunity to strengthen the criminal dimension of the protection of the environment.[228] On the contrary, the involvement of organised crime groups in cases of water pollution seems quite limited; hence, the silence of the Ship-Source Pollution Directive on the matter is less surprising.

Since organised crime groups show a growing interest in environmental crime, which has turned out to be very lucrative, it would be appropriate for the EU to also adopt effective legislation to 'follow the money' coming from these crimes. As far as money laundering linked to wildlife trafficking is concerned, still in 2018 the Commission signalled that '[l]ittle progress has been reported in investigations'[229] into this crime. Furthermore, until the end of the same year, the EU legal framework was quite unsatisfactory in that regard, since an express link between environmental criminal law and anti-money laundering law was missing.[230] The fact that environmental crime was not included among the predicate offences of money laundering in the fourth anti-money laundering (AML) Directive, as amended by the fifth AML Directive,[231] could

---

227 Article 8 of the PIF Directive.
228 See also Vagliasindi, 'The EU Environmental Crime Directive' (n 49) 50–51.
229 Commission, 'Report to the Council and the European Parliament. Progress report on the implementation of the EU Action Plan against Wildlife Trafficking' COM (2018) 711 final, 24 October 2018, 4.
230 V Mitsilegas, 'Contribution to Conclusions and Recommendations on Environmental Crime: Harmonisation of Substantive Environmental Criminal Law at EU level'. Study in the framework of the EFFACE research project (Queen Mary University of London 2016) 3. See also J Saunders and J Hein, 'EUTS, CITES and Money Laundering: A Case Study on the Challenges to Coordinated Enforcement in Tackling Illegal Logging'. A study for the EFFACE project (Chatham House 2015).
231 cf Article 3(4) of Directive (EU) 2015/849 of the European Parliament and of the Council of 20 May 2015 on the prevention of the use of the financial system for the purposes of money laundering or terrorist financing [2015] OJ L141/73 ('fourth AML Directive'). On this Directive, see V Mitsilegas and N Vavoula, 'The Evolving EU Anti-Money Laundering Regime. Challenges for Fundamental Rights and the Rule of Law' (2016) 23 *Maastricht Journal of European and Comparative Law* 261. The Directive was amended by Directive (EU) 2018/843 of the European Parliament and of the Council of 30 May 2018 amending Directive (EU) 2015/849 on the prevention of the use of the financial system for the purposes of money laundering or terrorist financing [2018] OJ L156/43 ('fifth AML Directive').

have hindered the effectiveness of environmental criminal law both within the EU and at the level of law enforcement co-operation with third states, as it was not always clear that proceeds from environmental offences need to be considered as proceeds of crime for the purposes of AML policies.[232]

The situation partially improved with the adoption in 2018 of the Directive on combating money laundering by criminal law,[233] which aims to harmonise national criminal legislation on money laundering and finally lists, among predicate offences, environmental crime, without any further requirement concerning penalty thresholds.[234] The Directive specifies that environmental crime 'includes' – and therefore is not limited to – the offences set out in the Environmental Crime Directive and the Ship-Source Pollution Directive. The expectation is that the explicit inclusion of environmental crime in the list of money laundering predicate offences can overcome differences in national legal approaches to the criminalisation of environmental crime and focus the mind of investigative and prosecutorial authorities on pursuing the proceeds of environmental crime.[235] Furthermore, EU legislation seems now aligned with the most known international (soft) law instrument in the field, namely the 40 FATF (Financial Action Task Force) Recommendations, which provide that environmental crime should be included among the predicate offences of money laundering.[236]

---

[232] As the Commission noted in its recent evaluation of the Environmental Crime Directive, '[c]ontrary to the recommendations of the Financial Action Task Force of the Organisation for Economic Co-Operation and Development, environmental crime is not expressly mentioned as "criminal activity" in Article 3(4) of the [fifth] Anti-money laundering Directive, and is therefore only covered if punishable by a minimum prison sentence of more than 6 months or a maximum of more than 1 year, depending on the case (see Article 3(4)(f) of the [fifth] Anti-money Laundering Directive). Not all Member States meet this threshold' (Commission, 'Commission Staff Working Document Evaluation of the Directive 2008/99/EC' (n 78) 67).

[233] Directive (EU) 2018/1673 of the European Parliament and of the Council of 23 October 2018 on combating money laundering by criminal law [2018] OJ 284/22.

[234] Article 2(1)(l) of Directive (EU) 2018/1673. It ought to be noted, however, that this Directive does not concern, like the other AML Directives, the preventive side of the fight against money laundering, but only the repressive one (ie harmonisation of definitions of, and penalties for, criminal offences).

[235] Mitsilegas, 'Contribution to Conclusions and Recommendations on Environmental Crime' (n 230) 7.

[236] In accordance with Recommendation No 3, 'Countries should apply the crime of money laundering to all serious offences, with a view to including the widest range of predicate offences'. Interpretative Note to Recommendation 3 explains that 'Whichever approach is adopted, each country should, at a minimum, include a range of offences within each of the designated categories of offences', and the General Glossary in turn clarifies that environmental crime falls within the notion of 'designated categories of offences'

Finally, the fight against the 'economic side' of environmental crime can be truly successful if the proceeds deriving from these illegal activities are confiscated, so that (environmental) 'crime does not pay'.[237] However, there are some gaps in the EU legal framework in that respect as well. Environmental crime is not mentioned in Directive 2014/42/EU, which establishes minimum rules on the freezing of property with a view to possible subsequent confiscation and on the confiscation of property in criminal matters.[238] Quite surprisingly, the list of offences already harmonised at the EU level to which the Directive applies does not contain any reference either to the Environmental Crime Directive or to the Ship-Source Pollution Directive, yet it mentions the offences covered by the 2008 Framework Decision on organised crime. This is considered to be 'practically unable to indirectly cover organised environmental crime',[239] not least because – as explained above – the mild choices of criminalisation adopted by the Member States do not always allow to consider environmental crime as falling within the broader concept of organised crime.

7 The Treaty of Lisbon and the Future of EU Environmental Criminal Law

In the wake of enhanced attention towards problems linked with global warming and climate change, the current European Commission is strongly committed to the protection of the environment. In December 2019, the Commission presided by Ursula von der Leyen, a few days after taking office, tabled a Communication on the 'European Green Deal', which has the ambitious goal of transforming the EU into 'a fair and prosperous society, with a modern, resource-efficient and competitive economy where there are no net emissions of greenhouse gases in 2050 and where economic growth is decoupled from

---

(FATF, 'International Standards on Combating Money Laundering and the Financing of Terrorism & Proliferation. The FATF Recommendations' (2012–2019) 10, 32, and 116).

237 Commission, 'Communication to the European Parliament and the Council. Proceeds of organized crime. Ensuring that "crime does not pay"' COM (2008) 766 final, 20 November 2008.

238 Article 1 of Directive 2014/42/EU of the European Parliament and of the Council of 3 April 2014 on the freezing and confiscation of instrumentalities and proceeds of crime in the European Union [2014] OJ L127/39. See also Commission, 'Commission Staff Working Document Evaluation of the Directive 2008/99/EC' (n 78) 71.

239 GM Vagliasindi, 'Contribution to Conclusions and Recommendations on Environmental Crime: Organised Environmental Crime'. Study in the framework of the EFFACE research project (University of Catania 2016) 5.

resource use'.[240] Although this comprehensive strategy goes far beyond the field of criminal justice and involves many EU policies, there is also a reference to environmental crime, since the Commission 'will promote action by the EU, its Member States and the international community to step up efforts against environmental crime'.[241] Furthermore, the Commission has conducted an assessment of the Environmental Crime Directive, focusing on waste and wildlife crime;[242] the results of this assessment were published in October 2020 and have been repeatedly mentioned throughout this chapter.[243] By the same token, the Council, as mentioned, decided to devote the eight round of mutual evaluation to the implementation of the Environmental Crime Directive.[244] The Finnish Presidency of the Council (second half of 2019) issued a report in October 2019 on the state of environmental criminal law in the European Union.[245] More than ten years after the adoption of the Environmental Crime and Ship-Source Pollution Directives, environmental crime is again in the limelight.

Due to the weaknesses of EU environmental criminal law, which have been examined in the previous sections, the European Commission plans to table a proposal to revise the Environmental Crime Directive by the end of 2021. The potential legal basis for this instrument is discussed in the next section, while section 7.2 presents a few issues that the revised directive should address to ensure that an up-to-date criminal legislation is in place at the EU level to effectively fight environmental crime.

---

240 Commission, 'The European Green Deal' COM (2019) 640 final, 11 December 2019.
241 ibid 23.
242 Commission, 'Evaluation Roadmap. Evaluation of the Environmental Crime Directive' (2019) <https://ec.europa.eu/environment/legal/crime/legis_en.htm> accessed 2 June 2021. Already in 2015, the Commission, highlighting the significant risks connected with environmental crime, claimed it would 'consider the need to strengthening compliance monitoring and enforcement, for instance by increasing training for enforcement staff, support for relevant networks of professionals, and by further approximating criminal sanctions throughout the EU' (Commission, 'The European Agenda on Security' COM (2015) 185 final, 28 April 2015, 18).
243 Commission, 'Commission Staff Working Document Evaluation of the Directive 2008/99/EC' (n 78).
244 See section 4.1 above.
245 Council Presidency, 'EU environmental criminal law – Presidency report' Council doc 12801/19, 4 October 2019. In other previous documents, the Council had called attention to environmental crime and the need to tackle it effectively at the EU level. See, for instance, 'Council Conclusions on countering environmental crime – Council conclusions (8 December 2016)' Council doc 15412/16, 12 December 2016.

7.1 Article 83 TFEU and Environmental Crime

The EU constitutional framework has changed compared to that in which the two existing Directives were adopted. Among the most relevant innovations of the Treaty of Lisbon, those enshrined in Article 83 TFEU need to be mentioned in this context. Article 83 TFEU allows the European Parliament and the Council to adopt directives providing for minimum rules concerning the definition of criminal offences and sanctions thereof. Since the choice of what to punish, and how to punish, is done at the EU level by means of a directive, which then needs to be implemented at the national level, some commentators have referred to such a competence as an 'integrated' one.[246] Others prefer to emphasise the fact that the EU is still not competent to lay down penal legislation *directly applicable* in the Member States; hence, they speak of an 'indirect criminal competence' of the EU in the aftermath of the Treaty of Lisbon.[247]

Article 83 TFEU offers two different options to the EU legislator. Article 83(1) TFEU confers upon the Union the competence to establish, by means of directives, 'minimum rules concerning the definition of criminal offences and sanctions in the areas of particularly serious crime with a cross-border dimension resulting from the nature or impact of such offences or from a special need to combat them on a common basis'.[248] Article 83(1) TFEU reflects what could be called the 'securitised criminalisation approach'[249] in determining EU competence in substantive criminal law. In other words, EU competence to criminalise is justified as necessary to combat specified areas of criminality the majority of which have been elevated after the Cold War by the international community and the Union as global security threats.

Such areas are enumerated exhaustively in Article 83(1) TFEU, and among them organised crime is included. Nevertheless, although in 2011 the European Parliament urged the Commission to submit a proposal for a directive on organised crime, acknowledging the failure of the 2008 Framework Decision in harmonising national legislation,[250] such a proposal has not yet been tabled. In the 'EU Strategy to tackle Organised Crime 2021–2025', the Commission only

---

246 R Sicurella, '«Prove Tecniche» per una Metodologia dell'Esercizio delle Nuove Competenze Concorrenti dell'Unione Europea in Materia Penale' in G Grasso, L Picotti and R Sicurella (eds), *L'Evoluzione del Diritto Penale nei Settori d'Interesse Europeo* (Giuffrè 2011) 6.
247 See, for instance, G Grasso, 'Il Trattato di Lisbona e le Nuove Competenze Penali dell'Unione Europea' in *Studi in onore di Mario Romano* (Jovene 2011) 2326.
248 Article 83(1) TFEU.
249 Mitsilegas, *EU Criminal Law after Lisbon* (n 15) 58.
250 European Parliament resolution of 25 October 2011 on organised crime in the European Union (2010/2309(INI)), para 7.

mentions that an external study was launched to assess 'whether the 2008 Council Framework Decision on Organised Crime is still fit for purpose'.[251]

Whereas it mentions organised crime, as well as money laundering, Article 83(1) TFEU does not include environmental crime. The Council may adopt – unanimously and after the consent of the Parliament – a decision identifying other areas of crime that meet the criteria mentioned in Article 83(1) TFEU, namely the cross-border dimension resulting from the nature or impact of the offences or from a special need to combat them on a common basis.[252] Similar criteria have led some commentators to argue that the justification for EU criminal law under Article 83(1) TFEU resides in its added-value function, drawing on a common capability to address the scale and nature of threats posed by transnational criminality.[253] In that regard, for instance, it can be easily argued that the trafficking of waste or endangered species has a cross-border dimension that would meet the legal basis requirements of Article 83(1) TFEU and comply with the principle of subsidiarity.

The applicability of Article 83(1) TFEU to areas of serious crime with a cross-border dimension resulting from the nature or impact of such offences or from a special need to combat them on a common basis must be read as conferring on the Union also the competence to define criminal offences and adopt criminal sanctions in areas of crime which have a cross-border dimension but which do not involve cross-border or transnational criminality as such. Examples of areas of crime with a cross-border dimension resulting from their nature or impact or need to combat on a common basis – but which may involve criminality conducted purely at national level – include terrorism and corruption. The same could be said with regard to some environmental offences, such as those cases of (national) pollution that can seriously affect the quality of (European or even global) air, water or soil. Similarly, serious cases of national wildlife trafficking could fall within this broad reading of Article 83(1) TFEU, especially when the number of specimens traded is considerable: in similar instances, wildlife trafficking can endanger ecosystems and biodiversity and could also facilitate the diffusion of diseases.[254]

---

251 Commission, 'EU Strategy to tackle Organised Crime 2021–2025' (n 206) 6.
252 See also Pereira, *Environmental Criminal Liability* (n 3) 202–203.
253 C Harding and JB Banach-Gutierrez, 'The Emergent EU Criminal Policy: Identifying the Species' (2012) 37 *European Law Review* 758.
254 EnviCrimeNet, 'Report on Environmental Crime' (n 97) 23. In an article on the World Bank's website concerning the risks of the recent Ebola virus disease, which is transmitted from animals to humans, it is stated that '[a]s wildlife is traded between hunters, middle marketers, and consumers, there are, quite literally, billions of opportunities for

In this way, the scope of Article 83(1) TFEU is broader than it appears at first sight.²⁵⁵

This broad scope of Article 83(1) TFEU is confirmed by the fact that EU competence is defined on the basis of *areas of crime*, rather than specific criminal offences. These areas of crime may correspond to a wide range of criminal offences. A clear example of the potential to overstretch EU criminal law competence under Article 83(1) TFEU involves the use of the concept of organised crime, which can also be used as a legal basis for harmonisation of a wide range of specific criminal offences and sanctions linked to the activities of a criminal organisation: this could be the case of (the most serious) environmental crimes, such as those forms of illicit trafficking that have proven to be very attractive to organised crime groups.²⁵⁶

More realistic possibilities for the EU to adopt harmonisation instruments concerning environmental crime are however rooted in Article 83(2) TFEU,²⁵⁷ which states that

> [i]f the approximation of criminal laws and regulations of the Member States proves essential to ensure the effective implementation of a Union policy in an area which has been subject to harmonisation measures, directives may establish minimum rules with regard to the definition of criminal offences and sanctions in the area concerned.²⁵⁸

Article 83(2) TFEU flows naturally from the Court of Justice's interpretation of the Union's (then the Community's) criminalisation competence under the first pillar in the above-mentioned *Environmental Crime* and the *Ship-Source Pollution* cases. Unlike the Court of Justice, the Treaty also provided the EU with the competence to harmonise criminal penalties.

---

disease transmission among wildlife, humans, and domestic animals each year' (T Bouley and S Thompson, 'Trafficking Wildlife and Transmitting Disease: Bold Threats in an Era of Ebola' [2014] <http://blogs.worldbank.org/voices/trafficking-wildlife-and-transmitting-disease-bold-threats-era-ebola> accessed 2 June 2021). On the opportunity to rely on Article 83(1) TFEU to strengthen the harmonisation of environmental criminal law in the EU, see Duțu and Duțu (n 82) 122–123.

255 Mitsilegas, *EU Criminal Law After Lisbon* (n 15) 59.
256 ibid. See also Giardi (n 123) 251ff; G Grasso, 'EU Harmonisation Competences in Criminal Matters and Environmental Crime' in Farmer, Faure and Vagliasindi (eds) (n 22) 28.
257 See also Pereira, *Environmental Criminal Liability* (n 3) 203; Vagliasindi, 'The EU Environmental Crime Directive' (n 49) 51ff; Lucifora (n 134) 234–240.
258 Article 83(2) TFEU.

Article 83(2) TFEU regulates what could be called a 'functional criminalisation'[259] or 'EU regulatory criminal law'.[260] Rather than assuming the status of a self-standing Union policy, criminal law is thus perceived as a means to an end, the end being the effective implementation of other Union policies. In light of the history of this provision and its strict relations with environmental matters, it can be claimed that the existing doubts on the exact interpretation of Article 83(2) TFEU – such as those concerning the meaning of 'essential' and 'effective' implementation of an area already harmonised[261] – do not concern environmental crime. On the contrary, the adoption of a new harmonisation instrument pursuant to Article 83(2) TFEU in the field of environmental crime is highly desirable, as noted by, inter alia, the Finnish Presidency of the EU in its 2019 report on environmental criminal law.[262] At the time of writing, the Commission has not yet issued a proposal to implement Article 83(1) or (2) TFEU as far as environmental crime is concerned,[263] yet it is expected to table a proposal to revise the Environmental Crime Directive by the end of 2021.[264]

In its recent evaluation of the Environmental Crime Directive, the Commission indicated a number of areas where there is room for improvement in terms of legislative reform. These include the interpretation of some legal terms needing further definition in practice; the standardisation of the level of sanctions across the Member States; the introduction of additional sanctions and sanctions linked to the financial situation of legal persons, reconsideration of linking the Directive's scope to the environmental instruments in its annexes; the extension of the Directive's scope to cover more or new areas of environmental crime; doing more to address cross-border cooperation and organised crime; and clarifying the relationship between criminal and administrative sanctions.[265] As discussed in the section below, a new directive would

---

259 Mitsilegas, *EU Criminal Law After Lisbon* (n 15) 60.
260 Öberg, *Limits to EU Powers* (n 51) 10.
261 See, eg, ibid 85–89.
262 Council Presidency, 'EU environmental criminal law' (n 245).
263 The adoption of a directive pursuant to Article 83 TFEU could be proposed also by a quarter of the Member States, which enjoy the right of initiative in the Area of Freedom, Security and Justice together with the Commission (Article 76(b) TFEU).
264 See the Commission's inception impact assessment available at <https://ec.europa.eu/info/law/better-regulation/have-your-say/initiatives/12779-Environmental-crime-improving-EU-rules-on-environmental-protection-through-criminal-law_en> accessed 2 June 2021.
265 Commission, 'Executive Summary of the Evaluation of the Directive 2008/99/ of the European Parliament and of the Council of 19 November 2008 on the protection of the environment through criminal law (ENVIRONMENTAL CRIME DIRECTIVE)' SWD (2020) 260 final, 28 October 2020, 3–4.

therefore be the ideal opportunity to bridge the existing gaps by taking a clear stance on different aspects; in doing so, the new instrument would ultimately contribute to strengthening the protection of the environment at the EU level.

7.2 A New Directive on Environmental Crime: Challenges and Opportunities for the EU Legislator

The adoption of a directive revising the Environmental Crime Directive should aim, first and foremost, to achieve a greater degree of legal certainty and foreseeability in EU environmental criminal law.[266] In the recent Commission's evaluation of the Environmental Crime Directive, it is stated that defining environmental crime by references to annexes is viewed as being complex and impracticable,[267] and failing to keep up with international developments in the field, in particular the link between environmental crime and transnational organised crime.[268] Furthermore, the current criminalisation by complex and multiple references to other instruments of EU secondary law on the protection of the environment presents challenges for legal certainty and the principle of legality as enshrined in Article 49(1) of the Charter and renders the task of transposition in Member States complex, leading to inconsistencies in implementation. Likewise, the Environmental Crime Directive's requirement to criminalise some conduces 'when unlawful' could be rethought, as its use and added value in practice are not self-evident.[269] It seems therefore necessary for the EU legislator to be clear on what should be defined as 'environmental crime'. The concept is neither homogenous nor monolithic as it covers several and different conducts. The EU needs to decide what it will prioritise in its criminal law response; it may perhaps consider whether 'less is more' in this field. In other words, the legislator could decide to focus on the most serious aspects of environmental crime, leaving the other forms of such criminality to the Member States. This may also ensure compatibility with the usual

---

266   See also Lucifora (n 134) 235–236. Further calls for clarity in environmental criminal law more in general can also be found in JL de La Cuesta, 'Protection of the Environment Through Criminal Law. Final Recommendations' (2016) 87 *Revue International de Droit Pénal – Protection of the Environment through Criminal Law* (ed by JL de La Cuesta et al) 343, 345.
267   Commission, 'Commission Staff Working Document Evaluation of the Directive 2008/99/EC' (n 78) 64.
268   ibid 70.
269   If the 'unlawfulness' requirement is instead kept, it would be appropriate to define it in a direct and express manner in the text of the directive itself, by focusing on specific categories of conduct and *mens rea* rather than on a list of legal instruments annexed to the Directive.

requirements of (EU) criminal law such as subsidiarity, proportionality, and *extrema ratio*.²⁷⁰

Second, further clarity in EU environmental criminal law would follow from setting clear boundaries between criminal and administrative law,²⁷¹ as also suggested by the GENVAL final report.²⁷² Once the EU will decide which conduct should be treated as criminal, the remaining ones should be treated as non-criminal (including administrative) infractions at EU level.²⁷³ This move may be considered as constituting legislative overkill especially by those who would not wish to reopen carefully worded legislative compromises at EU level. However, revising existing EU law in the field would provide the opportunity to modernise and address gaps in the current system. The clarification of respective mandates could ensure consistent approaches to the protection of the environment in Member States and contribute towards the respect of the principle of proportionality in criminal offences and sanctions enshrined in Article 49(2) of the Charter. EU institutions have embarked on a similar exercise post-Lisbon in the field of market abuse, where two parallel legal instruments – an administrative law Regulation and a criminal law Directive – have been adopted.²⁷⁴ Furthermore, the clarification of the relationship between criminal and administrative law on the protection of the environment may lead to decriminalisation, and to a careful examination of the possibilities offered by administrative enforcement in the field.²⁷⁵ In accordance with the principle of effectiveness of Union law, electing to treat conduct detrimental

---

270 For a more detailed analysis of the principles that any future EU intervention in the field of environmental criminal law should respect, see Pereira, *Environmental Criminal Liability* (n 3) 207ff.
271 For further remarks on the relations between administrative and criminal law, which bring to the fore further issues connected with *ne bis in idem*, see the following chapter.
272 'Another problem frequently identified in the evaluations was the lack of a clear distinction between crimes and misdemeanours and/or the regime of administrative or criminal penalties, in the absence of clear criteria for determining which regime should apply. Furthermore, in some cases the law does not appear to clearly and unambiguously stipulate when minor offences must be reported to the police or to the prosecutor. As a consequence, the prosecution authority may not investigate the case, leaving it to the competent administrative authorities to take appropriate action' (GENVAL final report (n 84) 56; see also ibid 57).
273 cf de La Cuesta (n 266) 345.
274 Regulation (EU) No 569/2014 of the European Parliament and of the Council of 16 April 2014 on market abuse (market abuse regulation) [2014] OJ L173/1; Directive 2014/57/EU of 16 April 2014 on criminal sanctions for market abuse (market abuse directive) [2014] OJ L173/179.
275 Mitsilegas, 'Contribution to Conclusions and Recommendations on Environmental Crime' (n 230) 7–8.

to the environment as an administrative – and not a criminal – offence would essentially limit Member States' capacity to treat the same conduct as a criminal offence at the national level.[276]

Third, the fight against environmental crime can be strengthened by addressing some of the issues that the two Directives – unlike the more recent EU substantive criminal law instruments, as well as the 1998 Council of Europe Convention – do not address, and namely: a) organised crime; b) sanctions for natural and legal persons; c) freezing and confiscation; d) statute of limitation; and e) investigations and jurisdiction. The opportunity to introduce a reference to *ne bis in idem* in the text of the revised Environmental Crime Directive is discussed in the next chapter.

The revised Environmental Crime Directive could expressly provide for an aggravating circumstance if environmental crimes are committed within the framework of a criminal organisation.[277] It should also harmonise sanctions for environmental crime[278] by introducing some rules on minimum maximum sanctions (eg maximum penalty of at least four years of imprisonment for serious cases of environmental crime).[279] So far, EU substantive criminal law instruments have never harmonised minimum penalties yet the new directive on environmental crime may at least relaunch the debate on whether this form of harmonisation is desirable. The issue is extremely sensitive, given that some Member States do not provide for specific minimum thresholds of imprisonment penalties.[280] Likewise, it may be discussed whether the harmonisation

---

276   See more in V Mitsilegas, 'From Overcriminalisation to Decriminalisation. The Many Faces of Effectiveness in European Criminal Law' (2014) 5 *New Journal of European Criminal Law* 415.
277   See also Grasso, 'EU Harmonisation Competences in Criminal Matters' (n 256) 29, who suggests that, as an alternative, the new directive could also introduce 'a rule which criminalises the "organised trafficking in waste". Such a rule–whose model can be represented by Article 260 of the Italian law no 152/2006 [now Article 452-quaterdecies of the Italian Penal Code]–should be then implemented in all the national legal systems by the competent legislative authorities' (ibid); Lucifora (n 134) 235–236.
278   See also Grasso, 'EU Harmonisation Competences in Criminal Matters' (n 256) 27–28; Vagliasindi, 'The EU Environmental Crime Directive' (n 49) 50–53.
279   Four years is the minimum maximum penalty provided for, eg, by the PIF Directive (Article 7(3)) and Directive (EU) 2018/1673 (Article 5(2)). In addition, the threshold of four years would both allow national competent authorities to rely on mutual recognition instruments without the need to ascertain dual criminality (see the next chapter) and lead to the application of EU and international instruments on organised crime, as discussed in section 6 above (Vagliasindi, 'Directive 2008/99/EC on Environmental Crime and Directive 2009/123/EC' (n 145) 18). See also Lucifora (n 134) 240.
280   See, for instance S Melander, 'Effectiveness in EU Criminal Law and Its Effects on the General Part of Criminal Law' (2014) 5 *New Journal of European Criminal Law* 274, 297. The

should extend to *penalties* for natural persons *other than imprisonment*, eg financial penalties. EU harmonisation instruments adopted so far do not cover financial criminal penalties for individuals and exclusively concern sanctions implying deprivation of liberty. It is true that most of the offences harmonised at the EU level are of such gravity that financial penalties would be too lenient, yet this argument seems less convincing when it comes to economic crimes, as most environmental crimes are. Financial penalties may also be imposed in addition to imprisonment in some cases, as emerges from the Preamble of the Directive on combating child pornography, according to which Member States 'are invited to consider providing for the possibility to impose financial penalties in addition to imprisonment',[281] when the offences are committed with the purpose of financial gain.[282]

The Member States' resistance to accept harmonisation of penalties which goes beyond imprisonment is also witnessed by the Directive on countering money laundering by criminal law (Directive (EU) 2018/1673). During the negotiations, some additional penalties for natural persons were added to the text, such as a temporary or permanent ban on entering into contracts with public authorities, a temporary disqualification from the practice of commercial activities, and a long-term ban on running for elections.[283] This provision would have not envisaged mandatory harmonisation, since it specified that Member States 'may also take'[284] such measures. On the contrary, and as is usually stated in EU harmonisation instruments, Member States were required to ('shall') 'take the necessary measures'[285] to ensure that criminal penalties are effective, dissuasive and proportionate, and that the most serious offences are punished with imprisonment penalties. In the text eventually approved, however, those additional penalties have been moved to the Preamble,[286]

2012 Commission's proposal for the PIF Directive had attempted to introduce a provision on the matter by requiring Member States to set out a minimum penalty of at least six months of imprisonment for some PIF offences, but this rule was eventually removed from the final text.

281 Recital 16 of Directive 2011/92/EU of the European Parliament and of the Council of 13 December 2011 on combating the sexual abuse and sexual exploitation of children and child pornography [2011] OJ L335/1.
282 Giuffrida, 'Effectiveness, Dissuasiveness, Proportionality' (n 135) 117.
283 Article 5(3) of the Commission's proposal in the version of January 2018 (Council doc 5504/18, 22 January 2018).
284 ibid.
285 ibid.
286 '... Member States should also provide for additional sanctions or measures, such as fines, temporary or permanent exclusion from access to public funding, including tender procedures, grants and concessions, temporary disqualifications from the practice of

whereas Article 5 of the Directive simply provides that 'Member States shall ... take the necessary measures to ensure that natural persons ... are, where necessary, subject to additional sanctions or measures'[287] without any further specification. Directive (EU) 2018/1673 could have been the first instrument of EU criminal law introducing the (optional) harmonisation of penalties for natural persons in addition to imprisonment, yet the sensitivity of the matter led Member States to confine such a new kind of harmonisation to the (not binding) Preamble.[288]

Perhaps even more importantly, the revised Environmental Crime Directive should regulate the liability of legal persons in a more detailed way than the two existing Directives. Fines are especially relevant in this context,[289] yet no EU criminal law instrument has so far set a minimum or maximum threshold nor there is any rule on how to calculate their amount.[290] The revised Directive could relaunch the debate in that respect as well. However, fines may not always be sufficient to deter companies from reoffending again (special deterrence) or other companies from committing the same crime (general deterrence). This is especially true for large and financially solid companies, which could even find it more convenient to violate the law and, if they are sanctioned, pay the criminal or non-criminal fines rather than complying *ex ante* with the requirements of environmental legislation.[291]

This therefore calls, on the one hand, for penalties that can be sufficiently tailored to the size and financial situation of legal entities. On the other, national legislation should provide for further effective and dissuasive sanctions against

---

commercial activities or temporary bans on running for elected or public office. That obligation is without prejudice to the discretion of the judge or the court to decide whether to impose additional sanctions or measures or not, taking into account all the circumstances of the particular case' (Recital 14 of Directive).

287   Art 5(3) of Directive (EU) 2018/1673.
288   Giuffrida, 'Effectiveness, Dissuasiveness, Proportionality' (n 135) 118–119.
289   'Some reports have pointed out that the fines for legal persons are not used sufficiently, and/or that they are too low compared to the potential profit that can derive from environmental crimes, including waste-related crimes. Several reports have pointed out that their amounts could be reviewed. Recommendations have therefore been addressed to the Member States concerned, with a view to making more use of corporate fines for environmental offences and increasing the levels of such fines' (GENVAL final report (n 84) 58).
290   V Franssen, 'The EU's Fight Against Corporate Financial Crime: State of Affairs and Future Potential' (2018) 19 *German Law Journal* 1221, 1243.
291   See, eg, P Stretesky, M Long and M Lynch, *The Treadmill of Crime: Political Economy and Green Criminology* (Rutledge Publishing 2014) 103; MJ Greife and MO Maume, 'Do Companies Pay the Price for Environmental Crimes? Consequences of Criminal Penalties on Corporate Offenders' (2020) 73 *Crime, Law and Social Change* 337, 350ff.

corporations. Post-Lisbon EU Directives on the harmonisation of substantive criminal law do not only require Member States to introduce criminal or non-criminal fines but do also list other penalties that national legislators can introduce. These sanctions are: (a) exclusion from entitlement to public benefits or aid; (b) temporary or permanent disqualification from the practice of commercial activities; (c) placing under judicial supervision; (d) a judicial winding-up order; and (e) temporary or permanent closure of establishments that have been used for committing the offence.[292] More recent instruments have introduced a sixth sanction, namely the temporary exclusion from access to public funding, including tender procedures, grants, and concessions.[293] The revised Environmental Crime Directive should be phrased in a similar way, although one cannot help but notice that EU legislation merely *suggests* these penalties to the Member States.[294] While 'it is perfectly conceivable that Member States meet the general standard of effectiveness, proportionality, and dissuasiveness without applying such sanctions',[295] a stronger wording providing for an obligation to introduce those further measures could be considered.

The fight against the economic facet of environmental crimes could also benefit from a provision on confiscation and freezing of proceeds deriving from these offences,[296] as was the case with the 1998 Council of Europe Convention,[297] or at least from the amendment of Directive 2014/42/EU in

---

[292] In a few Directives, however, the illustrative list of sanctions refers only to the liability that flows from the crimes committed by top management, while the EU legislator simply requires sanctions or measures that are effective, proportionate and dissuasive in the case of corporate liability following the commission of offences by other employees. Inherited by the pre-Lisbon legislation, this approach has however been abandoned in the most recent Directives. For further details, see Ligeti and Giuffrida (n 113).

[293] See, with negligible linguistic differences, Article 9(b) of the PIF Directive; Article 8(b) of Directive (EU) 2018/1673; and Article 11(b) of Directive (EU) 2019/713 of the European Parliament and of the Council 17 April 2019 on combating fraud and counterfeiting of non-cash means of payment and replacing Council Framework Decision 2001/413/JHA [2019] OJ L123/18.

[294] Just to name a few examples, Article 9 of the PIF Directive ('Sanctions with regard to legal persons') and Article 8 of Directive (EU) 2018/1673 ('Sanctions for legal persons') provide that the necessary measures to ensure that a legal person is punishable by effective, proportionate and dissuasive sanctions 'shall include criminal or non-criminal fines and *may* include other sanctions, such as...' (emphasis added), and then the list mentioned in the text follows.

[295] Franssen (n 290) 1243.

[296] cf M Faure, 'Limits and Challenges of Criminal Justice Systems in Addressing Environmental Crime' (2016) 87 *Revue International de Droit Pénal – Protection of the Environment through Criminal Law* (ed by JL de La Cuesta et al) 11, 23–24.

[297] See Article 7 of the 1998 Council of Europe Convention ('Confiscation measures').

order to include environmental crime within the remit of this Directive. The revised Environmental Crime Directive could therefore replicate the provisions of some recent EU Directives on the harmonisation of substantive criminal law requiring Member States to adopt the necessary measures to ensure that instrumentalities and proceeds of crimes are frozen and confiscated.[298] It ought to be added that the pre-Lisbon Framework Decision on drug trafficking, which is still in force, includes in the list of sanctions for legal persons also the confiscation of substances that are the object of those drug trafficking-related offences, as well as 'instrumentalities used or intended to be used for these offences and proceeds from these offences or the confiscation of property the value of which corresponds to that of such proceeds, substances or instrumentalities'.[299] The opportunity of introducing this sanction in the revised Environmental Crime Directive should be adequately considered, since it can represent an effective measure to neutralise the negative effects of environmental criminality.[300]

Furthermore, as it may take a considerable amount of time for an environmental offence to be discovered, investigated, and tried, Member States should ensure that such crimes do not become time barred in a too short timeframe that would jeopardise the outcome of investigations and prosecutions. Hence, the revised Environmental Crime Directive could also set out some rules on the statute of limitation (or prescription) of environmental crimes, along the lines of Article 12 of the PIF Directive.[301] Investigation and jurisdictional issues should also be regulated in the forthcoming piece of legislation. On the one hand, some recent EU instruments on the harmonisation of criminal

---

298 For instance, Article 10 of the PIF Directive ('Freezing and confiscation') reads as follows: 'Member States shall take the necessary measures to enable the freezing and confiscation of instrumentalities and proceeds from the criminal offences referred to in Articles 3, 4 and 5 [of the PIF Directive]. Member States bound by Directive 2014/42/EU of the European Parliament and of the Council shall do so in accordance with that Directive'. See also Article 9 of Directive (EU) 2018/1673 ('Confiscation'). On the importance of confiscation as a tool to ensure the effectiveness of environmental criminal law, see Pereira, *Environmental Criminal Liability* (n 3) 286–287.

299 Article 7(1)(f) of Council Framework Decision 2004/757/JHA of 25 October 2004 laying down minimum provisions on the constituent elements of criminal acts and penalties in the field of illicit drug trafficking [2004] OJ L335/8.

300 On confiscation as a penalty for corporations more in general, see G Vermeulen, W de Bondt and C Ryckman, *Liability of Legal Persons for Offences in the EU* (Maklu 2012) 99; Franssen (n 290) 1244–1246. Confiscation is already provided for among the penalties for legal persons in some legal systems, such as Italy's (Articles 9(1)(c) and 19 of Legislative Decree No 231/01).

301 See also Grasso, 'EU Harmonisation Competences in Criminal Matters' (n 256) 29.

legislation expressly require Member States to take the necessary measures to ensure that 'effective investigative tools, such as those which are used in organised crime or other serious crime cases, are available to persons, units or services responsible for investigating or prosecuting'[302] the relevant offences. This addition would be most welcome in the revised Directive, in the light of the current difficulties experienced by national law enforcement authorities in investigating and prosecuting this form of criminality.[303] On the other hand, provisions extending the jurisdiction of Member States on environmental crimes committed in the EU and by EU citizens outside the EU, or which have some kind of connection with the EU territory,[304] would likewise be appropriate to ensure that such crimes are duly prosecuted and punished.

Finally, an effective reaction against environmental crime also requires that, in line with the 'polluter pays' principle, the environment is restored to the extent possible.[305] Even when the prosecution is successful and the offender is punished by means of financial or imprisonment penalties, most of the times the damage to the environment as such would not be repaired.[306] The 1998 Council of Europe Convention contemplated the 'reinstatement of the environment'[307] among the penalties, although its introduction was optional.[308] The inclusion in the revised Environmental Crime Directive of a similar provision requiring Member States to introduce *restitutio in integrum* obligations would still fall within the remit of Article 83(1) or (2) TFEU. They could be considered 'sanctions' with respect to which the new instrument would establish minimum rules since they 'may have a punitive nature and stronger deterrent effect when they require restoration beyond the initial damage caused'.[309]

Irrespective of the formal qualification as 'sanctions', however, the revised Directive could still include these restorative measures, which were already envisaged in the 2007 Commission's proposal for a Directive on environmental crime but did not make it through in the final text.[310] Most post-Lisbon EU

---

302 Article 20(1) of Directive (EU) 2017/541 (terrorism). A very similar wording can be found in Article 11 of Directive (EU) 2018/1673 and Article 13(1) of Directive (EU) 2019/713 (fraud and counterfeiting of non-cash means of payment).
303 For an overview, see Mitsilegas and Giuffrida (n 1) *passim*. See also, inter alia, Faure, 'Limits and Challenges' (n 296) 17ff.
304 cf Pereira, *Environmental Criminal Liability* (n 3) 274–277. See section 4.2 above.
305 de La Cuesta (n 266) 345.
306 Faure, 'Limits and Challenges' (n 296) 23.
307 Article 8 of the 1998 Council of Europe Convention.
308 Pereira, *Environmental Criminal Liability* (n 3) 286.
309 ibid 285.
310 The obligation to reinstate the environment was included among the other sanctions or measures that could accompany the criminal sanctions for natural persons and the

directives on the harmonisation of criminal law lay down rules that do not concern criminal sanctions and definition of offences as such but are nonetheless meant to ensure a more effective protection of the legal interests at stake, such as those on jurisdiction-related issues, statute of limitation (PIF Directive), obligation to take the necessary measures to ensure the prompt removal of online content constituting a public provocation to commit a terrorist offence (Directive on terrorism),[311] and support to the victims.[312] After all, despite the (contentious) narrative of environmental crimes as 'victimless' crimes,[313] the environment should be considered the first victim of these offences, so that the inclusion of restorative measures in the revised Environmental Crime Directive would be appropriate.

8   Conclusion

The protection of the environment has always played a key role within the framework of the European Community, and then the EU. Irrespective of the precise meaning that can be attached to this broad notion, the 'environment' represents a legal interest that transcends national borders and that, in most cases, can be better protected by supranational (if not international) strategies and legislation. This chapter has focused on the EU substantive criminal law instruments that harmonise (some) offences against the environment. The pre-Lisbon inter-institutional disputes on the protection of the environment led the Court of Justice to decide two landmark cases, the *Environmental Crime* and the *Ship-Source Pollution* cases, which for the first time recognised the criminal law competence of the Community in the framework of the (then) first pillar. In the aftermath of these two seminal rulings, the European Parliament and the Council adopted two directives on the harmonisation of substantive criminal law provisions concerning environmental crime (Directive 2008/99/EC) and ship-source pollution (Directive 2009/123/EC).

---

fines for legal persons (respectively, Articles 5(5)(c) and 7(4)(a) of COM (2007) 51 final). On the possible content of measures adopted under Article 83 TFEU, cf Grasso, 'EU Harmonisation Competences' (n 256) 22–24.

311   Article 21(1) of Directive (EU) 2017/541.
312   cf Articles 18–20 of Directive 2011/92/EU (child pornography); Articles 24–26 of Directive (EU) 2017/541 (terrorism); Article 16 of Directive (EU) 2019/713 (fraud and counterfeiting of non-cash means of payment).
313   For further remarks and references on the misleading notion of 'victimless' crimes, see Mitsilegas and Giuffrida (n 1) 14–15.

Albeit dating back to more than ten years ago, these Directives still represent the two main instruments in the field. While they have unquestionably contributed to increase awareness on the challenges posed by environmental crime and to the partial harmonisation of national legislation on the matter, they also have a number of shortcomings, spanning from the silence on penalties for natural and legal persons to the lack of any reference to organised crime. Due to mounting international concerns for the protection of the environment, which are mirrored, inter alia, in the ambitious European Green Deal that the current Commission considers the first objective of its mandate,[314] discussions on the opportunity to amend the existing EU substantive criminal law framework have recently gained momentum.

In particular, the Commission's recent evaluation of the Environmental Crime Directive provides fresh impetus towards the reform of this Directive, which was adopted partly to reflect the important constitutional step by the Court of Justice to confer criminal law competence to the (then) Community under the (then) first pillar. With the three pillars now abolished by the entry into force of the Lisbon Treaty, the European Union legislators are called to reflect and deliberate on what forms of environmental crime must be criminalised at EU level in a way that is consistent with the Treaty legal bases and the need to fight serious environmental crime. In this process, it is essential that the main shortcomings of the current Directive – in particular in terms of legal certainty and foreseeability – are addressed, in order to provide a clear legal framework leading to a high level of harmonisation across the EU.

In this process, a way forward may be to define clearly in the text – along the lines of other EU instruments of substantive criminal law – a number of key environmental crime offences at EU level while at the same time introducing clear provisions on the link between criminal and administrative law on environmental protection where appropriate. While Article 83(2) TFEU appears the most appropriate legal basis for a new directive on environmental crime or a revised Environmental Crime Directive, the possibilities offered by Article 83(1) TFEU in relation to the criminalisation of organised crime – including in areas such as wildlife trafficking – should not be underestimated.

New legislation may ensure that Union law takes full account of international developments in the field and may provide the space for the Union to emerge as a leading global actor in the protection of the environment by criminal law. Now is an ideal opportunity to improve the quality and effectiveness

---

314 cf U von der Leyen (current President of the European Commission), 'A Union that strives for more. My agenda for Europe. Political guidelines for the next European Commission 2019–2024' (2019).

of EU environmental criminal law, especially with respect to the identification of what constitutes 'environmental crime' and the boundaries between criminal and administrative law, and to provide the EU with a strong and successful internal and external strategy to counter environmental criminality, while at the same time ensuring legal certainty and the respect of fundamental rights of the individuals.

CHAPTER 6

Environmental Crime at the EU Level
Judicial Cooperation, Conflicts of Jurisdiction and Ne Bis in Idem

1   Introduction

The previous chapter has examined the EU's role in the harmonisation of substantive criminal legislation on environmental crime. In this chapter, the analysis moves on to EU judicial cooperation in the fight against transnational environmental criminality. Investigations and prosecutions in this field are a complex task for national authorities. Environmental crimes are difficult to detect in the first place due to, inter alia, their nature of (allegedly) 'victimless' crimes[1] and the consequent scarce priority that national authorities and policy-makers tend to attach to them,[2] the usually short limitation periods after which they become time-barred, and the complexity of environmental (criminal) legislation.[3] Gathering evidence on the commission of such crimes is not easy either, especially when the damage they cause is to be proven in court,[4] and the investigative toolbox that is available to national authorities may not be as effective as that on which they rely when investigating other crimes.[5]

Furthermore, while the substantive criminal law Directives oblige the Member States to criminalise the conducts that affect the environment, with the failure to implement them being subject to infringement proceedings,

---

[1] For further remarks on this contentious notion, see EnviCrimeNet, 'Report on Environmental Crime' (2016) 5–6 <www.envicrimenet.eu/reports/> accessed 2 June 2021; V Mitsilegas and F Giuffrida, 'The Role of EU Agencies in Fighting Transnational Environmental Crime. New Challenges for Eurojust and Europol' (2017) 1 *Brill Research Perspectives in Transnational Crime* 1, 14.

[2] A Farmer, M Faure and GM Vagliasindi, 'Environmental Crime in Europe: State of Affairs and Future Perspectives' in A Farmer, M Faure and GM Vagliasindi (eds), *Environmental Crime in Europe* (Hart 2017) 330–331.

[3] See, eg, M Faure, 'The Evolution of Environmental Criminal Law in Europe: A Comparative Analysis' in Farmer, Faure and Vagliasindi (eds) (previous n) 288.

[4] See more in the previous chapter.

[5] Mitsilegas and Giuffrida, 'The Role of EU Agencies' (n 1) 12ff. As for wildlife crime, these and similar difficulties met by national authorities in investigating and prosecuting it are discussed by S Sina, C Gerstetter, L Porsch et al, 'Wildlife Crime' (2016) Study for the European Parliament's Committee on the Environment, Public Health and Food Safety, 95ff.

there is no obligation for national authorities to use the EU instruments of judicial cooperation. Their reliance on these instruments therefore depends on several factors: among the others, whether they are aware of the existence and added value of EU legislation on the matter; how they handle the case – for instance, if they focus only on the national aspect of a cross-border environmental crime, there would be no need to resort to EU instruments of judicial cooperation; and whether their system is based on the principle of discretionary or mandatory prosecution, with the former leaving them more freedom not to prosecute crimes that are not perceived as having high priority.[6]

This chapter sheds light on the main challenges that EU judicial cooperation in criminal matters faces in the fight against environmental crime. It first looks at the EU instruments of mutual recognition, especially the European Arrest Warrant (section 2). Section 3 analyses the issue of conflicts of jurisdiction: although they can be rather common when environmental crime has a cross-border dimension, EU legislation offers limited solutions. Finally, section 4 examines the principle of *ne bis in idem*, which prevents double prosecutions on the same facts and may be jeopardised when more than one country has jurisdiction on a given environmental crime. While this chapter does not address administrative authorities' investigations and sanctions, it provides however for some remarks on the possible violation of *ne bis in idem* when the same conduct against the environment is punished by criminal and administrative law.

2 Mutual Recognition Instruments to Fight Environmental Crime

One of the key constitutional objectives of the European Union is its emergence as an Area of Freedom, Security and Justice (AFSJ) without internal frontiers.[7] In the field of criminal law, European integration has moved forward not only by attempts at harmonisation of national law, but also, very prominently, by efforts to enhance inter-state cooperation with the aim of strengthening the enforcement capacity of Member States. While a key feature of the development of such an Area is the abolition of internal borders between Member States and the creation thus of a single European area where freedom of movement is secured, this single area of movement is not however accompanied by

---

6 See Faure (n 3) 293–297. Cf also R Pereira, *Environmental Criminal Liability and Enforcement in European and International Law* (Brill 2015) 303–306.
7 Article 3(2) of the Treaty on European Union (TEU) and Article 67(1) of the Treaty on the Functioning of the European Union (TFEU).

a single area of law. The law remains territorial, with Member States retaining to a great extent their sovereignty especially in the field of law enforcement. A key challenge for European integration in the field has thus been how to make national legal systems interact in the borderless AFSJ.

Member States have thus far declined unification of law in Europe's criminal justice area. The focus has largely been on the development of systems of cooperation between Member State authorities, with the aim of extending national enforcement capacity throughout the AFSJ in order to compensate for the abolition of internal border controls. The simplification of movement that the abolition of internal border controls entails has led under this compensatory logic to calls for a similar simplification in inter-state cooperation via automaticity and speed. Following this logic, the construction of the AFSJ as an area without internal frontiers intensifies and justifies automaticity in inter-state cooperation.[8] Automaticity in inter-state cooperation means that a national decision will be enforced beyond the territory of the issuing Member State by authorities in other EU Member States across the AFSJ without many questions being asked and with the requested authority having at its disposal extremely limited – if any at all – grounds to refuse the request for cooperation. The method chosen to secure such automaticity has been the application of the principle of *mutual recognition* in the field of judicial cooperation in criminal matters.

Mutual recognition is attractive to Member States resisting further harmonisation or unification in European criminal law as mutual recognition is thought to enhance inter-state cooperation in criminal matters without Member States having to change their national laws to comply with EU harmonisation requirements.[9] Mutual recognition creates extraterritoriality:[10] in a borderless Area of Freedom, Security and Justice, the will of an authority in one Member State can be enforced beyond its territorial borders and across this area. The acceptance of such extraterritoriality requires a high level of mutual trust between the authorities that take part in the system and is premised upon the acceptance that membership of the European Union means that

---

8   V Mitsilegas, 'The Limits of Mutual Trust in Europe's Area of Freedom, Security and Justice. From Automatic Inter-State Cooperation to the Slow Emergence of the Individual' (2013) 31 *Yearbook of European Law* 2012 319, 319–322.
9   V Mitsilegas, 'The Constitutional Implications of Mutual Recognition in Criminal Matters in the EU' (2006) 43 *Common Market Law Review* 1277.
10 K Nicolaidis and G Shaffer, 'Transnational Mutual Recognition Regimes: Governance without Global Government' (2005) 68 *Law and Contemporary Problems* 263; K Nicolaidis, 'Trusting the Poles? Constructing Europe through Mutual Recognition' (2007) 14 *Journal of European Public Policy* 682.

all Member States are fully compliant with fundamental rights norms. It is the acceptance of the high level of integration among Member States which has justified automaticity in inter-state cooperation and has led to the adoption of a series of EU instruments that in this context go beyond pre-existing, traditional forms of cooperation set out under public international law, which have afforded a greater degree of scrutiny to requests for cooperation. Membership of the European Union *presumes* the full respect of fundamental rights by all Member States, which creates mutual trust that in turn forms the basis of automaticity in inter-state cooperation in Europe's area of criminal justice.[11]

Framed in this manner, mutual recognition has emerged as the motor of European integration in criminal matters. As of 2002, a wide range of Framework Decisions putting forward a comprehensive system of mutual recognition in the field of criminal justice extending from the pre-trial (recognition of Arrest Warrants,[12] Evidence Warrants,[13] Freezing Orders,[14] Decisions on bail,[15] Investigation Orders)[16] to the post-trial stage (recognition of confiscation orders,[17] decisions on financial penalties,[18] probation

---

11 Mitsilegas, 'The Limits of Mutual Trust' (n 8) 322.
12 Council Framework Decision 2002/584/JHA of 13 June 2002 on the European Arrest Warrant [2002] OJ L190/1 (hereinafter 'EAW Framework Decision').
13 Council Framework Decision 2008/978/JHA of 18 December 2008 on the European Evidence Warrant [2008] OJ L350/72. Implemented by less than a half of the EU Member States, this instrument was not very successful and, after Lisbon, was replaced by Directive 2014/41/EU of the European Parliament and of the Council of 3 April 2014 regarding the European Investigation Order in criminal matters [2014] OJ L130/1 (hereinafter 'EIO Directive') for the Member States bound by such Directive, that is, all the EU countries except for Denmark and Ireland.
14 Council Framework Decision 2003/577/JHA of 22 July 2003 on the mutual recognition of orders freezing property or evidence [2003] OJ L196/45, which has been replaced, as regards the freezing of evidence, by the EIO Directive and, as regards the freezing of property, by Regulation (EU) 2018/1805 of the European Parliament and of the Council of 14 November 2018 on the mutual recognition of freezing orders and confiscation orders [2018] OJ L303/1 for the Member States bound by this Regulation, that is, all the EU countries except for Denmark and Ireland.
15 Council Framework Decision 2009/829/JHA of 23 October 2009 on the application, between Member States of the European Union, of the principle of mutual recognition to decisions on supervision measures as an alternative to provisional detention [2009] OJ L294/20.
16 EIO Directive (n 13).
17 Council Framework Decision 2006/783/JHA of 6 October 2006 on the mutual recognition of confiscation orders [2006] OJ L328/59, which has been replaced by Regulation 2018/1805 (n 14).
18 Council Framework Decision 2005/214/JHA of 24 February 2005 on the application of the principle of mutual recognition to financial penalties [2005] OJ L76/16.

orders,[19] and decisions on the transfer of sentenced persons)[20] have been adopted. The system of mutual recognition was completed pre-Lisbon by a Framework Decision on judgments in absentia, which amended a number of the previous Framework Decisions to specify when recognition of a judgment could or could not be refused in such cases.[21]

Before delving further into the mechanisms of mutual recognition and their relevance for the field of environmental criminal law, it is worth pointing out that, at the time of writing, the European Parliament and the Council are negotiating a regulation on European Production and Preservation Orders for electronic evidence in criminal matters.[22] The draft Regulation establishes a system that, if adopted, will compel private service providers offering services in the EU to produce or preserve electronic evidence, regardless of the location of data, upon receipt of orders issued by public authorities in EU Member States. Establishing a direct channel of communication between the issuing (public) authority and private service providers, the future Regulation, if adopted, would bring about a paradigmatic change: it envisages a system whereby co-operation takes place directly between a public authority in the issuing Member State and the private sector – thereby departing from the existing models of judicial cooperation and mutual recognition in EU law, which are based on cooperation and communication between public authorities in Member States.[23]

Against this backdrop, the sections below discuss the application of the principle of mutual recognition in criminal matters, with a focus on the functioning

---

19 Council Framework Decision 2008/947/JHA of 27 November 2008 on the application of the principle of mutual recognition to judgments and probation decisions with a view to the supervision of probation measures and alternative sanctions [2008] OJ L337/102.

20 Council Framework Decision 2008/909/JHA of 27 November 2008 on the application of the principle of mutual recognition to judgments in criminal matters imposing custodial sentences or measures involving deprivation of liberty for the purpose of their enforcement in the European Union [2008] OJ L327/27.

21 Council Framework Decision 2009/299/JHA of 26 February 2009, OJ L81/24.

22 See Commission, 'Proposal for a Regulation of the European Parliament and of the Council on European Production and Preservation Orders for electronic evidence in criminal matters' COM (2018) 225 final, 17 April 2018. Negotiations are ongoing at the time of writing.

23 V Mitsilegas, 'The Privatisation of Mutual Trust in Europe's Area of Criminal Justice: The Case of E-Evidence' (2018) 25 *Maastricht Journal of European and Comparative Law* 263, 263–264. For similar remarks on the increased importance of private parties' cooperation with law enforcement authorities see, in the context of the proposed revision of the Regulation on the European Union Agency for Law Enforcement Cooperation (Europol), section 2.5 of the next chapter.

of the European Arrest Warrant (EAW) system, which is the first and still most important instrument of mutual recognition in the EU and whose main features are largely replicated in all the other mutual recognition instruments. The analysis will bring to light the three most complex issues concerning the application of the principle of mutual recognition in the fight against environmental crime, namely dual criminality (section 2.1), the concept of 'judicial authority' (section 2.2), and the protection of fundamental rights (section 2.3).

2.1   Scaling Down Dual Criminality

The surrender procedure based on the European Arrest Warrant has replaced the political and cumbersome procedures of extradition among EU Member States. The EAW is a judicial decision issued by a Member State ('issuing Member State') with a view to the arrest and the surrender by another Member State ('executing Member State') of an individual for purposes of conducting a criminal prosecution or executing a custodial sentence or detention order.[24] The EAW Framework Decision regulates the procedure of issuing and executing the EAW, which is marked by automaticity and speed. A judicial authority of an EU Member State must give effect to a decision by a similar authority in another Member State with a minimum of formality: suspects or convicted persons must be surrendered as soon as possible, on the basis of completed forms, and ideally without the executing authorities looking behind the form.[25] The automaticity of the system is strengthened by the fact that the refusal to recognise and execute a European Arrest Warrant is allowed only for limited reasons. The Framework Decision includes only three, mostly procedural, mandatory grounds for refusal,[26] which are complemented by a series of optional grounds for refusal[27] and provisions on guarantees underpinning the surrender process.[28]

EAWs may be issued only 'for acts *punishable* by the law of the issuing Member State by a custodial sentence or a detention order for a *maximum period of at least 12 months* or, where a sentence has been passed or a detention order has been made, for sentences of at least four months'.[29] Therefore, the EAW cannot be used by national authorities when crimes are punished

---

24   Article 1(1) of the EAW Framework Decision.
25   V Mitsilegas, *EU Criminal Law* (Hart 2009) 121.
26   Article 3 of the EAW Framework Decision.
27   Article 4 of the EAW Framework Decision.
28   Articles 5, 27, and 28 of the EAW Framework Decision.
29   Article 2(1) of the EAW Framework Decision. Emphasis added.

with a lower penalty or a fine only, as may be the case for some environmental crimes.[30]

The threshold of the penalty for environmental crimes is also relevant under a different perspective. In order to further enhance the automaticity of the system, the executing authority shall not verify the existence of *dual criminality* for a list of 32 categories of offences listed in the Framework Decision.[31] This was one of the most ground-breaking innovations in the field of extradition (now surrender, in the EU) procedures. The list mentions 'environmental crime, including illicit trafficking in endangered animal species and in endangered plant species and varieties' and 'illicit trafficking in nuclear or radioactive materials'.[32] Although the EU legislator stresses the importance of environmental offences connected with trafficking activities, the choice of referring to a generic criminological category such as 'environmental crime' implies that in principle any offence falling within this category may justify the surrender without the verification of double criminality.[33] This is certainly positive for it allows the use of such an important mutual recognition instrument in the fight against this multifaceted – and often transnational – crime. Furthermore, in its recent evaluation of the Environmental Crime Directive, the European Commission (hereinafter: the 'Commission') stated that 'the criminalisation of environmental offences through the [Environmental Crime] Directive has contributed to attract higher public awareness and enabled more effective cross-border cooperation by creating an EU-wide set of environmental crimes that can be prosecuted in all Member States'.[34]

It should however be noted that the above-mentioned 32 categories of offences can lead to a surrender without the verification of double criminality

---

30   See also Pereira (n 6) 342.
31   Article 2(2) of the EAW Framework Decision.
32   ibid.
33   See, eg, S Manacorda, 'Le Mandat d'Arrêt Européen et l'Harmonisation Substantielle: Le Rapprochement des Incriminations' in G Giudicelli-Delage and S Manacorda (eds), *L'Intégration Pénale Indirecte. Interactions entre Droit Pénal et Coopération Judiciaire au Sein de l'Union Européenne* (Société de Législation Comparée 2005) 59.
34   Commission, 'Commission Staff Working Document Evaluation of the Directive 2008/99/EC of the European Parliament and of the Council of 19 November 2008 on the Protection of the Environment through Criminal Law' SWD (2020) 259 final, 28 October 2020, 59. This is however an indirect effect of the Directive since, as the Commission acknowledges, the Directive does not expressly deal with judicial cooperation in the fight against cross-border environmental crime and 'could not go as far as to set out specific provisions requiring the harmonisation of investigative tools or fostering specific means of cross-border cooperation' (ibid 14).

only when in the issuing Member State they are punishable 'by a custodial sentence or a detention order for a *maximum period of at least three years*'.[35] Therefore, if the national penalties for environmental crime fall below this threshold, or if they are only pecuniary, the surrender of the requested person should pass through a previous verification of the double criminality of the act, which can either delay the execution of the EAW or even lead to the refusal of the surrender, if in the executing Member State that specific act is not criminalised. In light of the differences among national laws with regard to the penalties for environmental crime,[36] automatic mutual recognition in the fight against environmental crime may be more difficult than in other areas of crime.[37]

The Court of Justice of the European Union (CJEU) has recently been called to decide whether the threshold of the maximum penalty of at least three years of imprisonment should be assessed by taking into account the law that was in force at the time of the commission of the offence or the law that was applicable when the EAW was issued.[38] The case concerned a rapper and composer who was convicted in Spain for some crimes, including glorification of terrorism and humiliation of the victims of terrorism, and then went to Belgium. At the time of the facts, this offence was punishable with a penalty of maximum of two years of imprisonment, yet when the EAW was issued, the maximum penalty had been increased to three years, which would have thus exempted the executing authorities from verifying dual criminality. Since the Belgian authorities took into account the legislation in force at the time of the facts, they assessed the double criminality and, due to the absence of a corresponding offence in Belgian law, they refused to execute the EAW. The CJEU

---

35 ibid. Emphasis added.
36 See more in the previous chapter. On the negative impact of low thresholds of penalties for wildlife crime on the functioning of the EAW system, see also Sina, Gerstetter, Porsch et al (n 5) 39–40.
37 cf GM Vagliasindi, 'The EU Environmental Crime Directive' in Farmer, Faure and Vagliasindi (eds) (n 2) 54. Back in 2007, the European Commission noted that '[c]urrent Member States legislation would not meet this three-year threshold in most cases and therefore the dual criminality test would apply. This creates difficulties because the discrepancies are currently significant between the legislation of Member States which in addition also still often recur to administrative sanctions' (Commission, 'Commission staff working document – Accompanying document to the Proposal for a Directive of the European Parliament and of the Council on the protection of the environment through criminal law – Impact assessment' COM (2007) 51 final, SEC (2007) 161, 9 February 2007, 31). See Pereira (n 6) 341–342.
38 Case C-717/18 *X (Mandat d'arrêt européen contre un chanteur – Double incrimination)*, EU:C:2020:142.

confirmed this is the right approach, since the threshold of penalty should be assessed by having regard to the law of the issuing Member State in the version applicable to the facts giving rise to the case in which the EAW was issued.[39]

This judgment is a testament to the importance of substantive criminal law for the smooth functioning of mutual recognition procedures.[40] If penalties are too mild, as is often the case for environmental crimes, the added value of EU legislation to counter cross-border criminality is largely lost. When environmental crimes are not punished with a maximum penalty of at least three years of imprisonment in the issuing Member State, the execution of EAWs shall pass the dual criminality test. While there is arguably some consistency across Member States' criminal laws with respect to the most serious forms of environmental crime such as waste trafficking, the existing differences in the definition of environmental offences and the limited attention that some legislators pay to the criminalisation of illegal conducts in this field may lead to a failure of the dual criminality test in some cases. This may also be due to the fact that, as the Commission noted back in 2007, some conduct can be subject to administrative – rather than criminal – penalties in some Member States.[41] More recently, in its evaluation of the Environmental Crime Directive, the Commission noted that some Member States communicated that 'in practice environmental criminal law is not applied in their country, but environmental offences are rather dealt with through the existing administrative sanction systems'.[42] In the same document, the Commission stated that one of the prerequisites for judicial cooperation is 'a common understanding of what constitutes an environmental crime'[43] – thus confirming the relevance of substantive criminal law (also) for the success of judicial cooperation.

It is arguably for all the above-mentioned reasons, coupled with the limited priority given to environmental crime and the difficulties often met by national authorities dealing with it,[44] that the use of EAWs in environmental

---

39 ibid, para 43.
40 In that respect, see also the caveat of the Finnish Presidency's report on environmental crime: 'Although it is necessary that Directives are limited to minimum standards and leave sufficient room for implementation in various types of legal systems, this variation may, in certain cross-border cases, entail shortcomings, in particular, in smooth police and judicial cooperation in criminal matters' (Council Presidency, 'EU environmental criminal law – Presidency report' Council doc 12801/19, 4 October 2019, 11).
41 COM (2007) 51 final, SEC (2007) 161 (n 37) 31.
42 Commission, 'Commission Staff Working Document Evaluation of the Directive 2008/99/EC' (n 34) 65.
43 ibid 14.
44 As mentioned, these difficulties span from low penalties and short limitation periods to limited investigative measures available, technical complexity of the legislation, and

crime cases is quite limited.⁴⁵ According to recent information shared by the European Union Agency for Criminal Justice Cooperation (Eurojust), between 2014 and 2018 only three EAWs were exchanged in environmental crimes cases in which Eurojust was involved.⁴⁶ Before leaving the EU, the UK used EAWs in environmental crime cases in at least two occasions, and both of them concerned persons who had been convicted in the UK of illegal waste dumping and then flew to Ireland.⁴⁷

It is worth noting that the same list of 32 conducts of the EAW Framework Decision, with the same exemption from the verification of double criminality if the crimes are punishable in the issuing State with a maximum penalty of at least three years of imprisonment, can be found in other EU instruments, such as the Framework Decisions on the mutual recognition of: i) judgments in criminal matters imposing custodial sentences or measures involving deprivation of liberty;⁴⁸ ii) judgments and probation decisions;⁴⁹ and iii) decisions on supervision measures.⁵⁰ In these cases, however, Member States retain the option not to abolish dual criminality and some of them have decided to exercise such an option.⁵¹ For those 32 categories of offences, furthermore, the

---

    obstacles in gathering evidence (Mitsilegas and Giuffrida, 'The Role of EU Agencies' (n 1) 12ff).

45   L Salazar, 'European Judicial Cooperation in the Fight against Environmental Crime' in 'Summary of the EFFACE Workshop "Environmental Crime and the Criminal Justice System"' (Catania, 23 June 2014) 6.

46   RS Mackor and FH Cassidy, 'International Cooperation from the EUROJUST Perspective' (2019) Presentation at the Joint Eurojust & ENPE Conference on Environmental Crime, 28–30 October 2019, slide 12 <https://www.environmentalprosecutors.eu/conference2019/conference-proceedings/index.html> accessed 2 June 2021.

47   The first case dates back to 2003–2004 and concerns two persons who dumped over 14,600 tonnes of waste in London and Essex (Pereira (n 6) 341). In the second case, an individual had been sentenced *in absentia* in the UK to 20-month imprisonment for dumping massive quantities of waste in the UK countryside (Environment Agency, ' "Plymouth's worst fly-tipper" jailed after 3 years on the run' (24 February 2020, press release) <www.gov.uk/government/news/plymouth-s-worst-fly-tipper-jailed-after-3-years-on-the-run> accessed 2 June 2021).

48   Article 7(1) of Council Framework Decision 2008/909/JHA.

49   Article 10(1) of Council Framework Decision 2008/947/JHA.

50   Article 14(1) of Council Framework Decision 2009/829/JHA.

51   See, respectively, Article 7(4) of Council Framework Decision 2008/909/JHA, Article 10(4) of Council Framework Decision 2008/947/JHA and Article 14(4) of Council Framework Decision 2009/829/JHA. For further details on the Member States that have used this option, see the 'Commission Staff Working Document. Tables "State of play" and "Declarations". Accompanying the document Report from the Commission to the European Parliament and the Council on the implementation by the Member States of the Framework Decisions 2008/909/JHA, 2008/947/JHA and 2009/829/JHA on the mutual

Framework Decision on the mutual recognition of decisions imposing financial penalties exempts the executing State from previously verifying the double criminality, even though in these cases – quite obviously since the matter concerns *financial* penalties – there are no reference to a minimum threshold of imprisonment to trigger the procedure of mutual recognition.[52] The list of 32 categories of crime is instead not provided for by the 2008 Council Framework Decision that requires each Member State to take into account, in the course of its criminal proceedings, previous convictions against the person who is subject to those criminal proceedings which have been handed down in any other Member State.[53] This Framework Decision applies to 'any final decision of a criminal court establishing guilt of a criminal offence',[54] thus also those concerning any environmental crime and without any further assessment of double criminality.[55]

The 2018 Regulation on the mutual recognition of freezing orders and confiscation orders,[56] which replaced previous Framework Decisions on the same subject-matter, and the Directive on the European Investigation Order (EIO) also provide for the same list of 32 categories of offences.[57] The EIO is a judicial decision issued by national judicial authorities of a Member State to have one or more specific investigative measure(s) carried out in another Member State, with the aim to obtain evidence. As the EAW, in practical terms the EIO is a form to be completed by a national competent authority, who will send it to the executing State where the needed evidence can be found. Once the EIO is executed, the executing authority shall, without

---

      recognition of judicial decisions on custodial sentences or measures involving deprivation of liberty, on probation decisions and alternative sanctions and on supervision measures as an alternative to provisional detention' COM (2014) 57 final, SWD (2014) 34 final, 5 February 2014.

52   Article 5(1) of Council Framework Decision 2005/214/JHA. This instrument adds however further categories to the 32 ones listed in the EAW Framework Decision. See G Vermeulen, W De Bondt and Y Van Damme, *EU Cross-Border Gathering and Use of Evidence in Criminal Matters* (Maklu 2010) 64.

53   Council Framework Decision 2008/675/JHA of 24 July 2008 on taking account of convictions in the Member States of the European Union in the course of new criminal proceedings [2008] OJ L220/32.

54   Article 2 of Council Framework Decision 2008/675/JHA.

55   Some authors noted that it 'is amazing that unanimity was found to demand [mutual recognition] of any conviction, which in practice includes the recognition of a conviction for behaviour not criminalised in own national criminal law provisions' (Vermeulen, De Bondt, and Van Damme (n 52) 65).

56   Article 3 of Regulation 2018/1805.

57   Annex D to the EIO Directive.

undue delay, transfer the evidence obtained or already in its possession to the issuing State.[58]

Soon after its adoption, the literature acknowledged the added value of the EIO Directive in the fight against environmental crime. Bachmaier Winter argued that the new instrument could make the request and exchange of expert evidence, which is key in environmental crime cases, quicker than in the past.[59] At the same time, however, the EIO is not a panacea as its use would be further strengthened and streamlined if there were, for instance, some consistency across the EU with respect to the standards for the appointment of experts and scientific methodologies considered as tested.[60] Likewise, the exchange of expert evidence may raise the issue of the costs of these measures which, according to the Directive, should be borne by the executing Member State. In case of exceptionally high costs, the executing authority may nonetheless consult with the issuing authority 'on whether and how the costs could be shared or the EIO modified'.[61] It boils downs therefore to

> [g]ood will, and again political will, [to] determine which costs will be paid to gather evidence that will make possible to prosecute a particular environmental crime. In the future it will be clarified which costs are considered 'exceptionally high', because the economic differences between EU member states are significant and there is also a risk that those economic differences may have a negative impact on the smooth implementation of the EIO. Common understanding on what are proportional requests and reasonable costs in the execution of EIOs should be reached to the purpose of creating an environment favourable to transnational cooperation in prosecuting environmental crimes.[62]

Recent data on EIOs confirm the success of this instrument from a law enforcement perspective. According to Eurojust's information, EIOs are used more often than EAWs in the fight against cross-border environmental crime: between 2014 and 2018, Eurojust dealt with 57 cases of environmental crime and EIOs were used in 25% of them.[63] This number is even more

---

58 Article 13(1) of the EIO Directive.
59 L Bachmaier Winter, 'Obstacles to Prosecution of Environmental Crime and the Role of Expert Evidence. A Comparative Approach' (2016) 87 *Revue International de Droit Pénal – Protection of the Environment through Criminal Law* (ed by JL de La Cuesta et al) 191.
60 ibid 214–215.
61 Article 21(2) of the EIO Directive.
62 Bachmaier Winter (n 59) 215–216.
63 Mackor and Cassidy (n 46), slide 12.

significant if one bears in mind that EIOs have been used since 2017 only.[64] In light of the cross-border nature of the most serious environmental crimes, which makes the collection and admissibility of evidence a sensitive issue, the increasing reliance by national authorities on EIOs is an encouraging signal for judicial cooperation and the effectiveness of the EU's response to environmental crime.

Finally, if environmental crimes are punished with a custodial sentence or a detention order for a maximum period of at least three years, they also fall within the remit of the Directive on passenger name record (PNR) data ('PNR Directive').[65] This directive was meant to regulate the transfer by air carriers of PNR data of passengers of extra-EU flights[66] but, upon decision of the Member States following the adoption of the Directive, it now applies to intra-EU flights as well.[67] The Member States can process such data – encompassing 19 categories of information listed in Annex I to the PNR Directive[68] – only for the purposes of preventing, detecting, investigating, and prosecuting terrorist offences and serious crime, which includes, when the threshold of penalty is met, 'environmental crime, including illicit trafficking in endangered animal species and in endangered plant species and varieties'.[69]

The exchange of PNR data is also subject to agreements between the EU and third countries, notably US and Australia.[70] The EU-Canada PNR agreement is currently under re-negotiation after a judgment by the Court of Justice

---

64 The deadline for the implementation by the Member States was 22 May 2017 (Article 36(1) of the EIO Directive).

65 Directive (EU) 2016/681 of the European Parliament and of the Council of 27 April 2016 on the use of passenger name record (PNR) data for the prevention, detection, investigation and prosecution of terrorist offences and serious crime [2016] OJ L119/32 ('PNR Directive').

66 Article 1 of the PNR Directive.

67 N Vavoula ' "I Travel, therefore I Am a Suspect": An overview of the EU PNR Directive' *EU Immigration and Asylum Law and Policy* (26 October 2016) <http://eumigrationlawblog.eu/i-travel-therefore-i-am-a-suspect-an-overview-of-the-eu-pnr-directive/> accessed 2 June 2021. Only Denmark does not participate in the Directive.

68 Among others, address and contact information, all forms of payment information, including billing address, complete travel itinerary, frequent flyer information, seat number and all baggage information.

69 Annex II to the PNR Directive.

70 Agreement between the United States of America and the European Union on the use and transfer of passenger name records to the United States Department of Homeland Security [2012] OJ L215/5 ('EU–US PNR Agreement'); Agreement between the European Union and Australia on the processing and transfer of Passenger Name Record (PNR) data by air carriers to the Australian Customs and Border Protection Service [2012] OJ L186/4 ('EU–Australia PNR Agreement').

declared the draft agreement incompatible with EU law,[71] while the Council of the European Union (hereinafter 'the Council) recently authorised the opening of negotiations on an EU-Japan PNR Agreement.[72] According to the EU-US PNR Agreement, the exchange of PNR data is authorised to prevent, detect, investigate, and prosecute terrorist offence or serious transnational crime. The latter is any offence that is transnational in nature and punishable by a sentence of imprisonment of at least three years.[73] The EU-Australia and draft EU-Canada PNR Agreements have the same applicability *ratione materiae* and keep the 'transnational in nature' requirement, yet they increase the threshold of minimum maximum penalty to four years.[74] As discussed in the previous chapter, while the transnational nature of environmental crime is often unquestionable, the penalty requirement may be more difficult to meet.

2.2 The Concept of 'Judicial Authority'

EAWs shall be issued and executed by 'judicial authorities' and such judicialisation of surrender represented a key evolution to the traditional system of extradition, since the actors involved in the process of surrender are now judicial and not executive authorities.[75] However, the definition of what constitutes a 'judicial authority' for the purposes of the EAW Framework Decision is not clear, with the CJEU attempting to treat the term as an autonomous concept of EU law in some cases.

In *Poltorak, Kovalkovas* and *Özcelik*, the CJEU treated the concept of judicial authority as an autonomous concept in EU law.[76] The Court ruled that

---

71 Opinion 1/15 (*Accord PNR UE-Canada*), EU:C:2016:656. For a commentary, see E Guild and E Mendos Kuşkonmaz, 'EU Exclusive Jurisdiction on Surveillance Related to Terrorism and Serious Transnational Crime: Case Review on Opinion 1/15' (2018) 43 *European Law Review* 583. The Draft Agreement between Canada and the European Union on the transfer and processing of Passenger Name Record ('EU–Canada PNR Agreement') can be found in Council doc 12657/5/13 REV 5, 23 June 2014.
72 Council Decision authorising the opening of negotiations with Japan for an agreement between the European Union and Japan on the transfer and use of Passenger Name Record (PNR) data to prevent and combat terrorism and serious transnational crime, Council doc 5378/20, 4 February 2020.
73 Article 4(1) of the EU–US PNR Agreement.
74 Article 3(1) and (3) of the EU-Australia PNR Agreement and Article 3(1) and (3) of the EU–Canada PNR Agreement.
75 See Article 6(1) and (2) of the EAW Framework Decision: '1. The issuing *judicial* authority shall be the *judicial* authority of the issuing Member State which is competent to issue a European arrest warrant by virtue of the law of that State. 2. The executing *judicial* authority shall be the *judicial* authority of the executing Member State which is competent to execute the European arrest warrant by virtue of the law of that State'. Emphasis added.
76 Case C-452/16 PPU *Poltorak*, EU:C:2016:858, para 32; Case C-477/16 PPU *Kovalkovas*, EU:C:2016:861, para 33; and Case C-453/16 PPU *Özcelik*, EU:C:2016:860, para 33. The

the words 'judicial authority' are not limited to designating only the judges or courts of a Member State, but may extend more broadly to the authorities required to participate in administering justice in the legal system concerned.[77] However, as regards the issuing of EAWs, the CJEU held that national police authorities and a national executive authority such as a ministry do not fall within this definition of judicial authority.[78]

The CJEU notes that the entire surrender procedure is covered by judicial supervision.[79] The issuing of an EAW by a non-judicial authority, such as a police service, or by an entity coming under the executive, does not provide the executing judicial authority with an assurance that the issue of that EAW has undergone judicial approval and cannot, therefore, suffice to justify the high level of confidence between the Member States which forms the very basis of the Framework Decision.[80] In *Özcelik*, which involved the issuing of a national warrant forming the basis of an EAW, the Court found however that a public prosecutor who has confirmed a warrant issued by a police service did fall within the concept of judicial authority for the purposes of issuing an EAW, as such confirmation provides the executing authority with an assurance that the EAW is based on a decision that had undergone judicial approval, thus justifying a high level of confidence between Member States.[81]

More recently, the CJEU has adopted a number of judgements on the question of whether a national public prosecutor's office can fall within the autonomous concept of 'judicial authority' for the purposes of issuing an EAW. This case law has been opened by two cases referred by the Irish Supreme Court, one concerning the German public prosecutor (*OG and PI*)[82] and one concerning the Lithuanian prosecutor's general office (*PF*).[83] In *OG and PI*, concerning the German public prosecutor, the CJEU found that the concept of judicial

---

following remarks draw upon V Mitsilegas, 'Autonomous Concepts, Diversity Management and Mutual Trust in Europe's Area of Criminal Justice' (2020) 57 *Common Market Law Review* 45, 63ff.

77 For the purposes of Article 6(1) of the EAW Framework Decision, see Case C-452/16 PPU *Poltorak*, para 33, and Case C-477/16 PPU *Kovalkovas*, para 34. For the purposes of Article 8(1)(c) of the EAW Framework Decision, see Case C-453/16 PPU *Özcelik*, para 32.

78 Case C-452/16 PPU *Poltorak*, para 34 and Case C-477/16 PPU *Kovalkovas*, para 35 respectively.

79 Case C-452/16 PPU *Poltorak*, paras 39–42 and Case C-477/16 PPU *Kovalkovas*, para 37.

80 Case C-452/16 PPU *Poltorak*, para 45; Case C-477/16 PPU *Kovalkovas*, para 44.

81 Case C-453/16 PPU *Özcelik*, para 36.

82 Joined Cases C-508/18 *OG* (*Public Prosecutor's office of Lübeck*) & C-82/19 PPU *PI* (*Public Prosecutor's office of Zwickau*), EU:C:2019:456.

83 Case C-509/18 *Minister for Justice and Equality v PF* (*Prosecutor General of Lithuania*), EU:C:2019:457.

authority is capable of including authorities that, although not necessarily judges or courts, participate in the administration of criminal justice, with public prosecutor's offices being capable of being regarded as participating in the administration of criminal justice.[84]

The CJEU emphasised the *dual level* of protection in the issuing of a national and European arrest warrant, and on the significant impact of the execution of the EAW on fundamental rights, in particular on the right to liberty.[85] The protection to be provided in the EAW process means that the judicial authority must review the observance of conditions necessary for the issuing of the warrant and examine proportionality in the issuing of the EAW.[86] Placing the analysis within a strong framework of fundamental rights protection, the CJEU went on to elaborate two constituent elements that must apply cumulatively for the autonomous concept of judicial authority for the purposes of issuing an EAW to be established.

The first constituent element is *independence*. According to the CJEU, the issuing authority must be capable of exercising its responsibilities objectively, without being exposed to the risk that its decision-making power be subject to external directions or instructions, in particular from the executive, such as that it is beyond doubt that the decision to issue an EAW lies with that authority and not, ultimately, with the executive.[87] The second constituent element of the autonomous concept of judicial authority is the availability of an *effective remedy* against the decision to issue an EAW, including the proportionality of such decision.[88]

Against this background, the CJEU found that the German public prosecutor's offices are exposed to the risk of being influenced by the executive and that it cannot be guaranteed that they act independently in issuing an EAW.[89] The CJEU stressed in this context that it cannot be ruled out that the executive can issue instructions to the prosecutors.[90] Importantly, the CJEU found that the existence of the second element of the concept of judicial authority in domestic law, namely the existence of effective remedies, does not remedy the fact that the first element of the concept, namely independence, is not ensured.[91] Thus, the German public prosecutor's office cannot be included

---

84   Joined Cases C-508/18 & C-82/19 PPU *OG and PI*, para 51 and paras 62–63.
85   ibid, paras 67–68.
86   ibid, para 71 (by reference to Case C-477/16 PPU *Kovalkovas*, para 47).
87   ibid, para 73.
88   ibid.
89   ibid, para 88.
90   ibid, paras 82–83.
91   ibid, paras 84–85.

within the autonomous concept of 'judicial authority' for the purposes of issuing an EAW.

In contrast, this is not the case with the Lithuanian prosecutor's general office. In the ruling on the latter,[92] the CJEU applied the same steps as in *OG and PI*, but on the basis of the facts reached a different conclusion regarding the independence of the Prosecutor General. The CJEU found that the requirement of independence is met in this case, stressing in particular that the responsibility for issuing EAWs lies ultimately with this authority,[93] that its independence is constitutionally enshrined, and that the prosecutor can act freely of any external influence.[94] However, fulfilling the requirement of independence is not enough for inclusion in the concept of judicial authority: the referring court must also determine whether the second constituent element of the concept stands, namely whether a decision to issue an EAW may be the subject of court proceedings that meet the full requirements inherent in effective judicial protection.

With the rulings in *OG and PI* and *PF*, the CJEU took the important decision not to exclude, in principle, public prosecutors from the concept of judicial authority. However, the CJEU can be seen as compensating for not excluding an authority that is not a judge or a court from the scope of a judicial authority issuing an EAW by setting out the provision of effective judicial protection as an additional requirement to that of independence. The CJEU leaves the final decision with national authorities, but the guidance given is more detailed than in its initial rulings concerning the development of the autonomous concept of judicial authority for the purposes of issuing an EAW and the inclusion of executive bodies within this concept. The decisions in the *OG and PI* and *PF* cases have been followed by further rulings on Austrian, Belgian, French, and Swedish public prosecutor's offices, with the CJEU stating that all of them meet the requirements of 'issuing judicial authorities' for the purposes of the EAW Framework Decision.[95]

This state of affairs has a number of implications for the fight against environmental crime. Since the most serious environmental crimes often have a

---

92   Case C-509/18 *PF*.
93   ibid, para 54.
94   ibid, para 55.
95   Respectively Case C-489/19 *NJ (Parquet de Vienne)*, EU:C:2019:849 (Austria); Joined Cases C-566/19 PPU & C-626/19 PPU *JR and YC (Parquet général du Grand-Duché de Luxembourg and Tours)*, EU:C:2019:1077 (France); C-625/19 PPU *XD (Openbaar Ministerie (Parquet Suède))*, EU:C:2019:1078 (Sweden); C-627/19 *ZB (Openbaar Ministerie (Procureur du Roi de Bruxelles))* PPU, EU:C:2019:1079 (Belgium).

cross-border nature, the efficient functioning of mutual recognition procedures is of the essence for an effective reaction by law enforcement and prosecuting authorities. Each legal system functions however in a different way and such differences do not only concern substantive criminal law but also procedural law and the organisation of the judicial system. As for the latter, the recent case law of the CJEU demonstrates that, despite the different approaches of each Member State, some common standards should be met to ensure, on the one hand, the effectiveness of the EAW system, and, on the other, the protection of fundamental rights of individuals whose surrender is sought.

It ought to be noted that other EU instruments – such as the EIO Directive and the Regulation on mutual recognition of confiscation and freezing orders – expressly allow for the issuing of mutual recognition instruments by authorities *other than courts*. According to the EIO Directive, 'issuing authority' indeed means:

(i) a judge, a court, an investigating judge or a *public prosecutor* competent in the case concerned; or
(ii) *any other competent authority* as defined by the issuing State which, in the specific case, *is acting in its capacity as an investigating authority in criminal proceedings* with competence to order the gathering of evidence in accordance with national law. In addition, before it is transmitted to the executing authority the EIO shall be validated, after examination of its conformity with the conditions for issuing an EIO under this Directive ... by a judge, court, investigating judge or a public prosecutor in the issuing State. Where the EIO has been validated by a judicial authority, that authority may also be regarded as an issuing authority for the purposes of transmission of the EIO.[96]

The definition of 'issuing judicial authority' in the Regulation on the mutual recognition of freezing and confiscation orders is almost identical.[97] These definitions, which are broader than those laid down in the EAW Framework Decision, allow an exchange of mutual recognition instruments among different actors of the criminal justice systems, potentially with less issues connected with their status, even though some judicial validation is still required. The addition of 'other competent authority' is noteworthy and bears special importance in the environmental field, where public prosecutors are not the only actors who can investigate and prosecute crimes.[98] The Court of Justice

---

96 Article 2(c) of the EIO Directive. Emphasis added.
97 See Article 2(8) of Regulation 2018/1805.
98 Despite its withdrawal from the Union, the UK is still worth mentioning as a case in point, since environmental agencies such as the Environmental Agency in England and Wales and the Scottish Environmental Protection Agency in Scotland play a pivotal role

has now held that Article 1(1) and Article 2(c) of the EIO Directive must be interpreted as meaning that the concepts of 'judicial authority' and 'issuing authority', within the meaning of those provisions, include the public prosecutor of a Member State or, more generally, the public prosecutor's office of a Member State, regardless of any relationship of legal subordination that might exist between that public prosecutor or public prosecutor's office and the executive of that Member State and of the exposure of that public prosecutor or public prosecutor's office to the risk of being directly or indirectly subject to orders or individual instructions from the executive when adopting an EIO.[99]

2.3 Protection of Fundamental Rights

Finally, one of the most pressing and recurring questions concerning the EAW is whether mutual trust, which is the theoretical underpinning of mutual recognition, can justify the recognition of judgments that may have a detrimental effect on the protection of the fundamental rights of the defendant, or the recognition of requests that appear disproportionate or contrary to the substantive criminal law of the executing Member State. Article 1(3) of the EAW Framework Decision states that this legal instrument 'shall not have the effect of modifying the obligation to respect fundamental rights and fundamental legal principles as enshrined in Article 6 of the Treaty on European Union',[100] yet it does not list non-compliance with fundamental rights as a ground to refuse to execute an EAW. There are two main ways in which fundamental rights concerns have been addressed in legislation: via the insertion of grounds of refusal on fundamental rights grounds in subsequent legislation; and via legislation addressing proportionality concerns.

---

in investigating and, if need be, prosecuting environmental crimes (see more in E Fasoli, 'Environmental Criminal Law in the United Kingdom' in Farmer, Faure and Vagliasindi (eds) (n 2) 249ff). The studies in the EFFACE project came to the conclusion that 'the public (criminal) prosecutor has in many countries (still) a central role in enforcement whereas specialised environmental agencies have the prior expertise and technical knowledge to investigate environmental crime. While in the United Kingdom this paradox has been solved by allowing administrative authorities to prosecute their own cases, other States use different models of cooperation' (M Faure, C Gerstetter, S Sina et al, 'Instruments, Actors and Institutions in the Fight Against Environmental Crime'. Study in the framework of the EFFACE research project, Berlin, Ecologic Institute (2015) 56). Cf Pereira (n 6) 302ff.

99   Case C-584/19 *A and others (Staatsanwaltschaft Wien)*, EU:C:2020:1002.
100 The EAW Framework Decision was adopted before the entry into force of the Lisbon Treaty, yet Article 6 TEU still represents – in the new version of the Treaties – the EU primary law provision on the protection of fundamental rights.

In terms of the use of fundamental rights as a *limit to mutual recognition*, some Member States added non-compliance of surrender with fundamental rights as an express ground of refusal in their national law implementing the EAW Framework Decision. Even more importantly, the EIO Directive and the Regulation on the mutual recognition of freezing and confiscation orders expressly include non-compliance with fundamental rights as a ground for refusal to recognise and execute requests for mutual recognition.[101]

As for the *proportionality* issue, concerns on the respect of this principle have been raised by governments and defendants alike and stem from the fear that mutual recognition instruments, and EAWs in particular, are issued for offences that are deemed to be minor or trivial in the executing State. In the light of the different approaches by Member States to environmental crime,[102] such concerns arise also in the field at stake. Calls for the introduction of a proportionality check in the operation of the principle of mutual recognition in criminal matters have been put forward in order to ensure that pressure on the criminal justice systems of executing Member States, and disproportionate results for the requested individuals, are avoided.[103]

Proportionality check requirements have thus been introduced in policy documents and secondary law. The prevailing view has thus far been for proportionality to be dealt with in the *issuing* and not in the executing Member State – this is for instance the interpretative guidance given in the revised version of the European Handbook on how to issue a European Arrest Warrant.[104] The requirement to introduce a proportionality check in the issuing State has also been introduced at EU level in the EIO Directive, which states that the issuing authority may only issue an EIO where this is necessary and proportionate and where the investigative measures indicated in the EIO could have been ordered under the same conditions in a similar domestic case.[105] The Directive thus links proportionality with the requirement to avoid abuse of law via the undertaking of 'fishing expeditions' by the authorities of the issuing

---

101   Article 11(1)(f) of the EIO Directive.
102   See the previous chapter.
103   For a discussion, see Joint Committee on Human Rights, *The Human Rights Implications of UK Extradition Policy*, Fifteenth Report, session 2010–12, 40–43. See also Case C-396/11 *Radu*, Opinion of Advocate General Sharpston, EU:C:2012:648.
104   'Commission Notice – Handbook on how to issue and execute a European arrest warrant' [2017] OJ C335/1, para 2.4. The role of proportionality in mutual recognition procedures has been recently examined in-depth by E Xanthopoulou, *Fundamental Rights and Mutual Trust in the Area of Freedom, Security and Justice. A Role for Proportionality?* (Hart 2020).
105   Article 6(1)(a) and (b) of the EIO Directive respectively.

State. In a similar vein, the Regulation on mutual recognition of freezing orders and confiscation orders provides that when issuing freezing orders or confiscation orders, 'issuing authorities shall ensure that the principles of necessity and proportionality are respected'.[106] Along the lines of the EIO Directive, the Regulation's Preamble clarifies that a freezing order or confiscation order should only be issued and transmitted where it could have been issued and used in a solely domestic case.[107]

In addition to the legislative measures adopted at the EU and national level, the relationship between fundamental rights, mutual recognition and mutual trust has been addressed by the Court of Justice as well, in a series of decisions opened by the *Aranyosi and Căldăraru*[108] case. Mr Aranyosi, who resided in Germany, was wanted for prosecution in Hungary and thus subject to two European Arrest Warrants issued by Hungarian authorities. As for Mr Căldăraru, who was also residing in Germany, an EAW issued by Romanian authorities was pending against him concerning the execution of a sentence of one year and eight months imposed on him. A significant feature of the cases is that the European Court of Human Rights (ECtHR) had condemned both Hungary and Romania for violation of Article 3 of the European Convention on Human Rights (ECHR) – prohibition of inhuman or degrading treatment or punishment – due to detention conditions in their jurisdictions. Consequently, the referring court considered that specific evidence suggested that the conditions of detention to which Mr Aranyosi and Mr Căldăraru would have been subjected, if they were to be surrendered to the Hungarian and Romanian authorities respectively, would not satisfy the minimum standards required by international law.

The Grand Chamber of the CJEU clarified that the protection of fundamental rights is key as the principle of mutual recognition is itself founded on the mutual confidence between the Member States that their national legal systems are capable of providing such protection in an equivalent and effective manner.[109] The Grand Chamber highlighted that limitations to the principles of mutual recognition and mutual trust between Member States could be made 'in exceptional circumstances',[110] and went on to provide guidelines as

---

106 Article 1(3) of Regulation 2018/1805.
107 Recital 21 of Regulation 2018/1805.
108 Joined Cases C-404/15 & C-659/15 PPU *Pál Aranyosi and Robert Căldăraru v Generalstaatsanwaltschaft Bremen*, EU:C:2016:198.
109 ibid, para 77.
110 ibid, para 82. See also the CJEU's Opinion 2/13 (*Accession of the European Union to the European Convention for the Protection of Human Rights and Fundamental Freedoms*), EU:C:2014:2454, para 191.

to how an executing judicial authority must proceed when assessing risks of inhuman or degrading treatments.

The Court envisaged a *two-step* approach. First, a *general* assessment of the risk must take place. Where the judicial authority of the executing Member State is in possession of evidence of a real risk of inhuman or degrading treatment of individuals detained in the issuing Member State, it is bound to assess the existence of that risk when it is called upon to decide on the surrender of an individual to the authorities of the issuing Member State.[111] However, in addition to a general assessment of the risk, it will also be necessary for the executing judicial authority to proceed to a further assessment, specific and precise, of whether there are substantial grounds to believe that the *individual* concerned will be exposed to that risk because of the conditions for his or her detention envisaged in the issuing Member State.[112] The Court found that if, on the basis of the information provided, the executing judicial authority finds that there is a real risk of inhuman or degrading treatment for the individual in respect of whom the EAW was issued, then the execution is postponed, but it cannot be abandoned.[113]

If, however, the information received by the issuing Member State permits to discount the existence of a real risk that the individual concerned will be subject to inhuman and degrading treatment in the issuing Member State, the executing judicial authority must adopt its decision on the execution of the EAW.[114] In its final step, the Grand Chamber grudgingly accepts that until obtaining supplementing information that would discount the existence of a risk of inhuman or degrading treatment, a decision on the surrender must be postponed, but if the existence of that risk cannot be discounted within a reasonable time, the executing judicial authority must decide whether the surrender procedure should be brought to an end.[115]

After *Aranyosi and Căldăraru*, other national courts have requested further clarification from the CJEU on the assessment they are required to make when deciding on the surrender of a person in execution of an EAW. In two further judgements, the CJEU has thus specified what kind of assessment the executing authority should carry out when evaluating the detention conditions in the issuing Member State.[116] In another case (*LM*), the question was

---

111   Joined Cases C-404/15 & C-659/15 PPU *Aranyosi and Căldăraru*, para 88.
112   ibid, para 92.
113   ibid, para 98.
114   ibid, para 103.
115   ibid, para 104.
116   Case C-220/18 PPU *ML* (*Conditions of detention in Hungary*), EU:C:2018:589; Case C-128/18 *Dumitru-Tudor Dorobantu*, EU:C:2019:857.

instead whether the dual-pronged test envisaged in *Aranyosi and Căldăraru* should also apply when the executing authority (Irish, in this case) doubts whether the issuing authority, which was Polish, enjoys sufficient independence.[117] The Court decided that the *Aranyosi and Căldăraru* principles apply also in this constellation. This has attracted some criticism, since it is not clear how the executing authority can assess the lack of independence of the issuing authorities in a specific case.[118] However, the Court of Justice has recently re-affirmed the applicability of the *Aranyosi* two-step test in cases involving concerns regarding serious rule of law deficiencies in the issuing State.[119]

In sum, the respect of human rights throughout the EU is crucial to ensure the efficient functioning of mutual recognition procedures. When environmental crimes have a cross-border dimension, effective investigation and prosecution of this form of criminality would usually require some cross-border cooperation, which may be hampered if (some) Member States are responsible for serious violations of human rights. The above-mentioned concerns over the threshold of penalties for environmental crimes, which national legislatures may set at a rather low level with negative consequences for judicial cooperation (section 2.1), are related to the perception that Member States have of the gravity and seriousness of environmental criminality–a perception that is often insufficient and overlooks the real dangers and problems connected with crimes against the environment. The concerns discussed in this section, which are related to human rights issues, go however beyond the Member States' approach to the fight against environmental criminality as they relate to broader systemic aspects of national criminal justice systems, such as detention conditions and independence of the judiciary. In other words, the effectiveness of the EU toolbox to curb environmental crime depends not only on the attention that each Member State and the EU pay to this field, but also on the more general compliance of national legal orders with fundamental EU principles and objectives.

---

117   Case C-216/18 PPU LM (*Minister for Justice and Equality – Défaillances du système judiciaire*), EU:C:2018:586.
118   See S Carrera and V Mitsilegas, 'Upholding the Rule of Law by Scrutinising Judicial Independence. The Irish Court's Request for a Preliminary Ruling on the European Arrest Warrant' (2018) CEPS Commentary <www.ceps.eu/ceps-publications/upholding-rule-law-scrutinising-judicial-independence-irish-courts-request-preliminary/> accessed 2 June 2021.
119   Joined Cases C-354/20 PPU and C-412/20 PPU *L and P (Openbaar Ministerie – (Indépendance de l'autorité judiciaire d'émission*), EU:C:2020:1033.

3 Conflicts of Jurisdiction in the European Union

In 2002, the oil tanker *Prestige* sank in Galician waters and 64,000 tonnes of oil were spilled, causing massive damages to the environment. Investigations into the facts were soon launched but a problem arose, namely the identification of the Member State in which the captain and the other persons allegedly responsible for the disaster should have been prosecuted (France or Spain). As will be discussed in the next chapter, Eurojust was instrumental in solving this conflict of jurisdiction and suggested that Spain was the country that was best placed to conduct investigations and launch prosecutions in that case. This example is illustrative of the inherent risks of conflicts of jurisdiction that are connected with most environmental crimes.[120] As the most serious among them do not know borders (such as pollution) or by definition involve more than one country (eg illegal trafficking of waste or protected species), the issue of which State has jurisdiction to deal with a given environmental crime is rather common.[121]

Currently, there is no centralised binding mechanism of jurisdiction allocation in criminal matters in the European Union.[122] This is rather unfortunate since concerns of prosecutorial forum shopping lurk behind such conflicts. When more than one Member State has jurisdiction on a given case, the risk is that the choice will fall on the system that yields more chances of conviction, while other relevant interests at stake, such as those of the defendants or of the victims, are neglected.[123] Conflicts of jurisdiction are usually classified in: a) 'positive', when two or more Member States wish to (or should) prosecute a given case, or are already dealing with it; and b) 'negative', which

---

120 See also Pereira (n 6) 276–277.

121 For less serious crimes, conflicts of jurisdiction may not arise if one or more of the countries that are affected by a given conduct that causes environmental damage do not criminalise that conduct but rather punish it with administrative sanctions (cf ibid 342).

122 V Mitsilegas, *EU Criminal Law after Lisbon. Rights, Trust and Transformation of Justice in Europe* (Hart 2016) 91ff, whereupon this section draws. See also A Klip, *European Criminal Law. An Integrative Approach* (3rd edn, Intersentia 2016) 455–456. Recently, some proposals to fill this gap have been put forward in the literature: see European Law Institute, K Ligeti and G Robinson (eds), *Preventing and Resolving Conflicts of Jurisdiction in EU Criminal Law* (OUP 2018) 42–76.

123 M Böse, 'Choice of Forum and Jurisdiction' in M Luchtman, (ed), *Choice of Forum in Cooperation Against EU Financial Crime. Freedom, Security and Justice and the Protection of Specific EU-Interests* (Eleven International Publishing 2013) 74–75. As far as the victims' role in this context is concerned, see M Simonato, 'What Role for Crime Victims in the Forum Choice?' in European Law Institute, Ligeti and Robinson (eds) (previous n) 283–304.

occur when no Member State is willing to deal with a crime, although two or more of them would have jurisdiction on it.[124] Positive conflicts of jurisdiction tend to flourish proportionately to both the growth of cross-border criminality and the number of national laws providing for extra-territorial jurisdiction.[125] A possible way to cope with positive conflicts of jurisdiction is the *transfer of proceedings*, which allows national competent authorities to divest themselves of a case and transfer it to the authorities of another Member State which are better placed to deal with it.[126] At the EU level, however, there is no legal instrument that regulates transfers of proceedings, which therefore take place mostly in accordance with non-EU rules.[127] A proposal for a Council Framework Decision on the matter was tabled in 2009 but did not have any follow-up.[128]

As the case of the shipwreck of the *Prestige* demonstrated, the (non-binding) powers of Eurojust with respect to conflicts of jurisdiction can play an important role in this context.[129] The Eurojust Regulation states that the Agency may ask the competent authorities of Member States 'to accept that one of them may be in a better position to undertake an investigation or to prosecute specific acts'.[130] Respectful of Member States' wish to maintain

---

124 See more in, inter alia, P Caeiro, 'Jurisdiction in Criminal Matters in the EU: Negative and Positive Conflicts, and Beyond' (2010) 93 *Kritische Vierteljahresschrift für Gesetzgebung und Rechtswissenschaft* 366, 369ff; 'Explanatory Note' in European Law Institute, Ligeti and Robinson (eds) (n 122) 16.

125 See, eg, Böse (n 123) 74. For some examples of EU criminal law instruments requiring the Member States to establish extra-territorial jurisdiction on crimes that are subject to EU harmonisation, see section 4.2 of the previous chapter.

126 See 'Transfer of Proceedings' (2016) 14 *Eurojust News* 1, 7–8; A Marletta, 'Report on the Field Research at Eurojust, February 2015' in European Law Institute, Ligeti and Robinson (eds) (n 122) 95–96.

127 Some EU Member States have ratified the 1972 European Convention on the Transfer of Proceedings in Criminal Matters, Strasbourg, ETS No 73. In addition to this instrument, other non-EU legal bases that are at times relied upon to transfer criminal proceedings are reportedly Article 21 of the 1959 European Convention on Mutual Assistance in Criminal Matters, Strasbourg, ETS No 30 and the 2000 United Nations Convention against Transnational Organized Crime ('Transfer of Proceedings' (previous n) 7–8).

128 [2009] OJ C219/7.

129 On Eurojust and conflicts of jurisdictions, see inter alia C Deboyser, 'Eurojust's Role in the Matter of Choice of Forum' in Luchtman (ed), *Choice of Forum in Cooperation Against EU Financial Crime* (n 123) 101–108; I Patrone, 'Conflicts of Jurisdiction and Judicial Cooperation Instruments: Eurojust's Role' (2013) 14 *ERA Forum* 215; Marletta, 'Report on the Field Research at Eurojust' (n 126).

130 Article 4(2)(b) of Regulation (EU) 2018/1727 of the European Parliament and of the Council of 14 November 2018 on the European Union Agency for Criminal Justice Cooperation

sovereignty in the initiation of investigations and prosecutions, Eurojust may only *ask* – but not oblige – national authorities to consider these issues. While Eurojust's contribution to the fight against environmental crime is discussed in the next chapter, at this stage suffice it to notice that, in 2003, Eurojust adopted a series of (non-binding) guidelines on 'which jurisdiction should prosecute'.[131] The Guidelines, which were revised in 2016,[132] call for a 'preliminary presumption'[133] that prosecution should take place in the jurisdiction where the majority of criminality occurred or where the majority of the loss was sustained. The Guidelines contain a series of criteria to take into account when identifying the Member State that should investigate or prosecute a given crime, including the location of the accused, capacity to extradite or surrender, centralisation of prosecutions of many suspects in one jurisdiction, attendance and protection of witnesses and victims. According to the Guidelines, the sentencing powers of the courts should not be a 'determining' factor in deciding where to prosecute, but availability and use of evidence is a relevant factor.[134]

Mechanisms and criteria of allocating jurisdiction do exist in further sectoral EU criminal law instruments.[135] This is not the case of the Environmental Crime and Ship-Source Pollution Directives,[136] although the Council Framework Decision that was annulled by the Court of Justice in the *Ship-Source Pollution* case listed some criteria to take into account in cases of maritime pollution involving more than one Member State.[137]

(Eurojust) and replacing and repealing Council Decision 2002/187/JHA [2018] OJ L295/138 ('Eurojust Regulation').

131 See Annex to Eurojust, 'Annual Report 2003' (2004) 60ff. On these guidelines, see A Marletta, 'Forum Choice in the Area of Freedom, Security and Justice' in European Law Institute, Ligeti and Robinson (eds) (n 122) 150–153.

132 Originally included in Eurojust, 'Annual Report 2016' (2017), the Guidelines are now a standalone document available on the Eurojust's website (<www.eurojust.europa.eu/practitioners/operational/pages/guidelines-on-jurisdiction.aspx> accessed 2 June 2021).

133 Eurojust, 'Guidelines for deciding "Which jurisdiction should prosecute?"' (previous n) 3.

134 ibid 3–4.

135 See, for instance, Article 19(3) of Directive (EU) 2017/541 of the European Parliament and of the Council of 15 March 2017 on combating terrorism and replacing Council Framework Decision 2002/475/JHA and amending Council Decision 2005/671/JHA [2017] OJ L88/6; Article 7(2) of Council Framework Decision 2008/841/JHA of 24 October 2008 on the fight against organised crime [2008] OJ L300/42.

136 For some remarks on jurisdictional issues connected with ship-source pollution in EU legislation, see A Pozdnakova, *Criminal Jurisdiction over Perpetrators of Ship-Source Pollution: International Law, State Practice and EU Harmonisation* (Brill 2012) 238ff.

137 See Article 7(4) and (5) of Council Framework Decision 2005/667/JHA of 12 July 2005 to strengthen the criminal-law framework for the enforcement of the law against ship-source pollution [2005] OJ L255/164.

Back in 2005, the Commission had launched the debate on whether there should be some common rules on conflicts of jurisdiction by linking the issue with the question of the development of an EU definition of *ne bis in idem*. In the Commission's Green Paper on conflicts of jurisdiction, published in December 2005,[138] the Commission floated the idea of creating an EU mechanism for the choice of jurisdiction and called for criteria on jurisdiction allocation to be listed in a future EU instrument. The Commission's Green Paper did not however lead to any relevant change in the status quo, and the situation has not been remedied by the adoption in 2009 of a Framework Decision on prevention and settlement of conflicts of jurisdiction,[139] which merely establishes channels of information exchange and consultation between national authorities.[140] The Framework Decision provides for a role for Eurojust where it has not been possible to reach consensus,[141] but Member States do not appear to have made wide use of this provision.[142] The text of the Framework Decision does not even list the criteria to take into account when competent national authorities assess and discuss which of them is better placed to deal with a given case. Only in the Preamble it is specified that they should consider 'relevant criteria', which may include those set out in the above-mentioned Eurojust's Guidelines, and take into account for example

> the place where the major part of the criminality occurred, the place where the majority of the loss was sustained, the location of the suspected or accused person and possibilities for securing its surrender or extradition to other jurisdictions, the nationality or residence of the suspected or accused person, significant interests of the suspected or accused person, significant interests of victims and witnesses, the admissibility of evidence or any delays that may occur.[143]

---

138 Commission, 'Green Paper On Conflicts of Jurisdiction and the Principle of *ne bis in idem* in Criminal Proceedings' COM (2005) 696 final, 23 December 2005.
139 Council Framework Decision 2009/948/JHA of 30 November 2009 on prevention and settlement of conflicts of exercise of jurisdiction in criminal proceedings [2009] OJ L328/42.
140 Articles 5–9 and 10–13 of Council Framework Decision 2009/948/JHA respectively. See inter alia Marletta, 'Forum Choice in the Area of Freedom, Security and Justice' (n 131) 145–148.
141 Article 12(2) of Council Framework Decision 2009/948/JHA.
142 Commission, 'Report from the Commission to the European Parliament and the Council on the implementation by the Member States of Framework Decision 2009/948/JHA of 30 November 2009 on prevention and settlement of conflicts of exercise of jurisdiction in criminal proceedings' COM (2014) 313 final, 2 June 2014, 4–5.
143 Recital 9 of Council Framework Decision 2009/948/JHA.

As often happens in EU legislation, the use of extensive preambular provisions is justified by the fact that legislators – or, in this case, the Member States within the Council – could not agree on real obligations in the operative part of the text.[144]

The entry into force of the Treaty of Lisbon may have provided new impetus towards the adoption of EU rules on conflicts of jurisdiction. Article 82(1)(b) of the Treaty on the Functioning of the European Union (TFEU) calls upon the European Parliament and the Council to adopt measures to prevent and settle conflicts of jurisdiction between Member States, while Article 85(1)(c) TFEU states that the tasks of Eurojust following the adoption of post-Lisbon secondary law may include the resolution of such conflicts.[145] However, little, if any, progress has been made thus far on the ground. At the time of writing, no use of Article 82(1)(b) TFEU has been made, while the Eurojust Regulation – adopted in 2018 – does not contain any major change in relation to the Agency's role in the resolution of conflicts of jurisdiction.[146] The 2013 Commission's proposal for a Regulation on Eurojust tried to enhance Eurojust's powers by providing that competent national authorities could decide not to follow Eurojust's opinions on conflicts of jurisdiction only upon justification of the reasons for this choice,[147] but the Member States did not agree and the obligation to give reasons in case of refusal to follow Eurojust's opinions has been eventually removed from the text of the Regulation.[148]

These developments reflect the reluctance of Member States to introduce EU-level binding rules that would limit their capacity to prosecute and their real and perceived power to deliver justice in criminal matters for their citizens. Binding EU powers in the field would indeed limit considerably the powers of Member States: in cases of positive conflicts of jurisdiction, a binding EU decision excluding one Member State from prosecuting would raise serious questions on its capacity to deliver justice domestically; in cases of negative conflicts of jurisdiction, a binding EU decision would have the effect of obliging a Member State to prosecute a case that it would not normally have

---

144 See H Nowell-Smith, 'Behind the Scenes in the Negotiation of EU Criminal Justice Legislation' (2012) 3 *New Journal of European Criminal Law* 381, 384.

145 For an in-depth analysis of these two provisions, see M Wasmeier, 'The Legal Basis for Preventing and Resolving Conflicts of Criminal Jurisdiction in the TFEU' in European Law Institute, Ligeti and Robinson (eds) (n 122) 102ff.

146 See more in the next chapter.

147 Articles 4(4) and 23 of Commission, 'Proposal for a Regulation on the European Union Agency for Criminal Justice Cooperation (Eurojust)' COM (2013) 535 final, 17 July 2013.

148 cf Article 4(6) of the Eurojust Regulation. In addition, Recital 14 of the Eurojust Regulation clarifies that the 'written opinions of Eurojust are not binding on Member States'.

prosecuted. While it may not be controversial from a Member States' perspective, the absence of EU binding rules on conflicts of jurisdiction can however cast doubt on the efficiency of the EU's reaction to cross-border crime, including environmental crime, as well as on its respect for the fundamental rights of the individuals, which are currently deprived of detailed and clear remedies vis-à-vis decisions on conflicts of jurisdiction.

4   Ne Bis in Idem

The only 'instrument' that can currently solve conflicts of jurisdiction in the EU is the transnational *ne bis in idem* principle. The right not to be tried or punished twice (*bis*) for an offence that has already been finally judged (*idem*) – expressed as the prohibition of double jeopardy in common law jurisdictions – is a fundamental principle in many, if not all, EU Member States.[149] In the context of EU criminal law, *ne bis in idem* has traditionally been related to the challenge of providing clear and legitimate answers to the question of how to achieve justice in cases of cross-border prosecutions.

In the AFSJ, transnational *ne bis in idem* had first been introduced in Article 54 of the Convention Implementing the Schengen Agreement (CISA or 'Schengen Convention')[150] and is now also enshrined in Article 50 of the EU Charter of Fundamental Rights (hereinafter: the 'Charter' or CFR). Since it is not coupled with a set of rules on jurisdiction, however, *ne bis in idem* has limited added value in solving conflicts of jurisdiction, since its application simply implies that the first Member State to adjudicate a case, as the 'sheriff who is quickest on the draw',[151] can prevent others from doing the same, 'even if someone was better placed to fire the shot'.[152]

---

149   V Mitsilegas and F Giuffrida, '*Ne Bis in Idem*' in R Sicurella, V Mitsilegas, R Parizot et al (eds), *General Principles for a Common Criminal Law Framework in the EU. A Guide for Legal Practitioners* (Giuffrè 2017) 209, whereupon this and the following sections partly draw.
150   Convention implementing the Schengen Agreement of 14 June 1985 between the Governments of the States of the Benelux Economic Union, the Federal Republic of Germany and the French Republic on the gradual abolition of checks at their common borders [2000] OJ L239/19.
151   J Spencer, 'Mutual Recognition and Choice of Forum' in Luchtman (ed), *Choice of Forum in Cooperation Against EU Financial Crime* (n 123) 71.
152   ibid. See also Caeiro, 'Jurisdiction in Criminal Matters' (n 124) 376; 'A Manifesto on European Criminal Procedure Law. European Criminal Policy Initiative' (2013) 11 *Zeitschrift für Internationale Strafrechtsdogmatik* 430, 432.

The inclusion of the *ne bis in idem* principle in the Schengen Convention, and subsequently in EU law as a consequence both of its inclusion in the Charter and of the incorporation of the Schengen *acquis* into the EU legal order by the Amsterdam Treaty,[153] is inextricably linked with rethinking territoriality in the European Union – in particular as regards the Schengen area. A person who is exercising free movement rights in a borderless area may not be penalised doubly by being subject to multiple prosecutions for the same acts as a result of him or her crossing borders. This represents another side of mutual recognition in criminal matters, the recognition of decisions finally disposing trials, and *ne bis in idem* in fact constitutes also a ground for refusal to execute EU mutual recognition instruments.[154]

Notwithstanding the inclusion of the *ne bis in idem* principle in primary and secondary EU legislation, there has been no further elaboration or clarification of the principle by EU legislation.[155] A number of questions have thus arisen regarding the precise definition of the elements of *ne bis in idem,* such as the definition of *idem,*[156] and the definition of *bis* – what is essentially meant by a trial being 'finally disposed of'.[157] This uncertainty has led to a series of references for preliminary rulings by national courts to the Court of Justice, which have resulted in the development of a quite substantial case law on *ne bis in idem* by the Luxembourg Court. The next section gives an overview of the main European legal texts in which the prohibition of double jeopardy is included, while the following sections look at the development of *ne bis in idem* – in its

---

153 Protocol annexed to the Treaty on European Union and to the Treaty establishing the European Community – Protocol integrating the Schengen *acquis* into the framework of the European Union [1997] OJ C340/93. A similar Protocol is annexed to the Treaty of Lisbon (Protocol (No 19) on the Schengen *acquis* integrated into the framework of the European Union [2012] OJ C326/290).

154 See, eg, Article 3(2) of the EAW Framework Decision, Article 11(1)(d) of the EIO Directive, and Article 8(1)(a) of Regulation 2018/1805.

155 The Greek Government tabled during its 2003 EU Presidency a proposal for third pillar legislation harmonising the definition of *ne bis in idem* ('Initiative of the Hellenic Republic for the adoption of a Framework Decision of the Council on the application of the "*ne bis in idem*" principle' Council doc 6356/03, 13 February 2003). Negotiations on the proposal were however suspended in 2004. The Commission has since tabled a Green Paper on conflicts of jurisdiction and *ne bis in idem* attempting to take the issue further (see n 138), without success.

156 Whether the principle applies to the 'same acts', or to the 'same offences', and what constitutes a 'same' act or offence.

157 Whether the application of the principle is limited to judicial decisions determining a person's guilt or innocence, or whether it has a broader application to include cases where a prosecution is terminated on procedural grounds (eg if dropped by a public prosecutor in cases such as plea bargaining).

cross-border dimension – as a fundamental principle of Union law (section 4.2).[158] The last section examines an issue that is extremely relevant in a field such as environment law where administrative (punitive) law plays a key role, that is, the recent case law on the application of the *ne bis in idem* principle – at the national level – to cases of administrative and criminal proceedings concerning the same facts (section 4.3).

4.1 The Principle of Ne Bis in Idem *at the European Level*

The *ne bis in idem* principle is provided for, in its transnational dimension (ie applying *across* Member States), by the CISA and the Charter, and by Protocol No 7 to the ECHR in its national version (that is, when it applies *within* a Member State). Article 54 of the Schengen Convention sets out the principle as follows:

> A person whose trial has been finally disposed of in one Contracting Party may not be prosecuted in *another* Contracting Party for the same acts provided that, if a penalty has been imposed, it has been enforced, is actually in the process of being enforced or can no longer be enforced under the laws of the sentencing Contracting Party. (emphasis added)

Article 54 of the Convention applies in all EU Member States and in four non-EU countries that are parties to the Schengen *acquis* (Iceland, Norway, Switzerland, and Liechtenstein).[159] As far as the applicability *ratione temporis* is concerned, the Court of Justice examined whether Article 54 CISA applies in cases where the Convention, at the time of the *first* proceedings, was not yet in force in the State that ruled on the case. Since *ne bis in idem* comes into play when investigations or prosecutions on the same facts are initiated *a second time*, the Court ruled that it is only necessary to assess whether the Convention was in force – at the time of the *second* proceedings – in the *second* State.[160]

---

158 On the importance of ensuring the respect of *ne bis in idem*, even beyond the EU and on the international level, when more than one country has jurisdiction over environmental crime cases, see G Vermeulen, 'International Environmental Norms and Standards: Compliance and Enforcement. Promoting Extensive Territorial Jurisdiction, Corporate Chain Responsibility and Import Restrictions' (2016) 87 *Revue International de Droit Pénal – Protection of the Environment through Criminal Law* (ed by JL de La Cuesta et al) 37, 46–47.

159 Articles 55–58 CISA lay down some limitations of, and further rules on, transnational *ne bis in idem*. For some remarks on these provisions, see PP Paulesu, '*Ne Bis in Idem* and Conflicts of Jurisdiction' in RE Kostoris (ed), *Handbook of European Criminal Procedure* (Springer 2018) 402–404.

160 Case C-436/04 *Van Esbroeck*, EU:C:2006:165, paras 18–24.

As for the Charter of Fundamental Rights, Article 50 reads as follows: 'No one shall be liable to be tried or punished again in criminal proceedings for an offence for which he or she has already been finally acquitted or convicted within the Union in accordance with the law'. The Charter resembles the Schengen Convention's text since it provides for the transnational version of *ne bis in idem* ('within the Union'), although it refers to the same 'offence' rather than 'same acts' and does not replicate the 'enforcement condition' of Article 54 CISA ('where he is sentenced, the sentence has been served or is currently being served or can no longer be carried out'). The issue of the enduring validity of this clause is discussed below.[161]

Finally, as far as the Council of Europe framework is concerned, the prohibition of double jeopardy is enshrined in Article 4 of Protocol No 7 to the ECHR. While Germany and the Netherlands have not yet ratified it, the Protocol is in force in the other EU Member States, as well as in the other 19 States Parties to the Council of Europe that are not EU countries. Article 4 of Protocol No 7, however, deals only with the *national* dimension of *ne bis in idem*: a final judgment issued by an authority of the *same* State where the second criminal proceedings are launched bars further prosecution or punishment of the same person in that State, while nothing is said with respect to investigations and prosecutions on the same facts in other countries.[162] In spite of its limited applicability, the right to *ne bis in idem* is of utter importance in the Council of Europe context for it falls among the fundamental rights that cannot be derogated even in time of emergency.[163]

4.2 Bis, Idem *and Enforcement Condition*

Pursuant to Article 54 CISA and Article 50 CFR, the principle of *ne bis in idem* applies when some conditions are met: i) a first set of criminal proceedings is finally closed and a second one is initiated (*'bis'*); and ii) both sets of proceedings concern the same facts and the same person (*'idem'*). Unlike Article 50 of the Charter, Article 54 CISA also requires that the sentence that has been issued at the end of the first proceedings has already been served, is in the process of being served, or can no longer be carried out ('enforcement condition').[164] The

---

161 See section 4.2.3 below.
162 'No one shall be liable to be tried or punished again in criminal proceedings under the jurisdiction of the *same State* for an offence for which he has already been finally acquitted or convicted in accordance with the law and penal procedure of that State' (Article 4(1) of Protocol No 7 to the ECHR). Emphasis added.
163 Article 4(3) of Protocol No 7 to the ECHR.
164 It follows that this condition does not come into consideration when the first set of proceedings ends with the acquittal of the defendant.

Court of Justice has so far ruled several times on these three components of *ne bis in idem*, as discussed in the sections below.

4.2.1 The *'Bis'* Element

The first decision of the Court of Justice on Article 54 CISA, *Gözütok and Brügge*,[165] dates back to 2003 and deals with the concept of 'finally judged'.[166] The cases involved the termination of prosecutions by the public prosecutor (in the Netherlands and Germany respectively) following *out-of-court settlements* with the defendants, which can be quite common when it comes to (minor) environmental offences.[167] The Luxembourg Court was asked to determine whether such termination was capable to trigger the application of the *ne bis in idem* principle. The Court answered in the affirmative, that is, *ne bis in idem* applies in such cases, which involve the discontinuation of prosecution by a public prosecutor – without the involvement of a court – once the accused has fulfilled certain obligations.[168]

The second decision of the Court on Article 54 CISA, *Miraglia*, concerns the *bis* element as well, but in this case the Court ruled that a decision of the public prosecutor to discontinue the prosecution 'on the sole ground that criminal proceedings have been started in another Member State against the same defendant and for the same acts, *without any determination whatsoever as to the merits* of the case'[169] prevents the application of Article 54 CISA. In similar circumstances, which can be defined of 'preventive' application of *ne bis in idem*,[170] the decision to discontinue the prosecution could not fall within the

---

165 Joined Cases C-187/01 & C-385/01 *Gözütok and Brügge*, EU:C:2003:87. For a commentary, see A Weyembergh, 'Comment on CJEU, 11 February 2003, Joined Cases C-187/01 and C-385/01 *Criminal Proceedings v Hüseyin Gözütok and Klaus Brügge*' in V Mitsilegas, A di Martino and L Mancano (eds), *The Court of Justice and European Criminal Law. Leading Cases in a Contextual Analysis* (Hart 2019) 199–211.

166 For an overview of the Court of Justice's case law on the *'bis'* element, as well as on the *'idem'* element and on the enforcement condition, see also A Weyembergh and I Armada, 'The Principle of *Ne Bis in Idem* in Europe's Area of Freedom, Security and Justice' in V Mitsilegas, M Bergström and T Konstadinides (eds), *Research Handbook on EU Criminal Law* (Edward Elgar 2016) 189–209.

167 cf Pereira (n 6) 303ff.

168 In Case C-505/19, *Bundesrepublik Deutschland (Notice rouge d'Interpol)*, EU:C:2021:376, the Court confirmed that *ne bis in idem* also applies to procedures whereby public prosecutors decide to discontinue the prosecution without the involvement of courts, provided that that decision is based on a determination as to the merits of the case (paras 73–74). As for the relevance of the assessment of the merits of the case for the application of the *ne bis in idem* principle, see immediately below in the text.

169 Case C-469/03 *Miraglia*, EU:C:2005:156, para 35. Emphasis added.

170 ibid, para 23.

concept of 'final judgement' of Article 54 CISA since this decision contained 'no assessment whatsoever of the unlawful conduct with which the defendant was charged'.[171] *Miraglia* therefore clarified that, in order to trigger the application of *ne bis in idem*, it is necessary that the first authorities have assessed the *merits* of the case. If they have done so, the outcome of the first set of criminal proceedings is then irrelevant, since also an acquittal for lack of evidence prohibits further prosecution against the same person for the same facts, as the Court ruled in *Van Straaten*.[172]

On the same day of *Van Straaten*, the Court handed down its judgment in *Gasparini*.[173] While in *Van Straaten* and *Miraglia* the Court argued that the final decision that bars further prosecution has to deal with the merits of the case, in *Gasparini* it held that also a final decision by which the accused is acquitted because prosecution of the offence is *time-barred* – thus without any possibility for the competent court to delve into the merits of the case – has the same effect for the purposes of Article 54 CISA. In *Gasparini*, therefore, the focus seems to shift from the 'merits' of the case to the 'final status' of national proceedings, with the Court suggesting that, in order to assess whether a decision is apt to trigger Article 54 CISA, it is crucial to look at the 'final' nature of such decision from a national perspective.

This interpretation of Article 54 CISA was openly adopted by the Court in *Turanský*.[174] The case concerned the applicability of Article 54 CISA to a decision by which 'a police authority, after examining the merits of the case brought before it, makes an order, at a stage before the charging of a person suspected of a crime, suspending the criminal proceedings which had been instituted';[175] in that case, which concerned the Slovak legal system, such decision did not bar further prosecution within that State. Recalling *Gözütok and Brügge*, the Court noted that the concept of 'finally disposed of' – to be found in Article 54 CISA – refers to those circumstances where 'further prosecution is definitely barred'.[176] In this decision, the Court stressed in particular that

> in order to assess whether a decision is 'final' for the purposes of Article 54 of the CISA, it is necessary first of all to ascertain ... that the decision in question is considered *under the law of the Contracting State* which

---

171   ibid, para 34.
172   Case C-150/05 *Van Straaten*, EU:C:2006:614.
173   Case C-467/04 *Gasparini and others*, EU:C:2006:610.
174   Case C-491/07 *Turanský*, EU:C:2008:768.
175   ibid, para 30.
176   ibid, para 32.

adopted it to be final and binding, and to verify that it leads, in that State, to the protection granted by the *ne bis in idem* principle.[177]

The principles laid down in *Turanský* have been confirmed in other judgements, beginning with *Mantello*.[178] In *Mantello*, the Court did not deal with Article 54 CISA but rather with Article 3(2) of the EAW Framework Decision, which lists *ne bis in idem* as a ground for mandatory non-execution of EAWs. The Court argued that the two provisions share the same objective to prevent a person from being prosecuted or punished twice for the same acts.[179] Against this premise, the Court confirmed the principles set out in *Turanský*, namely that the assessment of the 'final' nature of the first judgment shall be done in accordance with the law of the State where the judgment was delivered.[180]

The approach adopted in *Turanský* was then confirmed in recent decisions, *M* and *Kossowski*.[181] In the criminal proceedings against M, the Belgian authorities had issued an order of *'non-lieu'*, that is, they found that there was no ground to bring the suspect to judgment. In Belgium, this decision precludes new proceedings against the same person for the same facts, unless new facts and/or evidence come to light. In the case of *M*, the order of *'non-lieu'* had been confirmed by the Court of Cassation. The question arose as to whether this final decision of the Belgian authorities should forbid Italian authorities from investigating and prosecuting M for the same facts. The Court's *negative* answer – that is, *ne bis in idem* applies and Italian authorities should not deal with the criminal offences committed by M – relied on the previous judgments in *Miraglia* and *Turanský*, since the Court noted that Article 54 CISA applies when a decision concerns the merits of the case (*Miraglia*)[182] and when that decision is regarded as 'final' in the State where it was issued (*Turanský*).[183] The decisive factor for the applicability of *ne bis in idem* seems however to be the latter, ie the final nature of the decision according to the law of the first Member State. In *M*, the order making a finding of *'non-lieu'* became final and also concerned the merits of the case: it was a 'definitive decision on the inadequacy of ... evidence and exclude[d] any possibility that the case might be reopened on the basis of the same body of evidence'.[184] The defendant could not

---

177 ibid, para 35. Emphasis added.
178 Case C-261/09 *Mantello*, EU:C:2010:683.
179 ibid, para 40.
180 ibid, para 46.
181 Case C-398/12 *M*, EU:C:2014:1057; Case C-486/14 *Kossowski*, EU:C:2016:483.
182 Case C-398/12 *M*, paras 28 and 30.
183 ibid, paras 31–32.
184 ibid, para 30.

be judged again in Belgium for the same facts and on the basis of the same evidence. By interpreting Article 54 CISA in light of Article 50 of the Charter and Article 4 of Protocol No 7 to the ECHR, the Court then concluded that Article 54 CISA applies with regard to the Belgian order of *non-lieu*, which 'must be considered to be a final judgment, for the purposes of that article'.[185]

The Court seemed nonetheless to be aware that a '*non-lieu*' decision may not sit easily with the concept of 'final' judgment. Recalling a previous decision, *Bourquain*, the Court clarified that 'the sole fact that that criminal procedure would, under national law, have necessitated the reopening of the proceedings does not, *in itself*, mean that the judgment cannot be regarded as "final" for the purposes of Article 54 of the CISA'.[186] In *Bourquain*, the Court had to rule on a decision issued *in absentia* by a French military tribunal in Algeria in 1961, subsequently made void by an amnesty granted in 1968. However, French law imposed an obligation to hold a new trial if the person convicted *in absentia* reappeared before the date on which the enforcement of the sentence had become time-barred (twenty years from the date in which the decision had become definitive); in this case, the enforcement of the sentence would have become time-barred in 1981, but the defendant benefitted from the amnesty already in 1968. Hence, had Mr Bourquain reappeared in France between 1961 (time of the judgment) and 1968 (year of the amnesty), the penalty could have not been enforced, because a new trial would have been necessary, this time in his presence. Before affirming the compatibility of this scenario with the enforcement clause of Article 54 CISA,[187] the Court clarified that *ne bis in idem* also applies to decisions *in absentia* and – as in *M* – ruled that

> the sole fact that the proceedings *in absentia* would, under French law, have necessitated the reopening of the proceedings if Mr Bourquain had been arrested while time was running in the limitation period applicable to the penalty, and before he benefited from the amnesty ... does not, in itself, mean that the conviction *in absentia* cannot be regarded as a final decision within the meaning of Article 54 of the CISA.[188]

In other words, even if national law allows for the reopening of closed cases under certain circumstances – such as the discovery of new facts or evidence (*M*) or the physical presence in the State of a person who was previously

---

185   ibid, para 41.
186   ibid, para 34.
187   See more in section 4.2.3 below.
188   Case C-297/07 *Bourquain*, EU:C:2008:708, para 40. Cf Case C-398/12 *M*, para 34.

convicted *in absentia* (*Bourquain*) – this is not sufficient to deny the 'final' nature of the decision that was adopted at the end of the first proceedings.

Finally, in *Kossowski*, the applicability of Article 54 CISA to cases where public prosecutors terminate the criminal proceedings without any detailed investigation on the facts was discussed. The issue resembled that faced in *Miraglia* and the ruling of the Court is unsurprisingly similar: this decision of the prosecuting authorities does *not* fall within the scope of Article 54 CISA. In *Kossowski*, the Court pointed out a two-step procedure that national authorities should apply to assess whether the European right to *ne bis in idem* comes into play. First, national authorities should evaluate if a decision is *final* in the State where it was issued. In case of positive answer, the other question to face is whether that decision concerns the *merits* of the case: if not – as in the case of Kossowski – Article 54 CISA cannot apply.[189]

The Court's reasoning connects the dots of the previous decisions on the '*bis*' element. Dealing with the first assessment required from national authorities – the final nature of the first judgment – the Court recalls the *Turanský* principle[190] and confirms that Article 54 CISA applies also to those decisions that have been adopted without the involvement of a court (as in *Gözütok and Brügge*).[191] As far as the second step is concerned – whether the final judgment has dealt with the merits of the case – the Court suggest interpreting Article 54 CISA by taking into account the objective and the context of this rule.[192] The Court sticks to the traditional finding that Article 54 CISA aims to protect the freedom of movement and to ensure legal certainty.[193] As it did in *Miraglia* and *Turanský*, however, the CJEU underlines that the protective goal of Article 54 CISA must be coupled with the need to prevent and combat crime.[194] In light

---

189   Case C-486/14 *Kossowski*, paras 34 and 42. The Court of Justice confirmed the same two-step approach in Case C-505/19, *Bundesrepublik Deutschland* (*Notice rouge d'Interpol*), paras 79–81. The criterion concerning the merits of the case has recently been endorsed by the ECtHR to determine whether a judicial decision amounts to a 'conviction' or an 'acquittal' for the purposes of Article 4 of Protocol No 7 to the ECHR: see S Mirandola and G Lasagni, 'The European *Ne Bis in Idem* at the Crossroads of Administrative and Criminal Law' [2019] *eucrim* 126, 127 with reference to *Mihalache v Romania* App no 54012/10 (ECtHR, judgment of 8 July 2019), paras 97–98.

190   Case C-486/14 *Kossowski*, para 35: 'A decision which does not, *under the law of the Contracting State* which instituted criminal proceedings against a person, definitively bar further prosecution at national level cannot, in principle, constitute a procedural obstacle to the opening or continuation of criminal proceedings in respect of the same acts against that person in another Contracting State'. Emphasis added.

191   ibid, para 39.

192   ibid, para 43.

193   ibid, para 44.

194   ibid, paras 46–47. See Case C-469/03 *Miraglia*, para 34; Case C-491/07 *Turanský*, para 43.

of this further objective of Article 54 CISA, it is self-evident that a decision such as the one at stake in the criminal proceedings against Kossowski – by which the public prosecutor dropped the case without any investigation on the merits – could not be regarded as 'final'. More precisely, in those circumstances, there was

> a decision terminating criminal proceedings ... adopted in a situation in which the prosecuting authority, without a more detailed investigation having been undertaken for the purpose of gathering and examining evidence, did not proceed with the prosecution *solely because the accused had refused to give a statement* and the victim and a hearsay witness were living in Germany, so that *it had not been possible to interview them* in the course of the investigation and had therefore not been possible to verify statements made by the victim ...[195]

Should such a decision bar further prosecutions in other Member States, the aim to effectively prevent and combat crime within the Area of Freedom, Security and Justice would be seriously undermined.

In sum, the Court's case law on the *bis* element oscillates between cases where the Court emphasises the final nature of the first decision according to national law, even when this decision does not deal with the merits of the case, and cases where the key element is precisely such an assessment of the merits. The first approach is more protective towards the defendants' fundamental rights and the principle of legal certainty, while the second pays more attention to the need of ensuring security in the EU and avoiding impunity. The Grand Chamber's ruling in *Kossowski* shows a preference for this second approach: the final nature of the first decision according to national law is a necessary condition for the application of *ne bis in idem*, yet it is not sufficient, as an assessment of the merits of the case should also have been carried out at the time of the first criminal proceedings.

4.2.2 The '*Idem*' Element

The Court of Justice has dealt with the *idem* aspect of the right not to be tried or punished twice for the same facts in different judgments, where it has consistently put forward the same interpretation: individuals can rely on the right to *ne bis in idem* when the second criminal proceedings concern the same 'set of facts which are inextricably linked together, irrespective of the legal

---

[195] Case C-486/14 *Kossowski*, para 48. Emphasis added.

classification given to them or the legal interest protected'.¹⁹⁶ It goes without saying that, for the purposes of the application of the *ne bis in idem* principle, the person against whom new criminal proceedings are initiated should be the same that was subject to the first set of proceedings. In *Orsi and Baldetti*, which concerned a case of domestic legislation that combined administrative and criminal penalties for non-payment of Value Added Tax (VAT), the Court noted that *ne bis in idem* could not be invoked since the administrative penalty was issued against a company, whereas the criminal proceedings had been launched against natural persons (the legal representatives of the company).¹⁹⁷ Article 50 of the Charter, as well as Article 54 CISA, can only apply when the person involved in the two proceedings is the same.

The leading case on the '*idem*' element is *Van Esbroeck*, which concerned a case of illegal drug trafficking. When the crime of drug trafficking – or any other crime connected with trafficking activities such as illegal trafficking of waste or protected species – is transnational, the defendants could be charged for 'export' of drugs in the countries from which the drug is moved, whereas in those where the substances are received, they could be prosecuted for 'import' of drugs.

The answer to the question of whether similar conducts constitute 'same acts' for the purposes of Article 54 CISA depends on the criterion that national courts should apply in their assessment of the *idem* element.¹⁹⁸ If one looks at the legal classification of the conduct, the *ne bis in idem* principle could never apply in similar circumstances, since 'export' and 'import' of drugs are two different offences. The same goes if the evaluation focuses on the legal interests protected by the law. Assuming that drug trafficking affects inter alia the right to health and the public security of a given population, in case of transnational drug trafficking the right to health and the public security of (at least) two different populations – those of the importing and of the exporting country – are affected, so that the legal interests at stake are more than one.

Therefore, the only criterion that allows Article 54 CISA and Article 50 CFR to come into play in similar circumstances is that of the *same historical fact*: through the lens of the '*idem factum*', importing and exporting drugs do not represent two different facts but they are rather two sides of the same coin.

---

196 Case C-436/04 *Van Esbroeck*, para 42.
197 Joined Cases C-217/15 & C-350/15 *Orsi and Baldetti*, EU:C:2017:264.
198 As noted in section 4.1 above, the wording of Article 54 CISA and Article 50 of the Charter is different in that respect, with the former referring to the 'same acts' and the latter to the same 'offence', which corresponds the formulation of Article 4 of Protocol No 7 to the ECHR.

This view is endorsed by the Court of Justice in *Van Esbroeck*,[199] *Van Straaten*, *Gasparini*[200] and *Kraaijenbrink*.[201] The latter case involved money laundering-related convictions in Belgium and the Netherlands. While different acts giving rise to these convictions constituted 'the successive and continuous implementation of the same criminal intention',[202] it was not clear if they involved the same sums of money. In this context, the Court reiterated the earlier case law and stressed that the acts in question must make up 'an inseparable whole', but the Court noted that if the acts do not make up an inseparable whole the fact that they were committed with the same criminal intention does not suffice to meet the test of what constitutes 'same acts' under Article 54 of the Schengen Convention.[203] In other words, it is not sufficient that the facts are linked by the same criminal intention, since an objective link is also necessary.

On the same day of *Kraaijenbrink*, the Court also delivered the *Kretzinger* judgment,[204] in which it followed and expanded upon its earlier case law on the 'same facts'. The Court reiterated the *Van Esbroeck* test that the only relevant criterion is identity of the material acts, understood as the existence of a set of facts that are inextricably linked together, adding that that criterion applies irrespective of the legal classification given to those acts or the legal interest protected.[205] According to the Court, while the final assessment is for the national courts to make, the transportation of contraband cigarettes involving successive crossings of internal Schengen area borders – which was the offence at stake in the main proceedings – is capable of constituting a set of facts covered by the notion of the 'same acts'.[206]

In *Mantello*, finally, the Court extended its interpretation of the *'idem'* element to the EAW Framework Decision, underlining that such a notion 'must be given an autonomous and uniform interpretation throughout the European Union'.[207] This position has been recently upheld in the *X (Mandat d'arrêt européen – Ne bis in idem)* judgement.[208] This autonomous concept of Union law has also crossed the EU borders, since it has been endorsed also by the European Court of Human Rights. Even though in Article 4 of Protocol No 7 to

---

199   Case C-436/04 *Van Esbroeck*, para 35.
200   See Case C-467/04 *Gasparini*, para 54.
201   Case C-367/05 *Kraaijenbrink*, EU:C:2007:444, para 31.
202   ibid, para 18.
203   ibid, para 29.
204   Case C-288/05 *Kretzinger*, EU:C:2007:441.
205   ibid, para 29.
206   ibid, para 36.
207   Case C-261/09, *Mantello*, para 38.
208   Case C-665/20 PPU *X (Mandat d'arrêt européen – Ne bis in idem)*, EU:C:2021:339, paras 70ff.

the ECHR, like in Article 50 CFR, the term 'offence' is used (rather than 'facts'), the ECtHR's Grand Chamber ruled, in *Zolotukhin v Russia*, that the right to *ne bis in idem* applies when the second proceedings concern the 'same set of concrete factual circumstances involving the same defendant and inextricably linked together in time and space'.[209] *Zolotukhin* has reframed the Strasbourg Court's interpretation of *ne bis in idem* and strikingly offered a coherent interpretation of ECHR domestic and EU transnational *ne bis in idem*. It has been influential and a key reference point for subsequent Strasbourg[210] and Luxembourg[211] case law.

4.2.3 The Enforcement Condition in Article 54 CISA and Its Relations with Article 50 of the Charter

Article 54 CISA provides that, if a person has been convicted, *ne bis in idem* applies only if the penalty has been enforced, is in the process of being enforced or can no longer be enforced under the laws of the sentencing contracting Party. The Court of Justice has interpreted this enforcement clause in some judgments. In *Gözütok and Brügge*, the Court ruled that, when a defendant has complied with the obligations descending from an out-of-court settlement, namely paying a certain amount of money, the penalty can be regarded as 'having been enforced' for the purposes of Article 54 CISA.[212]

The enforcement condition is addressed also in *Kretzinger*, where the Court decided that, while a penalty is not to be regarded as 'having been enforced' or 'actually in the process of being enforced' where the defendant was for a short time taken into police custody and/or held on remand pending trial, the enforcement condition is instead to be considered fulfilled in cases of suspended custodial sentences.[213] The Court is thus prepared to extend *ne bis in idem* in cases of suspended sentences, implicitly accepting that this is a legitimate choice of penal enforcement by Member States which, if adopted at the domestic level, must be recognised as enforcement across the Schengen area for the purposes of Article 54 CISA.

---

209 *Zolotukhin v Russia* App no 14939/03 (ECtHR, judgment of 10 February 2009), para 84.
210 See, eg, *Glantz v Finland* App no 37394/11 (ECtHR, judgment of 20 May 2014); *Nykänen v Finland* App no 11828/11 (ECtHR, judgment of 20 May 2014); *Rinas v Finland* App no 17039/13 (ECtHR, judgment of 27 January 2015); *Österlund v Finland* App no 53197/13 (ECtHR, judgment of 10 February 2015); *Kapetanios et al v Greece* Apps nos 3453/12, 42941/12 and 9028/13 (ECt , judgment of 30 April 2015).
211 See Case C-398/12 *M*, para 39.
212 Joined Cases C-187/01 & C-385/01 *Gözütok and Brügge*, para 30.
213 Case C-288/05 *Kretzinger*.

Another relevant case on the enforcement condition is *Bourquain*. As mentioned above, Mr Bourquain had been convicted *in absentia* by the French military tribunal in 1961 and then benefitted from an amnesty in 1968. The penalty issued in 1961, however, could have never been enforced: according to French law, had the defendant reappeared in France, a new trial would have been necessary in his presence.[214] In such circumstances, the question is whether the enforcement condition is fulfilled, and consequently whether Mr Bourquain enjoys the right to *ne bis in idem*, if his case is reopened in another Member State. The Court replied in the affirmative, arguing that the clause of Article 54 CISA also encompasses cases where the penalty 'can no longer be enforced'. When the *second* proceedings begin, therefore, it is not relevant whether the penalty imposed with the first decision could have not been executed on the date when it was imposed – it is only necessary to assess whether, at the time of the second proceedings, that penalty has been, or is in the proceed of being, enforced, or can no longer be enforced. The latter is precisely the case of Mr Bourquain, who was again prosecuted in 2002 for the same facts for which he had been convicted in 1961. That penalty had become void with the amnesty of 1968 and, even without such an amnesty, according to the French law it could have not been served after twenty years from the decision, that is, as of 1981.[215] As a consequence, there is no doubt that the enforcement condition in similar cases is satisfied as the sentence against Mr Bourquain could no longer be carried out when the second proceedings began.[216]

The Court's fourth case on the enforcement condition, *Spasic*,[217] is rather problematic. This decision deals with two questions. The less sensitive concerns the application of the enforcement clause when a person, who is sentenced to both a custodial sentence *and* a financial penalty, has only paid the latter. The Court explains that Article 54 CISA, which provides for the singular form 'penalty', covers also the cases where a financial penalty *and* a custodial sentence have been imposed. Therefore, since in the case at stake only one of the two penalties had been 'enforced' (the financial penalty had been paid but the custodial sentence had not been served), the enforcement condition could not be regarded as having been fulfilled.[218]

The other issue dealt with by *Spasic* is more contentious. The Court was asked whether the enforcement condition of Article 54 CISA is compatible

---

214 See section 4.2.1 above.
215 For more details on this case, see the previous section.
216 Case C-297/07 *Bourquain*, paras 45–52.
217 Case C-129/14 PPU *Spasic*, EU:C:2014:586.
218 ibid, paras 80–82.

with the right to *ne bis in idem* as enshrined in Article 50 of the Charter, which does not make any reference to such a clause. The striking positive answer was based on the premise that Article 54 CISA is recalled in the explanations to Article 50 CFR; the explanations also provide that the limited exceptions to the right at stake, to be found in Articles 54–58 CISA, are covered by the horizontal clause of Article 52(1) of the Charter.[219] The latter provision regulates how the Charter rights can be limited. Similar limitations must: i) be provided for by law; ii) respect the essence of those rights; and iii) subject to the principle of proportionality, be necessary and genuinely meet objectives of general interest recognised by the Union or the need to protect the rights and freedoms of others. Assuming that the enforcement clause is a limitation of the right to *ne bis in idem*, the Court evaluated if the three conditions provided for by Article 52(1) of the Charter are met.

First, the enforcement condition is provided by the law, namely Article 54 CISA.[220] Second, the Court ruled that the condition laid down in Article 54 CISA does not call into question the *ne bis in idem* principle as such but is intended, inter alia, to avoid a situation in which a person definitively convicted and sentenced in one Contracting State can no longer be prosecuted for the same acts in another Contracting State and therefore ultimately remains unpunished if the first State did not execute the sentence imposed.[221]

The analysis then shifts to the proportionality of the enforcement clause. The Court's positive assessment is based on the claimed objective of Article 54 CISA, ie the general interest to prevent the impunity of persons convicted and sentenced in a Member State of the European Union.[222] According to the Court, by allowing, in cases of non-execution of the sentence imposed, the authorities of one Contracting State to prosecute persons definitively convicted and sentenced by another Contracting State on the basis of the same acts, the risk that the persons concerned would enjoy impunity by virtue of their leaving the territory of the State in which they were sentenced is avoided.[223]

In sum, the Court ruled out any incompatibility between the enforcement condition of Article 54 CISA and the right to *ne bis in idem* as enshrined in Article 50 of the Charter. The Court only added that, *in concreto*, when national authorities must assess if the enforcement clause is met, they can 'contact

---

219 'Explanations relating to the Charter of Fundamental Rights' [2007] OJ C303/31.
220 Case C-129/14 PPU *Spasic*, para 57.
221 ibid, para 58 and reference to Case C-288/05 *Kretzinger*, para 51. See Mitsilegas, *EU Criminal Law after Lisbon* (n 122) 89.
222 Case C-129/14 PPU *Spasic*, paras 61–63.
223 ibid, paras 63 and 64 respectively.

each other and initiate consultations in order to verify whether the Member State which imposed the first sentence really intends to execute the penalties imposed',[224] in light of the principle of sincere cooperation enshrined in Article 4(3) TEU.

The Court's approach in *Spasic* is striking, since the Court effectively introduces a security rationale within a fundamental right. The Court's interpretation opens the door towards divergent interpretations and levels of protection between domestic *ne bis in idem* cases involving the implementation of EU law (interpreted in conformity with Article 50 of the Charter) and transnational *ne bis in idem* cases under Article 54 CISA.[225] Especially when crimes have an inherent cross-border nature, or at least often concern more than one Member State – as is the case for environmental crime – such a scenario does not ensure sufficient legal certainty for the individuals who have been tried or sentenced for these crimes and raises the spectre of serious impediments to their enjoyment of free movement.[226]

4.3 Application of Ne Bis in Idem *to Criminal and Administrative Proceedings Concerning the Same Facts*

As the previous chapter has demonstrated, the protection of the environment is an illustrative example of a field where criminal law and administrative law go hand in hand. The final report of the eighth round of mutual evaluation carried out within the Council's Working Party on General Matters including Evaluations (GENVAL) acknowledges that all Member States 'have established a legal framework to tackle environmental crime ... defining related offences and penalties. However ... in certain Member States the potential of the law enforcement and criminal law systems is not being used to its full extent, in some cases most likely as *administrative* enforcement is seen as less problematic and more effective than judicial follow-up'.[227] Prosecutors can sometimes

---

224 ibid, para 73.
225 See further M Wasmeier, '*Ne Bis in Idem* and the Enforcement Condition: Balancing Freedom, Security and Justice?' (2015) 5 *New Journal of European Criminal Law* 534.
226 Mitsilegas, *EU Criminal Law after Lisbon* (n 122) 89–90. See also JAE Vervaele, 'Schengen and Charter-Related *Ne Bis in Idem* Protection in the Area of Freedom, Security and Justice: *M* and *Zoran Spasic*' (2015) 52 *Common Market Law Review* 1339, 1352ff.
227 GENVAL, 'Final report on the 8th round of mutual evaluations on "The practical implementation and operation of the European polices on preventing and combating Environmental Crime"' Council doc 14852/19, 5 December 2019 ('GENVAL final report') 13. Emphasis added. See more ibid 40–44 and 56–57. On GENVAL, see more in the previous chapter. On the enforcement challenges in the field of environmental law, also with regard to the complex interplay between administrative and criminal regulations, cf K Ligeti and A Marletta, 'Smart Enforcement Strategies to Counter Environmental Crime

doubt whether the administrative or criminal avenue is more appropriate to deal with a given case of environmental crime. This uncertainty seems justified not only by the unclear boundaries between the two fields but also by the argument put forward by some authors according to which the Environmental Crime Directive requires the criminalisation of a number of conduct yet it does not expressly require the *application* of criminal penalties in individual cases, when the concrete circumstances would suggest that administrative enforcement is more appropriate.[228] It is the Directive itself that in fact warns that it 'creates no obligations regarding the application'[229] of the criminal penalties that Member States are required to introduce in their legal systems to cope with environmental crime. Incidentally, this scenario is even more complicated since, in addition to these uncertainties *within* the Member States, there are also discrepancies *among* the Member States 'as regards the choice between criminal or administrative law to address environmental damage'.[230]

In the above-mentioned evaluation of the Environmental Crime Directive, the Commission acknowledges that many Member States 'rely on administrative sanctions in addition to criminal sanctions to address environmental offences, but this is often done without clear criteria on choosing one of the two systems'.[231] As the Commission notes, the consequences of this state of affairs are undesirable for both the protection of the environment and the individuals who are suspected of an environmental offence. The unclear boundaries between administrative and criminal law in this field result 'in overlapping regimes, unclear competences, and a risk of violating the *ne bis in idem* (double jeopardy) principle prohibiting an offender from being penalised twice for the same offence or a risk of ineffective proceedings due to a lack of coordination and clarity on the use of different types of sanctions'.[232]

The risk that the same conduct may be subject to different penalties and proceeding calls for a prompt and effective cooperation between criminal and administrative authorities – within the same country but also across the Member States. For instance, in the above-mentioned evaluation of the Environmental Crime Directive, it is stated that

---

    in the EU' (2016) 87 *Revue International de Droit Pénal – Protection of the Environment through Criminal Law* (ed by JL de La Cuesta et al) 133, 135–137 and 144–147.
228 See Pereira (n 6) 323–324 and 343–344.
229 Recital 10 of the Environmental Crime Directive.
230 Pereira (n 6) 342.
231 Commission, 'Commission Staff Working Document Evaluation of the Directive 2008/99/EC' (n 34) 83.
232 ibid.

The Commission could encourage Member States to improve cooperation between the different national authorities involved in enforcement. Cooperation between judicial, environmental and other relevant authorities (such as customs authorities and police) is essential to address environmental crime. This cooperation should also extend to competent authorities working in the area of money laundering, fraud and organised crime. This would ensure that investigations benefit from expertise in environmental law, criminal justice and finance. This is particularly important where profit is often the sole motivation for committing an environmental offence.[233]

Already the Council of Europe's Convention on the Protection of the Environment through Criminal Law acknowledged the strict relations between administrative and criminal law in the environmental field by requiring the State Parties to adopt the necessary measures to 'ensure that the authorities responsible for environmental protection co-operate with the authorities responsible for investigating and prosecuting criminal offences' (Article 10). The Environmental Criminal Directive does not replicate a similar provision. Due to the strict interplay between criminal and administrative law and the ensuing 'risk of overlap',[234] the same conduct could however be subject to criminal *and* administrative sanctions at the same time (so-called 'twin-track' or 'double-track' system).[235]

One may wonder whether the prohibition of double jeopardy applies in similar contexts. The GENVAL final report notes that similar problems may for instance arise where, as is the case in some Member States, 'environmental authorities also investigate crimes linked to [environmental] crimes (such as fraud and tax evasion) and the police also investigate the same crimes'.[236] This

---

233   ibid.
234   Faure (n 3) 299.
235   The criteria to decide which of the two penalties should be applied in a given case may also be unclear, as the GENVAL final report warns: 'Another problem frequently identified in the evaluations was the lack of a clear distinction between crimes and misdemeanours and/or the regime of administrative or criminal penalties, in the absence of clear criteria for determining which regime should apply. Recommendations have therefore been addressed to the Member States concerned, with a view to achieving more clarity and uniformity in the determination of the applicable legislation and penalty regime and to differentiating on the basis of precise predefined criteria between criminal offences and administrative infringements. This should allow each environmental offence to be addressed in the most appropriate way and to ensure judicial follow-up when a violation of environmental law results in criminal liability' (GENVAL final report (n 227) 56–57).
236   ibid 42. At least until 2015, however, the *ne bis in idem* principle seemed to be overall respected by EU Member States when dealing with environmental crime (GF Perilongo

is a dimension of *ne bis in idem* that is different from that discussed in the sections above: it has national scope, as criminal and administrative penalties can be issued against the same person within the same Member State, but it goes beyond criminal law *stricto sensu*.

As anticipated in the previous chapter, a reference to *ne bis in idem* in a potentially new EU directive on environmental crime or in an updated version of the current Environmental Crime Directive could therefore be added, along the lines of, for instance, the 2017 Directive on the fight against fraud to the Union's financial interests by means of criminal law ('PIF Directive').[237] The protection of the Union's financial interests, like that of the environment, is a field that traditionally straddles administrative and criminal law.[238] The Preamble of the PIF Directive therefore provides that the Directive

> does not affect the proper and effective application of disciplinary measures or penalties other than of a criminal nature. Sanctions that cannot be equated to criminal sanctions, which are imposed on the same person for the same conduct, can be taken into account when sentencing that person for a criminal offence defined in this Directive. For other sanctions, the principle of prohibition of being tried or punished twice in criminal proceedings for the same criminal offence (*ne bis in idem*) should be fully respected.[239]

A similar recital could be envisaged for a new or updated directive on environmental crime and, once more like the PIF Directive, could also be accompanied by a further caveat on the applicability of the 'traditional', transnational *ne bis in idem* in cases of cross-border environmental crimes.[240]

---

and E Corn, 'The Ecocrime Directive and Its Translation into Legal Practice. EU Green Offences and Their Impact at National Level According to the Results of a Recent Survey' (2017) 8 *New Journal of European Criminal Law* 236, 252).

237 Directive (EU) 2017/1371 of the European Parliament and of the Council of 5 July 2017 on the fight against fraud to the Union's financial interests by means of criminal law [2017] OJ L198/29. PIF is the acronym of '*protection des intérêts financiers*'.

238 The Commission calls for a consistent 'integrated policy to protect EU financial interests by criminal law and by administrative investigations' (Commission, 'Communication on the protection of the financial interests of the European Union by criminal law and by administrative investigations. An integrated policy to safeguard taxpayers' money' COM (2011) 293 final, 26 May 2011, 2). In the literature see, for example, V Covolo, *L'Émergence d'un Droit Pénal en Réseau. Analyse Critique du Système Européen de Lutte Antifraude* (Nomos 2015) 115ff.

239 Recital 17 of the PIF Directive.

240 Recital 21 of the PIF Directive reads as follows: 'Given the possibility of multiple jurisdictions for cross-border criminal offences falling under the scope of this Directive, the

The applicability of *ne bis in idem* to concurring administrative and criminal proceedings has recently been in the limelight due to an increasing number of cases decided by the Court of Justice and the European Court of Human Rights,[241] which have addressed the issue in a way that has changed over time. As the sections below illustrate, two phases in the case-law of the European courts can be identified: the CJEU and the ECtHR were first inclined to rule out the compatibility of double-track systems with *ne bis in idem*; after some years, however, they have partially modified and softened their approach.[242]

4.3.1 *Bonda, Fransson* and *Grande Stevens*: Incompatibility between Double-Track Systems and *Ne Bis in Idem*

In *Bonda*,[243] the Court of Justice dealt with the case of a Polish national who received an administrative penalty for some violations of Regulation No 1973/2004 on EU agriculture subsidies. He had declared a much bigger land than that he actually had and was therefore excluded from the subsidy for the subsequent year, pursuant to Article 138(1) of the Regulation. After the administrative penalty had been issued, the public prosecutor opened an investigation for fraud. Mr Bonda was convicted in first instance and acquitted in the second, whereas the Polish Supreme Court asked the Court of Justice to decide on the legal nature of the penalty provided for in Article 138(1) of Regulation No 1973/2004. If such a penalty were of a criminal nature, the Polish legislation on *ne bis in idem* would have applied and Mr Bonda should have been acquitted in the criminal proceedings. Relying on the *Engel* criteria used by the ECtHR in order to ascertain whether a given sanction can be considered of a criminal nature, the Court denied the criminal nature of penalties issued within the common agricultural policy. Even though this decision shows a positive convergence between the case law of the Court of Justice and that of the ECtHR on the qualification of penalties, it is surprising that the CJEU did not refer to Article 50 of the Charter, which is now the key provision in EU law setting out the principle of *ne bis in idem*.

Member States should ensure that the principle of *ne bis in idem* is respected in full in the application of national law transposing this Directive'. A further, albeit very generic, reference to *ne bis in idem* is to be found in Recital 28 of the same Directive.

241 See J Tomkin, 'Article 50' in S Peers, T Hervey, J Kenner et al (eds), *The EU Charter of Fundamental Rights. A Commentary* (Beck–Hart–Nomos 2014) 1405–1407.

242 For an analysis of the recent case law of the European Courts on the matter see, inter alia, K Ligeti, 'Fundamental Rights Protection between Strasbourg and Luxembourg: Extending Transnational *Ne Bis in Idem* Across Administrative and Criminal Procedures' in European Law Institute, Ligeti and Robinson (eds) (n 122) 160–181.

243 Case C-489/10 *Bonda*, EU:C:2012:319.

By contrast, *ne bis in idem* is looked at from the perspective of Article 50 of the Charter in *Fransson*,[244] where the Court assessed whether the Charter precludes a Member State, Sweden in that case, from imposing both a tax (formally non-criminal) penalty and a criminal sanction on the same person.[245] The Court of Justice argued that Article 50 of the Charter only applies if the two sets of proceedings concerning the same facts are of *criminal* nature. As in *Bonda*, the Court noted that the evaluation of whether a given penalty is 'criminal', and therefore apt to trigger the *ne bis in idem* principle, is to be done in accordance with the *Engel* criteria. In *Bonda*, however, one of the two penalties at stake – the administrative one – was to be found in EU legislation. Arguably because in *Fransson* all the relevant provisions were national, the Court did not itself proceed with the application of the *Engel* criteria to the Swedish legislation but it rather clarified that it is for the national competent authorities to assess the possible criminal nature of tax penalties.[246] When, as in the case of Fransson, the condition laid down in Article 51 of the Charter is met – 'The provisions of [the] Charter are addressed to … the Member States only when they are implementing Union law'[247] – domestic authorities are therefore obliged to disapply national legislation incompatible with the EU fundamental right to *ne bis in idem*, if they find that risks of its violation arise in the case before them.[248] In other words, in *Fransson* the Court of Justice clearly ruled out that a person could be subject to criminal and formally administrative – but in essence criminal – sanctions for the same tax violation.[249]

This conclusion was however partially revised in some decisions handed down by the Grand Chamber of the Court of Justice in March 2018. The partial *revirement* of the CJEU was in turn triggered by some developments in the European Court of Human Rights' case law. The ECtHR had dealt with the possible violation of the *ne bis in idem* principle in case of concurring administrative and criminal sanctions in a seminal judgment delivered in 2014, *Grande Stevens v Italy*.[250] In that case, the applicants had been punished, first, by the

---

244   Case C-617/10 *Åkerberg Fransson*, EU:C:2013:105.
245   See more in, eg, X Groussot and A Ericsson, '*Ne Bis in Idem* in the EU and ECHR Legal Orders' in B van Bockel (ed), Ne Bis in Idem *in EU Law* (Cambridge University Press 2016) 90–102.
246   Case C-617/10 *Fransson*, paras 32–37. For further possible explanations of the differences in the Court's approach in *Bonda* and *Fransson*, see PJ Wattel, '*Ne Bis in Idem* and Tax Offences in EU Law and ECHR Law', in van Bockel (ed) (previous n) 183–185.
247   Article 51(1) of the Charter. See Case C-617/10 *Fransson*, paras 26–27.
248   ibid, para 45.
249   ibid, para 34.
250   *Grande Stevens v Italy* App no 18640/10 (ECtHR, judgment of 4 March 2014).

Italian National Companies and Stock Exchange Commission (CONSOB) and, second, they were prosecuted for the same facts. Applying the *Engel* criteria, the ECtHR found that the proceedings before the CONSOB did involve a 'criminal charge' for the purposes of Article 6 ECHR; therefore, Article 4 of Protocol No 7 to the ECHR on *ne bis in idem* should have applied.[251] Since national authorities were called to adjudicate the same facts already punished by the CONSOB and did not stop the proceedings, the Court concluded that there had been a violation of the *ne bis in idem* principle. About two years and a half later, however, the Strasbourg Court delivered a judgment where it partially modified its approach, and this led to some changes in the CJEU's case law as well.

4.3.2   *A and B v Norway, Garlsson, Zecca and Di Puma,* and *Menci*: (Partial) Compatibility between Double-Track Systems and *Ne Bis in Idem*

In *A and B v Norway*,[252] concerning the field of tax offences, the European Court of Human Rights ruled that twin-track systems do *not* violate the *ne bis in idem* principle when some conditions are met. According to the ECtHR,

> States should be able legitimately to choose complementary legal responses to socially offensive conduct (such as ... non-payment/evasion of taxes) through different procedures forming a coherent whole so as to address different aspects of the social problem involved, provided that the accumulated legal responses do not represent an excessive burden for the individual concerned.[253]

A violation of Article 4 of Protocol No 7, therefore, does not occur in case of 'an integrated system enabling different aspects of the wrongdoing to be addressed in a foreseeable and proportionate manner forming a *coherent whole*, so that the individual concerned is not thereby subjected to injustice'.[254] Between the different procedures concerning the same person there should be 'sufficiently close connection ... in substance and in time',[255] and the Court then lists some factors to assess whether there is a sufficiently close connection in substance.[256] As for the connection in time, the Court argues that such connection must be

---

251   ibid, paras 94–101 and 222.
252   *A and B v Norway* Apps nos 24130/11 and 29758/11 (ECtHR, judgment of 15 November 2016).
253   ibid, para 121.
254   ibid, para 122. Emphasis added.
255   ibid, para 125.
256   They include:

'sufficiently close to protect the individual from being subjected to uncertainty and delay and from proceedings becoming protracted over time',[257] but does not give any further detail that may guide national authorities in the evaluation of whether administrative and criminal proceedings are close in time.[258]

The *A and B* judgment runs counter to the previous case law of the ECtHR (and of the CJEU), as demonstrated by the vehemently critical dissenting opinion by Judge Pinto de Albuquerque,[259] which captures the three main problems raised by *A and B*, namely its rejection of the principles laid down in *Grande Stevens*, the vagueness of the criteria endorsed (the close connection in time and substance),[260] and the consequences for the consistency between the jurisprudence of the ECtHR and the CJEU.

After *A and B*, the CJEU was required to rule again on the issue of *ne bis in idem* in case of administrative and criminal proceedings on the same facts and to clarify whether it would accept the new stance of the ECtHR or whether it would stick to the more protective *Fransson* approach. With some exceptions and without spelling it out, the CJEU seems to walk the first path. In *Menci*, the Court of Justice dealt with a case of a proprietor of a sole trading business who had been subject to a final administrative penalty for his failure to pay VAT within the time limit stipulated by law.[261] Criminal proceedings were

- whether the different proceedings pursue complementary purposes and thus address, not only *in abstracto* but also *in concreto*, *different aspects* of the social misconduct involved;
- whether the duality of proceedings concerned is a *foreseeable consequence*, both in law and in practice, of the same impugned conduct (*idem*);
- whether the relevant sets of proceedings are conducted in such a manner as to *avoid* as far as possible any *duplication* in the *collection* as well as the *assessment of the evidence*, notably through adequate interaction between the various competent authorities to bring about that the establishment of facts in one set is also used in the other set;
- and, above all, whether the *sanction* imposed in the proceedings which become final first *is taken into account* in those which become final last, so as to prevent that the individual concerned is in the end made to bear an excessive burden ... (ibid, para 132; emphasis added).

257 ibid, para 135.
258 See also Mirandola and Lasagni (n 189).
259 *A and B v Norway* Apps nos 24130/11 and 29758/11 (ECtHR, judgment of 15 November 2016), dissenting Opinion of Judge Pinto de Albuquerque, para 80.
260 See M Luchtman, 'The ECJ's Recent Case Law on *Ne Bis in Idem*: Implications for Law Enforcement in a Shared Legal Order' (2018) 55 *Common Market Law Review* 1717, 1728; Mirandola and Lasagni (n 189), who also note that the ECtHR's case law following the *A and B* judgment has not dispelled the several interpretative doubts raised by the vague criteria set out by the Strasbourg Court in that decision.
261 Case C-524/15 *Menci*, EU:C:2018:197.

subsequently initiated for the same facts. Had the *Fransson* principles applied, the case should have been dismissed by criminal law authorities upon verification of the criminal law nature of the administrative penalty. Endorsing to a certain extent the ECtHR's case law, however, the Court reaches a different conclusion through the following steps.

First, after clarifying that the matter falls within the scope of EU law,[262] the Court rules that – in light of the *Engel* criteria, which it had endorsed in *Bonda* – the administrative penalty issued against Mr Menci is of a criminal nature, due to its punitive purpose and its high degree of severity.[263] Second, the CJEU acknowledges that the facts that led to the imposition of the administrative penalty and those under prosecution were the same.[264] Had the Court stuck to the *Fransson* approach, the above findings would have been sufficient to conclude that the criminal case against Mr Menci, which was opened after the conclusion of formally administrative – but in essence criminal – proceedings, had to be dropped. The Court states instead that the duplication of proceedings and penalties constitutes a *limitation* of the fundamental right guaranteed by Article 50 of the Charter,[265] and it can therefore be legitimate as long as it complies with the conditions set out in Article 52(1) of the Charter.

As mentioned, any limitation on the exercise of the rights and freedoms recognised by the Charter must:[266] i) be provided for by law; ii) respect the essence of those rights; and iii) subject to the principle of proportionality, be necessary and genuinely meet objectives of general interest recognised by the Union or the need to protect the rights and freedoms of others. The CJEU addresses cursorily the first and second requirements, as well as that concerning the objectives of general interest. First, the criterion under i) does not raise any problem in this case, as the duplication is provided for by Italian law.[267] Second, the Court does not pay too much attention to the criterion under ii) either, since it simply acknowledges that the essence of the right to *ne bis in idem* is not jeopardised because national law allows the duplication of proceedings and

---

262   ibid, paras 17–25. See G Lo Schiavo, 'The Principle of *Ne Bis in Idem* and the Application of Criminal Sanctions: Of Scope and Restrictions' (2018) 14 *European Constitutional Law Review* 644, 649–650.
263   Case C-524/15 *Menci*, paras 26–33. The Court however clarifies that it is for the referring court to determine whether that administrative penalty has a criminal nature (ibid, para 33).
264   ibid, paras 34–39.
265   ibid, para 39.
266   See the analysis of the *Spasic* case in section 4.2.3 above.
267   Case C-524/15 *Menci*, para 42.

penalties under exhaustive and precise conditions.[268] Third, the CJEU accepts that the collection of all VAT due is an objective of general interest that may justify limitations to *ne bis in idem*.[269] The CJEU then moves on to the assessment of the *proportionality* of such limitation and lays down further criteria to apply.

More precisely, the respect of the proportionality principle requires that national legislation must: i) provide for 'clear and precise rules allowing individuals to predict which acts or omissions are liable to be subject to ... a duplication of proceedings and penalties'[270] – which, once again, was not contentious in the *Menci* case;[271] and ii) ensure that the disadvantages for the persons concerned following from such a duplication 'are limited to what is strictly necessary in order to achieve'[272] the objective of general interest that underlies that legislation (namely, in the *Menci* case, the collection of VAT). In turn, this second criterion calls for two further assessments: first, there should be rules that ensure *coordination* between administrative and criminal proceedings in order to 'reduce to what is strictly necessary the additional disadvantage associated with [the] duplication for the persons concerned';[273] second, there should also be rules to ensure that 'the severity of all penalties imposed corresponds with the seriousness of the offence concerned'.[274] While the Court delves into, and positively evaluates, the provisions of Italian law which allow the competent authorities to limit the severity of the penalties imposed on persons in the same situation as Mr Menci,[275] its assessment of the rules on the coordination between proceedings is not very convincing. In that respect, the Court merely states that Italian law provides for duplication of penalties and proceedings with respect to offences that are particularly serious (unpaid VAT for more than € 50,000) but does not consider whether there is any real coordination between proceedings.

In the light of this multi-step approach, the Court concludes by noting that it will eventually be for the referring court to 'assess the proportionality of the practical application of [national] legislation ... by balancing, on the one hand, the seriousness of the tax offence at issue and, on the other hand, the actual disadvantage resulting for the person concerned from the duplication

---

268 ibid, para 43.
269 ibid, paras 44–45.
270 ibid, para 49.
271 ibid, paras 50–51.
272 ibid, para 52.
273 ibid, para 53.
274 ibid, para 55.
275 See ibid, para 56.

of proceedings and penalties at issue in the main proceedings'.[276] Finally, the CJEU acknowledges that the level of protection guaranteed to the *ne bis in idem* principle, as interpreted by the Court itself, does not conflict with that ensured by the European Court of Human Rights, which in the *A and B* judgment did not rule out a duplication of administrative and criminal proceedings as long as they have a sufficiently close connection in substance and time.[277]

In *Menci*, the CJEU has therefore decided to partially follow the steps of the Strasbourg Court by overruling the *Fransson* decision – in the same way as the ECtHR had overruled *Grande Stevens* – and lowering the standards related to the *ne bis in idem* principle. On the same day of *Menci*, the Court handed down also the judgement in *Garlsson*,[278] which seems however to suggest that the CJEU still holds a more protective approach than the ECtHR. In *Garlsson*, the Court dealt with the same problem of *Menci* but in the opposite scenario: the criminal conviction – concerning market manipulation – had become final first and the competent national authorities were therefore uncertain whether an administrative penalty could be issued for the same facts. The CJEU approaches the matter with the same reasoning of *Menci* but reaches a different conclusion.

The decision begins with the acknowledgment that Article 50 of the Charter applies in the main proceedings, as the relevant national provisions on market manipulation constitute implementation of EU law for the purposes of Article 51(1) of the Charter.[279] Likewise, the Court claims that, in accordance with the *Engel-Bonda* criteria, the administrative penalty that can be imposed on the defendants is of criminal nature because of its punitive purpose and its severity.[280] After clarifying that the existence of the same offence for the purposes of Article 50 of the Charter is not contentious in this case either,[281] the Court embarks upon the multi-step assessment of whether the duplication of proceedings and penalties – which is a limitation of *ne bis in idem* principle – complies with the above-mentioned requirements of Article 52(1) of the Charter.

As in *Menci*, this limitation is provided for by Italian law,[282] respects the essence of the right not to be tried or punished twice for the same

---

276   ibid, para 59.
277   ibid, paras 60–62.
278   Case C-537/16 *Garlsson Real Estate and others*, EU:C:2018:193.
279   ibid, paras 21–27.
280   ibid, paras 28–35. The Court however clarifies that the power to qualify an administrative penalty as having a criminal nature lies with the referring court.
281   ibid, paras 36–41.
282   ibid, para 44.

facts,[283] and meets objectives of general interest, which in this context are the 'integrity of the financial markets of the European Union and public confidence in financial instruments'.[284] The difference with *Menci* lies however in the assessment of the *proportionality* of such limitation. In particular, while Italian law meritoriously provides for some coordination between the administrative and criminal proceedings,[285] the Court holds that the bringing of the proceedings relating to an administrative fine of a criminal nature *after* a criminal conviction for the same facts 'exceeds what is strictly necessary'[286] in order to achieve the objective of protecting the financial markets' integrity and the public confidence in financial instruments. And so it is even in those cases where, as in the main proceedings, the criminal penalty is extinguished as a result of a pardon.[287] With a reasoning that is not easy to combine with that of *Menci*, the Court seems therefore to assume that, if the criminal proceedings become final first, there is a sort of presumption that – arguably for the inherent higher severity of criminal sanctions – issuing administrative penalties for the same facts is excessive, and would therefore violate the right to *ne bis in idem*. In the opposite scenario, which was addressed in *Menci*, the Court seems instead to suggest that administrative proceedings and sanctions do not forbid ensuing criminal proceedings and penalties for the same facts.

No further clarity can be gleaned from the third judgment issued by the Court of Justice on the same day of *Menci* and *Garlsson*. *Di Puma and Zecca* originates from a request for a preliminary ruling lodged by Italian courts, which asked whether the final acquittal of the defendants in criminal proceedings would prohibit imposing on them administrative penalties for the same facts.[288] The Italian Code of Criminal Procedure (CCP) includes a provision, Article 654, according to which final judgments in criminal proceedings – be them acquittals or convictions – have the force of *res judicata* in administrative proceedings. As a consequence, since the defendants had been acquitted on the ground that the acts constituting the offence of insider dealing were not established, they could not be subject to any administrative penalty for the same facts. Nonetheless, Italian courts doubted that such provision respected

---

283 ibid, para 45.
284 ibid, para 46.
285 See ibid, para 57.
286 ibid, para 59. Again, the Court clarifies that it is for the national courts to finally ascertain that the duplication at hand does not comply with Article 52 of the Charter, and therefore violates Article 50 CFR (ibid, para 61).
287 ibid, para 62.
288 Joined Cases C-596/16 & C-597/16 *Di Puma and Zecca*, EU:C:2018:192.

the obligation resting upon the Italian Republic to punish insider dealing with effective, proportionate, and dissuasive administrative penalties, and at the same time wondered how to reconcile this obligation with the *ne bis in idem* principle.

The Court of Justice argues that Article 654 CCP does not violate either EU law or Article 50 of the Charter. The reasoning of the Court is however centred on the principle of *res judicata*, while *ne bis in idem* plays a secondary role. The Court unsurprisingly states that the duplication of penalties and proceedings is a limitation to the right enshrined in Article 50 CFR and, as in *Garlsson*, it claims that the bringing of proceedings for an administrative fine of a criminal nature after an acquittal in criminal proceedings 'clearly exceeds what is necessary to achieve'[289] the objectives of national and EU legislation on insider dealing, that is, protecting the EU financial markets' integrity and public confidence in financial instruments. The Court's conclusion in *Di Puma and Zecca* seems to confirm the contentious relevance of the time issue in double-track systems: as long as criminal proceedings come to an end first – independently of their outcome (acquittal or conviction) – the bringing of administrative proceedings of a criminal nature for the same facts is likely to violate the *ne bis in idem* principle. In the opposite situation, where administrative proceedings of a criminal nature terminate before criminal ones, there seems to be more margin of appreciation for national authorities to accept that criminal penalties may be issued for the same facts that have already been subject to administrative – but in essence criminal – penalties.

The case law of the European Courts on *ne bis in idem* in double-track systems is therefore complex and multifaceted. The CJEU and the ECtHR have abandoned their initial stance, which was more protective towards individuals, in favour of an interpretation of the *ne bis in idem* principle that tries not to turn upside down national legal orders that cherish the double-track punitive system. This has led both Courts to flesh out some – at times vague – criteria that national authorities should follow to assess whether *ne bis in idem* is violated. Although the conclusions they reach are similar, the two European Courts take an approach that is different in several aspects.[290] While the ECtHR has adopted the criterion of the close connection in substance and time, the CJEU prefers to focus on the proportionality of double-track systems, especially with respect to the overall severity of penalties.[291] If there is some correspondence

---

289 ibid, para 44.
290 See also Luchtman, 'The ECJ's Recent Case Law on *Ne Bis in Idem*' (n 260) 1732.
291 G Lo Schiavo, 'The Principle of *Ne Bis in Idem* and the Application of Criminal Sanctions: Of Scope and Restrictions' (2018) 14 *European Constitutional Law Review* 644, 657–660.

between the proportionality assessment and that on the close connection in substance,[292] it is instead unclear to what extent, if any, the CJEU values the connection in time for the purposes of Article 50 of the Charter.[293] These uncertainties do not bode well for legal certainty and put national authorities coping with environmental offences in a situation where they are confronted with different standards that are both relevant for their decisions.

5 Conclusion

Tackling transnational environmental crime remains a challenge for judicial and police authorities. As discussed in the previous chapter, national criminal laws on environmental crime still bear significant differences, especially as far as the definition of, and the penalties for, these crimes are concerned. This chapter has demonstrated that such discrepancies can have a negative impact on the efficient functioning of the procedures of judicial cooperation at the EU level. In particular, differences in the threshold of (imprisonment) penalties, together with the limited amount of such penalties, may hamper the application of the mutual recognition principle. The scenario may however improve if the revised Environmental Crime Directive – if and when adopted – will succeed in ensuring a higher degree of harmonisation throughout the EU.

The initial vision of national governments of mutual recognition with a high level of automaticity based on an almost blind trust in the justice systems of the Member States and the presumption of their compliance with fundamental rights has gradually been replaced with a more nuanced approach, putting the interests of the individual, and the need to comply fully with the Charter of Fundamental Rights, at the heart of the system. The centrality of human rights is reflected in the introduction of limits to recognition and the requirement for national authorities to examine the compatibility of the execution of a judgment with fundamental rights on the one hand, and in the imposition of standards safeguarding the judicialisation of cooperation on the other. Full compliance with fundamental rights must remain central in the development of cooperation between administrative and judicial authorities in the fight

---

292 When examining the proportionality principle, the CJEU mentions the importance of rules that provide for the coordination of different proceedings and of those that aim to ensure the proportionality of the severity of all penalties (cf Case C-524/15 *Menci*, paras 53–57; Case C-537/16 *Garlsson*, paras 55–58). Cf *A and B v Norway*, para 132.

293 Luchtman, 'The ECJ's Recent Case Law on *Ne Bis in Idem*' (n 260) 1732–1733; Mirandola and Lasagni (n 189).

against environmental crime, and the criminal law safeguards should not be circumvented by the back door.

Further obstacles to an effective EU reaction against environmental crime can flow from the absence of binding EU rules on conflicts of jurisdiction. The settlement of these conflicts is not only a pressing need from the perspective of the individuals concerned but is also a matter of efficient administration of justice. It would be unreasonable for the authorities of different Member States to exercise their jurisdiction with regard to the same facts, especially if they act in an Area of Freedom, Security and Justice that is allegedly founded on mutual trust. The only principle that can help solve conflicts of jurisdiction, although in an insufficient way, is *ne bis in idem*. The application of *ne bis in idem* in criminal matters, including in the surrounding grey area of 'administrative law of a criminal nature', which is of the utmost importance for environmental law, has represented one of the most debated issues in the development of the Area of Freedom, Security and Justice over the last years.

While the Lisbon Treaty could have prompted the adoption of new legal instruments concerning jurisdictional issues within the EU, there has so far been no political will for this. The Lisbon Treaty has nonetheless 'emancipated' the principle of *ne bis in idem* by elevating it to a fundamental right in the Charter. The constitutionalisation of *ne bis in idem* serves to remind us of the necessity to underpin any EU law or practice on choice of forum and conflicts of jurisdiction with clear and effective safeguards for affected individuals. As discussed above, and as stated by the Commission, it could therefore be appropriate to include a direct reference to the *ne bis in idem* in the text of the revised Environmental Crime Directive.[294]

Finally, the compatibility of double-track systems with the right to *ne bis in idem* is still a sensitive topic and will arguably continue to be at the centre-stage of further debates. The CJEU and the ECtHR have been asked to find a compromise that takes into account the well-established twin-track systems of several (EU) countries, which cope with some forms of criminality – including environmental criminality – by means a combined criminal-administrative approach, while at the same trying not to downplay the fundamental right to *ne bis in idem*. The outcome of this balancing exercise has generated some solutions that are not entirely convincing and, above all, not easily applicable by national authorities.

---

294 Commission, 'Commission Staff Working Document Evaluation of the Directive 2008/99/EC' (n 34) 84, where the Commission explains that such a refence would aim to 'exclude dual sanctions under certain circumstances, in accordance with CJEU case-law'.

CHAPTER 7

Environmental Crime at the EU Level

The Role of EU Agencies and Bodies

1 Introduction

This chapter examines the third dimension of the European Union's contribution to the fight against environmental crime. After the analysis of the EU's role in harmonising national criminal legislation and regulating mutual recognition procedures, the focus will now shift to the EU agencies and bodies that aim to foster police and judicial cooperation among national authorities that investigate and prosecute environmental crime. This chapter explores in particular the added value of the two most known EU agencies in the field, namely the European Union Agency for Law Enforcement Cooperation (Europol) and the European Union Agency for Criminal Justice Cooperation (Eurojust).[1] Their main features are illustrated in section 2, while sections 3 and 4 examine their activities to curb environmental crime. Section 5 discusses instead the potential role that the European Public Prosecutor's Office (EPPO) could play in this field in the future.

2 Europol and Eurojust: Structure, Functioning and Powers

The mission of Europol and Eurojust is to support and coordinate national law enforcement and prosecutorial authorities who investigate and prosecute cross-border crimes. Section 2.1 examines the competence of the two Agencies and provides for a classification of their tasks. The activities that Europol and Eurojust carry out to achieve their core mission are defined in this chapter as

---

1 The European Anti-Fraud Office (OLAF) may also be involved in cases that end up in investigations and prosecutions of environmental crime. See, for instance, European Commission, 'Commission Staff Working Document Evaluation of the Directive 2008/99/EC of the European Parliament and of the Council of 19 November 2008 on the Protection of the Environment through Criminal Law' SWD (2020) 259 final, 28 October 2020, 56 and 82. However, as the focus of this work is on the reaction to environmental crime by means of criminal law, OLAF's activities, which are of an administrative nature, are not analysed in this chapter. For further details on OLAF, see the chapter on EU agencies and bodies in V Mitsilegas, *EU Criminal Law* (2nd edn, Hart, forthcoming).

'operational', whereas the others are referred to as 'non-operational' or 'strategic'. The structure and operational activities of Eurojust are first discussed (sections 2.2 and 2.3), before moving on to the analysis of the Europol's structure and operational activities (section 2.4), as well as of the main changes to the Europol's legal framework envisaged in the proposal of the European Commission (hereinafter: the 'Commission') for a revised Europol Regulation (section 2.5). Section 2.6 zooms in on the strategic tasks of the two Agencies. Section 2.7 draws some conclusions on the overall role that Europol and Eurojust play in the Area of Freedom, Security and Justice, paving the way to the analysis of their contribution to the fight against cross-border environmental crime.

2.1 Competence of the Two Agencies and Classification of Their Activities

Despite their similar mission, the ways in which Europol and Eurojust achieve their objectives – as well as their history, structure, and powers – are different.

Europol was established with a Convention adopted in 1995,[2] which was repealed in 2009 by a Council Decision ('Europol Council Decision').[3] After the entry into force of the Treaty of Lisbon, the Decision has been replaced by Regulation 2016/794 ('Europol Regulation').[4] In December 2020, the Commission tabled a proposal to amend the Europol Regulation, which is currently under negotiation.[5] The idea of a European Union's Judicial Cooperation Unit (Eurojust) was instead conceived during the 1999 European Council

---

2   Council Act of 26 July 1995 drawing up the Convention based on Article K.3 of the Treaty on European Union, on the establishment of a European Police Office (Europol Convention) [1995] OJ C316/1. Different Protocols amended this Convention over the years: for further references, see the chapter on EU agencies and bodies in Mitsilegas, *EU Criminal Law* (n 1). Europol began its activities in 1999, replacing the previous Europol Drugs Unit, established in 1995 by the Joint Action 95/73/JHA of 10 March 1995 adopted by the Council on the basis of Article K.3 of the Treaty on European Union concerning the Europol Drugs Unit [1995] OJ L62/1.

3   Council Decision 2009/371/JHA of 6 April 2009 establishing the European Police Office (Europol) [2009] OJ L121/37.

4   Regulation (EU) 2016/794 of the European Parliament and of the Council of 11 May 2016 on the European Union Agency for Law Enforcement Cooperation (Europol) and replacing and repealing Council Decisions 2009/371/JHA, 2009/934/JHA, 2009/935/JHA, 2009/936/JHA and 2009/968/JHA [2016] OJ L135/53.

5   Commission, 'Proposal for a Regulation of the European Parliament and of the Council amending Regulation (EU) 2016/794, as regards Europol's cooperation with private parties, the processing of personal data by Europol in support of criminal investigations, and Europol's role on research and innovation' COM (2020) 796 final, 9 December 2020 ('Commission's proposal for a revised Europol Regulation').

meeting in Tampere.⁶ A Council Decision officially established Eurojust only in 2002⁷ and was later amended in 2003 and in 2009,⁸ before being replaced by Regulation 2018/1727 ('Eurojust Regulation').⁹

As far as their competence is concerned, Europol and Eurojust can exercise their powers with regard to the same areas of crime. Both Regulations provide that the two Agencies are competent with respect to the forms of 'serious crime'¹⁰ that are listed in an Annex to the two Regulations. Those listed areas of crime are identical and include terrorism, organised crime, drug trafficking, money-laundering activities, and trafficking in human beings.¹¹ They also include illicit trafficking in endangered animal species and in endangered plant species and varieties, as well as, more in general, 'environmental crime, including ship source pollution'.¹²

There is however a difference in the wording of the two Regulations on the Agencies' competence. The Europol Regulation requires these forms of serious crime to affect 'two or more Member States',¹³ while the Eurojust Regulation is silent in that respect.¹⁴ In line with Article 85 of the Treaty on the Functioning of the European Union (TFEU), on the basis of which the Eurojust Regulation was adopted, the Preamble of the Eurojust Regulation clarifies that the Agency's competence covers serious crimes affecting two or more Member States.¹⁵ Nonetheless, Eurojust can also exercise its powers when one of the

---

6   See the 'Presidency Conclusions of the Tampere European Council', 15 and 16 October 1999, Conclusion No 46.
7   Council Decision 2002/187/JHA of 28 February 2002 setting up Eurojust with a view to reinforcing the fight against serious crime [2002] OJ L63/1.
8   Respectively, Council Decision 2003/659/JHA of 18 June 2003 amending Decision 2002/187/JHA setting up Eurojust with a view to reinforcing the fight against serious crime [2003] OJ L245/44; Council Decision 2009/426/JHA of 16 December 2008 on the strengthening of Eurojust and amending Council Decision 2002/187/JHA setting up Eurojust with a view to reinforcing the fight against serious crime [2009] OJ L138/14.
9   Regulation (EU) 2018/1727 of the European Parliament and of the Council of 14 November 2018 on the European Union Agency for Criminal Justice Cooperation (Eurojust), and replacing and repealing Council Decision 2002/187/JHA, OJ L295/138.
10 Article 3(1) of the Eurojust Regulation and Article 3(1) of the Europol Regulation.
11 The list largely replicates the list of crimes for which EU instruments of mutual recognition can be used without need to verify double criminality. See more in the previous chapter.
12 See Annex I to both Regulations. In addition, both Agencies are also competent for crimes that are 'related' to those listed in the Annexes – see more in Article 3(4) of the Eurojust Regulation and Article 3(2) of the Europol Regulation.
13 Article 3(1) of the Europol Regulation.
14 cf Article 3(1) of the Eurojust Regulation.
15 Recital 3 of the Eurojust Regulation.

serious crimes listed in Annex I to the Eurojust Regulation 'requires prosecution on common bases'[16] – an expression that includes cases involving one Member State and a third country, or even a single Member State if the crime has repercussions at Union level.[17]

Environmental crime falls therefore within the competence of Eurojust and Europol mostly when it concerns two or more Member States. In exceptional cases, Eurojust can nonetheless deal with environmental crime cases even when they have a purely national dimension. The Annexes to the Europol and Eurojust Regulations also mention 'organised crime', which can thus cover the cases of transnational organised environmental crime.

With regard to the two Agencies' mission, Europol's objective is to 'support and strengthen action by the competent authorities of the Member States and their mutual cooperation in preventing and combating'[18] serious cross-border crime. Likewise, Eurojust aims to 'support and strengthen coordination and cooperation between national investigating and prosecuting authorities'[19] in relation to transnational criminality. The two Agencies do not have the 'coercive' powers of national authorities, eg those to arrest people, search houses, and launch their own investigations or prosecutions. The TFEU itself prevents the two Agencies from exercising such coercive powers: pursuant to Article 85(2) TFEU (on Eurojust), 'formal acts of judicial procedure shall be carried out by the competent national officials', whereas Article 88(3) TFEU (on Europol) provides that 'the application of coercive measures shall be the exclusive responsibility of the competent national authorities'. The two Agencies can only support national authorities in their investigations and prosecutions concerning transnational crime, but do not investigate and prosecute themselves.

Despite their similar objectives, the 'operational' activities of the two Agencies – namely the activities that Eurojust and Europol carry out to achieve their core mission – are different. While Eurojust's operational activities are meant to facilitate the coordination among national prosecuting authorities, Europol's ones are instead two-fold. Until the adoption of the Europol Regulation, Europol's core activity was the analysis of information and (personal) data that are relevant for national investigations. The Europol

---

16   Recital 11 of the Eurojust Regulation. On the similar possibility for Europol to deal with crimes that affect a common interest covered by a Union policy without the requirement of the cross-border dimension of the crime concerned – as envisaged in the Commission's proposal for a revised Europol Regulation – see section 2.5.
17   Article 3(5) and (6) of the Eurojust Regulation.
18   Article 3(1) of the Europol Regulation.
19   Article 2(1) of the Eurojust Regulation.

Regulation defines 'operational analysis' as encompassing 'all methods and techniques by which information is collected, stored, processed and assessed *with the aim of supporting criminal investigations*'.[20] This remains the thrust of Europol's identity.

Compared with the previous Council Decision, however, the Europol Regulation pays more attention to the *coordination* role that the agency can also play. The Europol Council Decision only stated that Europol should have the power 'to ask the competent authorities of the Member States concerned to initiate, conduct or coordinate investigations and to suggest the setting up of joint investigation teams in specific cases'.[21] On the contrary, the Regulation now mentions, among the tasks of the Agency, those of coordinating, organising and implementing 'investigative and operational actions to support and strengthen actions by the competent authorities of the Member States, that are carried out: (i) jointly with the competent authorities of the Member States; or (ii) in the context of joint investigation teams ...'.[22] Within these boundaries, which are consistent with the traditionally limited willingness of the Member States to surrender their sovereignty in the sensitive field of criminal law, the Regulation has enhanced the role that Europol could play in coordinating national authorities.

In sum, Eurojust's operational activities are those connected with its mission of coordinating national investigations and prosecutions. Such a coordination role falls also within the operational activities of Europol, even though the latter's main task remains the operational analysis of data provided by national law enforcement authorities.

Beyond this operational dimension, however, Eurojust and Europol carry out other activities, which mainly consist in gathering and spreading knowledge on areas of crimes within their competence, instruments to cope with them, and recurring legal problems in the framework of judicial and police cooperation. These activities can be defined as 'strategic' or 'non-operational'. An illustrative example can be found in the Europol Regulation: the Agency has the power to, inter alia, 'prepare threat assessments, strategic and operational analyses and general situation reports'.[23] More in detail, 'strategic analysis'

---

20 Article 2(c) of the Europol Regulation. Emphasis added.
21 Article 5(1)(d) of the Europol Council Decision.
22 Article 4(1)(c) of the Europol Regulation. The Commission had already suggested this wording when issuing the proposal for Council Decision 2009/371/JHA on Europol, but the Council opposed it (A De Moor and G Vermeulen, 'The Europol Council Decision: Transforming Europol into an Agency of the European Union' (2010) 47 *Common Market Law Review* 1089, 1109–1110).
23 Article 4(1)(f) of the Europol Regulation.

means 'all methods and techniques by which information is collected, stored, processed and assessed with the aim of *supporting* and *developing* a *criminal policy* that contributes to the efficient and effective prevention of, and the fight against, crime'.[24] The difference with the above-mentioned 'operational analysis' is evident: whereas the latter is meant to support (ongoing) criminal investigations, strategic analysis is a tool for the development of criminal policy.

Especially with regard to Europol, however, the alleged lack of coercive powers is highly debated in the literature: in some circumstances, the Agency's contribution to national investigations and prosecutions can be of such a relevance that is questionable whether it is still sound to claim that Europol does not have any coercive power.[25] As the following sections will demonstrate, environmental crime is an area where the support of the two Agencies can make the boundaries between the 'coercive' powers of national authorities and the (merely) 'supporting' ones of EU agencies quite blurred in practice. Likewise, the dividing line between 'operational' and 'non-operational' tasks of Eurojust and Europol, which is useful to categorise their powers, is quite difficult to draw in practice when looking more closely at their activities.

2.2 *Structure and Operational Activities of Eurojust*

With the exception of Denmark,[26] each Member State has its representative at Eurojust, the so-called 'national desk',[27] which is composed of the national member and at least one deputy and one assistant.[28] The national member is seconded by each of the 26 Member States for a (renewable) term of five years and, like his or her deputies, has the status of 'a prosecutor, a judge or a representative of a judicial authority with competences equivalent to those of a prosecutor or judge under their national law'.[29] All the national members form the College,[30] which then elects – from among the national members – the President and the two Vice-Presidents of Eurojust.[31] A representative from

---

24 Article 2(b) of the Europol Regulation. Emphasis added.
25 See S Gless, 'Europol' in V Mitsilegas, M Bergström and T Konstadinides (eds), *Research Handbook on EU Criminal Law* (Edward Elgar 2016) 464.
26 On the special status of Denmark vis-à-vis the EU measures concerning the Area of Freedom, Security and Justice see Protocol no 22 to the EU Treaties.
27 Recitals 21 and 22 and Articles 11(7) and 12(2)(b) of the Eurojust Regulation. Further references to Articles and Recitals in this section should be understood as referring to Articles and Recitals of the Eurojust Regulation, unless otherwise specified.
28 Article 7(2).
29 Article 7(4).
30 Article 10(1)(a).
31 Article 11(1).

the Commission takes also part in the College meetings yet such participation is limited only to those (parts of the) meetings 'when the College exercises its management functions'.[32]

In addition to its core operational tasks,[33] the Eurojust College has also management functions, such as adopting the budget and a document containing the agency's annual and multi-annual programming.[34] Over the last years, concerns had emerged on the excessive administrative burden of the College, which was largely prevented from focusing on its operational functions. In order to strengthen such functions and reduce the 'administrative workload of national members',[35] the Eurojust Regulation established an Executive Board. Composed of the President, the Vice-Presidents, two members of the College designated in accordance with a rotation system, and a representative from the Commission,[36] the Board is now responsible to take most of the Agency's administrative decisions.

Along the lines of the previous Council Decisions, the Regulation provides that Eurojust can act either through its national members or as a College, with the latter kicking in, inter alia, when a case involves investigations or prosecutions 'which have repercussions at Union level or which might affect Member States other than those directly concerned'.[37] While two separate provisions of the Eurojust Decision concerned the tasks of Eurojust acting through its national members and those of Eurojust acting as a College, the Regulation lists them in a single provision (Article 4) and clarifies that, in principle, Eurojust acts through one or more national members.[38] In particular, Eurojust may ask the competent authorities of the Member States concerned – giving its reasons – to:

(a) undertake an investigation or prosecution of specific acts;
(b) accept that one of them may be in a better position to undertake an investigation or to prosecute specific acts;
(c) coordinate between the competent authorities of the Member States concerned;

---

32 Article 10(1)(b).
33 See immediately below in the text.
34 Respectively, Articles 61(2) and 15(1).
35 Recital 9.
36 Article 16(4).
37 Article 5(2)(a)(ii).
38 Article 5(1). As mentioned above in the text, Eurojust will act as a College when the case has a strong transnational component.

(d) set up a joint investigation team in keeping with the relevant cooperation instruments;
(e) provide Eurojust with any information that is necessary for it to carry out its tasks;
(f) take special investigative measures;
(g) take any other measure justified for the investigation or prosecution.[39]

Therefore, Eurojust can *ask* Member States' authorities to undertake an investigation or prosecution of specific acts but cannot compel these authorities to do so. The possibility set out in the Treaty to entrust Eurojust with the power to initiate criminal investigations has not yet been implemented.[40] Eurojust was, and remains, a body that aims to support national authorities but does not exercise direct and coercive powers.

With regard to the issue of concurrent jurisdictions, which the previous chapter examined, suffice it to remember that Eurojust can ask national authorities to accept that one of them may be in a better position to undertake an investigation or to prosecute specific acts – yet it cannot take a binding decision on the matter.[41] Furthermore, where two or more Member States cannot agree on which of them should undertake an investigation or prosecution after a request from Eurojust, the Agency should issue 'a written opinion' on the case.[42] In accordance with the Preamble of the Regulation, Eurojust's written opinions 'are *not* binding on Member States'.[43] Even though the Treaty of Lisbon allows granting Eurojust the power to settle conflicts of jurisdiction,[44] the Regulation has not enhanced the Agency's role in that respect either. However, Eurojust can still be called to act as a 'broker' between Member States in cases of disagreement as to which jurisdiction should prosecute. At present, there are no binding rules on conflicts of jurisdiction at the EU level. Eurojust issued – and recently revised – its (non-binding) guidelines on determining which jurisdiction is best placed to prosecute.[45]

The Eurojust Regulation also clarifies the powers that national members shall have:[46]

---

39 Article 4(2).
40 Article 85(1)(a) TFEU.
41 For further remarks on the role of Eurojust in conflicts of jurisdiction, see the references in n 129 of the previous chapter.
42 Article 4(4) of the Eurojust Regulation.
43 Recital 14. Emphasis added.
44 Article 85(1)(c) TFEU.
45 See more in the previous chapter.
46 Article 8. Although the classification below among 'ordinary powers', 'powers exercised in agreement with a competent national authority', and 'powers exercised in urgent cases' was to be found in Articles 9b, 9c, and 9d of the Eurojust Council Decision and has not

i. 'ordinary' powers to facilitate mutual legal assistance and judicial cooperation, in particular those to: a) facilitate or otherwise support the issuing or execution of any request for mutual legal assistance or mutual recognition; b) directly contact and exchange information with any competent national authority, any other competent Union body and any international authority; and c) participate in joint investigation teams (Article 8(1) of the Eurojust Regulation);

ii. powers to be exercised *in agreement with a competent national authority*, namely: a) issue or execute any request for mutual legal assistance or mutual recognition; and b) order, request or execute investigative measures, as provided for in the Directive on the European Investigation Order (Article 8(3));

iii. powers to be exercised *in urgent cases*: when the case is urgent, ie it is not possible for Eurojust to identify or contact the competent national authority in a timely manner, national members can exercise *motu proprio* the powers mentioned in Article 8(3) above, although this could only happen, in principle, with the previous agreement of domestic authorities (Article 8(4)).[47]

Finally, Eurojust is now allowed to exercise its powers not only upon request of national authorities (or the EPPO) but also 'on its own initiative'.[48] Introduced by the Regulation, such a possibility could allow Eurojust to 'take a more proactive role in coordinating cases', for instance 'involving Member States that might not initially have been included in the case and discovering links between cases based on the information it receives from Europol, the European Anti-Fraud Office (OLAF), the EPPO and national authorities'.[49] This would also contribute to enhance Eurojust's role in producing guidelines, policy documents and casework-related analyses as part of its strategic work.

2.3 Eurojust in Practice: Coordination Meetings, Coordination Centres and Joint Investigation Teams

The section above provided for an overview of the main provisions of the Eurojust Regulation concerning the Agency's operational functions. In practice, however, the most efficient – and very common – way for Eurojust to cope

---

been replicated in the Regulation, it captures well the different powers that national members can exercise pursuant to the Eurojust Regulation.

47 For further limitations on Eurojust's powers in the cases provided for by Article 8(3) and (4), see Article 8(5).
48 Article 2(3).
49 Recital 12.

with the requests of assistance from national authorities involved in the same cross-border case is to gather all of them in order to find common solutions to the problems they encounter in investigating and prosecuting transnational crime. Barely touched upon in the Eurojust Regulation, the 'coordination meetings' are at the core of Eurojust's operational functions.[50] These meetings, which usually take place at Eurojust's premises and benefit from the agency's logistical and financial support, gather both the national authorities that investigate the same case and the representatives from the concerned Eurojust's national desks. The coordination meetings are an ideal platform for the competent national authorities to exchange views on ongoing investigations and (the possibility of) their coordination. OLAF, third states, and especially Europol can participate in the coordination meetings. In these circumstances, Europol has usually carried out a previous analysis on the case; on its basis, national authorities can gain a better understanding of the transnational dimension of the case, criminal network(s) involved, and possible links between offenders and crimes. Europol is arguably the most important partner of Eurojust and their relations are regulated by an Agreement signed in October 2009.

As an outcome of the coordination meetings, the competent national authorities can decide to carry out, contemporarily and in a previously agreed day (the 'action day'), measures such as arrests, seizures or searches. In these cases, a 'coordination centre' is usually set up at Eurojust: representatives of the involved national desks take part in it, with the aim to monitor the activities, facilitate communication between authorities on the ground, and solve possible issues raised by the ongoing actions. Once the action day is over, the authorities agree on the further steps of the investigations, with the support of Eurojust.[51]

Coordination meetings and coordination centres are highly valued by national authorities and represent the clearest example of Eurojust's added value in the fight against cross-border crime.[52] Yet sometimes they are not

---

50   Coordination meetings are only mentioned in Article 4(3)(a) of the Eurojust Regulation, where it is stated that 'Eurojust may also ... supply logistical support, including translation, interpretation and the organisation of coordination meetings'. See also M Coninsx, 'Eurojust' in Mitsilegas, Bergström and Konstadinides (eds) (n 25) 449; S Gless and T Wahl, 'A Comparison of the Evolution and Pace of Police and Judicial Cooperation in Criminal Matters: A Race Between Europol and Eurojust?' in C Brière and A Weyembergh (eds), *The Needed Balances in EU Criminal Law. Past, Present and Future* (Hart 2018) 346.

51   For an explanation of the functioning of coordination centres, see S Petit Leclair, 'Justice et Sécurité en Europe: Eurojust ou la Création d'un Parquet Européen' (2012) 20 *Cahiers de la sécurité* 38, 42.

52   GENVAL, 'Final report on the 6th round of mutual evaluations on "The practical implementation and operation of the Council Decision 2002/187/JHA of 28 February 2002

even necessary to allow the Agency to achieve its goals. Issues faced by national prosecutors can at times be rapidly solved once Eurojust is contacted: this can be through a meeting of the representatives of the involved desks or even by a simple exchange of information between them (eg the national desk at Eurojust can inform the requesting national authority on the person to contact in another country or could transmit the request for mutual assistance to another desk). This informal way of cooperation is highly appreciated by the practitioners, even though it makes the work of Eurojust not always transparent.[53]

Joint Investigation Teams (JITs) represent instead a more structured way of cooperation. Eurojust can ask the competent national authorities to set up a JIT.[54] Eurojust supports the establishment and the functioning of JITs also under a *financial* point of view, something that national authorities highly value as they are not requested to bear extra-financial costs in similar cases.[55] The establishment and functioning of JITs were regulated by Article 13 of the 2000 Convention on Mutual Legal Assistance (MLA Convention),[56] and later by a Framework Decision on Joint Investigation Teams (JIT Framework Decision).[57] These instruments enable the Member States to set up joint investigation teams 'for a specific purpose and a limited period, which may be extended by mutual consent, to carry out criminal investigations in one or more of the Member States setting up the team'.[58] The main advantages of JITs have been summarised as follows:

---

setting up Eurojust with a view to reinforcing the fight against serious crime and of the Council Decision 2008/976/JHA on the European Judicial Network in criminal matters'" Council doc 14536/2/14 REV 2, 2 December 2014 ('GENVAL final report on Eurojust') 45. For more details on GENVAL in general and how it works, see section 4.1 of chapter 5 of this book. In 2020, Eurojust organised 468 coordination meetings and 27 coordination centres (Eurojust, 'Eurojust Annual Report 2020' (2021) 58).

53 One of the recommendations of the GENVAL final report on Eurojust is 'to reflect on how to render more transparent the real workload of national members and national desks'· (GENVAL final report on Eurojust (previous n) 44).

54 Article 4(2)(d) of the Eurojust Regulation.

55 Article 60(4) of the Eurojust Regulation provides that Eurojust's expenditure includes, inter alia, operating costs, which includes funding for joint investigation teams.

56 OJ C197/1.

57 OJ L162/1. The Framework Decision largely replicates the text of the MLA Convention and was deemed necessary at the time because of the delay in the entry into force of the MLA Convention.

58 Article 13(1) of the MLA Convention; Article 1(1) of the JIT Framework Decision.

requests for mutual legal assistance are *no longer necessary*. Instead, if investigative action is required in a state that is party to the JIT, a team member from that country can instigate such an action directly, exactly as they would have done in their home country. Furthermore, team members can *freely exchange* all the information acquired.[59]

JITs have turned out to be a very useful instrument of cooperation, which is highly appreciated by the practitioners.[60]

2.4 Structure and Operational Activities of Europol

Whereas Eurojust has a collegial structure, Europol is organised in a hierarchical way, since it is headed by an Executive Director.[61] The other main organ of Europol, its decision-making body,[62] is the Management Board, which is composed of one representative per Member State (except for Denmark) and of the Commission.[63] Each Member State has its own representative at Europol, the so-called 'Liaison Bureau'.[64] The Bureau is composed of the Europol Liaison Officers (ELOs),[65] who are seconded at Europol from the Europol National Units (ENUs), ie those national offices that are located in each Member State and represent the *trait d'union* between the Agency and the national authorities. While the Member States can allow direct contacts between national authorities and Europol, the ENUs are conceived as the main liaison body.[66] Europol's Liaison Bureaux allow national authorities to get in contact with Europol and exchange information with the Agency, yet Europol's core activity (operational analysis) is mostly achieved through the work of the analysts, who process the data shared by national law enforcement authorities.

---

59   T Spapens, 'Joint Investigation Teams in the European Union: Article 13 JITS and the Alternatives' (2011) 19 *European Journal of Crime, Criminal Law, and Criminal Justice* 239, 249. Emphasis added. See also A Klip, *European Criminal Law. An Integrative Approach* (3rd edn, Intersentia 2016) 496–498.
60   GENVAL final report on Eurojust (n 52) 16 and 50–52.
61   Article 16 of the Europol Regulation. Further references to Articles and Recitals in this section should be understood as referring to Articles and Recitals of the Europol Regulation, unless otherwise specified.
62   G De Amicis, 'I Soggetti della Cooperazione Giudiziaria' in RE Kostoris (ed), *Manuale di Procedura Penale Europea* (Giuffrè 2014) 179.
63   Article 10.
64   This work intends to present only the main features of Europol (and Eurojust). For an in-depth analysis of the functioning of the two Agencies, see the chapter on EU agencies and bodies in Mitsilegas, *EU Criminal Law* (n 1) and further references therein.
65   Article 8.
66   Article 7.

The main tasks of Europol are 'to collect, store, process, analyse and exchange information, including criminal intelligence'.[67] Information-related tasks are central to the existence of Europol, which has been defined as an 'enormous data processing agency rather than a law enforcing police office'.[68] In the past, Europol had a complex system of processing data that encompassed different databases with different rules. The 2016 Regulation re-designed the processing architecture of Europol: the old pre-defined databases or systems are not mentioned in the Regulation anymore and a new 'privacy by design approach'[69] has been adopted. This approach 'would allow Europol to link and make analyses of relevant data, reduce delays in identifying trends and patterns and reduce multiple storage of data'.[70] As explained in the Europol Strategy for 2016–2020, the new Europol's legal framework introduced a new integrated data management concept, as a consequence of which

> Europol, in close consultation with [the Member States], will have the opportunity to use this flexibility to modernise its system's architecture and information-management strategy to ensure the best ways to manage criminal information and enhance the analytical capabilities of Europol based on [Member States] operational requirements. The integration of data will ensure that *links across crime areas will be more easily identified* and, therefore, analytical support will be of increased value.[71]

In essence, the rationale behind the Regulation is that, once (personal) data concerning criminal investigations are shared with Europol, the Agency can process and analyse them without the restrictions linked to the fact that that piece of information is included in a given database: interoperability – ie 'the

---

67 Article 4(1)(a).
68 Gless, 'Europol' (n 25) 465. Europol can also exchange information with private parties, under the conditions provided for by Article 26 of the Europol Regulation. For the proposed strengthening of such an exchange pursuant to the Commission's proposal for a revised Europol Regulation, see section 2.5.
69 Commission, 'Explanatory Memorandum' to the 'Proposal for a Regulation of the European Parliament and of the Council on the European Union Agency for Law Enforcement Cooperation and Training (Europol) and repealing Decisions 2009/371/JHA and 2005/681/JHA' COM (2013) 173 final, 27 March 2013, 8.
70 ibid.
71 Europol, 'Europol Strategy 2016–2020' (2016) 12. Emphasis added.

possibility to analyse one data set with another without additional procedural burden'[72] – should be the new guiding principle.

Europol is also responsible for the management of SIENA (Secure Information Exchange Network Application), an online platform that aims to facilitate the exchange of information among Member States, EU bodies (including Europol), third countries, and international organisations.[73] Empirical research has demonstrated that national authorities highly value the exchange of informational through SIENA.[74]

Finally, like Eurojust, Europol can (only) ask the national competent authorities to begin an investigation and can also take part in JITS,[75] and in the framework of JITS' activities it can process the relevant information with the consent and under the responsibility of the Member State that provided the information.

2.5   The Future of Europol in Light of the Revised Regulation

In December 2020, the Commission presented a proposal for a Regulation amending the Europol Regulation, with a view to enhancing Europol's mandate.[76] The proposal encompasses a wide-ranging revision of Europol's tasks. At the time of writing, negotiations on the text are ongoing.

Among its several objectives, the proposal aims to enable Europol to cooperate effectively with *private parties* in countering criminal offences committed in abuse of the cross-border services of private parties. The proposal aims to establish the Agency as a central point of contact in case of multi-jurisdictional or non-attributable datasets. Europol will be enabled to: a) receive personal data directly from private parties on a more regular basis; b) inform such private parties of missing information; and c) ask Member States to request private parties to share further information. These changes would constitute a

---

72 D Drewer and V Miladinova, 'The BIG DATA Challenge: Impact and Opportunity of Large Quantities of Information Under the Europol Regulation' (2017) 33 *Computer Law & Security Review* 298, 305.

73 Recital 24.

74 E Disley, B Irving, W Hughes et al, 'Evaluation of the implementation of the Europol Council Decision and of Europol's activities' (Rand 2012) <https://www.europol.europa.eu/publications-documents/evaluation-of-implementation-of-europol-council-decision-and-of-europol%E2%80%99s-activities-2> accessed 2 June 2021, 36.

75 Respectively, Articles 6 and 5.

76 Commission's proposal for a revised Europol Regulation (n 5). This section draws upon V Mitsilegas and N Vavoula, 'Strengthening Europol's Mandate. A Legal Assessment of the Commission's Proposal to Amend the Europol Regulation' (2021) Study for the European Parliament Committee on Civil Liberties, Justice and Home Affairs.

considerable paradigm shift for the Agency, which is line with the emergence of the trend in past years to establish direct channels of communication between law enforcement and private parties and foster a public/private partnership.

The proposal also aims to enable Europol to *process large and complex datasets* following the admonishment of the Agency by the European Data Protection Supervisor on 17 September 2020.[77] To face the 'big data challenge', Europol would be enabled to conduct 'pre-analyses' of large and complex datasets received and identify whether these concern individuals whose personal data may be processed by Europol in line with the Europol Regulation.[78] The prior processing would be limited to a maximum period of one year, which can be extended following authorisation by the European Data Protection Supervisor.

The proposal would also enable Europol to request the competent authorities of the Member States to initiate, conduct or coordinate an investigation of a crime that affects a common interest covered by an EU policy, *regardless of the cross-border nature of the crime.*[79] In the negotiations that followed the presentation of the Commission's proposal, this new Europol's power to request the initiation of investigations by national authorities has been met with great scepticism by the Member States, to the extent that at the time of writing it does not seem that this reform will take place. A large majority of Member States have considered that no further obligation to act at the request of Europol should be imposed on the Member States, as that would be disproportionate.[80]

Finally, the Commission's proposal also aims to strengthen Europol's cooperation with the European Public Prosecutor's Office (EPPO), by aligning the Europol Regulation with the Regulation that established the EPPO,[81] as well as with third countries, by enabling the Executive Director to authorise not only transfers, but also 'categories of transfers' of personal data to third countries or international organisations in specific situations and on a case-by-case basis.[82]

---

77   Decision of the European Data Protection Supervisor of 17 September 2020 on the own initiative inquiry on Europol's big data challenge.
78   Proposed Article 18(5)a of the Europol Regulation (Article 1(5) of the Commission's proposal for a revised Europol Regulation).
79   See the proposed new wording of Article 6(1) of the Europol Regulation (Article 1(3) of the Commission's proposal for a revised Europol Regulation).
80   Mitsilegas and Vavoula (n 76) 60.
81   Proposed Article 20a of the Europol Regulation (Article 1(8) of the Commission's proposal for a revised Europol Regulation). On the EPPO, see section 5 below.
82   See the proposed new wording of Article 25(5) of the Europol Regulation (Article 1(11) of the Commission's proposal for a revised Europol Regulation). The transfers of data by Europol are currently regulated by Articles 24ff of the Europol Regulation.

While the latter is a seemingly minor change in the Europol's legal framework, this reform may pose significant legal challenges if it ended up in broadening the remit of Europol's transfers of data – notably because it is not entirely clear what is meant by 'categories of transfers' – from criminal investigations on specific suspects to surveillance activities in general, thus changing Europol's powers.

In sum, the Commission's proposal entails some paradigm shifts in the way Europol operates and in its relationship with the Member States and third parties. The proposal aims to ensure the Agency can continue to play its key role in the fast evolving field of law enforcement, including in the fight against environmental crime, by strengthening its ties with traditional and new partners and entrusting it with powers that are sufficiently flexible and up to date to face new challenges and threats, yet this makes the strict compliance of the new Europol's legal framework with the EU *acquis* on fundamental rights and data protection all the more important.

2.6 *'Non-operational' Tasks of the Two Agencies and the Policy Cycle (EMPACT)*

Eurojust and Europol are ideally placed to collect and spread knowledge both on cross-border criminality and the best ways to curb it. For instance, Europol issues documents known as 'Threat Assessments', which offer an assessment of the main features of given crimes, as well as of the needs to counter them in an efficient way. The most known Threat Assessments are the SOCTA (Serious and Organised Crime Threat Assessment) and the IOCTA (Internet Organised Crime Threat Assessment).

Furthermore, in 2010, a scanning, analysis, and notification (SCAN) team had been established inside Europol, with the aim to provide 'national competent authorities and policy-makers at national and EU level with early warning notifications on new organised crime threats'.[83] Such notifications were usually brief documents knowns as 'OC-SCAN Threat Notices', which were disseminated among national authorities. As discussed below, some of these notices concerned environmental crime. However, at the time of writing, Europol has discontinued its practice of issuing and disseminating OC-SCAN Threat Notices.

It ought to be noticed that another objective of the above-mentioned Commission's proposal for a revised Europol Regulation is to strengthen Europol's role in the fields of research and innovation, namely a quintessential example of the 'non operational'/ 'strategic' tasks of the Agency. In accordance

---

83 Europol, 'Europol Review 2013' (2014) 14.

with the proposed text, Europol would for instance be able to process personal data for research and innovation matters for the development of tools, including the use of Artificial Intelligence for law enforcement.[84]

Eurojust plays a similar 'strategic' role, eg through the strategic or tactical meetings periodically organised by the Agency to allow national authorities to discuss some recurring problems in the field of judicial cooperation. These meetings have a further strategic function 'in that they are intended to promote Eurojust, demonstrating its added value to national authorities and therewith attracting more case referrals'.[85] Eurojust's strategic activity also encompasses the drafting of documents such as the Memorandum on Terrorism Financing and the Terrorism Conviction Monitor or the significant contribution of the Agency to the 'European Handbook on how to issue a European Arrest Warrant'.[86] Sometimes, Eurojust and Europol pool their expertise, as it happened with the Joint Investigation Teams Practical Guide, which Europol and Eurojust drafted at the end of a common project.[87]

The unique position of these bodies as central coordinators in the area of criminal justice and law enforcement allows them to play three other roles, which can fall within a broader understanding of 'non-operational' functions. First, they are 'trust promoter[s]':[88] gathering national authorities coming from (almost) all EU Member States in the very same building helps to foster the mutual trust among them. Second, Eurojust and Europol are in an ideal position to monitor the functioning of the instruments of judicial and police cooperation.[89] For instance, the Member States that are unable to respect the time limits for the execution of a European Arrest Warrant (EAW) have the obligation to report such a delay to Eurojust, pursuant to Article 17(7) of the EAW Framework Decision.

---

84 Proposed Article 33a of the Europol Regulation (Article 1(19) of the Commission's proposal for a revised Europol Regulation).

85 M Groenleer, *The Autonomy of the European Union Agencies. A Comparative Study of Institutional Development* (Eburon 2009) 318.

86 'Revised version of the European handbook on how to issue a European Arrest Warrant' Council doc 17195/1/10, 17 December 2010, which has been further revised in 2017 (OJ C335/1).

87 'Joint Investigation Teams Practical Guide' Council doc 6128/1/17, 14 February 2017.

88 J Vlastník, 'Eurojust–A Cornerstone of the Federal Criminal Justice System in the EU?' in E Guild and F Geyer (eds), *Security versus Justice? Police and Judicial Cooperation in the European Union* (Ashgate 2008) 38ff. See also Groenleer (n 85) 294 (on Europol) and 328ff (on Eurojust).

89 The 'monitoring function' of Eurojust is discussed by J Monar, 'Eurojust's Present and Future Role at the Frontline of European Union Criminal Justice Cooperation' (2013) 14 Era Forum 187, 193–194.

Third, as a further consequence of their role and expertise, it would not be unreasonable to imagine that Europol and Eurojust could (or even should) play a sort of 'lobbying/advising' role for the EU institutions, when the latter are called to legislate on matters related to the judicial or police cooperation. In that regard, however, Eurojust and Europol bear a significant difference.

As far as Eurojust is concerned, its role in 'policy development and strategy making'[90] has been quite limited, even though the Eurojust Regulation allows the Commission and the Member States to 'request Eurojust's opinion on all proposed legislative acts' concerning judicial cooperation in criminal matters and police cooperation.[91]

On the contrary, Europol's contribution to EU policy has recently become rather prominent. Reference is meant to the so-called 'EU policy cycle for organised and serious international crime', which is also known as EMPACT (European Multidisciplinary Platform Against Criminal Threats) Policy Cycle. The Policy Cycle is adopted by the EU 'in order to tackle the most important criminal threats in a coherent and methodological manner through optimum cooperation between the relevant services of the Member States, EU Institutions and EU Agencies as well as relevant third countries and organisations'.[92]

A first Policy Cycle covered the years between 2011 and 2013 and has so far been followed by three fully-fledged cycles for the periods 2014–2017, 2018–2021 and 2022–2025.[93] The functioning of the Policy Cycle is represented by the following image, available on the Europol website:[94]

---

90 P Jeney, 'The Future of Eurojust' (2012) Study for the European Parliament Committee on Civil Liberties, Justice and Home Affairs, 80.
91 Article 68 of the Eurojust Regulation. Coninsx underlined, for instance, the involvement of Eurojust in the adoption of Council Framework Decision 2008/919/JHA of 28 November 2008 amending Framework Decision 2002/475/JHA on combating terrorism [2008] OJ L330/21 (M Coninsx, 'Strengthening Interstate Cooperation: The Eurojust Experience' in AM Salinas De Frías, K Samuel and N White (eds), *Counter-Terrorism. International Law and Practice* (OUP 2012) 983–984).
92 'Council conclusions on the creation and implementation of a EU policy cycle for organised and serious international crime', Justice and Home Affairs Council meeting, 8–9 November 2010.
93 'Council conclusions on setting the EU's priorities for the fight against serious and organised crime between 2014 and 2017', Justice and Home Affairs Council meeting, Brussels, 6–7 June 2013; 'Council conclusions on setting the EU's priorities for the fight against organised and serious international crime between 2018 and 2021', Justice and Home Affairs Council meeting, Brussels, 18 May 2017; 'Council conclusions setting the EU's priorities for the fight against serious and organised crime for EMPACT 2022–2025' Council doc 8665/21, 12 May 2021.
94 See <https://www.europol.europa.eu/crime-areas-and-trends/eu-policy-cycle-empact> accessed 2 June 2021.

EU policy cycle – EMPACT

The first step of the policy cycle is represented by the Europol SOCTA, which identifies the main criminal threats in Europe; on the basis of Europol's assessment, the Council sets the EU's priorities in the fight against serious and organised crime. For each of them, Strategic Plans are then elaborated; they are implemented by means of Operational Actions Plans (OAPs), which should lead to more effective reaction against the crimes identified as priorities. At the end of the cycle, the activities are evaluated, in order to identify the new priorities for the next cycle. In the Policy Cycle, an important coordinating and monitoring role is played by COSI, the Standing Committee on Internal Security, which was established with the aim to 'ensure that operational cooperation on internal security is promoted and strengthened within the Union'.[95]

In the 2013 EU SOCTA, which informed the priorities of the 2014–2017 Cycle, environmental crime was not identified as a 'key threat' but as an 'emerging threat'.[96] The Council aligned its position with that of Europol; hence, in the conclusions setting the priorities for the 2014–2017 Policy Cycle, there was only

---

95 Article 71 TFEU. See 'Council conclusions on setting the EU's priorities for the fight against serious and organised crime between 2014 and 2017' (n 93) 4.
96 Europol, 'EU Serious and Organised Crime Threat Assessment – SOCTA 2013' (2014) 39.

one cursory reference to environmental crime.⁹⁷ In the 2018–2021 Policy Cycle, however, environmental crime was recognised as one of the eight priorities. In particular, the aim was to disrupt organised criminal groups involved in environmental crime, especially wildlife and illicit waste trafficking.⁹⁸ Finally, in the 2022–2025 Policy Cycle, environmental crime is again among the eleven EU's priorities, once more with the view of disrupting criminal networks involved in all forms of environmental crime, with a specific focus on waste and wildlife trafficking.⁹⁹ It is however added that also the disruption of 'criminal networks and individual criminal entrepreneurs with a capability to infiltrate legal business structures at high level or to set up own companies in order to facilitate their crimes'¹⁰⁰ now falls within such priority.

2.7 Exchange of Information with National Authorities and the EU Agencies' Evolving Role

The previous sections have examined the operational and non-operational facets of the two Agencies' activities, which are however two sides of the same coin, not least because they rely on the same prerequisite in order to be successful, that is, the willingness of national authorities to share their information and their cases with EU bodies. It is a well-known problem of EU judicial and police cooperation that domestic police and judicial bodies are sometimes reluctant to send the data at their disposal to Eurojust and Europol.¹⁰¹ Unsurprisingly, Member States are urged to share their information with EU agencies on a more regular basis. As far as environmental crime is concerned, for instance, the Commission highlighted this problem in the Staff Working Document accompanying the EU Action Plan against Wildlife Trafficking.¹⁰²

---

97   'The Council ... noting that all actors involved must retain a margin of flexibility to address unexpected or emerging threats to EU internal security, in particular regarding *environmental crime* and energy fraud' ('Council conclusions on setting the EU's priorities for the fight against serious and organised crime between 2014 and 2017' (n 93) 3, emphasis added).
98   For further details, see 'Implementation 2018–2021 EU Policy Cycle for organised and serious international crime: Draft Multi Annual Strategi Plan for Environmental Crime Priority' Council doc 11806/17, 7 September 2017.
99   'Council conclusions setting the EU's priorities for the fight against serious and organised crime for EMPACT 2022–2025' (n 93) 10.
100 ibid.
101 See, among the many, De Moor and Vermeulen (n 22); Groenleer (n 85) 296ff; Klip (n 59) 441.
102 Commission, 'Commission Staff Working Document accompanying the Communication on the EU Action Plan against Wildlife Trafficking' SWD (2016) 38 final, 26 February 2016, 50. Cf also M Morganti, S Favarin and D Andreatta, 'Illicit Waste Trafficking and Loopholes

Even though national authorities 'shall exchange' with Eurojust all information necessary for the performance of its tasks,[103] and the Member States – via the ENUs or national authorities, when allowed to do so – shall 'supply Europol with the information necessary for it to fulfil its objectives',[104] these provisions are sometimes disregarded in practice.[105] This may also be due to the fact that, being all in all 'young' institutions, Europol and Eurojust may not be largely known at national level, or at least their added value may be not always perceived. The Europol Regulation now faces directly this issue, tasking the ENUs with the duty to 'raise awareness of Europol's activities'.[106]

It is evident that the more the national authorities rely on Eurojust and Europol, the more the two Agencies are in position not only to carry out their operational tasks but also to collect useful information in view of the further diffusion of relevant knowledge and, at the same time, to make national authorities aware of the support they can provide. Similarly, if Eurojust and Europol manage to gain adequate expertise in the fight against cross-border crimes and succeed in raising adequate awareness on the added value of EU instruments and bodies of judicial and police cooperation, the chances of their future involvement in the coordination of national investigations grow accordingly. It follows that the boundaries between 'operational' and 'strategic' tasks have become quite blurred in practice, as the sections below will further demonstrate.

This is especially true with regard to Europol, the strategic activities of which lie at the core of its mission. Furthermore, the actions to be taken under the umbrella of the EMPACT Policy Cycle are based on the outcomes of the SOCTA, which is issued by Europol. Europol's role in policy making is therefore crucial and benefits from the interweaving between operational and strategic activities: the knowledge and the cases of Europol lead the Agency to detect the most urging threats, and consequently the Council to identify the EU's priorities in the fight against organised and international crimes. Comparing the key threats identified by Europol in the EU SOCTA 2013 with the priorities selected by the Council, it emerges that the Council

---

in the European and Italian Legislation' (2020) 26 *European Journal on Criminal Policy and Research* 105, 124.
103 Article 21(1) of the Eurojust Regulation.
104 Article 7(6)(a) of the Europol Regulation.
105 See, on Eurojust, GENVAL final report on Eurojust (n 52) 33–35; on Europol, see Disley, Irving, Hughes et al (n 74) 47–65.
106 Article 7(6)(c) of the Europol Regulation.

almost entirely aligned its position to that of Europol; it added just one priority that was not mentioned in the SOCTA.[107] Similarly, there is a high degree of convergence between the threats identified in the 2017 and 2021 SOCTAS and the priorities identified for, respectively, the 2018–2021 and the 2022–2025 Policy Cycles.

Not only the difference between the operational and non-operational facets of the two Agencies seems to be often unclear, but also that between the 'coercive' measures of national authorities and the allegedly non-coercive activities of the two Agencies has recently been called into question. The two Agencies' contribution to the activities of national investigating and prosecuting authorities is at times so relevant for the developments of investigations and prosecutions, if not altogether determinant in some instances, that one may reasonably expect that the 'coercive' activities of national authorities would have little success without the 'non-coercive' support by Eurojust and Europol. As the sections below demonstrate, this is often the case when the two Agencies are involved in national investigations and prosecutions concerning cross-border environmental crime.

3 Europol and Cross-border Environmental Crime

The role of Europol in the fight against transnational environmental crime will be examined by looking separately at the 'operational' and the 'non-operational' activities of the Agency. As anticipated, whereas the former encompass the so-called 'operational analysis' and the coordination of national investigations, the latter refer to Europol's strategic work.

3.1 *Operational Activities*

Europol's operational activities to counter environmental crime have become more prominent over the last years. In November 2017, Europol established the Analysis Project (AP) 'EnviCrime'.[108] In the previous data processing framework of Europol, 'Analysis Projects' were called 'Focal Points' but there was

---

107 That is, 'the risk of firearms to the citizen including combating illicit trafficking in firearms' ('Council conclusions on setting the EU's priorities for the fight against serious and organised crime between 2014 and 2017' (n 93) 4).

108 See Europol, 'Glass Eel Traffickers Earned More than Eur 37 Million from Illegal Exports to Asia', Press release (6 April 2018) <https://www.europol.europa.eu/newsroom/news/glass-eel-traffickers-earned-more-eur-37-million-illegal-exports-to-asia> accessed 2 June 2021.

none on environmental crime, although the need to create such a Focal Point had been voiced in several occasions.[109] Within the Analysis Projects, including AP EnviCrime, Europol specialists support law enforcement authorities in tackling organised crime and terrorism through:
- analysing related information and intelligence, to obtain as much structured and concrete information as possible for law enforcement authorities to 'hit' targets with;
- facilitating operational meetings between partners involved in cases;
- providing expertise and training to law enforcement authorities to support cases and share knowledge;
- deploying Europol mobile offices to the field for operations, giving live access to Europol's secure information exchange network and databases;
- providing support for judicial cooperation and for the tackling of other related criminal activities uncovered in the course of investigations, such as money laundering.[110]

Within AP EnviCrime, Europol specialists support law enforcement authorities coping with 'all environmental crime phenomena',[111] with a focus on waste trafficking and wildlife crime, which is in line with the priorities identified in the EU Policy Cycle. According to the information shared by Europol, AP EnviCrime is very active. In January 2020, Europol's Executive Director reported that the Agency was supporting around 400 cases concerning serious and organised environmental crime.[112]

---

109   For instance, in the framework of the consultation launched by the Commission in 2014 on the EU Approach against Wildlife Trafficking, Eurojust submitted a contribution where it stated that 'the opening of a Focal Point at Europol on environmental crime (including wildlife crime) would clarify trends, links with other crime areas, allow for precise threat assessments and ultimately also support coordination of investigation/prosecutions at judicial level' ('Eurojust's contribution to the Commission Communication on the EU approach against wildlife trafficking', Annex 4 to Eurojust, 'Strategic Project on Environmental Crime. Report' (2014)). As the summary of the responses to this consultation acknowledges, the establishment of a focal point on environmental crime, or at least a dedicated task force within Europol, was considered an important step also by five Member States and several NGOs ('Commission Staff Working Document. Summary of the Responses to the Stakeholder Consultation on the EU Approach against Wildlife Trafficking' SWD (2014) 347 final, 26 November 2014, 11).
110   Europol, 'Europol Analysis Projects' <https://www.europol.europa.eu/crime-areas-trends/europol-analysis-projects> accessed 2 June 2021.
111   ibid.
112   C De Bolle (Europol's Executive Director), 'How to Connect Dots in Davos' (22 January 2020) <https://www.europol.europa.eu/newsroom/news/how-to-connect-dots-in-davos> accessed 2 June 2021.

Europol's support to investigations concerning environmental crime however predates the creation of AP EnviCrime, although the absence of such an AP (or Focal Point) limited the Agency's operational activities in the field, notably its possibility to provide operational analysis of information gathered in the course of ongoing investigations. Even before the adoption of the Europol Regulation, Europol had already been involved in, and helped to coordinate, two major operations concerning environmental crime.

One was the so-called 'COBRA III' operation, which came to an end in June 2015. Organised by the ASEAN-WEN (Association of Southeast Asian Nations Wildlife Enforcement Network) and the Lusaka Agreement Task Force (LAFT),[113] its aim was to detect cases of transnational wildlife crime.[114] In March and May 2015, in all the 62 involved countries (among them, 25 EU Member States), some 'action weeks' were carried out: during those days, the police and other law enforcement authorities carried out checks and inspections, mainly at the borders and airports, in order to detect possible illegal trafficking of protected species. Globally, the outcome of the operation included seizures of 12 tonnes of elephant ivory and 119 rhino horns, with 139.7 kilos of corals and 5,067.9 kilos of wood seized only in the EU.[115]

During the COBRA III operation, national authorities carried out on the ground the investigations, checks and seizures. No personal data could be transmitted to, and processed by, Europol, due to the absence of an *ad hoc* Focal Point. Europol did however coordinate the operations at the EU level. This implied, first, a number of contacts with the ASEAN-WEN and LAFT to agree on the details of the operations. During the action weeks of 'COBRA III', Europol was the hub where all the information on ongoing operations in Europe were collected, since national authorities of the EU Member States were requested to report regularly on the outcomes of their activities. Europol was therefore able to monitor the ongoing activities and give reliable information at the end of the operation.[116]

---

113   On the LAFT, see EB Kasimbazi, 'The Lusaka Agreement Task Force as a Mechanism for Enforcement against Wildlife Crime' in M Faure, P De Smedt and A Stas (eds), *Environmental Enforcement Networks. Concepts, Implementation and Effectiveness* (Edward Elgar 2015) 239–262.
114   See also S Sina, C Gerstetter, L Porsch et al, 'Wildlife Crime' (2016) Study for the European Parliament, 91.
115   Europol, 'Operation COBRA III' (18 June 2015) <https://www.europol.europa.eu/activities-services/europol-in-action/operations/operation-cobra-iii> accessed 2 June 2021.
116   For further remarks on Operation COBRA III, see V Mitsilegas and F Giuffrida, 'The Role of EU Agencies in Fighting Transnational Environmental Crime. New Challenges for Eurojust and Europol' (2017) 1 *Brill Research Perspectives in Transnational Crime* 1, 95–97.

The other operation in which Europol coordinated the actions of national authorities was called 'Waste Trafficking' and was carried out by the Environmental Protection Unit of the Italian force *Carabinieri* in collaboration with Europol in 2014. Unlike 'COBRA III', this operation aimed to tackle illegal waste trafficking and concerned only the European Union. 14 Member States decided to participate in the operation.[117] As the final report explains, the core of the operation was an action week that took place in November 2014, during which the police forces of the involved countries made 'random checks on sites and/or input/output waste movements from/to those sites coming from third countries'.[118] During the action week, a coordination centre was set up at Europol.

Unlike COBRA III, Operation Waste Trafficking was coordinated by the Europol's Focal Point on Italian Organised Crime (ITOC).[119] As mentioned, due to the absence of a Focal Point on environmental crime, Europol was not allowed to analyse personal data on ongoing investigations concerning environmental crime, unless similar information was dealt with by focal points devoted to some other forms of crime which encompass, are connected to, or even overlap with environmental crime. In the 'Waste Trafficking' operation, this was the case of Italian organised crime, to which a Focal Point was indeed devoted.

With the entry into force of the Europol Regulation and the creation of the Analysis Project EnviCrime, the scenario has changed and Europol can now play a more prominent role in tackling environmental crime. The Agency has been involved in, or even coordinated, several operations tackling environmental crime, such as Operations 'Thunderstorm' (worldwide operation against wildlife trafficking, 2018),[120] 'Tarantelo' (international operation targeting illegal trafficking of Bluefin tuna, 2018),[121] 'Green Tuscany' (illegal trafficking

---

[117] See 'Report of the European action against the involvement of Organized Crime and Mafia-related crime in Waste Trafficking, in cooperation with Europol, owing to the emergence of the trans-national phenomenon' Council doc 16605/14, 8 December 2014, 67.

[118] ibid 66.

[119] ibid. Focal Point ITOC has now become Analysis Project ITOC (<https://www.europol.europa.eu/crime-areas-trends/europol-analysis-projects> accessed 2 June 2021).

[120] Europol, 'Wildlife Crime: European Seizures and Arrests in Global Operation Thunderstorm', Press release (21 June 2018) <https://www.europol.europa.eu/newsroom/news/wildlife-crime-european-seizures-and-arrests-in-global-operation-thunderstorm> accessed 2 June 2021.

[121] Europol, 'How the Illegal Bluefin Tuna Market Made over EUR 12 Million a Year Selling Fish in Spain', Press release (16 October 2018) <https://www.europol.europa.eu/newsroom/news/how-illegal-bluefin-tuna-market-made-over-eur-12-million-year-selling-fish-in-spain> accessed 2 June 2021.

of plastic waste in Europe, 2019),[122] 'Fame' (illegal trafficking of glass eels, 2019),[123] and 'Retrovirus' (illegal trafficking of sanitary waste in the context of the COVID-19 outbreak, 2020).[124]

Furthermore, Europol coordinates Operation 'Lake', which aims to curb trafficking of endangered species in the EU. The first edition of this operation took place in 2016 with only four countries. It has then been organised on an annual basis and has attracted increasing support, with 15 new law enforcement joining the operation in the fourth edition (October 2019–April 2020).[125] While 'operations' are structured law enforcement actions that Europol supports or periodically coordinates, the Agency – and notably the Analysis Project EnviCrime – also supports other investigations against cross-border environmental crime, such as those involving a few Member States only.[126]

To summarise the role played by Europol in the operations in which it has been involved in the last few years, two main trends are worth mentioning. First, while Europol is still not authorised to conduct investigations as such, nor to exercise coercive powers, its participation in investigative activities on the ground is increasingly common and relevant. Europol often deploys offices and forensic equipment to the Member States. For instance, in the context of the above-mentioned Operation Tarantelo, Europol deployed two mobile offices to Italy and Spain for on-the-spot support, including some Universal Forensic Extraction Devices.[127]

---

122 Europol, 'Trash Worth Millions of Euros', Press release (18 September 2019) <https://www.europol.europa.eu/newsroom/news/trash-worth-millions-of-euros> accessed 2 June 2021.

123 Europol, 'Over 5 Tonnes of Smuggled Glass Eels Seizer in Europe This Year', Press release (6 November 2019) <https://www.europol.europa.eu/newsroom/news/over-5-tonnes-of-smuggled-glass-eels-seized-in-europe-year> accessed 2 June 2021.

124 Europol, 'COVID-19 Waste Crime: Europe-Wide Operation to Tackle Unlawful Sanitary Waste Disposal', Press release (30 November 2020) <https://www.europol.europa.eu/newsroom/news/covid-19-waste-crime-europe-wide-operation-to-tackle-unlawful-sanitary-waste-disposal> accessed 2 June 2021.

125 Europol, 'The Most Recent Fishing Season Sees 108 Smugglers Arrested and Over 2 Tonnes of Glass Eels Seized in Europe', Press release (4 June 2020) <https://www.europol.europa.eu/newsroom/news/most-recent-fishing-season-sees-108-smugglers-arrested-and-over-2-tonnes-of-glass-eels-seized-in-europe> accessed 2 June 2021.

126 In 2020, for instance, Europol supported an investigation led by Spanish law enforcement authorities and involving other four EU countries, which dismantled a large organised crime group involved in wildlife trafficking (Europol, '355 Protected Reptiles Saved in Spain in Hit against Wildlife Traffickers', Press release (12 November 2020) <https://www.europol.europa.eu/newsroom/news/355-protected-reptiles-saved-in-spain-in-hit-against-wildlife-traffickers> accessed 2 June 2021).

127 Europol, 'How the Illegal Bluefin Tuna Market Made over EUR 12 Million a Year Selling Fish in Spain' (n 121). Likewise, in the action day of another operation that led to dismantling

THE ROLE OF EU AGENCIES AND BODIES 259

Second, and in line with the Europol Regulation, Europol's involvement in investigations now goes beyond the processing and analysing (personal) data, since the Agency is increasingly taking the lead in coordinating large cross-border operations, as demonstrated by the annual Operation Lake.[128] Both these trends show that the boundaries between 'coercive' measures that are reserved to national authorities and 'non-coercive'/'supporting' activities carried out by Europol are becoming increasingly blurred. As noted in the literature,

> ... although Europol does not have the competence to conduct any operations on its own, its tools and activities are of great importance for operational measures in Member States. Not only can its staff take part in national and joint investigations, but, more importantly, if Europol does its job correctly, *the information collected and analysed will set off operational measures in Member States*.[129]

The operations in which Europol took part are a prominent example of this trend, if one bears in mind that, for instance, the above-mentioned Operation Retrovirus led to approximately 278,300 inspections, 100 arrest, and seizure of € 800,000,[130] and Operation Fame to 43 arrests and the seizure of 737 kg of glass eels.[131] As Gless put it, 'gathering and processing information, as Europol does, generate "knowledge" and produces "evidence", which by *their very essence* are *no different* from a traditional house search conducted by a police unit using its operational power'.[132] Therefore, the recent Europol's experience in countering environmental crime shows that, while Europol is a not police authority, let alone a 'European FBI',[133] its operational functions cannot always be clearly distinguished from the proper coercive powers of national authorities.

---

    an organised crime network involving poachers and distribution companies responsible for food poisoning, Europol deployed 'an expert on-the-spot to cross-check operational information in real time' (Europol, '43 Arrested after 27 Poisoned by Clams in Spain', Press release (19 December 2019) <https://www.europol.europa.eu/newsroom/news/43-arrested-after-27-poisoned-clams-in-spain> accessed 2 June 2021).

128 Europol, 'The Most Recent Fishing Season Sees 108 Smugglers Arrested and Over 2 Tonnes of Glass Eels Seized in Europe' (n 125).

129 A Jonsson Cornell, 'EU Police Cooperation Post-Lisbon' in M Bergström and A Jonsson Cornell (eds), *European Police and Criminal Law Co-operation* (Hart 2014) 154. Emphasis added.

130 Europol, '355 Protected Reptiles Saved in Spain in Hit against Wildlife Traffickers' (n 126).

131 Europol, 'Over 5 Tonnes of Smuggled Glass Eels Seizer in Europe This Year' (n 123).

132 Gless (n 25) 464. Emphasis added.

133 JD Occhipinti, *The Politics of EU Police Cooperation. Toward a European FBI?* (Lynne Rienner 2003).

3.2 Non-operational Activities

In addition to its operational activities, Europol is also committed to collecting and sharing knowledge on environmental crime and the best instruments and strategies to cope with it. In 2010, Europol released a report in which some scenarios of the possible future involvement of organised crime groups in energy supply were discussed.[134] Such a report was 'not a threat assessment and [was] not intended to provide specific recommendations for operational responses',[135] it was rather a document to trigger further reflections on the issue, in line with the increasing 'concerns about global warming and other environmental threats [which] have brought increased public attention to energy issues in general'.[136]

In 2011, Europol issued four OC-SCAN Threat Notices related to environmental crime.[137] They all had the same structure: one-page documents, which contained, in the first part, the main findings on a given threat, and some recommendations to the national authorities in the second one.

Three of these OC-SCAN Threat Notices concerned general issues, notably trafficking in endangered species, use of improved illegal waste disposal sites, and trade in counterfeited and illegal pesticides in Europe.[138] They all emphasised the involvement of organised crime groups in these activities due to the expected high economic income. The recommendations to the national authorities concerned both operational aspects (such as the use of controlled deliveries as an instrument to disrupt organised crime groups or the launch of cross-border investigations) and strategic aspects, such as the need to undertake tactical analysis on the use of internet by organised crime groups trafficking in endangered species. The same pattern was followed also in the fourth OC-SCAN Threat Notice, which was issued in June 2011 and concerned

---

134 Europol, 'Organised crime & energy supply. Scenarios to 2020' (2010) <https://www.europol.europa.eu/content/publication/organised-crime-energy-supply-scenarios-2020-1505> accessed 2 June 2021.
135 ibid 3.
136 ibid.
137 On the OC-SCANs in general, see section 2.6 above.
138 Respectively, 'OC-SCAN Policy Brief for Threat Notice: 006-2010. Trafficking in Endangered Species by Organised Crime Groups' (31 March 2011); 'OC-SCAN Policy Brief for Threat Notice: 2521-88. Use of Improvised Illegal Waste Disposal Sites by Criminals and OC Groups in the EU' (30 June 2011); 'OC-SCAN Policy Brief for Threat Notice: 2521-93. Growth in the Trade in Counterfeit and Other Illegal Pesticides across Europe' (30 September 2011). These documents are available at <https://www.europol.europa.eu/crime-areas-and-trends/trends-and-routes#fndtn-tabs-0-bottom-2> accessed 2 June 2021.

a specific case of an Irish organised crime groups involved in the illegal trade of rhino horns.[139]

In 2011, a privileged partner of Europol in this field was established, ie EnviCrimeNet (Environmental Crime Network), an informal network of national law enforcement officers with expertise in the field of environmental criminality. EnviCrimeNet is a network without operational powers, as can be inferred from the Council Resolution on its creation, where it is defined as 'an appropriate platform and forum for exchanging non-operational information and experiences with a view to combating effectively and efficiently environment-related cross-border crime'.[140] Its General Meetings represent important occasions 'to discuss best practices, latest developments and challenges posed by environmental crime'.[141] Europol supports this Network and helps to coordinate its activities.[142] In the Europol Programming Document 2019–2021, the review of Europol's role under the Analysis Project EnviCrime in supporting EnviCrimeNet was expressly listed among the actions to be taken; hence, it remains to be seen how the cooperation between the Agency and the network will develop in the coming years.

As for the previous and current cooperation between Europol and EnviCrimeNet, a relevant example is the Intelligence Project on Environmental Crime, which they jointly carried out between 2014 and 2015. Before delving

---

139 Europol, 'OC-SCAN Policy Brief for Threat Notice: 2521-86. Involvement of an Irish Mobile OCG in the Illegal Trade in Rhino Horn' (11 July 2011) <https://www.europol.europa.eu/publications-documents/oc-scan-policy-brief-involvement-of-irish-mobile-ocg-in-illegal-trade-in-rhino-horn> accessed 2 June 2021.

140 Council Resolution on the creation of an informal network for countering environmental crime – "EnviCrimeNet" Council doc 10291/11, 20 May 2011. With similar purposes, also the European Network of Prosecutors for the Environment and the European Union Forum of Judges for the Environment were set up. On the latter, see L Lavrysen, 'The European Union Forum of Judges for the Environment' in Faure, De Smedt and Stas (eds) (n 113) 276–288.

141 See, for instance, Europol, 'Environmental Crime Experts Meet in Milan' (26 October 2015) <https://www.europol.europa.eu/newsroom/news/environmental-crime-experts-meet-in-milan> accessed 2 June 2021.

142 'The Council of the European Union … [convinced] that "EnviCrimeNet" … will benefit from the analytical skills and know-how of Europol' (Council Resolution on the creation of an informal network for countering environmental crime (n 140) 3); '[welcomes] the creation of an informal network for countering environmental crime called "EnviCrimeNet", supported by Europol' (ibid 4); '[invites] "EnviCrimeNet" to fully benefit from the Europol Platform for Expert (EPE) …, [invites] Europol to help to coordinate the activities of "EnviCrimeNet" in the fight against environmental crime' (ibid 5).

further into this Project, it ought to be noted that, after the adoption of the Policy Cycle 2014–2017, since environmental crime had been recognised as an emerging threat that required 'intensified monitoring',[143] Europol issued a Threat Assessment devoted only to environmental crime in 2013 (hereinafter the '2013 Threat Assessment').[144]

This document was drafted on the basis of information provided by the Member States and other Europol's partners and mainly dealt with illegal trafficking in waste and endangered species. In line with what the above-mentioned OC-SCANs had already pointed out, it highlighted that this kind of trafficking offences are driven by economic interest and usually not adequately investigated or prosecuted by the competent national authorities. Being 'high profit-low risk' activities, they had become particularly attractive to organised crime groups, even though sometimes also legitimate companies were involved.

Moreover, the 2013 Threat Assessment explained the reasons why, and the ways in which, these offences affect the EU. The issue was not self-evident in the case of wildlife trafficking, which could be perceived as a threat that does not regard directly (or at least seriously) Europe. However, the document showed that 'the EU is both a destination and source region'[145] for this form of trafficking. This conclusion was confirmed a few years later in the EU Action Plan against Wildlife Trafficking issued by the European Commission, in which it was stated that the EU is also a transit region.[146]

The 2013 Threat Assessment was one of the first EU documents where environmental crime and its challenges were analysed in-depth from a law enforcement perspective. Yet it had some gaps in describing the scenario at the EU level. Therefore, upon the COSI's request to EnviCrimeNet 'to report about their activities and to provide a scan in relation to environmental crime in the EU by the end of 2014',[147] the above-mentioned Intelligence Project on Environmental Crime (IPEC) was launched in May 2014. The aim was 'to gain a better knowledge on the types of environmental crimes impacting on EU

---

143   Europol, 'Threat Assessment 2013. Environmental Crime in the EU' (2013) 4.
144   Albeit briefly, the 2013 Threat Assessment also touches upon illegal, unreported and unregulated fishing and illegal sand mining (ibid 16).
145   ibid 14.
146   See Commission, 'Commission Staff Working Document accompanying the Communication on the EU Action Plan against Wildlife Trafficking' (n 102) 19–20. This Document mentions the 2013 Threat Assessment and adds further data on the impact of the phenomenon at stake on the EU (ibid 15–27).
147   EnviCrimeNet and Europol, 'Report on Environmental Crime in Europe' (2015) <http://www.envicrimenet.eu/reports> accessed 2 June 2021, 4.

Member States ..., their extent, and the obstacles which exist to fight these crimes'.[148]

In the framework of this Project, Europol and EnviCrimeNet collected information on environmental crime by, inter alia, reviewing the existing literature, interviewing stakeholders and practitioners, and participating in conferences and meetings of experts. In addition, a questionnaire was sent to national authorities of the Member States and some non-EU organisations and jurisdictions. The Project's main outcomes were two reports. Whereas the second mainly consists in a literature review of articles, studies, and other materials, the first illustrates the results of the interviews and the Project's main findings. The latter report was presented to COSI in December 2014, where the conclusion was the following: 'the Delegations acknowledged the growing importance of environmental crime in the EU, which was identified as an emerging threat in the EU SOCTA. Europol was invited to take the reports into account when preparing the 2015 Interim SOCTA'.[149]

Europol is also committed to facilitating the diffusion of existing knowledge on environmental crime through the development and maintenance of a secure online platform, the Europol Platform for Experts (EPE). This is an online environment thought to share 'best practices, documentation, innovation, knowledge and non-personal data on crime'.[150] The access to EPE can be granted only by invitation of Europol or ENUs and is open to law enforcement officers and experts in the field. Some sections of this platform are devoted to environmental crime. Therefore, it is one of the instruments that Europol can use to raise awareness and increase knowledge on the matter. The EPE has been also used by Europol with the aim to reinforce the multidisciplinary approach to organised crime.[151]

---

148 ibid 1.
149 'Summary of discussions of the meeting of 11 December 2014' Council doc 16163/14, 19 December 2014, 5. The 2015 Interim SOCTA was the document that was meant to report on the state of play of the Policy Cycle 2014–2017 after about one year from its launching.
150 'Europol Platform for Experts' <https://www.europol.europa.eu/activities-services/services-support/information-exchange/europol-platform-for-experts> accessed 2 June 2021. See also Disley, Irving, Hughes et al (n 74) 100.
151 'The EPE Administrative Approach tool was created in May 2012 ... It promotes the important role of administrative authorities as part of a multidisciplinary approach which is increasingly being used by Member States to combat organised crime. ... This electronic tool can help to put people in touch, spread awareness internationally and find answers to questions and problems as well as to reduce research costs and save time' ('Activity Report on the Administrative Approach to Prevent and Fight Organised Crime' Council doc 13498/13, 16 September 2013, 5).

Another online tool at the disposal of national authorities, but only focused on wildlife crime, is EU-TWIX (European Union Trade in Wildlife Information eXchange), to which Europol is also connected. It consists of two main components: a mailing list and a website that can only be accessed by designated officials. While the mailing list 'allows quick and efficient sharing of information between designated enforcement and management officials on seizures, and to exchange experience and expertise on illegal wildlife trade matters',[152] the website holds a database collecting information on wildlife trade seizures shared by national law enforcement authorities. Funded by the European Commission and some EU and non-EU governments, EU-TWIX is an initiative of the Belgian Federal Police, Belgian CITES Management Authority, Belgian Customs, and the NGO TRAFFIC, the wildlife trade monitoring network. All EU Member States are connected to EU-TWIX, as well as some other non-EU countries.[153]

In its 2018 Report on the implementation of the Wildlife Action Plan, the Commission pointed out that EU-TWIX is an effective tool to exchange information on wildlife trafficking and that the exchange of information through EU-TWIX triggered several cross-border investigations on wildlife crime.[154] On the contrary, the Commission reported that 'Member States' use of the SIENA platform for exchanging messages on wildlife trafficking varies greatly, depending on the authorities concerned'[155] and that this hampers effective cooperation and deprives Europol of 'precious information necessary to build a comprehensive intelligence picture of wildlife trafficking in the EU'.[156]

The relevance of Europol's non-operational activities in the fight against environmental crime was also highlighted by the Council, which, in its 2016 Conclusions on environmental crime, invited the Member States to monitor environmental crime and its systematic development, 'including though

---

152 'EU-TWIX. Trade in Wildlife Information Exchange. An Internet Tool to Assist the European Enforcement and Management Agencies in the Fight against Wildlife Trade Crime' (2019) <https://www.traffic.org/what-we-do/projects-and-approaches/supporting-law-enforcement/twixs/> accessed 2 June 2021.

153 For further information on EU-TWIX, see V Sacré, 'EU-TWIX: Ten Years of Information Exchange and Cooperation between Wildlife Law Enforcement Officials in Europe' in L Elliott and WH Schaedla (eds), *Handbook of Transnational Environmental Crime* (Edward Elgar 2016) 478–488.

154 Commission, 'Progress report on the implementation of the EU Action Plan against Wildlife Trafficking' COM (2018) 711 final, 24 October 2018, 6.

155 ibid. On SIENA, see more in section 2.4.

156 COM (2018) 711 final (n 154) 6.

regular collection and sharing of relevant information with all relevant partners both regionally and within the EU as a whole, *in particular via Europol*,[157] as well as to 'share relevant experience and knowledge with Europol in order to strengthen its expertise in the field of environmental crime'.[158]

In a similar vein, the Europol Programming Document 2021–2023 lists the identification of criminal trends and raising awareness on environmental crime among the expected results of Europol's action in this field, in addition to providing the necessary operational support to the Member States.[159] Arguably with the same aim of strengthening its strategic activities in this area, Europol has signed some Memoranda of Understanding with non-governmental organisations (eg Traffic, Wildlife Justice Commission, and Centre for Climate Crime Analysis) which will enrich the Agency's strategic knowledge – and enhance its role – in the fight against environmental crime.[160]

Finally, it is worth noting that the prominent operational role that Europol has increasingly played in countering environmental crime can only strengthen the Agency's non-operational activities. Operational and non-operational activities are inextricably linked to, and enhance, each other. Europol's operational activities inevitably end up providing the Agency with more operational but also strategic data (eg information on the *modus operandi* of organised crime groups, the routes they follow, etc) that can be used

---

157 'Council Conclusions on countering environmental crime' Council doc 15412/16, 12 December 2016, 5. Emphasis added.
158 ibid, 6. In parallel, the Council invited Europol to 'strengthen its expertise in the field of fighting environmental crime; ... regularly monitor and evaluate cross-border environmental crime, and provide information to Member States on the current trends in this illegal activity; ... encourage Member States to participate in the detection and investigation thereof, for example through the promotion of joint investigation teams; ... prepare and coordinate joint operations aimed at the detection of environmental crime, taking into account the priorities identified in the environmental crime assessment; facilitate the activities of EnviCrimeNet' (ibid, 6–7).
159 'Europol Programming Document 2021–2023' (2021) 54.
160 'Europol and TRAFFIC Join Forces to Fight Environmental Crime' (2 February 2017) <https://www.europol.europa.eu/newsroom/news/europol-and-traffic-join-forces-to-fight-environmental-crime> accessed 2 June 2021; 'Europol and Wildlife Justice Commission Team up against Environmental Crime' (13 March 2017) <https://www.europol.europa.eu/newsroom/news/europol-and-wildlife-justice-commission-team-against-environmental-crime> accessed 2 June 2021; 'Europol and the Centre for Climate Crime Analysis together against Criminal Activities Related to Air Pollution and Deforestation', Press release (4 May 2018) <https://www.europol.europa.eu/newsroom/news/europol-and-centre-for-climate-crime-analysis-together-against-criminal-activities-related-to-air-pollution-and-deforestation> accessed 2 June 2021.

for further operational and non-operational activities. And vice versa, gathering strategic information can lead to concrete actions that allow to obtain further data, which can be analysed and used for subsequent activities. While the fight against environmental crime at the EU level can only benefit from this virtuous circle, its perpetuation in the future requires Europol to keep its high level of commitment to fighting to environmental crime, and national authorities not to shy away from involving the Agency whenever its support may prove useful.

4   Eurojust and Cross-border Environmental Crime

Eurojust's role in countering cross-border environmental crime is examined in the two sections below, which will focus on both aspects of Eurojust's activities in the field, namely the operational and the non-operational ones.

4.1   *Operational Activities*

Eurojust's operational tasks encompass all the activities that the Agency carries out with a view to coordinating the investigations and prosecutions of environmental crime by national prosecuting authorities.

The number of environmental crime cases dealt with by Eurojust is relatively low, especially if compared with the overall number of the Agency's cases. Between 2014 and 2018, environmental crime cases represented less than 1% of the Eurojust's workload. About a half of these cases concerned wildlife trafficking and waste trafficking.[161] In 2019 and 2020, 12 and 20 new environmental crime cases were opened at Eurojust out of a total number of new cases amounting to, respectively, 3,892 and 4,200.[162] In the Report on its casework on environmental crime published in January 2021 (hereinafter: '2021 Report on environmental crime'), Eurojust itself acknowledged that the 'overall number of cross-border environmental crime investigations and prosecutions coordinated at the EU level is still very small'.[163] However, Eurojust's added value in supporting and coordinating the activities of national authorities that

---

161   Eurojust, 'Report on Eurojust's Casework on Environmental Crime' (2021) 7.
162   Eurojust, 'Eurojust Annual Report 2019' (2020) 28; Eurojust, 'Eurojust Annual Report 2020' (2021) 27.
163   Eurojust, 'Report on Eurojust's Casework on Environmental Crime' (n 161) 21. The European Commission drew similar conclusions in its evaluation of the Environmental Crime Directive (Commission, 'Commission Staff Working Document Evaluation of the Directive 2008/99/EC' (n 1) 56–57).

investigate and prosecute cross-border environmental crime has proven to be remarkable in the cases where Eurojust was involved.

For instance, activities of illegal trafficking in wild bird eggs affecting the UK, Finland and Sweden were discovered in 2013 (the 'Bird-Egg case'). Eurojust assisted the authorities of the latter two countries in setting up and funding a Joint Investigation Team.[164] One of the prosecutors involved in the case reported that Eurojust's support was 'invaluable in coordinating communication'[165] among the different authorities, even though such support should have been ideally sought at an earlier stage of the investigations. As another of the prosecutors involved said:

> [i]nternational communication and coordination *at the beginning* of the investigation may have achieved wide-ranging results. For example, Eurojust has a Liaison Prosecutor from the USA. Using Eurojust to facilitate contact between the UK, Sweden and out counterparts in the USA may have assisted in the coordinated engagement of all States at the same time.[166]

Eurojust's support can indeed be maximised if national authorities involve the Agency from the early stages of their investigations.[167] If contacted at a later stage, Eurojust can only play a limited role: for instance, if its intervention is requested just before the limitation period for national investigations expires, Eurojust would not have enough time to coordinate the operations. Similar problems can arise because of the different national rules on the discovery of evidentiary elements to the suspect. If the investigations are at an advanced stage in a Member State, and the suspect has already had access to the elements collected by the investigating authorities, it becomes problematic to coordinate the actions with the authorities of other countries where the investigations are still under secrecy. In these cases, Eurojust would do its best to find a solution to the issues that may arise, but it cannot as such overcome

---

164 On Eurojust's financial support to the establishment of the JIT, the at-the-time Swedish national member commented that 'the benefits ... are clearly demonstrated in this case when we see that the JIT funding enabled Sweden to hire the services of an expert, an ornithologist' ('The Bird-Egg case' (2013) 10 *Eurojust News* 16).
165 ibid 15.
166 ibid. Emphasis added.
167 The same need with regard to Europol's involvement in national investigations was underlined by S Chin and W Veening, 'Actors and Institutions Relevant to Fighting Environmental Crime'. Study in the framework of the EFFACE Project (Institute for Environmental Security 2015) 32.

national diversities. The 2021 Report on environmental crime restates the need to ensure Eurojust's *early involvement* in investigations concerning cross-border environmental crime cases since Eurojust 'is better situated to facilitate the detection or initiation of parallel or linked criminal proceedings and to assist in their coordination'.[168]

In the Bird-Egg case, Eurojust had also the opportunity to demonstrate another relevant contribution it can give to the success of cross-border investigations, namely supporting the setting up of Joint Investigation Teams and their activities from the beginning of the investigations until their conclusion. Due to the usual cross-border nature of serious environmental crime such as trafficking in waste or wildlife specimens, as well as the need to involve a whole range of national authorities to effectively counter such crimes, JITs are a very useful tool for national authorities:

> Considering the typical features of environmental crime, such as the involvement of trafficking routes across the EU and beyond, the high level of illegal profits, the low risk of detection and the involvement of organised crime and other crimes along with environmental crime, JITs are an efficient instrument to employ. JITs can include the whole range of competent national authorities, and can therefore ensure a multidisciplinary approach to the investigation. In addition, they allow for the exchange of information and evidence in a quick and direct manner across borders, thereby ensuring the possibility of a broader and stronger prosecution in the affected countries.[169]

However, the number of JITs supported by Eurojust in environmental crime cases has been overall limited so far. Two new JITs were set up with Eurojust's support in 2019, and three in 2020, out of the 177 new JITs established in the two years.[170] Since Eurojust's experience demonstrates that JITs can be truly effective in countering cross-border (environmental) crime, the Agency itself encourages national authorities to use the full potential of such an

---

168 Eurojust, 'Report on Eurojust's Casework on Environmental Crime' (n 161) 21.
169 ibid. For similar positive views on the use of JITs in the fight against environmental crime, see GENVAL, 'Final report on the 8th round of mutual evaluations on "The practical implementation and operation of the European policies on preventing and combating Environmental Crime"' Council doc 14852/19, 5 December 2019 ('GENVAL final report on environmental crime') 70.
170 The GENVAL final report on environmental crime similarly reports that JITs are underused in this area (ibid 70).

instrument.[171] The fact that environmental crime is part of the crime priorities of the 2022–2025 Policy Cycle may have a positive effect in that respect. In accordance with Annex II of the Eurojust's 'JITS Funding Guide', one of the criteria to take into account in the awarding of grants for the setting up of a JIT is indeed the inclusion of the crime to investigate among the priorities decided by the Council.[172]

In areas of crimes other than environmental crime, Eurojust has been supporting an increasing number of JITS involving also third countries over the last years. This could be relevant for environmental crime cases involving non-EU countries. In 2021, for instance, Eurojust was involved in the investigation of highly profitable illegal sales of metal waste, which were made possible by, inter alia, the activities of fictitious companies established in Turkey, Egypt, Pakistan, China, and Malaysia.[173] So far, however, the third countries that are more often involved in environmental crime cases opened at Eurojust are Switzerland and Norway.[174]

Another example of the JITS' added value is provided by a cross-border investigation that involved five European countries. In that case, large quantities of chicken eggs and egg products were contaminated with some insecticides.[175] In 2017, four of the EU countries involved in the case (Netherlands, Belgium, Germany and Italy) opened parallel criminal investigations and the competent

---

171 Eurojust, 'Report on Eurojust's Casework on Environmental Crime' (n 161) 21. Several authors emphasise the added value of JITS in the fight against cross-border environmental crime: see, for instance, Chin and Veening, 'Actors and Institutions Relevant to Fighting Environmental Crime' (n 167) 36; T Fajardo del Castillo, 'Organised Crime and Environmental Crime: Analysis of EU Legal Instruments'. Study in the framework of the EFFACE Research Project (University of Granada 2015) 17 and 35–36; K Klaas and S Sina, 'Contribution to Conclusions and Recommendations on Environmental Crime: Functioning of Enforcement Institutions and Cooperation between Them (MS/EU level)'. Study in the framework of the EFFACE Project (2016) *passim*.
172 Eurojust, 'JITs Funding Guide' (2018) <https://www.eurojust.europa.eu/jits-fundingguide> accessed 2 June 2021, 21. Before environmental crime was included among the priority crimes, some authors had argued that adding it to the list of priorities would have increased 'the probability that JITS set up for combating environmental crimes [were] eligible for funding by the grants from Eurojust' (Klaas and Sina (previous n) 4). On the EU Policy Cycle, see more in section 2.6.
173 Further details on the case are available on the Eurojust's website at <https://www.eurojust.europa.eu/massive-metal-waste-fraud-italy-halted-eurojust-support> accessed 2 June 2021. The relevance of the support by Eurojust (as well as Europol and the European Judicial Network) in dealing with environmental crime cases that involve third countries is also mentioned in the GENVAL final report on environmental crime (n 169) 67.
174 Eurojust, 'Report on Eurojust's Casework on Environmental Crime' (n 161) 7.
175 ibid 12.

national authorities asked for Eurojust's support. The Agency, together with Europol, supported the creation and funding of a JIT between the Belgian and Dutch authorities and took the necessary measures to ensure coordination between these authorities and those of the other three EU Member States involved in the case. To this end, Eurojust organised six coordination meetings to discuss and agree on a common strategy and facilitate the exchange of evidence; it also supported an action day to ensure coordinated seizures and arrests. As Eurojust reports, the Dutch-Belgian JIT 'continued to work together during the prosecutorial phase and included a financial investigation that led to the tracing and seizure of assets'.[176]

In that case, Eurojust also provided national authorities with a formal legal opinion on whether the opening of Italian and Belgian criminal proceedings would violate the *ne bis in idem* principle.[177] As discussed in the previous chapter, this is another area to which Eurojust can significantly contribute, due to its expertise and its role as an EU Agency that coordinates national criminal investigations. Eurojust proved its added value vis-à-vis jurisdictional and *ne bis in idem*-related matters already back in 2003, when it was involved in the notorious *Prestige* case, which was named after the oil tanker that sank in the Galician waters in 2002, causing impressive damages to the environment.

Among the many, another key issue in that case was the choice of jurisdiction, namely the choice of the Member State (France or Spain) where to prosecute the captain and the other persons allegedly responsible for the disaster. The national authorities sought Eurojust's support and the Agency managed to gather them together in two meetings: the first one mainly aimed at the collection and exchange of the necessary information and expertise to deal with such a complicate matter,[178] whereas the second faced the issue of jurisdiction. The latter meeting was intended to 'explore the possibility and draw on legal expertise to decide if it was possible, and if so how, to centralize the ongoing prosecutions into a single proceeding, to be led by one of the countries'.[179]

---

176   ibid.
177   ibid.
178   As reported by Eurojust, '[t]he purpose of the first meeting was to assist the magistrates in gathering experience about how to manage such a case, in which hundreds of victims have suffered loss. Colleagues leading similar investigations such as the shipwreck of *"Erika"* investigated in the Court of Paris and *"Mar Egeo"* investigated in the Court of La Corunna were invited to share their experience' (Eurojust, 'Annual Report 2003' (2004) 29).
179   ibid. For some remarks on the jurisdictional issues that arose in the case concerning the shipwreck of the tanker *Erika* (1999), see N Giovannini, L Melica, E Cukani et al,

Eurojust eventually suggested that Spain was in a better position to initiate the proceedings, and all the involved authorities accepted this recommendation. The adequate protection of the French victims was a sensitive topic, but as a result of the cooperation of the two countries those victims were treated 'as if they were Spanish victims. The French Public Prosecutor participated in the oral proceedings, sitting beside the Spanish prosecutor, and hearing the statements of some French victims'.[180] Eurojust's recommendation was mainly driven by pragmatic reasons, which were welcome by national authorities. As Pozdnakova explains, the main factors in Eurojust's decision were the following:

> first, more evidence had been gathered in Spain due to the direct contact from the start of the investigation between the Spanish authorities and the ship and crew; and second, more injured parties were situated in Spain than in France, with some of the French victims already having joined the judicial procedure in Spain.[181]

Therefore, Eurojust carried out a balancing act between the need to deliver justice in an effective way and the rights of the individuals concerned – the defendants avoided to be tried twice for the same facts and the interests of the victims were adequately taken into account.

Eurojust was also required to intervene in the Manure case (2012), which concerned illegal trading in manure. This case involved five EU countries and Eurojust set up a coordination meeting among national competent authorities, so that they could discuss the problems faced during the procedures of mutual assistance. They also agreed to organise an action day and the operations thereof were monitored at Eurojust by a coordination centre. The involvement of Eurojust turned out to be highly beneficial, insofar as 'several seizures of illegally obtained assets and administrative documents were made. Witnesses were heard in order to collect evidence'.[182]

'Addressing Environmental Crimes and Marine Pollution in the EU. Legal guidelines and case studies' (Droit au Droit 2013) <http://www.dadinternational.org/images/PDF/Guide-Web.pdf> accessed 2 June 2021, 26–30. See more in chapter 4 of this book.

180 'The Prestige case' (2013) 10 *Eurojust News* 14. Nevertheless, the case did not lead to any significant conviction (see ibid 15).

181 A Pozdnakova, *Criminal Jurisdiction over Perpetrators of Ship-Source Pollution. International Law, State Practice and EU Harmonisation* (Martinus Nijhoff Publishers 2013) 157.

182 'Report of the Strategic Meeting towards an enhanced coordination of environmental crime prosecutions across the EU: The role of Eurojust' Council doc 8101/14, 24 March

The illegal trading in manure had also led to a tax evasion of about € 8 million in the Netherlands. As Eurojust's experience demonstrates, cross-border environmental crimes are often related to other crimes, such as organised crime, money laundering, document forgery or, as in the Manure case, tax fraud.[183] While such links make Eurojust's involvement in cross-border investigations even more desirable so as to better tackle all the ramifications of environmental crime, they can have two – somehow opposite – effects on the effectiveness of the fight against environmental crime.

On the one hand, the connection between other crimes and environmental crime can be the very same reason why the latter is not sufficiently investigated in some cases. As Eurojust explains, there is a perception among the experts in the field that, if crimes connected to environmental crime are discovered (eg organised crime or money laundering), they 'become the "lead crimes" of the criminal proceedings, while environmental crime becomes ancillary and sometimes is not even investigated and prosecuted to its full potential'.[184] Eurojust's statistics seem to confirm this perception, although insufficient data is available to draw solid conclusions.[185]

On the other hand, the previous chapters have already pointed out some advantages, from a law enforcement perspective, of the links between environmental crime and other serious crimes, notably organised crime. Eurojust's recent assessment goes in the same direction and highlights the relevance of such links in view of the Agency's support to national authorities:

> If an environmental crime case is identified as a case involving cross-border *organised crime*, this qualification enables the case to be prioritised and a more extensive set of investigative measures to be used, including *special investigative tools* for organised crime. This qualification also

---

2014, 9–10. For other details on the Manure case, see also 'The Manure Case' (2013) 10 *Eurojust News* 16.

183 'Cross-border environmental crime is often highly organised crime that generates substantial illegal profits and goes hand in hand with other crimes such as tax fraud, forgery of documents and money laundering. In total, two thirds of the environmental crime cases referred to Eurojust concerned other crimes in addition to environmental crime' (Eurojust, 'Report on Eurojust's Casework on Environmental Crime' (n 161) 9).

184 ibid.

185 'The Eurojust statistics seem to confirm this perception because, indeed, none of these crimes appears as a crime associated with environmental crime in the cases referred to Eurojust. Unfortunately, this phenomenon could not be analysed based solely on the information that was available by virtue of the cases referred to Eurojust by the national authorities' (ibid).

enables national authorities to refer the case to Eurojust, so that cross-border coordination and cooperation is ensured in environmental crime cases on a more regular basis.[186]

Eurojust also pays due attention to the economic dimension of environmental crime. Currently, horizontal issues related to environmental crime are addressed by a subgroup of the Economic Crime Team of the Eurojust's College. Composed of members of the national desks, each Eurojust's Team is dedicated to a specific form of criminality or to some thematic issues concerning judicial cooperation. The Teams do not handle operational cases themselves, as they mainly represent a platform – inside Eurojust – to discuss some forms of crimes, possible activities to be undertaken by the Agency to raise awareness, and the like. The inclusion of environmental crime within the Economic Crime Team is a testament to the importance of the economic drivers behind environmental offences. Therefore, Eurojust urges national authorities to adequately address the economic consequences of environmental crime, especially in view of strengthening seizure and confiscation measures.[187]

In sum, Eurojust can play a key role in supporting national investigations and prosecutions of cross-border environmental crime, including in facilitating the exchanges of mutual legal assistance requests and streamlining mutual recognition procedures.[188] The above-mentioned examples show that Eurojust is ideally placed to address the main and recurring challenges faced by national authorities that investigate and prosecute transnational environmental crime. It is therefore regrettable that the involvement of Eurojust has been overall limited so far, but there are reasons to believe things will improve in the coming years.

4.2   *Non-operational Activities*

Eurojust's non-operational activities concerning environmental crime are likewise prominent. As discussed in the section above, in January 2021 Eurojust released a Report that examines the Agency's workload concerning

---

186   ibid 18. Emphasis added.
187   ibid 22.
188   'Legal advice and practical facilitation in applying international judicial cooperation instruments and tools (in most cases MLA and EIOs, but also the spontaneous exchange of information, JITs, asset freezing and confiscation, EAWs, extradition, transfer of proceedings, transfer of a sentenced person) at the various stages: from choosing the appropriate legal instrument or tool to drafting, transmitting, accepting for execution, prioritising multiple requests and orders, speeding up the execution process, mitigating delays and refusals and transmitting results' (ibid).

environmental crime in the period between 2014 and 2018. This Report illustrates the issues faced by national authorities when investigating cross-border environmental crime and Eurojust's role in this context, and includes some conclusions and recommendations that can contribute to strengthening the fight against this type of criminality.

This is however not the first report on environmental crime issued by the Agency. At the end of 2014, Eurojust issued the Report of the Strategic Project on environmental crime ('2014 Eurojust Report'),[189] which remains one of the clearest examples of the strategic role played by Eurojust in the field. Like the 2013 Threat Assessment of Europol, the 2014 Eurojust Report focused on trafficking in waste and in endangered species. Based on the evaluation of national legislation, a questionnaire sent to the Member States, and the outcomes of a strategic meeting on environmental crime held at Eurojust's premises in 2013,[190] the 2014 Eurojust Report offered an overview of the main features of the two above-mentioned criminal phenomena and the challenges faced by national authorities in the investigations and prosecutions thereof.

The Report presented some trends and assessments, which have been overall upheld by the 2021 Report on environmental crime: national legislation on the matter is usually complex and highly technical, on the one hand, and provides for too lenient sanctions on the other. The number of JITs active in the field is limited[191] and the cooperation among national authorities, and between them and the supranational ones, is sometimes insufficient and unsatisfactory. This alarming picture was even more problematic in light of the increasing links between organised crime and illegal waste and wildlife trafficking.[192]

Apart from the organisation of meetings and events dedicated to environmental crime,[193] another element of Eurojust's non-operational tasks in the field is represented by the establishment of a Contact Point for Environmental Crime, which was appointed for the first time in July 2014. The Contact Point is one of the Eurojust National Members and acts as part of the Eurojust's

---

189 Eurojust, 'Strategic Project on Environmental Crime. Report' (November 2014) <https://www.eurojust.europa.eu/strategic-project-environment-crime> accessed 2 June 2021.
190 See 'Report of the Strategic Meeting towards an enhanced coordination of environmental crime prosecutions across the EU: The role of Eurojust' (n 182).
191 Eurojust, 'Strategic Project on Environmental Crime. Report' (n 189) 34.
192 ibid 10–20.
193 For instance, Eurojust organised and hosted, together with the European Network of Prosecutors for the Environment, the 'International Collaboration and Cooperation in the Fight against Environmental Crime' in October 2019 (Eurojust, 'Report on Eurojust's Casework on Environmental Crime' (n 161) 5).

Economic Crime Team.[194] The Contact Point has mostly a strategic role, since environmental crime cases are dealt with by the national desks. The establishment of the Contact Point is meant to ensure that someone inside Eurojust pays special attention to this field and its developments and can act as a contact person for external stakeholders when issues related to environmental crime come to the fore. As the 2015 Eurojust Annual Report stated, the Contact Point 'follows up on environmental crime matters and shares expertise and best practice with practitioners and external stakeholders'.[195] He or she is also the Eurojust's representative associated with the Europol's Analysis Project EnviCrime[196] and ensures the cooperation among Eurojust and other actors in the field, such as Europol, EnviCrimeNet, and ENPE (European Network of Prosecutors for the Environment).

Another partner of Eurojust is the European Union Network for the Implementation and Enforcement of Environmental Law (IMPEL), which is composed of members of the environmental authorities of the EU Member States and other European countries. Among the others, IMPEL carried out a project – the IMPEL-TFS Prosecutors Project – which was useful to streamline and facilitate judicial cooperation. The Project aimed at establishing a database of decisions on illegal shipment of waste.[197] Even though the matter is regulated at the EU level, Member States' legislation still bears significant differences. Therefore, making the collection of the relevant national decisions available to all the interested practitioners was an attempt to answer the 'need for a systematic exchange of information and practices among countries'.[198]

The importance of such Project was demonstrated by some examples given during the 2013 strategic meeting on environmental crime organised at Eurojust: 'an English appellate court made references to a Dutch case concerning the definition of "transport" and a court in Göteborg, Sweden, used the Dutch experience as a tool to establish an appropriate penalty in a case concerning the illegal shipment of waste'.[199] Eurojust welcomes similar initiatives and already issues *ad hoc* reports aiming at collecting information on

---

194 ibid 10.
195 Eurojust, 'Annual Report 2015' (2016) 44.
196 Eurojust, 'Report on Eurojust's Casework on Environmental Crime' (n 161) 10.
197 See more on the dedicate page of the IMPEL's website (<https://www.impel.eu/projects/tfs-prosecutors-project/> accessed 2 June 2021).
198 Intervention of R De Rijck, responsible of the Project, during the 2013 Eurojust Strategic Meeting on environmental crime ('Report of the Strategic Meeting towards an enhanced coordination of environmental crime prosecutions across the EU: The role of Eurojust' (n 182) 5).
199 ibid.

cases and legislation concerning specific types of transnational crime, such as the above-mentioned Terrorism Conviction Monitor. However, nothing similar exists with regard to environmental crime for the time being.

Finally, one more example of Eurojust's non-operational role in the fight against environmental crime is represented by the contribution that Eurojust sent to the Commission Communication on the EU approach against Wildlife Trafficking in 2014, which Eurojust shared to 'provide a practitioner's point of view'.[200] In its contribution, the agency mentioned its limited involvement in environmental crime cases and acknowledged that one of the main obstacles for an effective EU action in the field was the lack of an adequate awareness by the Member States of the seriousness of the offences at stake.[201]

As discussed in the previous sections, the lack of awareness of the seriousness of environmental crime is at times coupled with a lack of adequate knowledge of EU instruments and bodies that can support national authorities in investigating and prosecuting cross-border crimes, including Eurojust itself. For instance, one of the prosecutors involved in the above-mentioned Bird-Egg case claimed that, '[K]nowing what I do now allows me to better inform my colleagues, and knowing how Eurojust can assist in a more coordinated approach will surely lead to better results'.[202] Therefore, while some national authorities may still have scarce knowledge of Eurojust's mission and services, they fully realise the importance of its activities when they have the opportunity to work with the Agency, and are arguably more inclined to rely on its support in future cases.[203]

In sum, Eurojust has the same opportunity as Europol to trigger a virtuous circle. The Agency's operational role has turned out to be – even though in an overall limited number of cases – of substantial importance for national investigations and prosecutions on cross-border environmental crime, at the same time providing Eurojust with an occasion to gather further strategic information and spread the knowledge of the Agency itself and its role in countering cross-border crimes. In turn, Eurojust seems increasingly committed to engaging with non-operational activities, as demonstrated by the 2014 Strategic Project, the 2021 Report on environmental crime, and the appointment of a

---

200 'Eurojust's contribution to the Commission Communication on the EU approach against wildlife trafficking', Annex 4 to Eurojust, 'Strategic Project on Environmental Crime. Report' (n 109).
201 ibid 93.
202 'The Bird-Egg case' (2013) 10 *Eurojust News* 16.
203 See also Chin and Veening, 'Actors and Institutions Relevant to Fighting Environmental Crime' (n 167) 36.

Contact Point for Environmental Crime. Further awareness of Eurojust's activities, including among the general public, can also derive from the Agency's involvement in some high-visibility cases, such as the *Prestige* case in 2003 or, more recently, the 'Dieselgate' scandal.[204] Against this backdrop, drawing a clear line between operational and non-operational tasks of the Agency, as well as between its activities and the coercive ones of national authorities, becomes an increasingly difficult task.

5   The European Public Prosecutor's Office

The European Public Prosecutor's Office (EPPO) is the EU body competent to investigate and prosecute crimes affecting the European Union's financial interests. Being the first EU office with direct powers vis-à-vis the individuals in the sensitive field of criminal law, the EPPO represents a Copernican revolution in the history of EU (criminal) law.

After years of political and academic debate, the Treaty of Lisbon finally provided for the legal basis for the establishment of this body. Article 86 TFEU allows the Council – with the previous consent of the European Parliament – to set up the EPPO by means of regulations. On the basis of this provision, Council Regulation (EU) 2017/1939 implementing enhanced cooperation on the establishment of the EPPO was adopted in October 2017. At the time of writing, 22 Member States participate in the EPPO, namely all EU Member States except for Denmark, Hungary, Ireland, Poland, and Sweden. The EPPO took up its investigative and prosecutorial functions on 1 June 2021.

While the in-depth analysis of the EPPO Regulation falls beyond the scope of this work,[205] a few key rules of the EPPO's functioning need to be examined before evaluating the role that the EPPO could play in the fight against environmental crime.[206] First, the EPPO is competent to investigate, prosecute and bring to judgment the perpetrators of, and accomplices to, criminal offences

---

204   For further details on the string of cases that have been generated by the 'Dieselgate' scandal, and Eurojust's contribution thereof, see the information available on the Eurojust's website at <https://www.eurojust.europa.eu/suspected-fraud-diesel-defeat-devices-germany-italy-and-switzerland> accessed 2 June 2021.
205   For more details on the EPPO and further references thereof, see the chapter on EU agencies and bodies in Mitsilegas, *EU Criminal Law* (n 1).
206   The following remarks draw upon F Giuffrida, 'Defence Rights and European Public Prosecutor's Office: Protecting the Individuals at the Intersection of EU and National Law' in S Allegrezza and V Covolo (eds), *EU Fair Trial Rights in Criminal Proceedings* (Hart forthcoming).

affecting the financial interests of the Union,[207] the so-called 'PIF offences'.[208] They include fraud affecting the Union budget, misappropriation of EU funds, corruption as long as it damages or is likely to damage the Union's financial interests, and money laundering of assets that derive from PIF offences.[209] The EPPO's competence – with the exception of VAT fraud – covers both national and cross-border PIF crimes.[210] In the future, as discussed below, the EPPO's mandate could however be extended to other serious crimes having a cross-border dimension, including environmental crime.[211]

Second, the EPPO has a *sui generis* structure. It is conceived as a single office, yet it is composed of two levels.[212] The central level is based in Luxembourg and includes the European Chief Prosecutor, one European Prosecutor per participating Member State (two of whom are appointed as Deputies to the European Chief Prosecutor), the College, where all the European Prosecutors and the European Chief Prosecutor sit, and the Permanent Chambers, which are composed of the European Chief Prosecutor (or one of his or her Deputies) and two European Prosecutors.[213] In addition to the central headquarters, the EPPO has decentralised ramifications in each participating Member State, where at least two European Delegated Prosecutors (EDPs) work for the EPPO.[214] The EDPs are appointed by the EPPO College among active members

---

207 Articles 4 and 22(1) of the EPPO Regulation. The trial will instead take place before the competent national courts. Further references to Articles and Recitals in this section should be understood as referring to Articles and Recitals of the EPPO Regulation, unless otherwise specified.
208 PIF stands for '*protection des intérêts financiers*'.
209 These offences are listed in Directive (EU) 2017/1371 of the European Parliament and of the Council of 5 July 2017 on the fight against fraud to the Union's financial interests by means of criminal law [2017] OJ L198/29, to which Article 22(1) expressly refers. The EPPO is also competent for offences regarding participation in a criminal organisation, if the focus of the criminal activity of such a criminal organisation is to commit PIF offences (Article 22(2)), as well as for any other criminal offence that is inextricably linked to PIF offences (Article 22(3), which refers to Article 25(3) for the conditions under which the EPPO can exercise its competence in these cases). On offences inextricably linked to PIF crimes, see more below in the text.
210 The PIF offences listed in the text fall within the EPPO's mandate irrespective of whether they concern one or more Member States. On the contrary, the EPPO can investigate and prosecute VAT fraud only when the latter is connected with the territory of least two Member States and involves a total damage of € 10 million (see Article 2(2) of Directive (EU) 2017/1371 and Article 22(1) of the EPPO Regulation).
211 See more immediately below.
212 Article 8.
213 Article 8(3).
214 Article 13.

of the public prosecution service or judiciary of the respective Member States and carry out their investigative and prosecutorial functions on behalf of the EPPO.[215] The EDPs play a central role in the EPPO: they conduct the investigations under the direction of the central Office and put in practice in their Member State the decisions taken at the EU level by the Permanent Chambers. The Regulation also envisages a *trait d'union* between the Chambers and the EDPs, that is, the supervising European Prosecutor. At the central level, the European Prosecutors therefore supervise the activities of the EDPs, and more precisely of the EDPs from their same Member State,[216] and advice accordingly the Permanent Chamber monitoring and directing the investigations.

Third, the Regulation lays down a number of provisions on EPPO investigations and prosecutions. Overall, the lion's share of the rules that apply to EPPO activities is however to be found in national law, for three main reasons. First, the Regulation does not address some key issues concerning pre-trial investigations and prosecutions (to mention one, duration of investigations), which, in accordance with Article 5(3) of the Regulation, continue to be regulated by national law.[217] Second, the Regulation itself, in several instances, refers back to national law rather than setting out rules that directly apply to the Office. For instance, the threshold to begin the investigations, that is, the 'reasonable grounds to believe that an offence within the competence of the EPPO is being or has been committed',[218] is to be determined in accordance with the applicable national law.[219] Pre-trial arrest follows national rules as well.[220] Third, the Regulation refers at times to the application of other EU instruments; as they mostly are directives and framework decisions, which need to be implemented by national legislation, it is again national law that determines the applicable rules.[221]

---

215   Article 17(2).
216   Article 12.
217   Article 5(3) reads as follows: 'The investigations and prosecutions on behalf of the EPPO shall be governed by [the EPPO] Regulation. National law shall apply to the extent that a matter is not regulated by this Regulation. ... Where a matter is governed by both national law and this Regulation, the latter shall prevail'.
218   Article 26(1).
219   ibid.
220   Article 33.
221   For instance, as mentioned above (n 209), the EPPO's mandate is identified by referring to the PIF Directive as implemented by national law (Article 22(1) of the Regulation). As for pre-trial detention in cross-border cases, the Regulation provides that the Framework Decision on the European Arrest Warrant, as implemented by national law, applies (Article 33).

For the purpose of this work, it should be first noted that, despite the current EPPO's competence is limited to PIF offences, in principle there could be cases where the EPPO could already exercise its powers vis-à-vis environmental crimes. The EPPO is indeed also competent for the crimes that are 'inextricably linked' to PIF offences.[222] In accordance with Recital 54 of the EPPO Regulation,

> The notion of 'inextricably linked offences' should be considered in light of the relevant case-law which, for the application of the *ne bis in idem* principle, retains as a relevant criterion the identity of the material facts (or facts which are substantially the same), understood in the sense of the existence of a set of concrete circumstances which are inextricably linked together in time and space.

It remains therefore to be seen whether, in practice, there will be cases where environmental crimes will be inextricably linked to PIF offences,[223] which may arguably be unusual.

As anticipated, however, the EPPO's competence could in the future include environmental crimes. In accordance with Article 86(4) TFEU, the European Council – acting unanimously after obtaining the consent of the European Parliament and after consulting the Commission – could decide to broaden the EPPO's competence in order to include 'serious crime having a cross-border dimension'.[224] Such an extension of the EPPO's mandate, while unlikely in the short term, may take place in the future. Europol's experience may be a useful term of comparison in this context. The Agency was originally competent for drug-related crimes only, but its mandate has been subsequently broadened; by the same token, the EPPO could begin to operate with a limited competence, which could be expanded when the Office will have demonstrated its added value.[225]

---

222 See n 209.
223 See R Sicurella, 'Article 86' in G Grasso, R Sicurella and V Scalia, 'Articles 82-86 of the Treaty on the Functioning of the European Union and Environmental Crime'. Study in the framework of the EFFACE research project (University of Catania 2015) 43; V Mitsilegas, 'Contribution to Conclusions and Recommendations on Environmental Crime. Harmonisation of Substantive Environmental Criminal Law at EU Level'. Study in the framework of the efface research project (Queen Mary University of London 2016) 5.
224 Article 86(4) TFEU.
225 See Klip (n 59) 460.

In the future, the EPPO could therefore become competent for cross-border environmental crimes such as trafficking in waste and protected species.[226] A similar extension of its competence could even be justified in light of some similarities between environmental crime and PIF crimes. First, they both attract organised crime groups for their nature of 'high profit-low risk' crimes.[227] Because of their common economic drivers, in some national systems the same specialised prosecution office deals with both these types of offences.[228] Second, environmental crimes and PIF crimes often have cross-border nature:[229] a prominent example of cross-border fraud to the detriment of the EU budget that falls within the EPPO's competence is VAT carousel fraud, which by definition affects more than one EU country. Third, both areas of crime are under-investigated and often not regarded as a priority by national prosecutors. Environmental crime is usually perceived as a victimless crime, which can often be neglected by domestic authorities.[230] Similarly, it has been argued that 'there is a perceived tendency to put complex European fraud cases involving cross-border cooperation on offences affecting the EU's financial interest "at the bottom of the pile"'.[231] Finally, Sicurella highlights the legal and axiological similarity between the two areas of crime, since the

---

[226] See GM Vagliasindi, 'Istituzione di una Procura Europea e Diritto Penale Sostanziale: L'Eventuale Estensione della Competenza Materiale della Futura Procura alla Criminalità Ambientale' in G Grasso, G Illuminati, R Sicurella et al (eds), *Le Sfide dell'Attuazione di una Procura Europea: Definizione di Regole e Loro Impatto sugli Ordinamenti Interni* (Giuffrè 2013) 206ff; Sicurella, 'Article 86' (n 223) 46–47; Mitsilegas, 'Contribution to Conclusions and Recommendations on Environmental Crime' (n 223) 5.

[227] See, with regard to fraud affecting the Union budget, the 'Commission Staff Working Document. Impact Assessment Accompanying Proposal for a Council Regulation on the establishment of the European Public Prosecutor's Office' SWD (2013) 274 final, 17 July 2013, 7.

[228] In the Netherlands, for instance, a specific branch of the Prosecution Service, the Functional Public Prosecutor's Office, is 'especially tasked to handle fraud and environmental cases' (W Geelhoed, 'Embedding the European Public Prosecutor's Office in Jurisdictions with a Wide Scope of Prosecutorial Discretion: the Dutch Example' in C Nowak (ed), *The European Public Prosecutor's Office and National Authorities* (Wolters Kluwer-CEDAM 2016) 94).

[229] 'Commission Staff Working Document. Impact Assessment Accompanying Proposal for a Council Regulation on the establishment of the European Public Prosecutor's Office' (n 227) *passim*.

[230] C Gerstetter, C Stefes, A Farmer et al, 'Environmental Crime and the EU. Synthesis of the Research Project "European Action to Fight Environmental Crime" (EFFACE)' (2016) 37ff.

[231] 'Commission Staff Working Document. Impact Assessment Accompanying Proposal for a Council Regulation on the establishment of the European Public Prosecutor's Office' (n 227) 19.

environment – like the Union's budget – is 'a proper "supranational" legal interest'[232] that should fall within the competence of an EU prosecuting authority.

With a few exceptions in political[233] and academic circles,[234] however, there is little discussion on the extension of the EPPO's competence to cross-border environmental crimes for the time being, while other areas – notably terrorism – have already been identified as ideal candidates for such an extension.[235] Should the EPPO be made competent for cross-border environmental crimes, this would imply direct criminal law enforcement at EU level. It would be a remarkable paradigm shift compared to the current situation, where EU bodies only support national authorities in their investigations and prosecutions of environmental crime. However, the EPPO would still need to cooperate with Europol and Eurojust to ensure the efficiency of its activities. The EPPO's relations with the two Agencies are regulated by some provisions of the respective Regulations,[236] as well as by the working arrangements concluded by EPPO

---

232   Sicurella, 'Article 86' (n 223) 47.
233   See the recent call for an 'EU Green Prosecutor' by a Member of the European Parliament (V Gheorghe, 'Why the EU now needs a "Green Prosecutor"' *euobserver* (7 July 2021) <https://euobserver.com/opinion/152345> accessed 2 June 2021).
234   In addition to the authors mentioned in the previous footnotes, the following have also examined the issue: C Di Francesco Maesa, 'EPPO and Environmental Crime: May the EPPO Ensure a More Effective Protection of the Environment in the EU?' (2018) 9 *New Journal of European Criminal Law* 191; L Seiler, 'L'Extension de la Compétence Matérielle du Parquet Européen' in C Chevallier-Govers and A Weyembergh (eds), *La Création du Parquet Européen. Simple Évolution ou Révolution au Sein de l'Espace Judiciaire Européen ?* (Bruylant 2021) 429–431.
235   The European Parliament supports the extension of the EPPO's competence and the Commission issued a Communication in September 2018, in which it proposed such competence to cover serious cross-border terrorism crimes (COM (2018) 641 final, 12 September 2018). See also the European Parliament's Resolution of 25 October 2016 on the fight against corruption and follow-up of the CRIM resolution (2015/2110(INI)), P8_TA (2016) 0403, para 54. In the political arena, the extension of the EPPO's competence to cross-border terrorism has at times be mentioned over the last few years, for instance by the current French President Emmanuel Macron who, in his speech at the Sorbonne University in late September 2017, included such an extension of the Office's mandate among his proposals for relaunching the European Union ('Les Principales Propositions d'Emmanuel Macron pour Relancer le Projet Européen' *Le Monde* (27 September 2017) <https://www.lemonde.fr/europe/article/2017/09/26/les-principales-propositions-d-emmanuel-macron-pour-relancer-le-projet-europeen_5191799_3214.html> accessed 2 June 2021).
236   See Articles 100 ('Relations with Eurojust') and 102 ('Relations with Europol') of the EPPO Regulation; Article 50 of the Eurojust Regulation ('Relations with the EPPO'). The Commission's proposal for a revised Europol Regulation (n 5), when adopted, would introduce a new provision in the Europol Regulation concerning the relations between the Agency and the EPPO.

and Europol in January 2021 and the EPPO and Eurojust in February 2021.[237] If the EPPO's competence will end up covering crimes on which Eurojust and Europol are already particularly active, such as terrorism, but also, as demonstrated, environmental crimes, these bodies should aim to avoid any duplication and overlap of their activities.

6 Conclusion

The EU's contribution to the fight against environmental crime through the activities of its agencies is arguably more visible than the contribution examined in the previous chapters. In the field of substantive criminal law, it is still national legislation that defines environmental crime and sets out the amount of the penalties thereof, with the EU providing for some harmonisation. As for procedural criminal law, national authorities are competent to investigate and prosecute environmental crime and can rely on EU instruments of judicial cooperation when these offences have a transnational nature. Member States' competent authorities also decide which of them should investigate and prosecute when more than one Member State could exercise its jurisdiction on the same facts, or none of them is inclined to exercise it. This chapter has however demonstrated that, in these dynamics of cross-border cooperation, the EU can also play a more active role through agencies such as Eurojust and Europol. In the future, such a role can be further strengthened if the EPPO's mandate will be extended to cover cross-border environmental crime, yet this does not seem likely for the time being.

Despite their different structure, power, and mission, both Eurojust and Europol can provide invaluable support to national investigating and prosecuting authorities in cross-border environmental crime cases. The above analysis has shed light on at least three common features. First, the activities of Eurojust and Europol in the area of environmental crime have rapidly increased over the last few years. The establishment of the EnviCrime Analysis Project at Europol and the Contact Point for Environmental Crime at Eurojust, together with the noteworthy strategic and operational activities examined in the previous sections, are a testament to the importance that has been recently attached to the fight against environmental crime at the EU level, in line with (and partially triggered by) the inclusion of this area of crime among the EU priorities for the

---

237 The text of both working arrangements is available on the EPPO's website at <https://www.eppo.europa.eu/documents> accessed 2 June 2021.

2018–2021 and 2022–2025 Policy Cycles. It will gain further momentum due to the expected revision of the Environmental Crime Directive and the EU actions and initiatives in the framework of the 'European Green Deal'.[238]

Second, the strategic and operational activities of Europol and Eurojust have been highly appreciated by national authorities and were conducive to remarkable results in the fight against transnational environmental crime.[239] In several cases, the involvement of Eurojust or Europol, or both of them, has significantly contributed to the success of national investigations and prosecutions. When the two Agencies are able to properly support ongoing activities by national authorities, their smooth participation in such activities creates a scenario of intertwined powers, services, information, and instruments between the national and EU level in which the Agencies' contribution is sometimes even necessary to allow national authorities to adopt their measures. Even though the Member States remain in the driving seat of investigations and prosecutions of environmental crime, while Eurojust and Europol do not have coercive powers, the distinction between the different roles may become in practice less prominent than it is in theory. In other words, in the same way as the dividing line between the agencies' operational and non-operational tasks seems quite blurred in practice, as demonstrated above, the difference between the merely 'supporting' role of Europol and the Eurojust and the 'coercive' powers of national authorities is increasingly fading away in the day-to-day reality of criminal investigations and prosecutions.

Finally, despite the increased awareness of the seriousness of environmental crime and the added value of relying on the two Agencies' support in cross-border cases, the involvement of Eurojust and Europol in investigations and prosecutions of environmental crime remains all in all limited. In the literature, it has been argued that this is due, inter alia, to the 'lack of an un-ambiguous definition of environmental crime at the European and the international level ... in particular what kind of offences have to be considered environmental crimes'[240] – in this way demonstrating that the three dimensions of the EU's

---

238   Commission, 'The European Green Deal' COM (2019) 640 final, 11 December 2019. On the expected revision of the Environmental Crime Directive, see section 7.2 of chapter 4.
239   See GENVAL final report on environmental crime (n 169) 15.
240   M Faure, C Gerstetter, S Sina et al, 'Instruments, Actors and Institutions in the Fight Against Environmental Crime'. Study in the framework of the EFFACE research project (Ecologic Institute 2015) 64. These authors argue that '[o]ne of the reasons for the very low number of cases of environmental crime registered by Eurojust ... is the limited ability of national law enforcement authorities to recognize what constitutes environmental crime and to report it as such, and also to properly address and deal with initiatives/requests for judicial cooperation in this field' (ibid). See also Eurojust, 'Report on Eurojust's Casework

contribution to the fight against environmental crime analysed in this work are interlinked. Be that as it may, it is telling that, in January 2021, Eurojust still reported the 'hesitation on the part of national authorities, in some Eurojust cases, to initiate parallel criminal proceedings, to take part in a [coordination meeting] or a [coordination centre] or to establish a JIT'.[241] The way ahead in the fight against environmental crime looks therefore complex and requires some improvements, yet the positive examples of cooperation between EU agencies and national authorities examined in this chapter bode well for a stronger protection of the environment at the EU level.

on Environmental Crime' (n 161) 22. As for Europol, similar difficulties due to the lack of a harmonised definition of organised crime are discussed in De Moor and Vermeulen (n 22) 1098–1099; Disley, Irving, Hughes et al (n 74) 71.

241 Eurojust gave the following example: 'in a multilateral case concerning illicit trading in fuel oils and related hazardous chemical pollution, where parallel investigations were identified and were ongoing in several Member States, the national authorities of the Member States concerned were not interested in participating in a [coordination meeting] and in establishing a JIT, as proposed by the Member State that opened the Eurojust case' (Eurojust, 'Report on Eurojust's Casework on Environmental Crime' (n 161) 13).

CHAPTER 8

Conclusion

The Regulation of Environmental Crime in International and EU Law: Coming of Age?

This book has attempted to provide a holistic, comprehensive and in depth analysis of the international and EU framework on environmental criminal law. The analysis has demonstrated that this is a dynamic field, which has in recent years been growing and developing its own distinct identity. With policy and legislative responses being centered increasingly on the protection of the environment as a common, global good, the question of the role of criminal law in enforcing environmental protection becomes more topical. The book has mapped the evolution of measures related to environmental crime at international level (where a distinct focus on criminal law is slowly emerging) and at EU level (where the protection of the environment by means of criminal law is now a well-established avenue of intervention and where the debate is currently focused on its reform), and highlighted instances where international and EU law interact. Environmental criminal law is part of a system of multi-level governance of environmental protection, and is itself multi-layered and multifaceted: there is no homogenous definition of environmental crime, a term that covers a wide variety of conduct ranging from wildlife trafficking to pollution at sea to illicit waste disposal and management. We hope that the book will be published as a timely contribution to the current international and European debate on how best to protect the environment by means of criminal law, including by identifying a number of key questions and challenges in need of attention. These challenges are as follows:

1 The Extent and Scope of Criminalisation

With international law paying increasing attention to the aspect of criminal law enforcement in environmental protection, and the European Commission currently considering a possible revision of the EU framework on environmental criminal law, a key question in need of addressing is the extent to which the use of criminal law is the optimal means for the protection of the environment. From the perspective of criminal law, a key question in this context is which criminalisation of conduct deemed detrimental to the environment will comply with the *ultima ratio* principle, namely that criminal law should only be used as a last resort. A further question that has arisen prominently in the context of the implementation and evaluation of the EU Directive on environmental crime is the extent to which criminalisation complies with the principle of legality and the requirement of legal certainty and foreseeability of criminal offences and sanctions. The challenges arising in the field of the protection of the environment by means of criminal law have been linked largely to the lack of definitional and conceptual autonomy of environmental offences. In EU law, criminal offences are defined and criminal sanctions are imposed by reference to breaches of underlying environmental regulations – something that has led to considerable legal uncertainty in terms of the scope and aims of criminalisation. The situation is complicated by the choice to link environmental criminal law with serious breaches of administrative environmental standards. Continuing to link criminal and administrative law without giving further thought on the necessity and justification of the use of criminal law for the purposes of the protection of the environment may prove to be a missed opportunity in terms of the need to define a clear justification, scope and limits to the use of criminal law for the protection of the environment and to achieve legal certainty in a complex field. The adoption of autonomous environmental criminal law instruments at international and EU law level may provide an opportunity for a meaningful debate on the best use of criminal law for the protection of the environment.

2   The Organised and Financial Crime Dimension

Throughout this book, we have attempted to place emphasis on the organised and financial crime dimension of environmental crime. This dimension has been gradually recognised by the international community, with specific initiatives targeting in particular wildlife crime. The recognition of the links between environmental and organised crime, as well as of the profit-making incentives underlying many forms of environmental crime, is key towards developing a joined-up approach in terms of both legislative and agency intervention as well as enforcement. The analysis has demonstrated potential synergies in international law between the environmental conventions and instruments such as the Palermo Convention on Transnational Organised Crime (UNTOC) and the UN Anti-Corruption Convention (UNCAC), as well as the potentially stronger role for UNODC and the UN Security Council. At EU level, these links are more explored at the level of the work of agencies such as Europol and Eurojust. We believe that the organised and financial crime aspects of environmental crime must be addressed as a matter of priority. This can be done under a multi-level approach. Environmental crime can appear more clearly and prominently in horizontal legislative initiatives on organised and financial crime (including as money laundering predicate offences and in confiscation measures); new legislation focusing specifically on organised environmental crime (such as wildlife trafficking) should be considered; and the work of law enforcement agencies can be focused more directly on the organised and financial aspects of environmental crime.

3   Compliance, Enforcement and a Multi-agency Approach

Throughout this book, we stressed the importance of ensuring effective implementation and enforcement of environmental crime legislation at national level. Together with developing and clarifying international and EU law on environmental crime, ensuring its effective implementation and enforcement is key to achieve the objectives of the legal framework against environmental crime. A multi-agency approach has been emerging at international level and increasingly at the level of EU criminal justice bodies and agencies. However, more can be done towards ensuring effective compliance and implementation of international and EU standards at the domestic level. In the European Union, the European Commission has exercised its powers as the 'guardian of the treaties' to conduct a detailed evaluation of the effectiveness and implementation of the environmental crime *acquis* and initiatives towards further law reform are awaited. At international level, further emphasis can be placed on compliance and implementation of international commitments. In both cases, however, an essential pre-requisite for effective implementation is clarity in terms of the scope of criminalisation obligations and the objectives pursued by the legislation. At the EU level, the pending revision of the environmental crime Directive is a first-class opportunity to strive towards such clarity.

Index

Bamako Convention   76, 77, 77n108, 77n110
Ban Amendment   61, 61n24, 61n27, 71
Basel Convention   v, 1, 2, 2n11, 3, 6, 9n11, 22n84, 23n87, 55, 55n1, 56, 56n6, 57, 57n10, 57n7, 58, 58n11, 59, 59n13, 59n16, 59n17, 59n18, 60, 60n19, 60n20, 60n21, 60n22, 61, 61n24, 61n25, 61n27, 61n28, 62, 62n34, 63, 63n35, 64, 64n41, 65, 65n42, 65n44, 66, 66n47, 66n48, 67, 67n50, 68, 69, 70, 70n71, 71n79, 72, 73, 73n92, 74, 74n94, 74n96, 75, 75n100, 75n101, 77, 78, 78n115, 78n116, 78n118, 78n120, 79, 80, 81, 81n133, 81n135, 81n136, 82, 82n137, 82n139, 83, 84, 84n148, 85, 85n158, 86, 86n164, 87, 87n168, 87n170, 88, 88n172, 88n175, 89n177, 89n178, 90, 91, 92, 93, 94, 112, 112n6, 130, 130n88

CITES   v, 1, 2, 2n11, 3, 6, 7, 7n1, 8, 8n5, 8n6, 8n7, 9, 9n9, 10, 11, 11n14, 11n15, 11n17, 12, 12n21, 12n23, 13, 13n24, 13n25, 14, 14n30, 14n31, 15, 15n34, 17, 18, 19n58, 20, 20n65, 20n66, 21, 21n73, 21n75, 22, 22n78, 22n80, 22n81, 22n82, 23, 23n85, 24, 24n88, 25, 25n90, 25n93, 26, 26n94, 26n97, 27, 27n101, 27n99, 28, 28n107, 28n108, 28n109, 29, 30, 31, 31n123, 31n124, 31n125, 31n126, 32, 32n131, 33n134, 34, 34n144, 34n147, 35, 36, 36n153, 37, 37n156, 40, 40n172, 41, 41n177, 42, 43, 43n186, 43n187, 43n188, 43n190, 44n193, 45, 45n201, 45n203, 46n204, 46n205, 46n206, 47, 48, 48n214, 48n216, 49, 49n217, 50, 50n219, 51, 51n222, 51n225, 52, 52n229, 53, 54, 57, 72, 86, 108, 112, 112n6, 125, 125n73, 130, 130n91, 264

Covid-19   48, 48n215, 49, 49n216, 49n217, 49n218, 51, 51n223, 53, 53n231, 54, 73, 73n92

ENFORCE (Environmental Network for Optimizing Regulatory Compliance on Illegal Traffic)   2n11, 4, 23, 24, 32n130, 40n175, 73, 77, 85n158, 91, 91n189, 91n190, 92, 92n192, 92n194, 95, 108

Environmental Crime Directive   4, 13, 13n28, 16n42, 29, 29n116, 29n117, 29n119, 38n160, 67, 67n53, 71, 82, 83n144, 83n145, 121, 121n48, 122, 122n49, 122n51, 122n52, 123n58, 123n59, 124, 124n61, 124n62, 124n63, 125, 125n71, 125n72, 126n74, 127, 127n76, 127n77, 128n80, 128n81, 129n85, 130, 131n94, 131n96, 132, 133n106, 134, 134n107, 134n108, 134n112, 134n114, 135, 135n120, 136n125, 137, 138n131, 138n133, 139, 140, 141, 142, 143, 151, 156, 156n228, 157, 157n232, 158, 159, 159n242, 162n257, 163, 164, 166, 166n278, 168, 169, 170, 171, 172, 173, 181, 182n37, 183, 219, 219n229, 221, 231, 232, 266n163, 284, 284n238

EPPO (European Public Prosecutor's Office)   6, 233, 241, 247, 247n81, 277, 277n205, 278, 278n207, 278n209, 278n210, 279, 279n217, 279n221, 280, 281, 282, 282n235, 282n236, 283, 283n237

ESM (Environmentally sound management)   59, 59n14, 59n15, 60, 62, 66, 72

Eurojust   5, 17n50, 64n39, 110n1, 128n82, 136n123, 152n211, 175n1, 184, 184n46, 186, 198, 199, 199n126, 199n129, 200n130, 200n131, 200n132, 200n133, 201, 202, 202n147, 202n148, 233, 234, 235, 235n10, 235n12, 235n14, 235n15, 235n7, 235n8, 235n9, 236, 236n16, 236n17, 236n19, 237, 238, 238n27, 239, 239n38, 240, 240n41, 240n42, 240n46, 241, 241n47, 242, 242n50, 242n51, 243, 243n52, 243n53, 243n54, 243n55, 244, 244n60, 244n64, 246, 248, 249, 249n88, 249n89, 250, 250n90, 250n91, 252, 253, 253n103, 253n105, 254, 255n109, 256n116, 266, 266n161, 266n162, 266n163, 267, 267n164, 268, 268n168, 269, 269n171, 269n172, 269n173, 269n174, 270, 270n178, 271, 271n180, 271n182, 272, 272n183, 272n185, 273, 274, 274n189, 274n190, 274n191, 274n193, 275, 275n195, 275n196, 275n198, 276, 276n200, 276n202, 277n204, 282, 282n236, 283, 284, 284n240, 285n241, 287

European Arrest Warrant   5, 176, 178n12, 180, 194, 197n118, 249, 249n86, 279n221
Europol   5, 17n50, 64n39, 110n1, 132n98, 149n195, 150, 150n200, 151n203, 175n1, 179n23, 233, 234, 234n2, 234n3, 234n4, 234n5, 235, 235n10, 235n12, 235n13, 236, 236n16, 236n18, 237, 237n20, 237n21, 237n22, 237n23, 238, 238n24, 238n25, 241, 242, 242n50, 244, 244n61, 244n64, 245, 245n68, 245n69, 245n71, 246, 246n72, 246n74, 246n76, 247, 247n77, 247n78, 247n79, 247n81, 247n82, 248, 248n83, 249, 249n84, 249n88, 250, 251, 251n96, 252, 253, 253n104, 253n105, 253n106, 254, 254n108, 255, 255n109, 255n110, 255n112, 256, 256n115, 256n116, 257, 257n117, 257n120, 257n121, 258, 258n122, 258n123, 258n124, 258n125, 258n126, 258n127, 259, 259n128, 259n130, 259n131, 260, 260n134, 261, 261n139, 261n141, 261n142, 262, 262n143, 262n147, 263, 263n150, 264, 265, 265n158, 265n159, 265n160, 267n167, 269n173, 270, 274, 275, 276, 280, 282, 282n236, 283, 284, 285n240, 287

ICCWC (International Consortium on Combating Wildlife Crime)   2n11, 3, 14, 19n56, 31, 37, 43, 43n188, 44, 44n194, 45, 45n201, 46, 46n206, 47, 50, 54
Intertanko   124, 124n66, 125n67, 140, 140n142, 143, 144n164, 144n165, 145n170, 146n174, 146n175, 146n178, 147, 147n179, 148, 149

Lusaka Agreement   25, 25n92, 43n186, 256, 256n113

MARPOL   vi, 1, 2, 4, 6, 95, 96, 97, 97n13, 97n16, 98, 99, 100, 100n25, 101, 101n31, 102, 102n33, 103, 103n35, 104, 104n43, 105, 106, 107, 108, 109, 119, 119n40, 140n143, 141, 141n146, 142n149, 144, 144n162, 145, 146, 146n174, 149n193

PIC (prior informed consent) procedure   62, 65n44, 66, 81

Rotterdam Convention   2, 2n6, 68n56

Ship-Source Pollution Directive   4, 140, 140n143, 141n144, 141n145, 141n146, 142, 142n147, 142n148, 142n149, 142n150, 142n151, 142n152, 142n153, 143, 143n154, 143n155, 143n156, 143n157, 151, 156, 157, 158
Stockholm   68, 68n57, 74, 74n96, 80, 87n170, 89n177

UNCAC (United Nations Convention against Corruption)   20, 21n71, 21n72, 22, 52n229, 73, 73n88, 287
UNODC (United Nations Office on Drugs and Crime)   2n11, 7n1, 9, 10n13, 14n31, 14n33, 15, 15n34, 15n35, 15n38, 16n41, 19n56, 19n59, 20, 20n64, 21, 21n76, 21n77, 27, 27n101, 27n103, 28, 30, 30n122, 36, 36n154, 37, 37n159, 38n161, 38n162, 38n164, 38n165, 39, 39n170, 40n171, 40n174, 41, 41n176, 41n178, 41n179, 41n180, 43, 43n190, 44, 44n193, 44n195, 45, 45n198, 45n199, 45n202, 46, 47n209, 49n218, 53, 55n1, 55n2, 56n5, 69, 91, 287
UNTOC (United Nations Convention against Transnational Organized Crime)   17n51, 18, 20, 22, 52n229, 53, 72, 152, 287

Waigani Convention   76, 76n107